WILLIAM F.
WINTER
and the New Mississippi

WILLIAM F. WINTER

and the New Mississippi

—— *A Biography* ——

Charles C. Bolton

University Press of Mississippi / *Jackson*

Willie Morris Books in Memoir and Biography

www.upress.state.ms.us

The University Press of Mississippi is a member
of the Association of American University Presses.

Jacket photo from the collection of William F. Winter

First printing 2013

∞

Library of Congress Cataloging-in-Publication Data

Bolton, Charles C.
William F. Winter and the new Mississippi : a biography /
Charles C. Bolton.
p cm. — (Willie Morris books in memoir and biography)
Includes bibliographical references and index.
ISBN 978-1-61703-787-0 (cloth : alk. paper) — ISBN 978-1-61703-788-7
(ebook) 1. Winter, William F. 2. Governors—Mississippi—Biography.
3. Mississippi—Politics and government—1951– I. Title.
F345.3.W56B65 2013
976.2'063092—dc23
[B]   2013004132

British Library Cataloging-in-Publication Data available

For Leslie, Laura, and Ben

CONTENTS

WILLIAM F. WINTER
and the New Mississippi

MISSISSIPPI RIVER

MISSISSIPPI DELTA

·Senatobia

·Oxford

·Tupelo

·Greenville ·Greenwood

·Grenada

Columbus
·

Philadelphia
·

·Meridian
·

·Vicksburg

★
Jackson

·Magee

·
Laurel

·Natchez

·
·McComb ·Hattiesburg

MILES
0 20 40 60 80

Biloxi

Gulfport Pascagoula

Map of Mississippi

INTRODUCTION

On Monday, September 12, 1966, black children in Grenada, Mississippi, attempted to integrate the local public schools and a riot erupted. In the worst instance of racial violence associated with school desegregation attempts in Mississippi, a white mob assaulted black schoolchildren and white reporters while local law enforcement looked the other way. Racial confrontation had simmered in Grenada for months before this incident. During the summer of 1966, local black activists had launched a broad-based boycott against Grenada merchants who had failed to abide by the Civil Rights Act of 1964 and end racial segregation in places of public accommodation; whites responded with counter demonstrations of their own.[1]

In the week before the school disturbance, William F. Winter, Mississippi's state treasurer, traveled to Grenada to talk to some of the local white business leaders about forming a biracial committee to help solve some of the city's problems. Winter hailed from Grenada County and knew most of the local businessmen well. They listened politely to Winter's suggestion and promised to consider it. Just before he began his return to the state capital in Jackson on Friday afternoon, Winter heard that black protestors planned to march to the high school football stadium before a game that evening between the white Grenada High School and a rival school from nearby Charleston, in Tallahatchie County. Tensions were high, and rumors circulated that groups of whites from both Grenada and Tallahatchie Counties would come to the game armed and ready to challenge any black protestors who tried to disrupt their Friday football contest. Winter and three ministers—Emett Barfield of Grenada's First Presbyterian Church and two Methodist preachers, Bowen Burt and Jamie Houston—went to the Belleflower Baptist Church, a black church where the protesters were assembled, to discourage the black citizens from staging their march. Winter told the leaders of the planned protest that he had tried to do whatever he could "to diminish the strife that was tearing

3

the town apart and that was now threatening to get some black kids killed or injured." He promised to continue working for the formation of a biracial committee in the city, although he had to admit that the white merchants did not seem enthusiastic about the idea. The black leaders said the march was already planned and they could not back down. Winter and the three ministers, however, managed to talk out their concerns long enough that the leaders eventually called off the march because the game had already started.[2]

Although Winter helped defuse one racial confrontation in Grenada on that Friday evening, he could only listen in horror as the reports came in on the radio and from his Grenada friends about the riot that erupted on the Grenada school grounds the following Monday morning. The next day, Winter drove down to talk with McComb newspaper editor, Oliver Emmerich, about how McComb had stopped the wave of racial violence that had swept the town in 1964. Emmerich told Winter that a community group had gotten business leaders to sign a petition supporting law and order in the city. Winter returned to Jackson and immediately wrote a similar petition, denouncing the violence and calling on "all law-abiding citizens" to join together to resolve the racial conflict that had divided the city. The petition also urged the "reestablishment of communication between the white and Negro communities." Winter took the petition to Grenada, and by himself, walked around town soliciting signatures. Most of the local businessmen, sobered by the violent school unrest, eagerly affixed their names to the document. Not all whites, however, deplored the recent violence or appreciated Winter's efforts. While walking around the town square with his petition, Winter received cold stares from some white observers, and one shouted from an upstairs window, "Nigger lover, go back to Jackson."[3]

At the time, Winter was contemplating a run for governor of Mississippi, with the election less than a year away. Attempting to mediate Grenada's racial conflict did not seem a wise move politically, especially in Mississippi, the southern state generally perceived as the most resistant to the civil rights revolution then underway. Winter, however, was no political novice. He had already served almost two decades in state politics, during a time when tumultuous battles over black civil rights dominated Mississippi life. During those years, Winter walked a tightrope of Mississippi's racial politics. In a system in which almost all blacks were excluded from participation in the political process (until 1965) and whites remained determined to use every method at their disposal to preserve white supremacy, Winter managed to survive politically, even though he had established himself as a white voice of reason and compromise on racial matters.

First elected to the Mississippi state legislature in 1947, Winter had entered politics at a time when much of the Mississippi political establishment embraced the Dixiecrat campaign to block all efforts by black citizens and the federal government to end racial segregation and black disfranchisement. After the U.S. Supreme Court decision in *Brown v. Board of Education* (1954) declared segregated schools unconstitutional, white attitudes hardened, and the official policy of Mississippi became one of massive resistance to any attempts to alter the racial status quo. Not all white Mississippians actively supported this course of opposition. Many simply tried to ignore the racial conflict swirling around them. As historian Jason Sokol has noted in his study of white attitudes during the civil rights era: "Most white southerners identified neither with the civil rights movement nor with its violent resisters. They were fearful, silent, and often inert."[4] Some white moderate politicians in the state, including William Winter, also rejected the massive resistance approach and cautiously advocated instead for compromise and gradual change as a way to move forward.

Both before and during the civil rights movement, every southern state had its white moderates or liberals who offered dissent from the white orthodoxy on race.[5] These individuals were primarily preachers, journalists, and intellectuals, but their ranks included some political leaders as well. Scholars who have studied these southern dissenters note that they typically critiqued the South's existing racial arrangements largely in the interest of steering the region in a direction they believed would ensure southern progress. They envisioned a different future for the South than one shaped by poverty and racial conflict. Most also recognized that the South's system of racial apartheid was not immutable and would eventually be dismantled. The racial views of these white Southerners varied, and the nature of their criticism of existing social arrangements or their expressions of sympathy for the plight of southern blacks differed depending on individual circumstances and experiences. As historian Morton Sosna explains, "Each arrived at an island of tolerance in a sea of hate."[6]

When the black civil rights movement gained momentum in the late 1950s and early 1960s, most white moderates throughout the South preferred some kind of accommodation to black demands, but they largely remained on the sidelines as the equal rights struggle unfolded. The nature and timing of any changes they supported typically remained vague, and they proved generally unwilling to campaign actively for racial moderation, especially compared to those whites who vigorously advocated massive resistance to racial change. In 1963, Martin Luther King Jr. charged in his famous letter from the Birmingham jail that white moderates undermined the black effort to achieve civil rights. Recent studies that have examined the white segregationist opposition to the civil rights movement have echoed King's analysis: that white moderates had more than a benign presence during the civil rights era. These scholars suggest that some whites who adopted a measured approach to civil rights did so because they recognized this strategy as a more practical and effective way to preserve white privilege in the face of black demands and federal pronouncements for adjustments in the South's existing racial arrangements.[7] While this analysis offers a useful way to understand how some whites made the transition from "never" to "maybe a little" on the issue of black rights during the 1960s, it does not adequately explain the nature or the importance of the racial moderation of William Winter.

Like other white southern racial moderates, and especially those who occupied public office, William Winter did not aggressively press his position as the fight over black civil rights raged. Yet, his response to the racial battles of the era did not represent a cynical calculation about the best way to maintain white prerogatives. Rather, Winter's rejection of massive resistance and his support for racial moderation grew out of his early life experiences, spoke to his concerns about how best to advance progress in his native state, and reflected his own basic moral discomfort with the unfairness of segregation and disfranchisement.

Winter's moderation developed in part from his upbringing as a youth in rural Grenada County during the Great Depression and as a student at the University of Mississippi (Ole Miss) in the early 1940s. Both environments shaped Winter's conception of government as a place where citizen leaders came together to solve their common problems. While in the Army during World War II, Winter's work as a trainer of black troops and service in one of the Army's experimental integrated officer corps led him to understand that the global conflict had raised black expectations for the fulfillment of rights as American citizens. Although Winter continued to support racial segregation well into the 1960s—political survival in Mississippi required nothing less—he also believed that the South's racial arrangements would be adjusted in time. He knew that while states like Mississippi spent most of their energies fighting racial change that would inevitably come, they devoted little attention to the serious educational and economic problems that plagued them, deficiencies created in part because of the system of racial apartheid they continued to defend so vigorously. For Winter, education always held the key to Mississippi's progress. A better-educated citizenry would lead to economic improvements, which would enhance the lives of everyone in the state.

The fight to end racial segregation and black disfranchisement, however, complicated this equation. Winter initially preferred a compromise of Mississippi's ongoing racial conflicts in the interest of addressing the state's other serious problems. That compromise included support both for equalization of existing separate services for black Mississippians and for quiet and gradual acceptance—rather than outspoken defiance—of federal directives to end segregation and disfranchisement. This moderate position made Winter one of the most racially progressive white public officials in Mississippi at the time. However, the dedication and sacrifice of activists demanding basic civil rights for blacks (with increasing support from the federal government) eventually forced more fundamental racial change on the state. James Meredith's successful integration of Ole Miss in the fall of 1962 signaled the beginning of the end of the old way of life. After this event, Winter spoke out for an even bolder position: white Mississippians had to accommodate the demands of the state's black citizens for an end to segregation, and Mississippi had to follow federal law.

From the perspective of the twenty-first century, Winter's stance during the civil rights era might not look particularly effective or courageous; it did little to bring about the important racial transformation that has reshaped Mississippi and other southern states. As a segregationist during the early part of his political career, Winter sometimes took actions that we would now judge as prejudiced and even distasteful, yet it is important to remember that such attitudes were widely shared by most whites at the time, not just those in the South or Mississippi. Although Winter did not directly challenge racial segregation during the 1950s and early

1960s, he did favor racial change. The pace and the shape of that change remained poorly defined, but Winter envisioned a future beyond the racial caste system that had defined Mississippi life for almost a century. The nature of Winter's racial moderation also evolved over time, and as the civil rights movement won victories, Winter increasingly advocated positions that helped whites negotiate the transition to a New Mississippi, from a world where Jim Crow defined all aspects of life to one that accepted black civil rights.

The path to a New Mississippi proved a rocky one. Winter lost his first race for governor in 1967 to an outspoken segregationist. The New Mississippi had only begun to emerge, largely as a result of the 1965 Voting Rights Act, and Winter's racial moderation proved an untenable political position at that pivotal moment of change. Winter lost another gubernatorial campaign in 1975 but won on his third attempt in 1979. He became one of the New South Democrats who assumed political power in the South in the 1970s and early 1980s, a group of white moderate leaders—including Jimmy Carter and Bill Clinton—who sought to work with both black and white constituencies to further the transition to a post–civil rights South of racial equity and justice. During Winter's gubernatorial administration, he helped restore some of Mississippi's tarnished reputation, which during and after the civil rights struggles had hardened into the image of an ignorant, bigoted backwater. Winter also pushed through an education reform bill that represented one of the state's greatest legislative achievements in the twentieth century and that moved the state beyond the racial divisions that had long diminished public education in Mississippi. Winter's administration suggested the possibility of a new political future for Mississippi, one in which whites joined newly enfranchised black citizens in a political alliance to address some of the many problems the state faced, including educational deficiencies and widespread poverty. That coalition, however, had its difficulties, even during Winter's years as governor, as many black Mississippians had recurring reasons to suspect that their new white political allies still had a long way to go in truly embracing the principle of black equality. Despite the problems, the state Democratic Party managed to hold on to enough white voters while adjusting to black enfranchisement that it continued to thrive through much of the 1990s. The politics of moderation that Winter embodied clearly helped Mississippi move forward in the initial post–civil rights period, although the political coalition of white moderates and blacks has diminished in Mississippi in recent years.[8]

After Winter left the governor's office in 1984, he continued to champion the causes that defined his political career. He persisted as an advocate for educational improvement and economic change for Mississippi and the South, working through a variety of initiatives and organizations. He also remained on the front lines of the effort to improve race relations in Mississippi and throughout the nation. Winter served in the 1990s on the advisory board of President Bill Clinton's One America in the 21st Century: The President's Initiative on Race, and he chaired the 2000 commission created by Mississippi Governor Ronnie Musgrove to propose an alternative to the state flag, with its controversial and divisive Confederate symbol. In the years after he left public office, Winter's ideas about race continued to evolve and moved far beyond his earlier position of merely making accommodation to civil rights changes. He became a steadfast proponent for addressing the "unending work of racial reconciliation" in Mississippi and the rest of the nation. A relatively small number of white Mississippians joined the former governor in pursuing this task; as he had throughout his life, Winter continued to represent one of the most progressive white positions in the state on the matter of resolving the thorny racial issues that still plagued social life there and elsewhere.

I

GRENADA FARM

In the winter of 1932, William F. Winter, just shy of his ninth birthday, boarded a train in Grenada, bound for the state capital. Earlier that day, Winter had left his family's farm in an isolated section of Grenada County, located in north-central Mississippi, east of the Delta. Winter travelled to Jackson to visit his father, Aylmer Winter, a member of the Mississippi State Senate. During his visit, Winter sat with his father at his Senate desk and listened to the legislative debates, many of which revolved around how the state would respond to the Great Depression that had left the state government deeply in debt. Lawmakers considered and eventually passed a state sales tax, after a contentious three-month debate of the measure that included protests against the tax in the streets of Jackson by distressed, out-of-work people. Following one mass meeting, a group of angry citizens marched to Governor Mike Conner's office in the State Capitol, and one member of the crowd shouted out: "What are you peckerwoods waiting for? Let's get that _____ Governor." Conner calmly walked out of his office and through the threatening crowd untouched, an action that seemed to deflate the mob's ire. When William Winter returned to the Grenada County farm, he dreamed about becoming a politician one day, perhaps a state senator like his father, or even governor of Mississippi like Conner.[1] Winter's boyhood aspirations would eventually be fulfilled, and his family background and somewhat uncommon experiences growing up in rural Grenada County during the Great Depression would help shape the political path he would follow.

The Winters of Grenada County had an impressive pedigree. They could trace their American roots back to the late seventeenth century. Starting from humble origins in England and Ireland, the Winter ancestors had steadily improved their fortunes by migration to the colony of Maryland and, then in the early nineteenth century, by a second migration to the southwestern cotton frontier. In 1815, William Winter's great-great-grandfather, William Hooe Winter, who had married Catherine Stark Washington, a cousin of the first president of the United States, left the mid-Atlantic and relocated to Williamson County, Tennessee, south of Nashville. The couple had a growing family and ten black slaves. A year later, William claimed that he was "very much attached to the situation that I have bought," and he told his mother that "I am in hopes I am settled for life." Yet, within two years, the Winters had moved again, this time joining the rush of white settlers who headed to north Alabama to try to secure part of the new cotton lands recently taken from the Creek Indians and made available at public auction. In January 1819 William Winter observed the "cotton fever" that gripped north Alabama and noted that new arrivals from the Carolinas, Georgia, Kentucky, and Tennessee were "flocking" to the area "like blackbirds to a corn field." He advised anyone back east who thought of moving west "to make haste & bring with them Negroes to cultivate." Winter purchased some of the valuable lands, and the family, which eventually included fourteen children, settled in Tuscumbia, west of Huntsville. The Winters prospered and became one of the leading families in the area. In 1823, William Winter built a large home in Tuscumbia—Locust Hill—which still stands today.[2]

New lands even further west beckoned to the next generation of Winters. In the late 1830s, William Hooe Winter Jr., accompanied by twelve black slaves, relocated to Hinds County, Mississippi, near the capital of Jackson, where he farmed and also taught school. Around 1840, he moved north to Yalobusha County and acquired part of the land recently appropriated from the Choctaw Indians by the federal government under the Treaty of Dancing Rabbit Creek. Within a few years, he had developed a successful cotton plantation on the lush bottomlands of the Yalobusha River, ten miles west of the town of Grenada. By 1850, forty slaves worked the property, and in 1860, sixty-six slaves lived in fifteen cabins on the two-thousand-acre farm. An overseer, Lewis Key, handled slave management, and in 1860 the plantation produced 267 bales of cotton as well as 4,000 bushels of corn. In addition to the extensive cotton plantation on the Yalobusha River, William Winter also acquired land in a number of nearby counties during the 1850s. On the eve of the Civil War, he owned land valued at over $50,000, with tracts not only in Yalobusha County but also in the counties of Tallahatchie, Sunflower, and Coahoma in the Mississippi Delta, at that time still largely an untamed wilderness. In 1858, Winter bought Morrison Heights, a two-story house in Grenada, and moved his family there, primarily to ensure that his eight children received a proper education, since schools of any kind did not really exist out in the county.[3]

Ephraim S. Fisher owned one of the neighboring plantations in Yalobusha. A recent migrant from Kentucky, Fisher joined the numerous white settlers crowding into the new Choctaw cession. In 1842 Fisher married the daughter of a Yalobusha planter, acquired slaves, and established his own plantation on the Yalobusha River near the Winter place. Fisher also established a home in Coffeeville, eighteen miles away, where he began his law practice. He became a respected political leader in Yalobusha County, serving in the legislature during the 1840s. In 1851 the voters elected him to the Mississippi High Court of Errors and Appeals, known later as the Supreme Court, where he served eight years, before resigning and returning to his plantation. After the Civil War, in 1869, the Winter and Fisher families united when William Brown Winter married Amelia Fisher— William F. Winter's grandparents.[4]

During the 1840s and 1850s, both William H. Winter and Ephraim Fisher supported the Whig political party. When talk of secession dominated political discussion in the winter of 1860–1861, both men vigorously opposed the action. Like many other wealthy Whig planters, Winter and Fisher had too much to lose by what seemed a hotheaded response to the election of the Republican Abraham Lincoln. In addition, Winter's brother-in-law, former governor Henry S. Foote, had long been a prominent opponent of disunion; he had helped shape the famous Compromise of 1850, which derailed an earlier secession attempt by southern fire-eaters. However, once Mississippi seceded in January 1861, Winter and Fisher offered their support to the southern cause. Both men were in their forties when the conflict began and never joined the Confederate army. Winter and Fisher helped out where they could, supplying Confederate officials with intelligence of enemy movements; leasing slaves to help Confederate engineers; and serving in the Home Guard, organized to protect the local population from Yankee attackers, Confederate deserters, and restive slaves.[5]

The male children of Winter and Fisher shared little of their fathers' conservatism and anxiously embraced the chance to get in the fight with the North. Armistead Fisher, the judge's oldest son, was only fifteen when the war commenced, but in January 1864, the boy joined the Third Regiment of the Mississippi Cavalry and fought in Mississippi, Tennessee, Georgia, and Alabama, including several engagements alongside Nathan Bedford Forrest's famous cavalry unit. William Brown Winter, thirteen in 1861, longed for the day when he could join the fray, and in the last year of the conflict, just sixteen years old, William signed on as a private in Company C of the Eighteenth Mississippi Cavalry, which was a part of the forces of Nathan Bedford Forrest. Winter joined in time to see action at the Battle of Brice's Cross Roads in northeast Mississippi in June 1864, where the Rebels captured sixteen hundred Union prisoners along with large caches of artillery and supplies. Two months later, Winter and other members of his company were in Forrest's famous cavalry raid on Memphis. Winter's company was in an advance group, led by Bill Forrest, one of General Forrest's younger brothers. On the outskirts of Memphis, the horsemen rode through a camp of black Union troops and shot it up. They then rode to the Gayoso Hotel in Memphis, searching for Union General Stephen A. Hurlbut. The company rode straight into the hotel's lobby on horseback, but General Hurlbut had already made his escape from the establishment.[6]

After the war, white Mississippians struggled to come to grips with the new order, a world where blacks had not only gained their freedom but also challenged white supremacy in both economic and political matters. Black troops stationed in Grenada at the end of the war profoundly angered local whites. The new Freedmen's Bureau established an office in the town, and the agency upset white citizens when it tried to mediate disputes between former slaves and their old masters, or in rare instances, subjected local whites to trials for abusing freedpeople. Beginning in 1867, former slaves registered to vote and became politically active. Whites responded by organizing the Ku Klux Klan, and the sons of Winter and Fisher, unable to accept the South's defeat and the changed social conditions that followed, became leaders in the new organization. Hal Fisher, another son of the judge, assumed leadership of the Tallahatchie den of the Klan, while William B. Winter headed the local organization at Pea Ridge. Members of the group "took an oath to put down negro supremacy," and their methods ranged from simple intimidation to murder. They tried to turn away blacks who sought to exercise their newly won suffrage rights and "visited" black Republicans and other black leaders in their homes. William B. Winter, years later, recounted one incident where his Klan group went to Hardy Station, six miles north of Grenada, "to deliver a warning to a negro who had been guilty of misconduct." When the black man fired on the night riders, the hooded white men captured and hanged him. Although Winter claimed the death was accidental, that the group had only meant to scare the black man, the Klan's methods led to numerous black deaths in Yalobusha and around the South.[7]

Ephraim Fisher counseled both his own son and his new son-in-law that their involvement in the Klan had gotten out of hand. Fisher approached Reconstruction with a much different attitude than his young kin. In the fall of 1865, he ran for governor in the first state election after the war. All the candidates were moderates prepared to accept the Confederacy's defeat and some accommodation with the government in Washington. Fisher lost the election by thirty-five hundred votes to Benjamin Humphreys, a former Civil War general who had fought at Gettysburg. When the Republicans came to power later in the decade, Fisher supported the Republican biracial coalition, and Governor James L. Alcorn appointed him to a circuit judgeship in 1869. As judge, Fisher sought to control the white violence that plagued the state in the late 1860s and early 1870s. Fisher's entreaties for moderation apparently calmed his son-in-law's radicalism, but his own son Hal left for Texas in the early 1870s to avoid arrest after federal pressure led to a crackdown on the Klan throughout the South.[8]

In the midst of these tumultuous Reconstruction years, William B. Winter and Amelia Fisher married. They established a household during the early 1870s on land acquired from both of their fathers, eventually totaling about five hundred acres, located in what was now Grenada County (a new county established from parts of Yalobusha and Carroll Counties in 1870). The union produced four boys, but only William Aylmer, born in 1872, survived childhood. William B. Winter reestablished on a smaller scale the Grenada County farming operation of his father and father-in-law. He resumed cotton farming and had several tenants who also worked the place. Winter, however, struggled to prosper during what proved difficult financial times for all southern farmers in the late nineteenth century.[9]

Despite their economic problems, the Winters were determined that their only remaining son get the best education possible. He initially went to Center Point School, several miles away. Since this school ended at the sixth grade, Aylmer's father did what his own father had done decades earlier: he moved the family to Morrison Heights to take advantage of the Grenada school, leaving the farming operation largely in the hands of the tenants. Aylmer proved a gifted student, and after graduation from high school, he left Grenada for northeast Mississippi to attend Iuka Normal Institute, a private, co-ed college founded in the early 1880s, which offered course work in four areas: Classics, Science, Teacher Training, and Music. Aylmer pursued the teaching track and graduated at the top of his class in 1891 at the age of nineteen. After graduation Aylmer Winter stayed on a year to teach at Iuka. He then took a teaching job at Cascilla, six miles north of his father's farm. There, Aylmer boarded with the Whitten family, who so admired their young guest that when a son was born during the year, they named him Aylmer. This child later had a son, Jamie Whitten, who would serve as a U.S. congressman from north Mississippi for almost fifty-four years, the second-longest tenure for a U.S. representative in Congress.[10]

Aylmer Winter, however, soon abandoned teaching. After a year in Cascilla, he returned home to run his father's Grenada farm. At the time, William and Amelia lived in Grenada at Morrison Heights, where William worked as a salesman and Amelia kept house for several boarders. Out in the county, Aylmer worked hard to make the Grenada hill farm profitable, but success continued to prove difficult with a series of crop failures during the 1890s. Essentially alone on the isolated farm, Aylmer spent much of his spare time avidly reading everything he could, especially history and the classics. He longed, however, for something more challenging to do with his life. Soon after the turn of the twentieth century, Aylmer told his father he wanted to explore new opportunities. He set out to find work in the Mississippi Delta, a booming area that had recently become the center of the cotton-producing world. In many ways, the Delta at that time was a frontier region, complete with its share of hard drinkers, reckless gamblers, and dangerous gunmen. Aylmer Winter, however, remained sober and businesslike. He worked for several plantation stores for a number of years, including one in Doddsville owned by the Eastland family. He later became a cotton buyer for textile mills in the Carolinas. He had established a successful life in the Delta, but by 1910, Aylmer's parents once again needed help. They had sold Morrison Heights in 1909 and returned to live full-time on the farm. Amelia had also suffered a paralyzing stroke. Back in Grenada County, Aylmer took over management of the place and resolved to dedicate himself to making a good living on the ancestral farm.[11]

A few years after returning to Grenada County, he decided to run for political office and won election without opposition to the Mississippi House of Representatives in 1915. Since the legislature met for only a few months every other year, he could continue farming. Two other notable freshmen joined Winter in the 1916 legislature: Walter Sillers, from the Delta county of Bolivar, and Mike Conner, a twenty-five-year-old Yale Law School graduate from south Mississippi. The House elected Conner Speaker during his first term in the legislature, and Sillers would go on to serve fifty years in the legislature, the last twenty-two as House Speaker. At the time Aylmer Winter entered the legislature, state government remained quite small. In 1912, the total appropriation for all purposes by the state government had totaled only $7.7 million, with $3.9 million of that amount for public education and almost $1 million for Confederate pensions.[12]

As a legislator, Winter recognized that the state of Mississippi had to do more to address its pressing problems, but he remained unwilling to raise taxes to support all the necessary improvements. Winter had three brothers die as infants or young children because of the state's woeful health care. He knew that economic development would require both better schools and better highways. As a former teacher, he understood the problems faced by the state's schools, black and white. Winter also knew that the automobile age just on the horizon required significant transportation improvements. Without paved roads, Aylmer's own trip to Jackson to attend the legislative sessions remained an arduous one. When the roads became muddy, as they often did when the Yalobusha and its numerous creeks overflowed its banks, it might take almost three hours to get from the Winter farm to Grenada by horse and buggy to catch the train to Jackson. The 1916 legislature, with Winter's support, passed a number of measures to solve some of these problems, including the establishment of a tuberculosis hospital in Magee and a highway department. Winter, however, was a frugal man personally, and he thought government should also be prudent. He became one of only nine representatives to oppose the creation of a tax commission in 1916, designed to help collect the funds necessary to finance these very beginnings of a more activist state in Mississippi.[13]

In 1921, at the age of forty-nine, Aylmer Winter married for the first time. His bride was Inez Parker, a thirty-two-year-old teacher originally from Big Creek, in Calhoun County. Like the Winters, the Parkers had been pioneer white settlers of Mississippi, arriving in the 1840s from North Carolina. Inez's mother, Emma Smith, married Abraham Parker, who had a successful career as a farmer and a merchant in Big Creek, although he died when Inez was not yet ten years old. Emma continued to run her husband's business and the family farm, as well as raise seven children. Inez, the oldest of six daughters, helped tend to her five younger sisters, and all six of the Parker girls eventually became teachers, collectively serving a total of almost 150 years in the Mississippi public schools. In the late nineteenth and early twentieth centuries, Inez taught in several schools in both south Mississippi and the Delta. While teaching in the Delta county of Quitman, she met Aylmer Winter, the cotton broker, and they married several years later. After the wedding, Aylmer brought his new wife to the Winter farm, where they lived with the aging Civil War veteran, William B. Winter, Aylmer's mother having recently died. Two years later, on February 21, 1923, Inez gave birth to the couple's only child, William Forrest Winter. The proud grandfather suggested the middle name, the surname of his hero—his commander during the Civil War, Nathan Bedford Forrest.[14]

By the time of William Winter's birth, Aylmer Winter had established both a successful political career and a prosperous farming operation. He served three terms in the Mississippi House, from 1916 to 1924 and 1944 to 1948, as well as three nonconsecutive terms in the Mississippi Senate, spanning the years 1924 to 1944. As a legislator, Aylmer Winter provided a progressive voice on many issues, though not all, and while he proved at times to be an independent thinker, he remained sensitive to the attitudes of his Grenada constituents. During the 1926 session, Winter became the Senate leader for a House bill that created a State Forestry Commission. Since the late nineteenth century, industrialists had clearcut much of the state's vast pine forest. Winter was among the earliest of the state's political leaders to recognize the value in conserving and managing these valuable natural resources. In addition to creating the commission, the new law also provided funds for the prevention of forest fires and authorized the acquisition by the federal government of up to twenty-five thousand acres to create a national forest. Another prominent issue that session concerned the question of evolution and its teaching in the public schools. When a House bill reached the Senate that proposed to prohibit "the teaching that man descended, or ascended, from a lower order of animals," Winter proposed an amendment that he thought might satisfy religious conservatives while not attacking scientific thinking, and at the same time, guard against political radicalism. The amendment proposed to substitute the anti-evolution language with the following: "That it shall be unlawful to teach disrespect to the Holy Bible, or to teach that ours is an inferior form of government." Winter's amendment failed, and the Grenada County legislator ended up voting against the original anti-evolution law, although the measure passed.[15]

Although Aylmer Winter's more progressive positions often placed him at odds with many of his constituents, they regularly returned him to Jackson because they widely viewed him as a man of superior intellect, fiscal responsibility, and steadfast integrity. An insight into Winter's basic decency in his dealings with others can be gleaned from an incident during his legislative campaign in 1939. For the first time in five races, Winter had opposition. During a campaign event in Water Valley, one of Winter's opponents, a man who "was a poor talker," spoke last on the program. The sizeable audience quickly evaporated during the man's presentation, and by the end of his remarks, only Aylmer and Inez Winter and one other man remained. Afterwards, the three remaining spectators went up to congratulate the man at the end of his speech. This kind of gracious respect for others, even one's political opponents, would later be a hallmark of William Winter's own political career.[16]

In addition to serving in the legislature, Aylmer Winter developed a prosperous farm in Grenada County. He acquired ownership of his father's farm, about five hundred acres, and added an additional four hundred acres in the late 1920s. By the 1930s, Aylmer also managed an adjoining six hundred acres owned by Blanche Winter, the unmarried sister of his father, bringing the entire Winter farm to approximately fifteen hundred acres. Cotton, corn, and hay were the primary crops, and farming was done the old-fashioned way, relying largely on power provided by man and mule. While the Yalobusha bottom lands continued to produce valuable cotton crops, in the 1920s Aylmer Winter began to convert some of the hilly terrain to pastureland, and he became one of the first farmers in the county to focus significant efforts on raising beef cattle. The Winter farm provided for much of the family's needs and also produced a modest cash income, at least during the good crop years. In 1941, for instance, the farm produced cash receipts of just over $1,800 (about $26,000 in 2008 dollars).[17]

The Winter farm, nestled in a rural community along Long Creek Road, included a patchwork of small, family-owned farms alongside several larger holdings worked by tenants. Wash Winter, a black man whose slave ancestors had worked for William H. Winter, owned a homestead close to the Winter place. By the 1930s, ten to twelve tenant families worked the Winter land. Most of them were black, but there were also a couple of white households. Most of the tenants who rented the land owned their own mules and farm equipment. They paid rent as a fourth of the cotton crop and a third of the corn produced. The others were sharecroppers, who paid half the cotton crop to Aylmer Winter. In addition to land, Winter supplied them with livestock and equipment. For both renters and sharecroppers, he provided a number of other items during the year, which he then deducted from the proceeds acquired through the sale of the cotton crop. In addition to farming their plots, some of the tenants provided special services for the Winters in exchange for additional compensation. Odie Jackson, who had farmed for William B. Winter for many years, worked as a servant around the Winter home during the 1930s. Irene Hamer, the wife of black tenant Walter Hamer, who had also farmed on the Winter place for decades, was the family cook and washerwoman.[18]

Aylmer Winter had the reputation of an honest landlord. At a time when unscrupulous white landlords frequently cheated tenants, especially black ones, by both overcharging for expenses and fudging on the actual amounts yielded from crop sales, Aylmer Winter treated his tenants fairly. One son of a small black landowner from the neighborhood remembered in the 1980s that "the Winters in the old days were known as friends of the black people." When the Agricultural Adjustment Act (AAA) of 1933, in an effort to boost falling farm prices, required that part of the South's cotton acreage be taken out of cultivation in exchange for a government payment, many landlords pocketed the entire amount; some used the forced downsizing to evict tenants off the land. Winter, however, kept all his tenants at work and distributed to them their share of the parity payment. In 1935, the AAA payment to the farm was $122.25; Winter distributed $67.42 of that amount to his twelve tenant families. Aylmer Winter, unlike many white landlords, also encouraged his black tenants to send their children to school, although the local facilities did not provide an education beyond the sixth grade. The Winter tenants managed to make a living without facing the inequities that many tenants typically endured. Because Winter dealt with his tenants in good faith, many of them farmed their plots year after year, even as large numbers of their fellow impoverished agriculturists, black and white, regularly left the state in the hopes of a better life outside the South.[19]

As a child growing up on the Grenada farm, William Winter had a number of white friends, especially Bryan Baker, whose family owned a large farm nearby, but many of his most frequent companions were the black tenant children on the farm: Roy, Elmo (Cricket), Peaches, John Henry, Excel, Josh, Dude, Man-Son, and Joe Louis. Despite the harsh system of racial segregation that existed throughout the South during the 1920s and 1930s, social relations in rural areas followed a different rhythm than that of the region's towns and cities; rural blacks and whites lived near each other and worked together interacting on a more intimate and personal level than the Jim Crow paradigm dictated. Winter became fast friends with his black contemporaries. They fished and swam together in nearby Long Creek. They visited in each other's homes. They played baseball on a makeshift diamond in a pasture down the road from the Winter home. In the fall and winter, the boys hunted rabbits and squirrels together. Winter's grandfather probably had strikingly similar experiences on the same piece of land with the slave ancestors of Roy, Cricket, and many of the other black boys of William's youth. William Winter's attitude toward his black contemporaries was shaped by his parents' teachings, which included adherence to the Golden Rule, as well as a sense of paternalism and noblesse oblige. They encouraged their son to treat all people with respect and to help those less fortunate.[20]

William Winter's parents, especially his mother, also instilled him with a strong sense of religious faith. The Winters had long belonged to the Presbyterian denomination. Indeed, William H. Winter had been one of the early members of the First Presbyterian Church in Grenada, established in

1837. During the 1930s Winter and his mother regularly attended Sunday
school and church services at First Presbyterian, often traveling to town
with Bryan Baker and his mother and sister. On some Sundays, especially when road conditions made the trip to town an arduous one, the
Winters and Bakers went instead to Bethel Presbyterian Church, located
only a few miles from the farm. Aylmer Winter, although he shared his
wife's religious values, did not generally join the family on their trips to
church. In large part, his absence stemmed from his dislike of the fact
that organized religion at that time focused so much attention on the
personal conduct of its members. A number of churches in the 1930s
pressed for members to sign a pledge that they would not drink alcohol.
Aylmer Winter never drank liquor throughout his life, although he had
an occasional beer. Even though his personal conduct remained beyond
reproach and others signed the pledge even if they sometimes took a
drink, Aylmer Winter refused to be bullied into signing an abstinence
promise. He remained a member of First Presbyterian and embraced its
teachings, but he rarely attended services.[21]

William Winter's parents both came from families that had always
emphasized the importance of education, and they passed on this value
to their only son. Aylmer and Inez Winter both read avidly. In addition
to receiving the *Memphis Commercial Appeal* six days a week, the Winters
subscribed to *Time, Life, Liberty, Christian Herald, National Geographic*,
and the *Saturday Evening Post*. Aylmer Winter had also built an extensive
library, which included books of all descriptions, both fiction and nonfic-
tion. By the time William was ready to attend school, he had already read
fifteen books. Over the years, he devoured the American Biography set his
father purchased for him, starting with the narrative of one of his father's
political heroes, Thomas Jefferson.[22]

William's mother provided his first formal schooling. Although the
Kincannon School, a county-sponsored, one-room, six-grade school, was
located on the Winter property, William's mother, a former teacher, set up
a makeshift school for his first year in an abandoned ten-by-twenty foot
shed, which at an earlier time had housed a Winter servant but had most
recently served as a storage place for hay. The following year Kincannon
hired Inez Winter as its only teacher, so William attended school there,
along with nine other children, enrolled in the first through sixth grade.
Classes met for half a day, and the other children attending included those

from the white tenant farms on the Winter place and the offspring of other white landowners in the area. The course of study included reading, spelling, arithmetic, English language, and writing.[23]

Kincannon was not the kind of school that could ever provide a strong education. The Winters would have likely migrated back to Grenada to educate their boy, much as the previous two generations had done, but the following year, in 1930, the county of Grenada worked out an arrangement with the Grenada city school system to transport county children into town to attend Grenada's more modern schoolhouse. Beginning with the third grade, Winter caught a bus along with other neighborhood children and endured a daily round trip of thirty-two miles to attend the Grenada city schools, a ride he would make until his graduation from high school in May 1940. As a result, Winter received a solid education. By the early 1920s, the Grenada city schools, under the leadership of Superintendent John Rundle, widely regarded as one of the top school superintendents in the state, had developed into one of the better public school systems in north Mississippi.[24]

Winter's bus rides into Grenada provided his first inkling about the unfairness of the South's racial arrangements. While his black friends walked two miles to a one-room school, Jackson Chapel, which went only to the sixth grade and operated for only five months (the light agricultural months from November to March), Winter rode a bus to Grenada to attend a modern, nine-month, twelve-grade school. Many mornings Winter's bus would pass Cricket, Peaches, and the others trudging the dirt roads to their schoolhouse. At those moments, Winter later remembered, he felt that segregation was wrong, but he also thought "it was a lot better to be a white boy."[25] School segregation thus reinforced the sense of white privilege, while also creating at least the slightest pangs of doubt about the equity of Mississippi's "separate but equal" school system.

Winter excelled in the Grenada public schools. In elementary school, he earned As" in all subjects, except for an occasional B or C in writing or music. Although his formal writing perhaps needed some polishing in the estimation of his teachers, he clearly had, from a very early age, a precocious awareness of the wider world, developed from the many and varied reading materials he had already encountered. Beginning with the fourth grade, Winter assumed "his long-to-be-held stand at the head of the class," according to a student-written history of Grenada High's 1940 graduating class. At the beginning of fifth grade, he took an achievement test, and the results suggested that he could skip ahead to the sixth grade, but he and his parents decided to keep him with his classmates. Winter's academic prowess continued throughout junior high and high school. During his senior year, Winter was both class president and valedictorian and also won the Good Citizenship Award from the local Daughters of the American Revolution. Winter was popular among his fellow students, who in high school called him Woods, a playful allusion to his middle name.[26]

The teacher who had the greatest influence on Winter during his school years was his high school English instructor, Estelle Turner, from Durant. She had high standards and urged Winter to work harder to improve his writing. She assigned him summer reading each year during his high school career, designed to expand his choice of books and authors, by including European writers such as Thackeray and Dickens. One fall during Winter's high school years, Turner also introduced him to the writings of Ralph Waldo Emerson, which made a strong impression on the boy. She assigned Winter the transcendentalist's essay, "Self-Reliance," which urged men to "trust thyself," rather than the prevailing opinions of others. At a time when Mississippians did not exactly prize independent thinking as a personal attribute, Emerson's words insisted that "nothing is at last sacred but the integrity of our mind." Winter later recalled that the reading of this essay represented the real beginning of his education.[27]

During Winter's high school years, he led a more isolated existence than most of his classmates, who typically resided in town. Living so far from Grenada, he did not have the chance to participate in many extracurricular activities, which typically occurred after school hours, although he did get involved in both the Newspaper Club and the Dramatic Club. Winter had an abiding love of sports, but he did not become a high school athlete, in part because of his inability to stay after school for practice, but also because as a high school student, Winter remained relatively small, having not yet reached his adult height of 5'11" and weighing at the time only 120 pounds. Despite not participating in organized sports, Winter remained physically active and fit. He had his chores on the farm, and decades before jogging became a national craze, Winter would run for miles through the countryside of Grenada County. Relatively shy around young girls, Winter had few dates until his senior year in high school; for a time that year he went out with Caroline Whitaker, the daughter of the editor of the local newspaper, the *Grenada County Weekly*.[28]

From an early age, Winter also received another kind of education, about the world of politics. His first foray into that arena came during the presidential election of 1928, when he traveled to vote with his grandfather at the Mims precinct at Kincannon School, where fewer than thirty whites usually voted. The old Confederate veteran asked his five-year-old grandson, "Would you like to vote?" "Yes, sir!" Winter answered, and none of the election officials objected when the old man pulled off an extra ballot and showed his young charge how to mark an "X" by the name of Al Smith, Democratic candidate from New York. William completed his ballot and dropped it in the box, becoming undoubtedly the youngest voter to cast a ballot in that year's presidential contest. That night, the Winters went to the home of a cousin, who lived a few miles away and who had just purchased a radio, to listen to the election returns. As the news came in, William could see the distressed look on his father's face as it became clear that the Republican candidate, Herbert Hoover, would win the race. Even though Smith was a "wet" Yankee, Aylmer Winter valued loyalty to the Democratic Party.[29]

William's budding interest in politics received a real boost three years later, when he traveled with his parents to Jackson to attend the inauguration of Governor Mike Conner. Conner was replacing Theodore G. Bilbo, and the contrast could not have been more striking. Bilbo came to power as the diminutive, self-proclaimed and outspoken champion of Mississippi's "rednecks," while Conner seemed shy and scholarly by comparison. He had twice lost contests for the governor's seat, before winning on his third try. On inauguration day, Winter and his parents watched the ceremony on the grounds of the Capitol. Viewing the festivities, William asked his father if he might meet Conner. The following morning Aylmer and his son went back down to the Capitol and waited outside the governor's third-floor office with an assembly of people battered by the Great Depression, all hoping to land a much-needed job in the new administration. When the Winters finally got in to see Conner, Aylmer told his old legislative colleague, "Governor, my son has come all the way down here from Grenada to attend your inauguration, and he wants to meet you." Conner shook William's hand and invited him to sit in the governor's chair. Looking at the young boy with his feet dangling from the seat, Conner told Aylmer Winter, "You know, that chair just fits him." The next day, William and his mother returned to the Grenada farm, and William tried to explain his exciting encounter to his friends, but most of them had no idea who Mike Conner was. The parents of most of his white friends generally favored Bilbo, and of course the parents of his black friends could not even vote.[30]

By the time Winter got to junior high school, he clearly had aspirations for a career in politics. When one of his teachers had the students write an autobiography, Winter concluded his assignment with a look "into the future," a view that predicted his political success:

> A man stood on a platform in the center of a crowded park, mak-
> ing a speech. There was very little noise, as the speaker talked on
> and on. He was a brilliant, young lawyer from Grenada, Missis-
> sippi, and next senator from his district. Four years later this same
> man walked into the House of Representatives at Washington,
> congressman from Mississippi. His name was William F. Winter.
> He achieved fame in the Mississippi legislature where he engi-
> neered the passing of a very important bill.[31]

Winter had a number of political role models growing up, starting with his father, whom the young boy greatly admired. Even decades later, having far surpassed the elder Winter's political achievements, William Winter recalled his father as his hero—"the most impressive man that I ever knew." In addition, Mike Conner also became a political hero. Conner's political career combined intellectual breadth with dogged persistence in achieving the state's highest office, a path similar to the one William Winter would travel. Growing up, Winter also looked to the political examples among Mississippians he read about or that his father described to him, most notably his ancestor Judge Fisher but also men like Edward C. Walthall, a U.S. senator from Grenada; L. Q. C. Lamar, another U.S. senator, member of the Grover Cleveland cabinet, and U.S. Supreme Court justice; and John Sharp Williams, U.S. senator and ardent supporter of President Woodrow Wilson.[32]

In addition to his interest in politics, sports often occupied Winter's thoughts and imagination as a youth. Winter imagined that one byprod-uct of a successful career in politics would be the opportunity to get to

know the sports stars of the day; in his 1936 autobiography, that celeb-
rity was his classmate Charles Calloway, whom Winter had cast in his
tale as the "leading pitcher of the world-champion Detroit Tigers." Other
than a political career, Winter's other youthful ambition was to become
a sportswriter. From an early age, he avidly followed sports, especially
baseball. Decades later, Winter told writer Willie Morris that he was "one
of the original baseball children." Winter first became interested in the
sport during the 1934 World Series, when the St. Louis Cardinals faced
the Detroit Tigers. Since the Winters did not own a radio, they listened
to game four of the series at the Grenada town square, where a local merchant had installed a loudspeaker for people to take in the game.[33]

The Winter family got its own radio the following year, a battery-
operated set with a fifty-foot antenna, and it altered the social life of the
family, which before had largely revolved around reading or sitting on the
porch talking to neighbors and each other. Many evenings had passed
with Aylmer Winter recounting interesting stories to his wife and son: of
his political career; of the Civil War tales his own father had told him; of
the unique things he had seen and heard during his life, such as Secretary
of War William Howard Taft talking with Filipino natives at the 1904 St.
Louis World's Fair. With the arrival of the radio, however, the family now
listened to nightly newscasts by Lowell Thomas; *National Barn Dance*, a
weekly comedy and country-music program; the *Grand Ole Opry*; and
radio serials, including the popular comedy program, the *Lum and Abner
Show*, about two white Arkansas hillbillies. Sports programming also
dominated the listening habits of the Winters. In addition to baseball
and college football, the Winters tuned in for the numerous prize fights
broadcast to a national audience during the 1930s. When the black heavyweight champion Joe Louis fought, the black tenants living on the Winter
place gathered on the Winters' lawn to hear the action. They were especially jubilant on that June evening in 1938 when Louis knocked out the
German boxer Max Schmeling in less than three minutes, two years after
the German defeated the black boxer for the first loss in his heavyweight
career. The voices of political leaders also filled the airwaves, everything
from the fireside chats of President Franklin D. Roosevelt to the rants of
Adolf Hitler.[34]

The radio brought a wider world to William Winter, as did a number
of trips he took as he entered his teenage years. Winter and Bryan Baker

went with legislators on a 1934 trip to the Mississippi Gulf Coast; on the way, the two boys visited a pickle factory in Wiggins and saw a Civilian Conservation Camp in Stone County. In the fall of 1935, Winter made two memorable trips, one to the state fair in Jackson, and the other to New Orleans, aboard *The Rebel*, the South's first streamlined passenger train, operated by the Gulf, Mobile, and Ohio Railroad. In New Orleans, William saw the Mississippi riverfront, the French Quarter, the Cabildo, and the Chalmette Battlefield, where Andrew Jackson had defeated the British at the end of the War of 1812. The following spring, Winter and Baker went to Greenwood to hear a lecture by noted admiral Richard E. Byrd, explorer of the North and South Poles. Winter's travels remained confined to the South until the summer of 1939, when he went with his Winter relatives from Jackson to attend the New York World's Fair. In addition to New York City, the three-week excursion included stops in Chicago, Niagara Falls, and Washington, D.C. It was the kind of trip that few Mississippians at the time had the means or opportunity to take, and to the sixteen-year-old boy, the trip was "mind-blowing."[35]

Winter needed no broadening of his horizons to understand the Great Depression that hovered over his formative years. He saw firsthand how the economic crisis adversely affected southern families and how Franklin D. Roosevelt's New Deal tried to solve the problem. For the Winters, the economic crisis began in the fall of 1930, when crops failed after a prolonged drought. Every tenant on the place ended up in debt, unable to repay their furnish (the advances of supplies and food) from what little the year's crop had yielded. The Depression years proved to be difficult economic times for William Winter's entire neighborhood. Several farms in the area faced foreclosure, and creditors sold them for debt. Somehow Aylmer Winter managed to avoid this fate, a testament to his economic savvy and frugality. During the 1930s, the Winter household became a temporary refuge for a succession of relatives down on their luck. In 1930, a cousin of Aylmer Winter came to claim some land in Grenada County after losing his job in Charlotte, North Carolina. The cousin's family lived with the Winters while they constructed a dwelling on the only thing of value they still owned. Since William B. Winter had died the previous fall, the Winters had a spare room to offer. In 1931, the family of one of Inez Winter's sisters moved to the Grenada farm, after the father of this household lost his job. Another of Inez Winter's cousins lived with the Winters for awhile in 1935 after he became unemployed.[36]

William Winter had the opportunity to observe the New Deal in action in his own backyard. In 1935, the Resettlement Administration, one of FDR's short-lived federal agencies, started an experimental farm for displaced white sharecroppers on land adjoining the Winter property; the agency launched similar projects around the South in 1935 and 1936, with the goal of transforming southern tenants into landowners. Eventually, the government settled fifteen or so families on the place and provided them tools, farm animals, and a furnish to live on while raising crops. Winter remembered them as "the poorest white people that I can ever recall having seen." The Winters visited these families on Sunday afternoons, and the children of the tenants rode the bus with William to the Grenada city schools. A number of them became his friends.[37]

During the summer of 1937, Winter had another opportunity to observe firsthand how the federal government had helped to move Mississippi and the South into the modern era. Aylmer Winter suggested that the family travel to northeast Mississippi and northwest Alabama. William, fourteen at the time of this excursion, drove the family car. Licensing for drivers did not exist at the time, but William and one of his black friends had taught themselves how to drive a couple of years earlier. On the way north, the family saw the beginnings of Governor Hugh White's 1936 highway program, which had paved many state highways for the first time. When the Winters arrived in northeast Mississippi, Aylmer hardly recognized it as the place where he had attended college forty years before. One of the New Deal's signature programs, the Tennessee Valley Authority (TVA), had rapidly transformed the rural areas in this part of state, bringing electricity and all its associated benefits. (The Winter farm would not receive electricity until 1949.) The family drove on to Muscle Shoals, Alabama, on the Tennessee River, to see the Wilson Dam, built in the 1920s but by then part of the TVA system. Aylmer Winter questioned the cost of some of FDR's many programs, but he could not deny the improvements the TVA had brought to this corner of the South. William Winter, for his part, thought that the TVA had finally created the kind of economy Henry Grady envisioned when he had preached about the coming of a New South in the decades following the Civil War.[38]

The New Deal provided William Winter with yet another political role model: President Franklin D. Roosevelt. Although Aylmer Winter had initially embraced the Democrat Roosevelt when he arrived on the national scene in the early 1930s, his zeal for the president cooled somewhat as Roosevelt rolled out a host of expensive federal programs to try to solve the economic crisis. Aylmer Winter believed FDR's interventions went too far in terms of government involvement in economic life. Mike Conner, despite his progressive credentials as governor, also did not support FDR. William Winter's opinion of the president and his programs, however, diverged from that of his two political heroes. He felt that FDR's New Deal tried to help "restore people" and brought "hope and optimism" to people battered by difficult economic circumstances. The younger Winter admired the president, who further bolstered his belief "that politics is a worthy profession."[39]

Although William Winter grew up in an isolated part of rural Mississippi during the Great Depression, much about his family background and his experiences as a youth in Grenada County prepared him well for the career he would later have in Mississippi politics. His family had deep roots in the state and were part of an established social and political elite. Although the Civil War and the Great Depression had battered the Winters economically, their moderate lifestyle enabled them to weather the hard times better than the vast majority of Mississippians, black and white. For William Winter, this economic security and his love of reading provided the opportunity to see something of the possibilities life offered beyond the backwoods of rural Mississippi. In addition, Winter's parents instilled key values in the young boy—the significance of public service, the importance of education, the need to treat others fairly and show them a measure of basic respect—all of which would profoundly shape the future political leader. William Winter also developed an understanding that dedicated citizen leaders, people like his father, Mississippi governor Mike Conner, and President Franklin D. Roosevelt, could work effectively to solve the problems of their day through government service.

2

COLLEGE AND CAMPAIGNING

William Winter graduated from Grenada High School in the spring of 1940, and shortly thereafter, he won an oratorical contest sponsored by the state American Legion. As a result, the organization chose Winter to give a speech at a patriotic meeting organized for early September in Greenville. Winter's speech at the program praised President Franklin D. Roosevelt as "a great leader," who "is guiding our feet along the way to a still more perfect freedom." He urged Americans to avoid complacency about the dangers posed by the war in Europe, noting that "the indifference of the American people is the deadliest enemy we have today. God grant that someday the people of America will learn that eternal vigilance is the price of liberty." Winter ended his short address by noting that he and his peers were likely to "be sent forth to die on the fields of honor. If this becomes necessary it only means that once more we shall make good with our lives and fortunes the great faith to which we were born."[1] Winter would eventually enter military service, like so many of the young men of his generation. Although he never saw combat in World War II, the conflict did have a major impact on him. Before his service in the U.S. Army began, however, Winter spent three years at the University of Mississippi, the state institution that typically provided higher education to the state's political and economic leaders. During an abbreviated undergraduate career, Winter demonstrated considerable leadership abilities and further expanded his intellectual skills. He also had the chance, during the summer of 1942, to participate in his first statewide political campaign.

In the early 1940s Ole Miss was a small, close-knit campus. Fewer than fifteen hundred students enrolled in the fall of 1940. Classes were held every day but Sunday, and students rarely went home more than once or twice a semester, since few had automobiles. Indeed, on the infrequent occasions when Winter returned to his parents' home, only fifty miles away, he typically hitchhiked. Winter joined Phi Delta Theta with a number of his Grenada classmates. Although Winter's fraternity brothers selected him "outstanding pledge" during his first semester on campus, the fraternity did not become the primary focus of his college experience. He had only a passing interest in the parties and dances sponsored by the fraternities and sororities. Because of his interest in sports, however, Winter actively participated through his fraternity in a variety of intramural sports: track, softball, and touch football. He also served as the freshman trainer for the Ole Miss track team.[2]

During his years at Ole Miss, Winter became involved in an array of other campus activities. As a freshman, he joined the Hermean Literary Society, which held literary discussions and participated in campus debates. In December 1940, Winter represented the Society in a debate that proposed "that a two-party system is desirable in the South." Winter furthered honed his public speaking skills as a finalist in the annual freshman declamation competition, when he presented a stock speech, "The Monster in the Public Square," which warned of the dangers of political demagogues. Winter participated in the International Relations Club and the Freshman YMCA. He also joined the Committee of 100, which brought speakers to campus to talk about religious topics.[3]

By his junior year, Winter had assumed leadership positions in several organizations on campus. He became the president of the Hermean Literary Society; Phi Eta Sigma, a national scholastic fraternity; and the International Relations Club. He was also elected in the fall of 1942, along with eight others, to Omicron Delta Kappa, a national leadership fraternity, which regularly held speaker forums. These events, initiated by history professor Jim Silver in 1940, brought a variety of speakers to the Ole Miss campus, many of whom were controversial. One of the first forums Winter helped organize, and over which he presided, looked at "Mississippi farm problems" and featured a debate between Owen Cooper, from the Mississippi Farm Bureau, and an official from the federal Farm Security Administration.[4]

Work on the campus newspaper, *The Mississippian*, consumed most of Winter's free time during his undergraduate years. Assigned to cover sports, Winter put in long hours at the paper, frequently working late into the evening and then studying after that, often past midnight. One account at the time noted that "when other reporters quit, Winter remained at his typewriter doing more than his share of reporting the results of Ole Miss athletic events." Winter's first byline in *The Mississippian* appeared in November 1940 with a feature about Henry and George Kinard, then finishing up their football careers at Ole Miss, who were the brothers of Frank "Bruiser" Kinard, a two-time All-American at Ole Miss in the 1930s who later went on to a Hall of Fame professional football career. The following month, working with sports editor Charlie Haile from Natchez, Winter's writing began to appear in a weekly column, "Haile in the Winter," and the following year he had his own sports column, "A Rebel Writes." In February 1942 Winter defeated Harold Brownstein by a count of 638 to 281 in the election for managing editor of the paper, and then the following year, after winter break, when the editor of *The Mississippian* left to concentrate on his studies in medical school, Winter was elected without opposition to succeed him.[5]

Despite an active extracurricular life, Winter, a history and political science major, was a serious student. At the end of his first semester, he was one of only 106 students to make the Honor Roll, and he would finish his undergraduate career at Ole Miss with a record of all As and Bs. Winter's professors recognized his intellect but challenged him to do more. For instance, surviving papers from Winter's English classes show that his teachers praised his writing abilities, especially how he drew on his observations of local history and culture, but his professors still offered ample criticism of how the young man could further improve his skills as a writer. Professors at Ole Miss also frequently pointed out perhaps uncomfortable truths to students raised on a diet of Lost Cause myths. For one of Winter's history papers, entitled "What Happened to France in 1940," which received a grade of OK+, Winter had included as part of his analysis of French failures the fact that French deputies were sometimes elected by a much smaller part of the electorate than in the United States. His professor wrote in the margin, "how about our own South?"[6]

Several of Winter's history and political science professors made strong impressions on the student and deeply influenced his thinking. During his first semester, Winter encountered H. B. Howerton, a fairly conservative political science teacher but one who introduced Winter to the possibilities of political reform and who stressed the importance of "efficient, honest administration of government." Howerton tried to teach students "something of good citizenship, good government," and he later remarked, after Winter had been involved in politics for almost two decades, that "William Winter epitomizes the idea that I tried to present." Winter made the only A on the final examination in Howerton's course during that first semester at Ole Miss.[7]

The following year, Winter enrolled in the classes of history professor James Silver, whom Winter later described as "not in the conventional mode. He challenged a lot of shibboleths, the old conventional ideas of the Deep South." Silver had come to Ole Miss in 1936, and from the beginning, he questioned the validity of Mississippi's racial caste system, with its claims of white superiority and black inferiority. Silver "puzzled over my advanced students who seemed to have little doubt of the Negro's inherent inferiority." In his classes, he introduced Winter and other students to a host of new and controversial ideas and viewpoints on race and other matters. Silver also encouraged his students to think for themselves, and for Winter, the history professor raised the possibility that all things, including the South's seemingly immutable social arrangements, could potentially be changed. Silver and his wife frequently hosted groups of students in their homes for meals and informal discussions and, in the process, developed close relationships with a number of students, including Winter. Silver and Winter became lifelong friends.[8]

World War II transformed the Ole Miss campus, especially after the Japanese attack on Pearl Harbor in December 1941. Enrollment at the university had already begun to decline at the beginning of the fall 1941 term, but after the attack, male students began to leave to enroll in the armed forces. Even Chancellor A. B. Butts left the following summer to work in the army's judge advocate general's office. Beginning with the spring 1942 semester, instructors adapted courses "for the war situation and defense training"; students endured practice blackouts to prepare them for possible air raids by enemy planes; and later in the spring, the dining hall began to ration food items. By the fall of 1942 the campus observed "meatless" Tuesdays as a "patriotic action." That same semester, the U.S. Army located its first Administration School at Ole Miss, which brought would-be sergeant-majors and section clerks to campus for five-week training sessions. The soldiers took over eight of the school's fourteen men's dormitories, occupied one-half of the cafeteria for meals, and attended classes in three buildings set aside for the army's use. The soldiers generally remained segregated from the student body in housing, eating, and classroom facilities, although army personnel mingled with faculty and students in a variety of social settings. The arrival of the soldiers gave Ole Miss the increasing feel of an army training facility rather than a peacetime university.[9]

U.S. entry into World War II also put the graduation of Winter and his male classmates in serious doubt. Most of the male students remaining at Ole Miss, including Winter, had already enrolled in campus Reserve Officers' Training Corps (ROTC) units. After Pearl Harbor, they began the wait for their activation orders. When Winter started his junior year in the fall of 1942, he and his ROTC colleagues doubted that their stay at Ole Miss would extend beyond Christmas. In January 1943, however, Winter learned that juniors in his ROTC unit would be allowed to finish the school year before being placed on active duty. Winter looked forward to entering the fray, telling his parents in March 1943 that "I'm more anxious than ever to leave this place."[10]

The preparation for war affected every aspect of campus life, including Winter's work on *The Mississippian*. In November 1942, soon after he became managing editor, the paper announced that it would cut its size, due to declining enrollments and falling advertising revenues. By the time Winter assumed the duties of editor a few months later, he sometimes found that he had little help putting out the weekly publication. He told his father that the completion of one edition "worked me pretty hard, since I had to do most of the writing myself. . . . I put out this paper just about by myself, and in my spare time at that." Yet, Winter loved newspaper work. He felt that it "was the only work that I've ever done that I would willingly stay up all night to do." As editor of the paper, Winter focused much of his efforts detailing the changes that the war continued to bring to campus, including the fact that because of the departure of most of the male student body, which would be almost complete by beginning of the 1943–1944 academic year, female students were poised to take over leadership positions at both *The Mississippian* and in student government.[11]

The upheaval surrounding war preparations also caused Winter and other Ole Miss students to consider how the conflict might impact the South. White leaders around the South, already concerned about how the New Deal had transformed the region, pondered how the war might further alter time-honored traditions in the region. When a group of Deep South governors suggested in 1943 that the South might need to create a new political party because FDR's actions had not upheld the principles cherished by the white South, Winter editorialized in *The Mississippian* that he was not sure the South needed a new political party, especially in the midst of a war. He did, however, sympathize that "the breaks are still unequal, and that the South is still not coming in for its rightful share of the voice in running the government." He noted that after the war southern leaders would indeed need "to remove the political and economic shackles from the South," a problem complicated by "the presence of the negro and the backward white."[12]

The war also raised questions among Ole Miss students about the fate of southern race relations. For example, one of the campus groups that Winter participated in, the United Sons of the South, discussed this issue in the spring of 1942. The organization believed that "the racial situation in Dixie is today far from satisfactory" and that racial changes were needed. The group supported granting blacks "equal status with the white in an ECONOMIC sense" but conceded little else. Equality in the legal system meant black juries and judges, which posed "too many complications . . . to be achieved in the near future by peaceful negroes." Ending segregation would lead to social equality, as well as "lynchings, racial hatred, and bloodshed." Granting "immediate enfranchisement" to blacks would bring back the "Tragic Era" of Reconstruction, a view of that event no doubt still emphasized in some of the student's history classes, since it remained the dominant interpretation of the post–Civil War period among most academic historians at the time. Although the United Sons of the South realized that blacks would likely press for racial changes in the aftermath of the war, likely at the urging of "agitators," the group emphasized that the South would have "to settle her own southern problems in her own southern way! If the South is not let alone, history gives proof of consequences too dreadful to elaborate." This position on the race question actually represented a fairly progressive position among white Mississippians of the time. Winter, who served as secretary of the organization in 1942, accepted this formula for a limited, gradualist approach to racial change, a line of thinking that would continue to inform his ideas on race for many years to come, even as his experiences in World War II would challenge his beliefs on this issue.[13]

Although Winter agreed that the South needed to change, he remained sensitive to criticism of his native region from outsiders and to the negative images of the South promoted by the national media. In April 1943, *Time* magazine, in its "U.S. at War" section under the heading "Mississippi," published a picture of Phil Bell, an ex-bootlegger in overalls from Webster County who was running for the state legislature, along with a poorly written letter from the would-be politician. Winter fired off an editorial in *The Mississippian* claiming that *Time* had presented an unfair image of the state. While admitting that people like Phil Bell were "a staunch and dependable part of our citizenry," Winter noted that "we resent the Yankee magazine's implying that we are all Phil Bells." Winter said that Mississippians "admit our shortcomings, and they are many, but the North has its shortcomings, too." In a letter to the magazine, Winter claimed that its first mention of Mississippi in months represented little more than a "L'il Abner comic strip." The editor of the *Webster Progress*, Ned Lee, criticized Winter for protesting too much in his *Time* editorial. Lee told Winter, in a letter printed in *The Mississippian*, "I have a suspicion that some of you fellows sporting fraternity pins and a kind of false polish put on you by our country club universities live in mortal fear of ridicule by some damyankee up north." Lee said the more appropriate response would be to "get up on hind legs, admit your shortcomings, and tell them to go to hell." Winter countered Lee's attack with a defense of Ole Miss as one of the best universities in the country, whose students "are not the products of a country club by a long shot." Winter also reminded Lee that many of the university's men had already "gone out into the hard places of the world to prove their loyalty to a greater alma mater."[14]

⁂

During his Ole Miss years, Winter had a couple of summer jobs that proved beneficial to his future political career. After his freshman year, he secured a job with the U.S. Department of Agriculture, measuring crop acreage as part of the crop reduction program initiated during the New

Deal. In a 1930 model Chevrolet he bought for $75, Winter traveled to every farm in the northwest part of Grenada County, recording the exact dimensions of each planted field. The summer of 1941 was hot, and the work was grueling physically, but it paid the new federal minimum wage, forty cents an hour. The job also provided Winter with valuable political allies for the future. He visited with local farmers, who had survived the Great Depression and now looked for more prosperous days ahead. They sometimes invited him to stay for lunch, and each stop offered an opportunity for conversation about "crops and politics." At the end of the summer, Winter sold the well-worn automobile for $150, netting a 100 percent profit.[15]

Even more important to his political aspirations, Winter secured a summer job in 1942 as driver for James O. (Jim) Eastland in his first U.S. Senate campaign. In the spring of 1942, William Winter told his father that he would like to be involved in the campaign. As a young man, Aylmer Winter had worked for a time at the Delta plantation store of Woods Eastland, Jim Eastland's father, and considered the elder Eastland "one of the best friends I have in the world." Aylmer Winter called up the candidate and asked for a job in the campaign for his son. Aylmer told Joe Brown, Eastland's campaign manager and Natchez district attorney, that his son could write well and would work hard.[16]

Winter started working for the campaign at the beginning of June. Instead of filling a job behind the scenes at a campaign office, however, Eastland selected Winter as his driver to motor him around the state in a late-model Chevrolet. During Winter's first week on the campaign, he traveled all over north Mississippi, with stops in New Albany, Bruce, Calhoun City, Houston, Vardaman, Duck Hill, Greenwood, and Ruleville. Winter helped by talking to local leaders in each town to "find out how they stand and how much strength Senator Eastland has." By mid-June, Eastland had begun his speaking tour, and the campaign made up to eight stops a day. A typical week would begin with a mid-morning appearance on Monday and end with a final speech on Saturday night. A sound truck preceded the candidate's car and announced to the local population that the candidate would soon arrive to address the crowd. While Eastland spoke, typically for forty minutes or more, Winter would sometimes nail the candidate's posters all over town. After the speech ended, Eastland would shake hands with the crowd, and the caravan would leave for the next stop. The schedule was tight, and Winter often had to drive fast to make it to the next location, frequently traveling along the many unpaved roads that remained in the state. Although the state had few highway patrolmen around at the time to flag speeding drivers, had any troopers stopped the Eastland car, they would have likely issued no ticket. Governor Paul Johnson backed Eastland, and the governor frequently had the highway patrol out delivering the candidate's campaign literature. Every time Winter would make it to a scheduled stop despite being pressed for time, Eastland would compliment him for his driving skills. At night, Eastland and Winter would stay at a local inn or at the home of one of Eastland's many supporters.[17]

As Winter drove, the aspiring senator often talked with the young man about his political experiences. At other times, Eastland spent the time in the car preparing for his next appearance, frequently by combing *Time* magazine for the latest news of the day. Sometimes Joe Brown would come along for the ride, and especially at the end of a long day of campaigning, the two men in the back of the car would pull out a bottle, and the drinking would lead to stories and tall tales about Mississippi politics, which Winter enjoyed immensely. During one ride, Brown, a good-humored fellow who liked to tease Eastland, suggested a new campaign strategy: "Jim, I'll tell you what we're going to do. Let's get us a helicopter and go to northeast Mississippi and fly over those folks out there in the fields and swoop down and say, 'Mississippians, this is the Lord speaking. If you do not vote for Jim Eastland, you will be stricken in your fields!'"[18]

Four other men vied for the U.S. Senate seat that summer. Eastland's most formidable opponents were two men who had significant congressional experience, Wall Doxey, who had served for fourteen years as a U.S. representative before moving to the U.S. Senate in 1941 after the death of Pat Harrison, and Ross Collins, an eighteen-year veteran of the U.S. House of Representatives. The major debates of the campaign revolved around how each candidate proposed to support the war effort and how each candidate planned to assist the Mississippi economy, especially the agricultural sector. Eastland had long been a member of the Theodore Bilbo faction of Mississippi politics, having served as one of Bilbo's legislative floor leaders during his gubernatorial term from 1928 to 1932 and having campaigned for Bilbo during his 1940 Senate campaign. In the

1942 Senate campaign, however, Bilbo backed Doxey, a change in political alliances that Jim Eastland used to his advantage.[19]

Eastland's well-orchestrated campaign paid off. Although he began the race as an underdog to both Doxey and Collins, Eastland campaigned hard and gradually emerged as the frontrunner. In the first primary vote at the end of August, Eastland finished first, polling 37 percent of the vote and gaining a plurality in forty-six of eighty-two counties. The next closest candidate, Wall Doxey, got almost 29 percent of the ballots but won only nineteen counties. When the two men faced off in a second primary three weeks later, Eastland accused Bilbo, who continued to back Doxey, of trying to "dictate elections." In effect, Eastland could still attract Bilbo supporters because of his past support for the "redneck" champion while also distancing himself from the controversial politician, whom many Mississippians, such as William Winter's father, disliked intensely. In the second primary, in which voter turnout reached the lowest point in almost fifteen years, Eastland won almost 57 percent of the vote and carried sixty counties.[20]

Winter received $50 a month for his summer job, in which he drove approximately thirty thousand miles. Eastland told Aylmer Winter that his son "was one of the smartest young men I have ever seen. He has a head full of common sense and will certainly go places." More important to William Winter than the pay and Eastland's praise was the experience of traveling around the state, much of which he had never seen, and meeting people in every locale. As Winter's summer job in 1941 had connected him to people in Grenada County who would become life-long political supporters, the 1942 summer job of driving for Jim Eastland introduced Winter to political power brokers around the state, some of whom would be Winter allies for years to come. Winter's work in the 1942 campaign further sparked his long-standing desire to have a political career of his own one day. Preparing to go back to Ole Miss that fall, he told his mother, "I'm sorry the campaign is over." Over the summer, the young man had heard the candidate deliver a version of the same speech scores of time. By the end of the campaign, he could recite large portions of Eastland's discourse from memory. Winter recalled that on a brief visit home before returning to Ole Miss he practiced the Eastland speech on his father's cows, "as I envisioned myself someday waging a campaign for public office."[21]

ⓒⓞ

As Winter completed his third year at Ole Miss, he and thirty-one of his fellow ROTC classmates received orders to report in June 1943 to Camp Shelby in Hattiesburg for processing and assignment to an Infantry Replacement Training Center. After being inducted as a private, Winter discovered that a recent army order allowed any advanced ROTC students who could finish their college degrees over the summer to do so before reporting for their active duty assignment. Winter lacked twenty-seven hours to graduate, so he and several of his ROTC comrades returned to Ole Miss for a summer session crammed with courses. Attending summer school as a soldier, Winter was subject to military oversight and some-times restricted to his dorm quarters because of infractions by his fellow soldiers. He also took part in physical training with the Army Specialized Training Program (ASTP) at Ole Miss. The ROTC cadets ran the stadium steps, participated in a calisthenics program, and went on regular mile runs. Winter, however, found time in between his heavy course schedule and the physical exercise regimen to play softball on one of the ASTP teams. He told his father that "I'd rather play baseball or softball than any-thing I can think of." Because of the change of plans, Winter got to spend some extra time with his parents in Grenada County and heard that racial trouble had erupted that summer at Camp McCain, recently constructed outside the town of Grenada. At his graduation ceremony at the end of the summer, Winter wore his cap and gown over his military uniform. He missed graduating with distinction by .2 of a point, a shortcoming he attributed to the long hours he put in at *The Mississippian*. A week later, after a final visit with his parents, Winter left for Camp Blanding, Florida, to begin basic training and his service in a war that would have a major impact on him and many of his fellow Mississippians.[22]

3

WORLD WAR II

World War II transformed the South. New war industries and military camps boosted an impoverished economy and brought American soldiers from all over the country into the region to train. At the same time, southern agriculture, already reshaped by New Deal farm policies, experienced further strains, as black and white workers abandoned the countryside for the military or to search for war jobs. Black military service and the United States' rhetoric against the racist Nazi regime encouraged black Americans to question more stridently the South's system of racial segregation and black disfranchisement. Military service exposed Southerners, both black and white, to a wider world of people and ideas and gave them a new perspective on their region and its institutions.[1] William Winter, serving for over three years in the U.S. Army, witnessed many of the changes World War II created, while also further honing his leadership skills in diverse settings.

Immediately after graduation from Ole Miss in September 1943, Winter and his fellow ROTC members headed for seventeen weeks of basic training at Camp Blanding, Florida, where he got his first glimpse of the nation's true diversity. Most of the Ole Miss boys were placed with each other in platoons of the Sixty-Fifth Regiment, but Winter's platoon was filled with strangers. Winter's first impression of his fellow soldiers was that they were a collection of "low type of men," many "sorry Yankees from Minnesota, Pennsylvania, Illinois, and Missouri." Gradually, he overcame his parochial prejudices to appreciate the unique collection of individuals he encountered; indeed, by the end of basic training, Winter had many friends among what he viewed initially as a motley mass of humanity.[2]

Winter's opinion of his immediate superior at Camp Blanding, Sergeant. Chuberko, underwent a similar evolution. A recent east European immigrant from Czechoslovakia, Chuberko held a particular hatred for the Nazis, who had invaded his native country and murdered some members of his family. Winter reported that Chuberko's "mastery of the English language is open to argument." Despite his verbal limitations, Chuberko "incited terror" among the recruits in his charge. The sergeant apparently sought retribution against the Nazis by creating the toughest soldiers he possibly could. Winter told his father soon after arriving that Chuberko was "the nearest thing to Simon Legree that I have ever seen." Chuberko led his troops on long marches through the sand and muck of north Florida and rode them for every small infraction against military discipline. To prepare his soldiers for the rigors of combat, Chuberko would wake his platoon at three in the morning for a brisk run around the sand flats of Camp Blanding. Despite his original impressions, Winter came to recognize Chuberko as "fair and sincere." After a month at Blanding, Winter described the sergeant as an "A-1 fellow."[3]

The instruction at Blanding consisted of blocks of training. First came the basics of how to "march, shoot, and salute." Winter spent his first couple of weeks "drilling, drilling, drilling, rolling packs, hearing lectures, taking calisthenics, and cleaning rifles." Instruction in infantry weapons and tactics followed, with focus on advanced training in a specific aspect of warfare, in Winter's case heavy weapons. The last two weeks of training involved field exercises, where the recruits left the relative comfort of camp for a taste of what real infantry life might entail. Winter excelled at all aspects of the training regimen. After bayonet drill, Sergeant Chuberko cited Winter for having "the best form in the platoon," and during rifle training, Winter proved to be a first-rate marksman.[4]

The rigorous physical training gave Winter little problem. Early on, after a five-mile hike with full packs and rifles, he noted how "some of those poor fellows [were] dragging that last mile in ankle-deep sand." During the daily exercise regimen, many of the older soldiers in Winter's platoon (some in their late twenties or early thirties) had to drop out before the sessions ended. The fact that Winter did not drink or smoke undoubtedly aided his physical conditioning, as did his workouts with the army the summer before at Ole Miss.[5]

Winter's performance during the first six weeks of training earned him promotion to acting corporal of a squad. Although the temporary upgrade meant more work, Winter understood that the promotion also meant his superiors recognized his talents. His lieutenant rated Winter as "the top man in the platoon." Sergeant Chuberko agreed. Despite the acclaim Winter received from his superiors, halfway through his time at Camp Blanding, he began to hear troubling reports that getting into Officer Candidate School (OCS) at Fort Benning, Georgia, might be difficult, as the army already had a ready supply of infantry officers, and the number of American casualties had not reached the levels earlier predicted.[6]

At the end of basic training, Winter and the other members of the Ole Miss ROTC group were ordered to return to Oxford to join the Army Specialist Training Program and await further instructions about OCS vacancies. As Winter prepared to leave Blanding, he reflected on his experience by describing it as difficult but noting that "I know of no comparable time that was more interesting and memorable." He also concluded, "You learn a lot more than just how to fire a machine gun in the army, and if I am fortunate enough ever to become an officer, I know that I shall be a better one for having had this basic training." Back at Ole Miss, Winter enrolled in a couple of classes. He investigated shifting to the air corps but found out that it also had a surplus of potential officer candidates. Although generally restricted to campus, Winter got passes to visit his mother in Grenada and to travel to Jackson to sit in with his father for a part of the Mississippi House's 1944 legislative session.[7]

When Winter finally joined an OCS class at Fort Benning soon after the D-Day invasion, he found even greater diversity than at Camp Blanding. Only one of his Ole Miss ROTC friends, Curtis Richardson, from Tippah County, Mississippi, was in his class, while over half of the student-soldiers in Winter's company were from Puerto Rico. Initially they impressed Winter as "rare birds, but fine fellows. They are mostly college men and well-informed, but there are some who mutter some unintelligible sounds that pass for English." Although Winter eventually counted some of the Puerto Rican candidates among his friends in the company, he did not embrace them as readily as the collection of European immigrants he encountered at Blanding. Many of the Puerto Rican recruits did not survive the training process. At the six-week mark, almost 90 of the 210 men in the company, most coming from the Puerto Rican cohort, were dismissed for inadequate performance. Even more noteworthy in terms of diversity were the two black soldiers in Winter's initial class of 210 men. One, Willie Williams, an ROTC student from the Agricultural and Technical College of North Carolina, had the bunk next to Winter. The other black candidate was an ROTC student from Texas named Kemp. Sharing living quarters with blacks was a new experience for Winter and most of his fellow white soldiers. Although relatively few black men were in Benning's OCS classes, the post housed large numbers of black soldiers. By the summer of 1944, more than 80 percent of all black troops in the World War II army had passed through the Fort Benning Reception Center. In addition, the fort was the home base for the 555th Parachute Infantry, an all-black outfit that began training at Benning in December 1943. In May 1944 Benning had approximately twenty thousand white soldiers and ninety-five hundred black troops.[8]

Winter's OCS training coincided with a pivotal moment in American race relations, when war demands increasingly challenged the South's racial segregation and black disfranchisement. From the beginning of the conflict, blacks had recognized that America's "fight for freedom" against Nazi Germany's racism offered an excellent opportunity to press the United States to end its own racial apartheid. A. Philip Randolph's threatened march on Washington, D.C., in 1941 prompted President Roosevelt to issue Executive Order 8802, prohibiting racial discrimination in companies with federal war contracts. The *Pittsburgh Courier* led the call for a "Double-V" campaign: victory against fascism abroad and racism at home.[9]

By the spring of 1944, the white South was on the defensive about its racial arrangements. After the U.S. Supreme Court outlawed the white primary as a disfranchising mechanism in its *Smith v. Allwright* decision, Mississippi politicians, including Aylmer Winter, sought ways to circumvent the court mandate. Mississippi Democrats considered withholding their support for Franklin D. Roosevelt's fourth race for the presidency, primarily because he supported an anti-poll tax bill then under debate in the U.S. Senate. That spring while awaiting his OCS assignment, William Winter noted that the "negro issue is cropping up more frequently and more seriously than ever before, and I fear increasing trouble over the thing."[10]

The army made some accommodation to black demands for a relaxation of its policy of segregation. In part, the army responded to the racial unrest and violence that had gripped southern army posts since the beginning of the war, such as the 1941 lynching at Fort Benning of a black soldier in uniform and a number of high-profile incidents in the summer of 1943, including the assault on Duck Hill by black soldiers from Camp McCain near Grenada, Mississippi. Officer training had already been integrated by 1942, in part to save costs, although the number of black officer candidates remained small. Soon after Winter began his OCS training, the army took a further step when it ordered an end to racial segregation in post theaters and exchanges and on army transportation between army bases and surrounding communities. Negative stories in the black and white press revealed the poor travel arrangements provided by the army for black soldiers, and Fort Benning had been cited as one of the worst offenders. Black soldiers in 1943 had reported the transportation there as "rotten and terribly inadequate. Colored soldiers must walk long distances to get small space in [a] bus." The racial segregation at Benning seemed particularly unfair because German prisoners of war received more respect than black American soldiers. While black soldiers at the camp were restricted to the one black theater on base or to the black section of another theater, the German prisoners of war had unrestricted access to all camp theaters.[11]

Deep South politicians and white citizens berated the army for its attack on local racial customs, such as the commissioning of black officers and the integration of OCS companies. In May 1942, the Mississippi congressional delegation had signed a joint petition asking that no black officers be stationed in the state. In 1943, the leader of a Georgia White Supremacy League had denounced the fact that white officer candidates at Fort Benning "have to eat and sleep with Negro candidates." He deemed the practice "the most damnable outrage that was ever perpetrated on the youth of the South." But the presence of the two black candidates in Winter's class and the completely integrated living and eating arrangements, while a new experience for Winter and the other white soldiers, elicited no animosity or sense of impending doom among the white soldiers. The officer candidate schools were the army's first experiment with an integrated military, and on the whole, this new test in race relations proceeded smoothly, according to reports both during and after the war. According to Winter, the southern whites in his company seemed to be more at ease with their black colleagues than the northern boys. For those white Southerners in OCS who established friendships with the black candidates, the experience proved eye-opening. A wartime report on OCS integration claimed, "The reaction of southern men to this enforced intimacy with Negro classmates was very interesting. In most cases they reached an enlightening knowledge of a type of Negro that they had never known before," an analysis that certainly described Winter's own experience.[12]

About halfway through the OCS training cycle, Winter's platoon, which included both of the black soldiers in his class, planned a weekend party at a restaurant in nearby Columbus. When making arrangements, the white soldiers discovered that the establishment would not admit blacks. Some of the white soldiers, including Winter, suggested that the platoon cancel the party. When the two black soldiers heard about the controversy, however, they urged their white colleagues to go ahead with the planned event. Halfway through OCS, Williams and Kemp had little interest in stirring up an altercation over the issue of off-base segregation in Georgia. The white soldiers held the party without their black comrades.[13]

Although Winter's OCS class suggested the more racially integrated future that lay ahead for the South, the larger segregation controversy that played out at Fort Benning during the summer and fall of 1944 intruded little on Winter's consciousness. The rigorous OCS training consumed most of his time. Whereas the instruction at Blanding had been primarily a physical ordeal, the training for the officer candidates at Benning included additional attention to the intellectual and leadership abilities of the men to judge their suitability for second lieutenant bars. As at Camp Blanding, Winter excelled in all aspects of OCS training. The first exam for the candidates was a two-hundred-question general information test, on which Winter made a perfect score. His IQ was calculated at 149, which placed him in the highest 1 percent in the entire Army and undoubtedly as one of the smartest members of his company. Nearly every week, candidates had one or more examinations, covering topics such as map reading, compass operation, communications, and the details of various weapons and tactics. Winter aced practically every one of the exams but had difficulty with the advanced machine gun test. After the first month of instruction, a major portion of OCS training consisted of frequent bivouacs, which simulated combat problems in the field. Despite

all this required activity, Winter still found time to write for Fort Benning's OCS newspaper, the *Shavetail*. As at Ole Miss, Winter's fellow soldiers recognized him as a leader. The company elected Winter one of six
members of an honor committee, charged with addressing "undesirable
activities" in the company.[14]

Winter spent whatever free time he had away from camp primarily with
Troy Middleton, a fellow candidate who had come from the Louisiana
State University ROTC program. Middleton's father, Troy H. Middleton,
a distinguished general in the army, had served as colonel in World War
I. During the Second World War, he had returned to the army to command the Forty-Fifth Infantry Division in Sicily and Italy and then head
the army's VIII Corps, which fought in France during the summer of
1944. Winter and the younger Middleton frequently took weekend liberty
together. During one trip "to see a couple [of] colonel's daughters" on the
outskirts of Columbus, the two stayed out too late, and, failing to secure
a hotel room, they had to spend the night "on raincoats in a thicket of
woods." Middleton's aunt lived in Columbus, and some weekends, the
two went there for a home-cooked meal and the chance to spend the
night in her large private residence. At other times, they would visit with
officers stationed at Benning who were friends of Middleton's father.[15]

At the end of the seventeen weeks of OCS, only one third (71) of Winter's original class of 210 finished the program, a much smaller graduating
class than usual. Richardson and Middleton had made it through, as had
Williams and Kemp. At the graduation ceremony, Winter was recognized
as the top graduate of his class. His parents could not attend the event,
because Inez Winter was teaching and Aylmer Winter was busy harvesting
his crop. Troy Middleton's mother and his sister did attend the graduation
event, and after the ceremony, General George Weems, who had pinned
on Winter's lieutenant bars, invited Winter and the Middletons to dinner at the officers' club. Sporting his brand new shiny gold bars, Winter
basked in his accomplishment.[16]

After graduation Winter had a ten-day leave before his next assignment,
at the Infantry Replacement Training Center (IRTC) at Fort McClellan,
Alabama. When he arrived home, he found that the war had affected even
this isolated corner of the globe. Most notably, the war had led to a short-
age of labor on the farm, as many of the tenants either left for the war or
for better-paying jobs in the numerous war industries around the country.

However, those tenants who did remain stood to make money as a result of a good harvest and higher prices for their crops. As Aylmer Winter noted, some "made more money than they have ever before made in one year." Though the visit was brief, Winter and his parents relished the reunion. Soon after Winter returned to his next army assignment, Aylmer Winter wrote him, "I have missed you very much since you returned to Camp. It is lonesome here without you."[17]

Arriving at Fort McClellan at the end of October 1944, Winter's superiors assigned him to command a platoon in the Second Battalion of the First Regiment, one of two all-black regiments undergoing basic training at McClellan. White officers staffed the First Regiment at the time, except for a handful of black noncommissioned officers. An older black man named Jones, an ex-professional boxer from Harlem, served as Winter's platoon sergeant. Army officials likely picked Winter for this particular assignment because they believed southern white officers would better know how to deal with black soldiers.[18]

The army had only recently provided some instructions for white officers assigned to black units, information designed to highlight the problems that might arise in the interracial training and to reiterate the official army policy of nondiscrimination. One directive given to the white officers declared, "Sometimes prejudice against the Negroes flares up in the Army. It is not a problem, however, in a camp where it is well understood that a soldier in the United States uniform is a *soldier*, not a white or Negro, Christian or Jew, rich man or poor, but a soldier, and as such is worthy of respect." White officers, however, often had difficulties leading black troops. Winter recalled that many of northern white officers in his regiment remained extremely uncomfortable around black soldiers, since as civilians they had had few dealings with black people. Of course, many white southern officers also struggled to obey the army's nondiscrimination orders, although some, like Winter, generally succeeded in adhering to the directive.[19]

As a platoon leader, Winter earned respect in part because he was not a rigid authoritarian. In general, he "tried to be a friend of the enlisted man." He told his parents at the time that he had no interest in using "what little rank this bar holds to exercise domination over men less fortunate than I." In large part, the paternalistic view of black/white relations Winter had absorbed growing up in Grenada County shaped his approach to dealing with black soldiers. His leadership style worked better with some platoon members than with others in a unit that contained black soldiers from all over the country. Having grown up in a world where whites regularly asserted their "superiority," southern blacks proved more willing to accept orders from a white officer, especially one with a friendly demeanor. On the other hand, Winter had less preparation to deal with the non-southern black trainees, who rejected white paternalism and were less deferential. One soldier in Winter's platoon, from Detroit, who clearly resented taking orders from a southern white officer, continually complained about the hard training. As was common practice by black NCOs of black units led by white officers, Sergeant Jones assisted with disciplinary matters and enforced adherence to Winter's orders. Although Lieutenant Winter initially did not know about his NCO's techniques, Jones would have recalcitrant privates who balked at obeying commands join him behind the latrines for individual sessions, where the sergeant would use his "fistic prowess" to encourage a change in attitude.[20]

A more common problem than the occasional discipline issues was a situation that Winter had often seen at Camp Blanding, recruits so badly out-of-shape that they struggled with the physical demands of basic training. Many of the southern black soldiers, used to back-breaking labor on southern farms, seemed better prepared than their northern counterparts.

Winter hoped that his McClellan assignment would be a temporary posting, in part because he was eager to see combat. While he waited for his chance to be sent to the front lines, he resolved to do his best job with the assignment he had. His father, confident that Winter would succeed, told his son, "Those young Negroes, who have the stamina and intelligence to complete basic training, will likely develop into good soldiers, when they get into the routine of Army discipline." Winter's superiors asked for "unceasing effort," and he did not disappoint. A month after Winter's arrival, the regiment leaders recognized Winter's stellar performance by assigning him the tasks of both battalion drill instructor and battalion physical training officer. Winter worked his charges hard, taking them on successive four-mile runs. While many of the soldiers "had lain down by the roadside ere half the run was over," Winter continued to push them to achieve good physical condition. At the same time, Winter established a rapport with many of the black soldiers in his platoon and throughout his battalion. At one point, he arranged a boxing exhibition for the entire outfit. As physical training instructor, Winter knew the best athletes, so he set up the pairings and then served as master of ceremonies for the event. Fifteen hundred soldiers, including the commander of McClellan's IRTC, attended. Winter thought, "These black boys had a big time, and produced some good fighters."[21]

Winter's disappointment with his assignment also grew out of his understanding about the fate of the black soldiers he trained. Since the army had typically assigned black infantry units to support roles, he knew that his black charges would likely never see combat. For many white Southerners, the Army's discriminatory assignments merely confirmed their deeply-held beliefs about black inferiority. At the officers' club one day, Winter met a captain from Mississippi who had fought in the Pacific for twenty-seven months. The captain, "filled with disgust at having to put up with these blacks," told Winter he considered "the idea of making infantrymen out of them" laughable. He claimed that, while in the Pacific, the all–black Ninety-Third Infantry Division had only been "used on the docks at Port Moresby and other ports to unload ships," a statement that ignored the role that racism played in the Army's decision to relegate much of the 93rd to a support role in the Pacific fighting. Winter despaired over the futility of his assigned task, reflecting, "There is little consolation to me in the fact that I am training troops for combat, when I know that these negroes will never be anything but laborers for the quartermaster corps."[22]

When the Allied march across Europe bogged down in the winter of 1944 in the face of a Nazi counterattack, even more of the lieutenants at Fort McClellan received orders to report to Western Europe, but Winter's name never appeared on the list of those bound for overseas duty. The fact that Winter did such a good job as an instructor, in effect, diminished his chances of being sent to a theater of war. His regimental superiors gave him the highest efficiency rating among the officer corps. Captain Snyder, the captain of his company, did not hesitate to call on him when a problem arose, telling him, "Winter, you're one man around here that will get this done right, so here it is." Winter had performed so well that his battalion commander wanted to recommend him for a promotion, although Winter had not been a second lieutenant long enough to warrant such an upgrade. By late January 1945, with the German counteroffensive in Europe largely turned back, Winter became resigned to the fact that he would probably miss out on the war in Europe. He still had hopes that he might make it to the Pacific and lead an infantry unit there before the fighting concluded. Displaying a common racial attitude pervasive since Pearl Harbor, Winter assuaged his disappointment over missing the fight against Germany by noting that "no American soldier can have a greater destiny than to help our country avenge the infamous deeds of those yellow-bellied sons of Nippon—to help obliterate that race of traitorous creatures who attempt to pass as civilized human beings." In mid-February 1945, however, Winter was assigned to work in regimental headquarters at McClellan as the scouting and patrolling instructor. The new assignment meant that Winter typically spent at least five nights a week "in the woods."[23]

When Winter moved to regimental headquarters, he found himself part of another of the army's limited experiments with racial integration. Because so many white officers had been sent to Europe, the army assigned underutilized black officers to help with the training of the two all-black regiments at Fort McClellan. At the end of 1944, the army had only 210 black infantry officers, 170 of those holding the rank of lieutenant. The scarcity of higher-ranking black officers sprang from army decisions that limited their deployment to noncombat roles. Although the army trained black officers to command, army headquarters remained skeptical throughout the war about their leadership capabilities. Many white officers, whether from the South or elsewhere, tended to take every mistake of a black officer as confirmation of general incompetence. Army leaders frequently accused black officers of fraternizing too closely with black enlisted men, but part of that perception might be explained by the fact that black enlistees, not entirely free of entrenched notions of racial hierarchy themselves, often did not show black officers the same respect as they did their white leaders. In addition, black NCOs often clashed with black officers, thinking lieutenants and captains lorded their status over lower-ranked blacks.[24]

Observers during the war and subsequent army studies claimed that the kind of officer corps created at McClellan in early 1945, a staff of mixed black and white officers, faced particularly acute problems. By late spring 1945, more than half of the officers in Winter's regiment were black. The black and white officers lived together, ate at the same mess, and shared some recreational facilities, per the army's anti-segregation orders of 1943. Outside of the officers' quarters, where sleeping locations were assigned, self-segregation continued to exist. As one army report completed right after the war noted, "Segregation was hardly less real under rules which sought to prevent it than it would have been had the rules not existed." As on many other bases, the white officers at McClellan refused to share all of their privileges, specifically their officers' club. Black officers quickly established their own club at Fort McClellan. Overall, however, desegregation at McClellan created less conflict than at other locales with mixed officer groups.[25]

Winter later recalled that Fort McClellan "was something of an oasis in the South," and some compelling evidence backs up this claim. Late in 1943, six months before the army had issued its anti-segregation directive, a black preacher from Chicago, James L. Horace, visited eight army camps in the Deep South to examine the treatment of black troops. Talking with black soldiers throughout Louisiana, Mississippi, Alabama, and Georgia, he found their experiences overwhelmingly negative, except at Fort McClellan. Horace concluded that the Alabama fort harbored "less segregation" than elsewhere. He also felt that McClellan had "more Democracy than any. The spirit of fair play seems to be present." His conversations with black soldiers convinced him as well that their relations with the civilians at Fort McClellan ranged "from good to excellent" and "a sense of appreciation" existed.

To be sure, Fort McClellan had its share of racial conflicts. One eighteen-year-old black enlistee from New York, stationed at McClellan in the summer of 1944, complained, "I expected to find jim crow & discrimination in the south, but never as bad as it is here." In January 1945, after three white soldiers attacked a black soldier who entered the white service club at Fort McClellan, three hundred black soldiers gathered at the club and threatened to "clean up" the white soldiers. The MPs arrived and averted a confrontation. In another incident, black soldiers at the base hospital in the spring of 1945 charged that a white officer had said that he had more respect for the German prisoners housed on base than the black soldiers working with him at the hospital. The white officer reportedly said, "If I had my way I would line them [the black soldiers] all up together and shoot them with my forty-five."[26] Even if Fort McClellan did have a better racial climate than the typical Deep South army base during World War II, it still simmered with racial friction, as blacks and whites interacted in ways that departed from the typical patterns of daily life in the region.

Because of his new regimental duties, working sixteen- to twenty-hour days, William Winter had limited time to interact socially with the new black officers, but the integration of the officer corps affected him on a highly personal level. When Winter did fraternize with his fellow black officers off the training field, he was impressed. Most of them, he said, were "well-trained, hard-working, [and] highly dedicated." The black officers arrived at Fort McClellan from all around the country, most having graduated from some of the nation's best higher education institutions: the University of Michigan, Cornell University, West Point. In fact, they were men very much like Winter and most of the other white officers and similar to the two black officer candidates Winter had encountered in his OCS class at Fort Benning.[27]

Winter became friends with several of the black officers, although others remained a bit suspicious of the white Mississippian. One northern white officer, who had a particular dislike for Southerners, would approach Winter when he was in the company of black officers and say, "Tell them about your friend Bilbo." Of course, most of the black officers did not need anyone to tell them about Bilbo; in 1944 and 1945, the senior senator from Mississippi had made loud pronouncements about the need to send all black Americans back to Africa and had filibustered the appropriation for the Fair Employment Practices Committee. Somewhat less well known but also prone to making outrageous statements on the subject of race toward the end of the war was the other Mississippi senator, Jim Eastland, close friend of the Winter family, including Lieutenant Winter. Winter veered away from the subject of Mississippi politics with his new black colleagues, but sometimes the conversation turned to the topic of race. All the black officers believed that Jim Crow's days were numbered, that significant racial change would come quickly in the postwar years. Winter, knowing how entrenched the racial mores of his region were, doubted that change would come so easily. After all, Bilbo and Eastland talked the way they did largely because they knew that such rhetoric would win them votes (and cost them few) in a state like Mississippi.[28]

As Winter became acquainted with black officers, he recognized that he could not have a regular friendship with them. They could not meet at either of the two segregated officers' clubs on base, and they certainly could not go together into nearby, strictly segregated Anniston for a meal or a movie. Even the ride into town might pose problems. Although the army officially prohibited segregation on transportation between McClellan and Anniston, civilians ran the bus line and oftentimes enforced local customs by ordering black officers to the back of the bus. Winter was uncomfortable with the contradiction of this situation: he could have one kind of relationship—based on presumed equality and mutual respect—with his black officer friends at most places on base, but that relationship had to change immediately outside the camp. As a result, Winter began to understand, on a very individual level, "how unreal was the world in which I had grown up, the segregated world." That realization would have a profound effect on Winter when he returned to civilian life.[29]

In mid-July Winter found that his name had finally made it to the top of the list for a new assignment. He thought he would head to the Pacific to join a planned invasion of Japan, one that military intelligence suggested could result in more than one hundred thousand U.S. casualties. However, in early August, Winter and other Americans discovered that "a Japanese madness has come to a devastating end in the unbelievable fury that is the atomic bomb." Winter realized he would have "the inevitable tour of occupation duty." He had to accept that despite two years of active military service, he had missed the actual fighting and had "been denied a share of whatever glory and satisfaction there is in being a combat infantryman." He also worried that his stateside military service might be "a killing blow" for his future political aspirations. Even many of the black tenants on the Grenada farm had seen overseas duty. For instance, all five of James Robinson's sons had enlisted in the military during the war and spent several years in various theaters of the war. Aylmer Winter tried to reassure his son that no "fair-minded" person would hold the young Winter's wartime assignment against him, since he could only "serve to the best of your ability, where you were ordered to serve." Winter eventually made his peace with what he frequently considered a second-class assignment. A month after he left Fort McClellan, Winter realized that many soldiers disliked their role in the war: "The poor wretch on the battle lines is only too glad to take a softer spot; the unsung wearer of the blue in an Alabama training camp feels that the war is missed." And looking back on his McClellan tour while stationed in the Pacific in 1946, Winter recalled, "a year ago I was spending full days training colored soldiers and enjoying the work—even though I may not have admitted it at the time."[30]

At the end of August, Winter received his orders to proceed to Fort Ord, 125 miles south of San Francisco on Monterey Bay. He left on September 2—the same day the Japanese formally surrendered to General Douglas MacArthur in Tokyo Bay—for a long train ride cross country. In late September, Winter, along with 250 officers and almost 1,100 enlisted men, left Long Beach, California, for Manila, Philippines on the *Kota Baroe*. The six-thousand-mile trip took twenty days.[31]

Arriving in Manila Bay, the men were placed in the Twenty-Fourth Replacement Depot. Winter hoped to be assigned to a war crimes investigation team, but once again his excellent record in the military worked against him. After being interviewed by the commanding colonel, Winter was driven to a headquarters in the southern part of Manila, where he would serve as "assistant aide-de-camp" to Major General F. E. Uhl, commanding general of the Replacement Command in the Pacific.[32]

Winter disliked his new assignment and his new boss. He complained to his parents about "being groomed for the job of houseboy and apple polisher for this general who walks like a man but who speaks only to God and a fish-faced major." After a week working in Uhl's operation, Winter filed a formal request for reassignment and asked for "duty with Infantry troops." He explained that he had trained as an infantryman, that he had no experience with headquarters administration, and that he wanted "to serve the Army in the best possible manner." A few days later, General Uhl summoned Winter and roared, "What do you mean by requesting a change of assignment?" Winter repeated the reasons he listed in his written request. After a short lecture from the general, Winter secured his release and returned to the Twenty-Fourth Replacement Depot. Winter's brief stay at Uhl's headquarters led him to question the entire nature of military hierarchy. Although he recognized "the necessity for an officer's retaining and holding the respect and esteem of his men," Winter also deplored "the system of privileges which mark the gap between the two classes."[33]

Winter's new assignment landed him in the Eighty-Sixth Division, which had briefly fought in Europe at the end of the war against Germany before being redeployed to the Philippines. By the time Winter joined the outfit, the division primarily worked with Filipino army outfits to ferret out a few Japanese stragglers from the Filipino countryside. Many of the Eighty-Sixth's soldiers had little to do and felt that "their coming to the Philippines was rather useless." Winter served in the G-3 section as an assistant responsible for planning and coordinating the operations of the division. The planning centered on "keeping the soldiers occupied" through recreational and education programs, supplying the various outposts in Luzon working with Filipino soldiers, and overseeing the reestablishment of communications and transportation on the island.[34]

Winter's overall impression of the island and its people reflected his belief in a racial hierarchy of white civilization and Asian backwardness. Winter told his father that the Filipinos resembled "southern negroes in their living conditions and in their lack of industry, although their personal habits and morals are on a slightly higher plane." He thought that whatever success the Philippines had experienced had occurred because of "American capital" and "American leadership" and concluded that "without the United States this would be another island of primitive Orientals." Aylmer Winter confirmed his son's images of the Filipino people by recalling his visit, as a young man, to the 1904 Louisiana Purchase Exposition in St. Louis, where Aylmer, along with thousands of other Americans, had seen the ethnological displays, which included various Filipino groups, including members of the Igorot tribe. He remembered them as "the most primitive people and lowest in the scale of civilization I had ever seen."[35]

After a few months, Winter's work in the G-3 section of the Eighty-Sixth Division's Headquarters focused primarily on the demobilization of the Pacific forces. Each week, qualifying members of the Eighty-Sixth division shipped home, and Winter made the necessary arrangements for the return journeys and reassignment of new soldiers shifted to the Eighty-Sixth. The demobilization proceeded much too slowly for many of the three hundred thousand American soldiers stationed in the Philippines as 1946 began. In early January, the army announced that the difficulty in securing voluntary replacements would slow the relief of occupation forces then in place. In the Philippines, thousands of American soldiers took to the streets in two days of protests, which culminated with an "orderly though wildly enthusiastic" mass meeting of twenty thousand soldiers in a central plaza in Manila. Soldiers speaking at the meeting claimed that the occupation force on the Philippine Islands was much larger than necessary to carry out essential tasks, which new recruits could handle in any event. Many also asserted that the large force wrongly remained in place to guard against potential internal problems that might develop as the Philippines moved toward national elections and independence from the United States later in 1946. One leaflet distributed before the mass meeting declared, "The State Department wants the army to back up its imperialism." A soldiers' committee, claiming to represent almost 140,000 troops, later met and drew up a list of questions to present to Secretary of War Robert Patterson on his upcoming visit to Manila. The army squelched the soldier complaints by threatening participants with military discipline, but the protests succeeded in pressuring politicians to speed up the demobilization process. As part of the demobilization operation, Winter knew about the problems that necessitated a slower pace of demobilization. Yet he understood the feelings of the disgruntled soldiers:

> It was not mutiny; it was not desertion; it was simply the voice of loneliness, of homesickness, of longing for the one-mule farm in South Georgia or the tenements of Chicago's South Side; it was the outpouring of the intense wanting to be away from all that is the army by a group of very un-internationally minded "little people" who have fought and won this war. That to them is enough.

In Winter's estimation, the protestors had little concern "that the Flips don't shoot each other or that a sawmill in the wilds of Luzon isn't carried off by bandits." In the final analysis, however, he concluded a soldier had to accept the decisions of his commanders, and "with very rare exceptions I don't think this GI complaining is justified."[36]

Demobilization soon proceeded more smoothly, and Winter took advantage of the more relaxed pace of work to satisfy his intellectual curiosity by exploring Luzon. In February, he secured a 105-foot boat from a general and organized an expedition of twenty-five officers to Corregidor, the island fortress at the mouth of Manila Bay and the last piece of the Philippines surrendered to the Japanese in 1942. The following weekend, Winter and two other officers returned to the area by jeep for a more thorough tour of the Bataan peninsula, where during the winter and spring of 1942, American and Filipino forces had held out for four months before succumbing to the Japanese invaders. Captain Pete Reed, a graduate of Harvard Law School and a Boston attorney, became Winter's most frequent companion on weekend jaunts around the island of Luzon. A few weeks after the Bataan trip, Winter and Reed visited a jungle site near

Lipa, where the locals showed them a mass grave of hundreds of Filipino civilians at the base of a cliff, apparent victims of Japanese soldiers who had forced them over the precipice at the point of bayonets. The two officers also visited Cabanatuan, the site of the Japanese POW camp where Americans were imprisoned after the Bataan Death March, and Balete Pass, an isolated, mountainous site, where a crucial battle took place in 1945 during the liberation of the Philippines. On another trip, they saw Baguio, designated the Philippine summer capital by the Americans soon after the conclusion of the U.S.-Filipino War, and native villages in remote parts of the island. Passing through an Igorot village, Winter exchanged some army C-rations for an Igorot spear. In addition to weekend excursions around the island, Winter also used his free time to stay in top physical shape by maintaining a regimen of regular exercise and participating in organized sporting events. He ran the half-mile in the division track meet and played first base and pitched on the headquarters officers' baseball team.[37]

In late June Winter had the most memorable of his many excursions around Luzon. Learning that General Emilio Aguinaldo lived south of Manila, Winter and Reed set out to see if they could gain an audience with the seventy-seven-year-old warrior. Few of Winter's fellow soldiers likely understood the centrality of Aguinaldo to the history of the Philippines. He had led the Filipinos in their war against the United States at the turn of the twentieth century. He had cooperated with the Japanese during World War II, and at the end of the war, the Filipinos arrested him as a collaborator. Aguinaldo served several months in prison before receiving amnesty from the Filipino government. The two American soldiers found Aguinaldo's home, which had a sign out front that read, "Philippine Independence Proclaimed Here June 12, 1898." They knocked on the door and were greeted by a servant, who took them directly in to see Aguinaldo. The Filipino general spent more than an hour with the Americans. His English was not good, but from what the officers understood, he talked primarily about his exploits in the revolution against the Americans. As the two officers prepared to leave, Aguinaldo pointed out a bottle of wine that he had saved since 1903, which he planned to drink a few days later when the Philippines officially received independence from the United States.[38]

Winter was present on July 4 for the Independence Day ceremonies. In a drenching rain, Winter joined a large crowd in Manila to watch the

American flag come down after forty-eight years of U.S. rule, replaced by
the new standard of the Republic of the Philippines. Filipino President
Manuel Roxas and General MacArthur made speeches, and a "mammoth
parade" followed. The Philippine Army led the procession, followed by
two miles of soldiers and vehicles from the Eighty-Sixth Division. General
Aguinaldo also marched in the parade and carried the revolutionary flag
of 1898 at the head of a contingent of older soldiers who had fought for
independence against the United States decades earlier. After the parade
spotting Aguinaldo gathered with some of his former comrades, Winter
speculated that they were drinking Aguinaldo's wine. Two weeks later,
Winter left the Philippines and headed back to Mississippi.[39]

As Winter returned home, the postwar world and the United States
faced numerous problems, including a world food emergency, political
uncertainty in international affairs, the unknown status of the postwar
U.S. military, a housing crisis, and thousands of striking American workers. The South and Mississippi faced an additional problem: challenges to
the region's racial arrangements. Black soldiers returned home determined
to change established racial customs. Just before Winter left the Philippines, he received the news that Mississippians had reelected Theodore
Bilbo to the U.S. Senate. Winter could not understand why his fellow
citizens would make this choice, since he viewed Bilbo as someone who
"has done our state irreparable harm in the eyes of the nation." Winter
believed that Bilbo "is thoroughly corrupt and incompetent, and he has
made a monster out of the racial problem by continually hammering at
the issue. We can never hope to cope with the negro question with any
degree of satisfaction with the like of Bilbo in the driver's seat." Although
the war had challenged Winter's ideas about race, he had not abandoned
his belief in white supremacy. In fact, in the Senate contest he had supported Tom Ellis, a man he thought "stands as clearly and uncompromis-
ingly for white supremacy as Theodore claims to stand," but someone
who "could be a real asset to the state in Washington." Yet, because of
his wartime experiences, especially his service at Fort McClellan, Winter
would find it increasingly difficult to defend Jim Crow wholeheartedly.
The experience of working and living with black officers clearly his equal
in intelligence and ability did not lead Winter to conclude that racial
segregation would and should be soon eliminated, but these experiences
caused him to question the fairness of segregation and challenge the belief

common among white Southerners that all blacks accepted the racial status quo. At the same time, Winter had political ambitions, and he could not easily abandon overnight the racial mores of his native state. Indeed, figuring out how to assert a position more in keeping with his racial awakening during World War II, without jeopardizing his political future in Mississippi, would occupy a good deal of Winter's early political career.[40]

4

MODERATE IN THE
LAND OF THE DIXIECRATS

In the summer of 1947, William Winter and fifteen other Ole Miss students won election to the state legislature. Most had served in the military during World War II before entering Ole Miss, either as new or
returning students. These young legislators hoped to make their mark
in Jackson by enacting legislation that would help move Mississippi
forward in the postwar period. Many of them had moderate views on
racial matters and thought that some limited reforms to the state's system of racial segregation and black disfranchisement might be possible.
By the time the new legislature assembled in January 1948, however,
the possibility for any change in the area of race relations had narrowed
considerably. In December 1947, President Harry Truman released the
report of his President's Committee on Civil Rights, which called for
far-reaching reforms to advance the civil rights of black Americans.
Fielding Wright, the state's new governor, responded with an inaugural
address on January 20 that blasted the Truman administration's civil
rights agenda as an attack on the South. He argued that the defense
of white supremacy from an increasingly "meddlesome" federal government should be Mississippi's top priority and might require a bolt
from the national Democratic Party. Wright and others from the Deep
South did eventually defect from the party to form the States' Rights
Party, or Dixiecrats, and Wright ran as vice president on the new party's
ticket in the 1948 presidential election. The vast majority of white Mississippians embraced the Dixiecrat effort to protect the South's established racial arrangements from a perceived challenge from the national

Democratic Party and the federal government. In this atmosphere of heightened tension over the mere possibility of racial change, William Winter launched his political career.[1]

After the conclusion of his military service in the Philippines, Winter returned to Ole Miss in the fall of 1946 to attend law school. He found the school transformed. Over 3,200 students were enrolled, more than double the number there when Winter first entered in 1940. Designed for a maximum enrollment of 1,500, the facilities of the university were seriously stressed. The number of students enrolled at the law school totaled almost 250, with a freshman class of 120. Most of the freshman law students were veterans taking advantage of the GI Bill, which paid most of their educational costs. Admission standards for law school were minimal, but the curriculum was fairly rigorous. After the fall semester, about a third of the first-year students dropped out of the program. Winter himself found the classes "difficult," but he finished the first term among the top in his class.[2]

Although law school studies occupied much of his time, Winter eagerly resumed his involvement in campus affairs. He was elected president of the Omicron Delta Kappa (ODK) leadership fraternity and became chairman of the group's sometimes controversial speakers' forum. He helped bring a string of noteworthy lecturers to campus, both international figures and local notables: Alexander Kerensky, leader of the Russian provisional government that replaced the czar in 1917 prior to the Bolshevik Revolution of October 1917; Kurt von Schuschnigg, Austrian chancellor at the time of the 1938 Nazi coup; Ralph McGill, racially moderate editor of the *Atlanta Constitution*; John Rankin, long-time reactionary congressman from Mississippi's First District; and George McLean, progressive editor of Tupelo's *Northeast Daily Journal*.[3]

No ODK speaker was more controversial than Hodding Carter, the editor of the Greenville *Delta Democrat-Times*, invited to speak at Ole Miss in December 1946. Carter had won a Pulitzer Prize that year for his editorials "on the subject of racial, religious, and economic intolerance." One of his targets was Theodore G. Bilbo, who encouraged white Mississippians concerned about renewed efforts by black Mississippians to vote in 1946 to visit them the night before the election, a thinly veiled advocacy for real or threatened lynching. Shortly before Carter's scheduled appearance at Ole Miss, a telegram from a group of Gulfport alumni urged Chancellor J. D. Williams to cancel the engagement because the "radical"

Carter was "unfit for the students in this college." Williams met with Ole Miss history professor James Silver and Winter, both of whom argued that academic freedom had to be preserved. Williams agreed and allowed the event to go forward.[4]

On December 12, an enthusiastic and welcoming crowd packed Fulton Chapel (in marked contrast to the "cold" reception Carter had received weeks earlier at Mississippi State College.) As master of ceremonies, Winter opened his remarks by triumphantly announcing, "Academic freedom prevails at the University of Mississippi." Carter's talk, entitled "The Liberal Spirit and the South," began with a reference to the opposition his appearance had generated: "Any university that has the right to invite John Rankin to speak has the right to invite me." Carter also sarcastically admitted that he did belong to several "subversive" groups, including the American Legion and the St. James Episcopal Church. Carter then called for improvements in the economic, health, and educational status of Mississippi blacks, though he emphasized he supported changes "within the pattern of racial segregation." In effect, Carter advocated for greater equalization of the state's separate but supposedly equal arrangements. He also said he did not favor universal voting rights for blacks, although he did note that "it is coming whether we like it or not."[5] Carter's views represented one of the most progressive positions of white Mississippians at that time.

Carter's voice of moderation on the race issue in many ways mirrored Winter's own thinking, which had evolved over the course of the 1940s out of his experiences as a Ole Miss undergraduate and as a result of his military service. This moderate position emphasized that Mississippi needed to take action to improve the lives of its black residents as part of the overall effort to help the state advance. Neither Carter nor Winter advocated wholesale abandonment of racial segregation or black disfranchisement, but both recognized that such changes would inevitably occur in the near future. But as the controversy over Carter's Ole Miss appearance suggests, many white Mississippians viewed even temperate calls for adjustments in the racial status quo as wild anarchy. When a Greenville businessman and friend of Aylmer Winter wrote William Winter to deplore "the harmful influences" that speakers such as Hodding Carter "brought to bear upon our young people in State Institutions of learning," Winter responded that Carter represented one of many voices that ODK brought to campus and that Ole Miss students, many of whom were veterans, could "do their own thinking." Winter also observed that the ODK forums sought to offer students a "changing menu of ideas," rather than "a starvation diet of one-track thinking. In what better way can we overcome the narrow, bigoted minds that have so often been a stumbling block to constructive leadership in this country."[6]

In addition to organizing the ODK forums, Winter took on other leadership roles upon his return to Ole Miss. A new history club on campus, the Claiborne Society, named for noted Mississippi historian J. F. H. Claiborne, selected Winter as its first chairman. The freshman class at the law school chose Winter as its class president. Commenting on his selection, Winter's father predicted that he was "going to be within the next few years one of the leaders of Mississippi." While Aylmer Winter was quite prescient about his son's political future, in the spring semester of 1947, William Winter experienced electoral failure when he ran for student body president. He finished second in the initial balloting and lost in the runoff to James Barnett, nephew of Ross Barnett, a successful damage-suit lawyer, future governor of the state, and one of Winter's opponents in his 1967 gubernatorial race.[7]

After three years in the army, Winter also welcomed a return to the Ole Miss social life, including the intramural sports he had enjoyed so much before. Although he had dated a number of girls over the years, he never really had a serious girlfriend. During his first semester back at Ole Miss, however, he met his roommate Joel Varner's younger sister. Elise Varner, who had just begun her junior year at Ole Miss after two years at Northwest Junior College in Senatobia, was an attractive and personable young woman. The three would often have meals together and attend campus events as a group. Before long, however, Winter began to see Elise as more than his roommate's little sister. What started off as a casual acquaintance gradually developed into a romance. By the spring semester of 1947, the two were dating on a regular basis. Winter thought Elise Varner "the prettiest girl I ever met," but he also found in her a kindred spirit. The two shared similar values, "how we viewed life and how life ought to be lived." For both, family and church were the bedrock structures that shaped their lives. Elise also majored in history and political science, and she admired many of the same professors Winter had first encountered several years earlier, including Silver and H. B. Howerton.

In many ways, William Winter and Elise Varner also had similar family backgrounds. Like Winter, Elise and Joel had a grandfather, C. P. Varner, who was a Civil War veteran and who had lived with them during their youth. The Varners, like the Winters, also had a history of public service. One of C. P. Varner's cousins was G. D. Shands, who served as lieutenant governor of Mississippi from 1882 to 1890. E. W. Varner, Elise's father, was a pharmacist who had opened a small store in Senatobia in 1911, where Elise worked occasionally during her youth. He had recently been elected mayor of the small town, a post he would hold until his death in 1962. Much like Aylmer Winter, E. W. Varner had concern for those less fortunate than him. As a pharmacist during the Depression years, he dispensed medicine to customers who could not pay, on the slim hope that one day they might have the resources to reimburse him.[8]

Many of the war veterans returning to Ole Miss in 1946 would frequently get together between classes and in the evenings to talk about current events and ponder what the future might bring. As early as that first fall, some of the returning veterans talked about running for the state legislature in 1947, including Brinkley Morton, H. M. Ray, Noah "Soggy" Sweat Jr., Boyce Holleman, and William Winter. Winter and his father had corresponded about the younger Winter's future in politics during his stay in the Philippines, and on a visit home in the fall of 1946, Winter discussed his political options with his father. Aylmer Winter thought his son "could probably be elected" to the House but advised him to finish law school before embarking on a political career.[9]

In fact, Winter had limited political options in Grenada County. The county's Senate seat was a "floater"—it traditionally alternated between a resident of Grenada and Yalobusha Counties—and the seat was rotating back to Grenada County in 1947. However, Winter would be only twenty-four by the time the legislature met in 1948, two months shy of the minimum age of twenty-five required by the Mississippi Constitution for members of the State Senate. In addition, Grenada County had only one House seat available in 1947, since Grenada's second House position was also a floater, which the elder Winter had been elected to in 1943, and which would go back to Montgomery County in 1947. Ed McCormick, a farmer, occupied the lone House slot up for grabs. After much discussion with his father and others, Winter decided to enter the available House race, although conventional wisdom held that he did not have much of a chance against the incumbent McCormick, first elected to his post in 1927. Some local political observers noted that the campaign would at least help Winter become better known among the citizens of Grenada County.[10]

After completing his first year of law school in the spring of 1947, Winter returned to the farm in Grenada County for the summer to run for his first political office. The campaign was a low-budget operation, in which Winter personally visited almost every house in the county to solicit votes. He had handbills printed that proclaimed Winter as the candidate "for able, alert, aggressive representation." Though never stated explicitly, Winter's status as a World War II veteran proved a definite advantage, as it did for all political candidates that year. Campaign expenses totaled less than $200, including gasoline, the handbills, and an ad he ran in the Grenada paper the week before the election. He gave few speeches during the race and took the stump only when one of the five gubernatorial candidates passed through Grenada. At these rallies, local candidates would each receive a few minutes to make their pitch.[11]

Winter did speak on the opening day of the July circuit court in Grenada, a traditional venue for aspiring candidates to address local citizens. J. P. Coleman served as the circuit judge for Grenada, but he had arranged to have a fellow circuit court judge, John C. Stennis, fill in that day, as a way of helping Stennis, himself an aspiring politician, gain some recognition in Grenada County. The charge Judge Stennis gave to the Grenada County grand jury, a collection of farmers and small businessmen, captivated Winter. As he later recalled, Stennis painted "a picture of the sanctity of the law, the nature of our system of justice, and the vital role which they had to play in maintaining the integrity of that system." At the noon recess, Winter met Stennis on the streets of Grenada. The judge complimented the young man on his remarks made earlier in court. Winter expressed his admiration for the judge and inquired about his political plans, widely rumored to involve a run for the U.S. Senate should the ailing Theodore Bilbo not survive his battle with throat cancer. Stennis indicated he would run should the opportunity arise, and Winter pledged his support.[12]

On election night in August, Winter followed the results at the town square of Grenada, where a big blackboard under the Confederate monument kept score. The first precinct that came in was from Elliott Station on the Montgomery County line, a polling station that largely contained the votes from a single extended family. The precinct went for Winter 42 to 2. While the later boxes did not bring in such big majorities for Winter, he ended up handily beating McCormick, by a vote of 2,160 to 597.[13]

In addition to resuming his law studies at Ole Miss after the election, Winter played a significant role in the U.S. Senate campaign of John Stennis that fall. Theodore Bilbo died a few days after Winter's election to the legislature, and the next day, Winter called Stennis and renewed his offer to help with his bid for the U.S. Senate. Before returning to Ole Miss, Winter helped gather petitions to qualify Stennis for the special election scheduled for November 1947. Once back at Ole Miss, Winter became head of a Stennis for Senate campus organization. Aylmer Winter suggested that his son "not take the stump" for Stennis, probably because Walter Sillers, the Speaker of the House of Representatives that Winter would soon join, supported William Colmer, a U.S. representative from the Gulf Coast and one of the other candidates in the 1947 U.S. Senate contest. Winter, however, genuinely admired Stennis. His campaign avoided the race issue and attracted the racially moderate faction of white voters. Ignoring his father's opinion in this case, Winter participated actively and publicly in the Stennis campaign by making several speeches for the judge. Although few prognosticators gave Stennis much of a chance at the outset, he won election in the six-candidate race by surpassing the next closest contender, Colmer, by more than six thousand votes. Special elections required only a plurality at the time, and Stennis won the race with only 27 percent of the vote. The new senator was grateful for Winter's support, and thus began a lifelong political alliance and personal friendship. Speaker Sillers, on the other hand, fumed at the outcome of the senatorial contest and pushed through a bill during the 1948 legislative session that required that a candidate receive at least 50 percent of the vote to win in future special elections.[14]

The legislature that Winter joined in January 1948 had a decidedly new look. Of the 140 members, 37 were World War II veterans, 32 were younger than 30, and 78 members were first-timers. Service in the legislature remained a part-time job; the lawmakers met every other year for three or four months, with occasional special sessions in-between. The pay in 1948 was $1,500, payable in three installments, from which members had to cover their living expenses in Jackson. For housing, Aylmer Winter suggested that his son get a "good room close to the Capitol," as the elder Winter had done during his legislative days, but William opted to rent a room at the Edwards Hotel, where many legislators stayed during the session. The hotel advertised itself as "Mississippi's Finest" and came with amenities such as a twenty-four hour "Coffee Room" and "Circulating Ice Water in every room." Winter bunked with Brinkley Morton, and the shared room cost each man $2 a night. Legislators also received ten cents a mile for one round-trip to Jackson from their home. Winter, however, did not have a car, so he traveled between Jackson, Grenada, and Oxford by train or bus, by riding with friends, or sometimes by hitchhiking. The new legislator also arranged with the *Grenada County Weekly* to write a weekly column during the session, reporting on legislative happenings and offering explanations of legislative procedures.[15]

As a longtime legislator, including three terms in the Mississippi House, Aylmer Winter had plenty of ready advice for his son as he embarked on his first stint as a lawmaker. He looked over legislation the younger Winter had drafted in advance of the session. He also suggested possible legislation, such as a bill about land surveys along the Yalobusha River, for which he promised "to have something prepared for you to introduce on the subject." William Winter's father also advised him on dealing with local politicians who clamored for the new legislator to introduce bills to aid their particular cause. When a county supervisor urged William Winter to push for a one-cent increase in the gasoline tax to help with the upkeep of county roads, the experienced legislator warned his son to "not make any positive commitment" and reminded him that "all departments and institutions, including schools, colleges, public welfare, etc." would be asking for additional funds, and "all you can do is to to [sic] do the best you can for them, within the budget limitations." Finally, Aylmer Winter counseled his son on the fine points of legislative etiquette and hoped that his own many contacts in the legislature might lead to good committee appointments for his son. William's father reminded him that "the courteous thing to do [was] to address all former senators in the House, by their title as 'Senator.'" Aylmer also talked to several of his longtime friends in the House about his son. After a conversation with Hilton Waits, longtime chairman of the House Ways and Means Committee, Winter's father felt certain that Waits would recommend the younger Winter to the Speaker for appointment to the influential committee, which Aylmer considered "a high honor for a new member."[16]

Aylmer Winter and Speaker Sillers were longtime friends and legislative colleagues. Both men had joined the Mississippi House as freshmen during the session of 1916. Sillers, a conservative Bolivar County planter who in 1948 was beginning his ninth consecutive term in the House and second as Speaker, was perhaps the most powerful person in state government. William Winter recalled in the 1970s that Speaker Sillers "ran a pretty tight ship." He "checked out the philosophy of the members before appointments were made to committees and once the committees were appointed exercised a good deal of influence with the chairmen." Karl Wiesenburg, who served in the House in the 1950s and 1960s, remembered that the Speaker handed out the committee chairmanships to his "henchmen, sworn to fealty." Since William Winter had been a frequent visitor to the House chamber, dating back to his three-week visit during the 1932 session, the Speaker already knew a good deal about Aylmer Winter's only child. It is likely that Winter put in a good word for his son with Sillers after the 1947 elections. Indeed, when Sillers distributed legislative appointments early in the 1948 session, William Winter fared well. In addition to an appointment to the House Ways and Means Committee, Sillers also named Winter to the Agriculture Committee; Judiciary B (all lawyers and law students were appointed to one of the judiciary committees by rule); the Military Affairs Committee, which contained a large number of World War II veterans; and as chair of the Interstate Cooperation Committee, which conducted relatively little business.[17]

Many of the new, young members, veterans of the world war, hoped to use their positions to bring about change in the areas of the state's economy and educational system. Several of the freshman legislators also believed some limited, gradual change to Mississippi's racial caste system would help the state move forward. One potential action that some of the moderates had discussed was repeal of the poll tax, one of the state's disfranchising measures. Campaigns to repeal the tax had begun during World War II and had already generated substantial opposition from white Southerners, so it seems unlikely that a proposal to eliminate the poll tax would have succeeded, even if the Dixiecrat movement had not mobilized in 1948. Winter thought that Mississippi might begin to admit blacks to previously all-white graduate and professional schools, as other southern states had recently done. Few among the legislature's leadership appointed by the conservative Sillers, however, shared this youthful zeal for change, especially their ideas about making even limited adjustments in the area of race relations.[18]

Winter and his young colleagues, whatever they might have thought about reforms in the area of the state's racial arrangements, realized after hearing Governor Wright's inaugural address that the defense of racial segregation from outside attack now required their total support; otherwise, they would have been discounted from the outset. Following Wright's speech, the House passed a resolution pledging that "Mississippians and Southerners will no longer tolerate these abuses and efforts to destroy the South and her institutions, and hereby pledge our full support to the Governor in his efforts to protect and uphold the principles, traditions, and way of life of our beloved Southland." Only one representative dissented, Thamus Stephens, a middle-aged farmer and labor union member from Lauderdale County. All of official white Mississippi quickly fell in line to defend the racial status quo. When newly elected U.S. Senator John Stennis initially questioned the effectiveness of Wright's plan to oppose the national party leadership on civil rights, most of the Mississippi press condemned him roundly, and Stennis soon joined the united defense of white supremacy. Over the course of the first half of 1948, the Dixiecrat movement in Mississippi convinced most of the state's white citizens that white supremacy was under attack from the federal government. Any attempt to alter existing racial arrangements would mean unmitigated disaster, so whites had to close ranks and prevent any efforts to promote racial change.[19]

In the first couple of weeks of the 1948 session, the House considered a number of resolutions that expressed the dedication of the legislature to resist federal efforts to force racial change on the South. House leadership authored these documents and then gave them to various House members to introduce. On one occasion, the Old Guard selected Winter and his roommate, Brinkley Morton, to present a resolution expressing "opposition to recommendations of the President's Civil Rights Committee," which had proposed a permanent Fair Employment Practices Commission, a federal anti-lynching law, and an anti-poll tax measure. The resolution railed against the proposed legislation as leading to "the subjugation of the majority to the demands of various minority groups, and not least among these recommendations, certain ones whose effect would be to deprive the states of their rights with regard to suffrage and elections laws, and passing this power to the federal government for their dictates." The House quickly passed the resolution, and once the Senate concurred, the legislature forwarded the document to President Truman and the U.S. Congress. Winter noted to his constituents in Grenada County that the resolution he introduced put the legislature "on record in condemning the vicious recommendations of the President's Civil Rights Committee."[20]

Throughout the 1948 legislative session, states' rights indignation gripped the halls of power. Democrats held a statewide mass meeting at the Jackson city auditorium on February 12, Lincoln's birthday, to chart the state party's opposition to the national Democratic Party, which had seemingly capitulated to the cause of black civil rights. Five thousand people, including the entire legislature, attended the event, described by the *Jackson Daily News* as "the most memorable and history-making gathering that has been held in Jackson since the adoption of the ordinance of secession." The assembly passed resolutions promising to oppose national civil rights initiatives and to "quit the Democratic party under its present leadership." According to the Jackson press, "There was no dissension, not even slight differences of opinion." A week after the Jackson states' rights meeting, Winter traveled to Oklahoma City to represent the House in an interstate meeting to discuss oil and gas legislation—including the use of severance taxes—with representatives from other southern and southwestern states. In addition to these discussions, the assembled politicians from Louisiana, Arkansas, Texas, and Oklahoma also discussed the "Southern movement" among Democrats. Winter told Grenada County voters that "considerable support" for the Dixiecrats existed among leaders from all these locales.[21]

While fending off the national assault on Mississippi's racial prerogatives, the legislature also tried to short-circuit the incipient civil rights movement within the state. During the 1948 session, after Gladys Noel Bates, a black Jackson schoolteacher, launched an equal pay lawsuit against the city school board, the legislature approved a $25,000 appropriation to help defend the white school officials in the case. The vote in the House was 134 to 0, and Winter joined his colleagues in voting for the funding to defend segregation. The legislature also unanimously approved another $25,000 of funding for tuition grants to "provide instruction" for

Mississippi black students in colleges and universities outside the state, an effort to deflect lawsuits against the state for not providing graduate or professional education for blacks in its so-called "separate but equal" arrangements. Finally, the legislature attempted to tighten voting requirements through a controversial constitutional amendment, which would have required voters "to sustain a good moral character." Although the amendment did not mention race, its proponents admitted the measure sought to keep blacks from voting, since as one supporter noted, 90 percent of blacks "live in bigamy and adultery." The proposed amendment ran into a snag when Boyce Holleman, freshman legislator from the Gulf Coast, raised concerns that the "moral character" clause might be used against anybody, including members of the legislature. His impassioned arguments garnered enough support to defeat the measure on the House floor, with fifty-nine negative votes, although Winter voted in favor of the amendment. Speaker Sillers took the House into executive session to reconsider the vote. According to Holleman, Sillers admonished the legislators that anybody who voted against the amendment was voting against the white race and was perhaps not even really white. Afterwards, another vote was held, and only Holleman and thirteen other stalwarts continued to resist the action. Mississippi voters, however, shared the dissenters' concerns, as they voted against the proposed constitutional amendment in the statewide election that fall.[22]

Following the 1948 legislative session, the Dixiecrats continued to advance their political movement. A big states' rights convention in Jackson in early May featured South Carolina Governor Strom Thurmond, the emerging leader of the Dixiecrat forces, who urged a party bolt if the national Democrats embraced civil rights measures. Winter was away at Fort Benning for two weeks of training as part of his army obligations and missed this meeting. When he returned from Georgia, Winter continued to watch the Dixiecrat drama unfolding in Mississippi, but with the legislative session over, he tried to avoid the Dixiecrat mania as much as possible. Although elected as a delegate to the state Democratic convention in June, Winter chose not to attend. He knew that the main function of the convention would be to sanction Dixiecrat political objectives, and he had no interest in actively supporting them. Walter Sillers and Fielding Wright firmly controlled the state Democratic Party, and as expected, Mississippi delegates to the Democratic National Convention received orders to reject the national party if it nominated Truman or adopted a civil rights plank. Weeks later, Winter listened on the radio to the national convention proceedings in Philadelphia. When the Mississippi delegates walked out of the meeting, Winter did not cheer. In the end, however, he voted for the States' Rights ticket of Strom Thurmond and Fielding Wright, largely out of a sense of loyalty to Wright, who had been a legislative colleague of his father. The southern challenge, much as Winter anticipated, proved to be an exercise in futility. The Dixiecrats carried only four Deep South states—including Mississippi—and failed to prevent the reelection of Harry Truman.[23]

Some of Winter's legislative actions in 1948 and his vote for the States' Rights Party in November might suggest that he differed little from the true believers in the Dixiecrat cause. Other evidence, however, suggests that Winter had reservations about the Dixiecrat campaign and that his support for the states' rights protest was more a function of political survival than heartfelt belief. On the weekend after Winter and Morton presented their anti-civil rights resolution in the Mississippi House, they traveled to southwest Mississippi to see the sights. Among the places they visited was Alcorn Agricultural and Mechanical College, a publically supported black school in Lorman, established in 1871. Neither of the men had ever seen the college. When the legislators arrived on campus, they asked to meet the president, and President William Harrison Pipes soon arrived to greet them. A native of the Mississippi Delta and a son of sharecroppers, Pipes had received a high school diploma and undergraduate degree from Tuskegee Institute. He then went to Michigan State and received the first Ph.D. in speech earned by a black student in the United States. As the men discussed Alcorn's future, Pipes told them that he wanted to move Alcorn forward but was limited in what he could accomplish, especially when he could not even vote. This encounter gave Winter pause, as he heard firsthand of the injustice of black disfranchisement and contemplated the consequences of his own legislative action and inaction.[24]

Although the 1948 legislature passed numerous measures designed to protect Mississippi's system of racial apartheid, Winter and his more moderate-minded colleagues did mount at least one successful effort to dampen the Dixiecrat racial obsessions that dominated legislative proceedings. On March 1, the Executive Committee of the Mississippi Democratic Party indicated that its delegates to the national convention would not support any candidate who favored black civil rights and that it would instruct its delegates to walk out of the convention if the party approved a civil rights plank in its platform. When Dixiecrats in the legislature offered a resolution the following day endorsing the action of the state Democratic Party, Winter and several other young legislators met privately with the Speaker and voiced their opposition to what they viewed as an extreme measure: having the legislature endorse the abandonment of the national party because of possible civil rights reforms. Although Sillers agreed with the proposed resolution, as demonstrated by his actions at the state Democratic Party convention two months later, he agreed to kill the measure, perhaps because the young moderates had approached him privately and because failure to pass the resolution actually made little difference. Sillers assigned the offending resolution to his own Rules Committee, from which it never reemerged.[25]

In less political settings, Winter clearly favored a more reasoned approach to the emerging issue of civil rights, a position more consistent with the ideas he had developed during his college and military years. Soon after the 1948 legislative session ended, Winter wrote a short piece in the *Mississippi Law Journal* about South Carolina's recent efforts to evade the U.S. Supreme Court's 1944 ruling in *Smith v. Allwright*. This decision outlawed the white primary that Democratic parties throughout the South had used to keep blacks from voting in the only election that mattered in the one-party region. After detailing the legal background of the case, Winter came to the conclusion "that any attempt through party machinery, unfettered by statutory provisions, to keep negroes from voting will be declared by the federal courts to be state action and thus a violation of the Fourteenth and Fifteenth Amendments." Winter doubted that a new primary law adopted by the Mississippi legislature in 1947, designed to preserve white supremacy in elections, would succeed, since "it is evident that any effort, whether by state or party, which the courts can interpret as a move to disfranchise negroes as such, will be held to be state action and therefore illegal." This analysis calmly laid out the existing legal landscape and suggested the impracticality of efforts to evade the changes embraced by the federal courts, a position at odds with Dixiecrat dogma.[26]

Winter and other young racial moderates in the Mississippi legislature did not challenge the Dixiecrats publically in 1948 in large part because they wanted to remain politically viable. Although Winter's World War II experience at Fort McClellan had suggested to him that blacks would seek changes in their status after the war, he underestimated how rapidly pressure would build after the war for rapid and effective change to advance black civil rights and how fiercely whites would resist any alteration in the racial status quo. In the racially heightened atmosphere of 1948, it would have been difficult for a young legislator with any political ambition to actively oppose the Dixiecrats. As Winter noted later, he believed that voting against tactics designed to protect segregation and disfranchisement at that time "would have killed me in politics forever." The moderates also did not press for racial reform because it represented only a minor part of the many pressing problems they believed demanded legislative attention. In 1948, Winter did not fully share the Dixiecrats' heightened fear of racial change or their strategies for resistance, but his commitment to even incremental adjustments in Mississippi's racial arrangements remained vaguely formed and a secondary concern.[27]

Despite the obsession with guarding racial boundaries that hung over the entire 1948 session, Winter and others managed to push through progressive legislation to address other concerns, most notably by passing a workmen's compensation law. In 1948, Mississippi was the only state without such a statute. Various legislators had tried to engineer the passage of a workmen's compensation law for more than twenty years, including Aylmer Winter, whose 1940 bill died in a Senate committee. The measure had actually passed in the 1946 House but also died in the Senate. In 1948, Winter and three of his young colleagues, H. M. Ray, Soggy Sweat, and Lowell Grisham, crafted a workmen's compensation bill. After a long struggle in both the House and Senate, the bill passed, and Governor Wright signed it into law. Since Mississippi was the last state to pass this basic safeguard for workers, the law Winter and his compatriots crafted built on previous efforts, and they designed a model piece of legislation, one that was, in the estimation of Kenneth Toler of the *Memphis Commercial Appeal*, "the most liberal of any of the statutes in the other 47 states."[28]

In addition to workmen's compensation, Winter promoted other progressive legislation, including two measures that angered church groups around the state. One sought to eliminate a longstanding state blue law that prohibited leisure activities, such as movies and sporting activities, on Sundays. Many locales, such as Jackson and even Grenada, selectively enforced the restrictions, which made the law seem arbitrary and unfair in places that did strictly construe the law. Its inconsistent enforcement led to class inequities as well. Wealthy Mississippians could go to a country club and play golf on a Sunday afternoon, while poorer ones in small towns could not take in a movie or play baseball on the Sabbath. Winter, along with Brinkley Morton and Phil Mullen, authored the "Sunday movie" bill, as it became known. Winter was a religious man, but he always rejected the notion that one should "equate sectarian dogma with political orthodoxy." He thought it wise "to recognize that on most major public issues conscientious and faithful Christians may hold deeply felt differences of opinion." After the legislators introduced the Sunday movie bill, an outcry from religious groups commenced, although the law still prohibited movies and sporting events before 1:00 p.m. on Sundays. As Winter later remembered, "It was as if we had legislated against motherhood." Mullen noted at the time that most of the opposition's arguments boiled down to a simple equation: "Vote for God!" The *Mississippi Methodist Advocate* editorialized that the bill would "desecrate the holy Sabbath Day," and various congregations around the state held prayer meetings to pray for the bill's defeat. Debate on the House floor was intense. One opponent of the measure claimed that passage would lead to an increase in promiscuity and adultery. In the end, the Sunday movie bill passed, with seventy-two yeas to fifty-eight nays.[29]

The other issue that perennially aroused the ire of church groups was the effort to end Mississippi's alcohol prohibition. When a bill to legalize liquor through a local option mechanism reached the House floor in 1948, the debate, as usual, was passionate. Winter recalled that one of the most effective defenders of prohibition "had fortified himself for the battle with several stiff drinks." Another representative reportedly received a new car from illegal whiskey dealers in exchange for his vote against legalization. The bill died when Sam Allred offered a successful amendment that eliminated the enacting clause in the bill. Another anti-prohibition measure came before the House later in the session, this one providing for a referendum on the issue of legalizing liquor sales. Although it passed the House by a two-to-one margin, it failed in the Senate. Winter supported both attempts to liberalize the liquor laws, for two reasons. First, legalization of liquor would raise additional revenue for the state, $20 million a year by one estimate. Second, the continuation of prohibition merely promoted the illegal liquor trade. As Winter noted at the time: "If there was ever an unholy alliance in this state, it is that which exists between the blind church folks and the shrewd bootleggers who use the church people to further their own (bootleggers) interests."[30]

Winter's performance in the 1948 legislature garnered the respect of Speaker Sillers and other political observers. Winter's role as one of the young members that pushed through the workmen's compensation bill certainly attracted notice. Icey Day, a House veteran first elected in 1916 along with Aylmer Winter, believed that William Winter and his colleagues' work on the legislation "was by far the best presentation of a bill of any this session." J. K. Morrison, a long-time friend of Aylmer Winter and a business lobbyist who supported the passage of the workmen's compensation law, praised Winter and H. M. Ray because "they have kept their head and not joined the Anti Delta club." Indeed, Winter did nothing during the session to undermine the Speaker's admiration for his young colleague, and Sillers appointed Winter to a number of special tasks in the two-year hiatus between legislative sessions.[31]

In December 1948, Sillers chose Winter to represent the legislature at the ninth biennial meeting of the Council of State Governments meeting in Detroit, a three-day meeting of nearly one hundred public officials from almost every state in the nation. For a young politician, the meeting proved an event, he told his parents, "I could not have afforded to miss." Winter met a number of governors and members of the U.S. Congress, as well as the British ambassador to the United States. One of the issues discussed at the meeting was the increasing role of the federal government and encroachments on states' rights. Coming from Mississippi, Winter had heard much about this issue in the preceding months as the Dixiecrats debated their strategy, but the participants in Detroit considered the topic from a wide range of perspectives not discussed in the Mississippi legislature. Speaker Sillers would not have anticipated the lessons Winter took from these discussions. Reporting on the conference in an article for the *Grenada County Weekly*, Winter said one of the most impressive aspects of the meeting was the realization that leaders with different "local problems" could "sit down together in a spirit of friendly cooperation." Having witnessed the Dixiecrat hysteria of the preceding months, he clearly appreciated the value of moderation and compromise.[32]

At the request of Sillers, Winter also attended a February 1949 conference in Birmingham, sponsored by the American Legion, on subversive activities. He hitchhiked the first leg of his journey, from Oxford to Tupelo, and then caught the train to Birmingham. The meeting brought together delegates from all over the South and a slate of anticommunist speakers, including Benjamin Gitlow, vice-presidential candidate in 1924 and 1928 for the Communist Party, and Elizabeth Bentley, the Soviet spy who defected to the United States in 1945 and who would later testify against Ethel and Julius Rosenberg. During a break in the meeting, Winter had a chance to meet privately with Bentley, when the two enjoyed sodas and conversation at a local drug store. Overall, the conference heightened Winter's concern that a potential "Communist menace" threatened the country. At the conclusion of the two trips, Aylmer Winter told his son that Speaker Sillers "has certainly been nice to you. He has shown his appreciation of your ability and your loyalty."[33]

In addition to these periodic political duties, Winter spent the year after his first legislative session finishing his law degree at Ole Miss. Back at the university, he resumed his typical harried schedule. In addition to courting Elise and keeping up with his studies, Winter spent many hours working on the *Mississippi Law Journal* and resumed his work on the ODK forums. The law school faculty selected Winter, a top student in his class, to the prestigious position of editor-in-chief of the *Mississippi Law Journal* for the 1948–1949 year. His earlier experience working for *The Mississippian* prepared him for the demands of putting out four issues during the year, highlighted by the March 1949 issue, devoted entirely to the new workmen's compensation law he had helped author and engineer to passage. At the University's Centennial Commencement in May 1949, Winter received, by a vote of the law school faculty, the school's highest honor, the Phi Delta Phi Award as the outstanding graduate. Aylmer Winter, in declining health, could not attend the ceremony, but in a letter, he praised his son on the achievement, writing that "nature has endowed you with an analytical and judicial mind." And, as always, he gave him advice: "You should aim for a place on the Mississippi Supreme Court and prepare yourself accordingly."[34]

Since legislative service provided only a low-paying, part-time position, Winter considered how to best put his law degree to use. He initially hoped to "work under" Judge Andrew Carothers in Grenada, a lawyer who had practiced in the town for almost four decades. Winter had known the attorney for many years, since Carothers served as an elder at First Presbyterian Church in Grenada. Aylmer Winter went to see the judge on his son's behalf, but Carothers, who already had one young associate, did not think his firm could support another. Although a number of other senior lawyers in Grenada discouraged Winter from coming back to the town to practice law, he decided to open a law office in downtown Grenada in June 1949. He bought a library from a Jackson lawyer and saved on expenses by living on the family farm. Winter soon discovered that the opportunities for lawyers in the small town "were adequate, but also adequately served." Clients for the new practice were "few and far between." One of Winter's first clients was a former neighbor who, having experienced some economic setbacks, stole his mother-in-law's safe. With the man facing ten years in Parchman, the state penitentiary, Winter negotiated with the Grenada district attorney for a reduced sentence of eighteen months. His client balked, claiming that "Parchman ain't no place for a gentleman." Winter finally convinced the man to accept the generous plea bargain. The man paid Winter for his work with a plot in a local cemetery. In late summer, Senator Stennis asked Winter to join his Washington staff to replace Frank Smith, who had resigned his position to run for Congress. Winter agreed to take the job at the conclusion of the 1950 session of the legislature.[35]

Before the session began, Senator Stennis publicly announced that he had hired Winter to join his staff once the legislature adjourned. The legislature of 1950, in contrast to Winter's first one, was relatively quiet on the race issue. The major actions included measures to fund a long-range highway program and to establish and fund a four-year medical school, the University of Mississippi Medical Center, in Jackson. Winter coauthored the latter bill. Another bill that Winter authored, along with Brinkley Morton, proposed a commission to study changes in the organization of state government in order to streamline a system that included 103 administrative agencies. The legislature approved a version of the measure, and the commission created by the law issued a report calling for substantial government reorganization.[36]

The Red Scare haunted the 1950 session. In early February, a week before Senator Joseph McCarthy made his Wheeling, West Virginia, speech that ignited a nationwide anticommunist panic, Soggy Sweat introduced the

"Subversive Act of 1950," which essentially proposed to create a state loyalty program, requiring all current and future state employees, as well as candidates for political office, to sign an "anti-subversive certificate," pledging they were not "subversive persons" and did not belong to "subversive organizations," both of which the proposed statute defined broadly. Sweat asked every House member to sign the legislation, and a number of his colleagues, including William Winter, did endorse it. Winter, after attending the conclave in Birmingham, had come away with a greater apprehension about domestic subversion.[37]

Even though Winter, like many other Americans in the early 1950s, had real concerns about domestic security, he also questioned those who exaggerated claims of disloyalty at home. Soon after Sweat introduced his bill, House member Hamer McKenzie, a twenty-six-year-old law student, took the floor and, McCarthy-like, began waving a document claiming to prove that a number of Ole Miss professors should be considered subversives for "molding the minds of students along socialistic lines." The House adjourned into a two-hour executive session, in which McKenzie accused five Ole Miss professors of being Reds. Among those named was Winter's teacher and friend, Jim Silver. Mississippi leaders had suspected the history professor of various forms of unorthodoxy for a number of years, and the previous year, the General Legislative Investigating Committee, which had broad powers to investigate state agencies and employees, had looked into whether Silver had ties to communists and found no evidence to substantiate the charge. McKenzie, however, declared that Silver was "a card-carrying member of the Communist Party" and also suggested that through the ODK forums Silver had brought radical speakers to the university. Winter rose to defend his mentor and ODK. He later told the press that in his six years at Ole Miss, he "never detected anything communistic, subversive, or un-American" at the university. "Great harm" might be done to the school by embarking on "an irresponsible witch hunt," he cautioned. Winter informed his Grenada County constituents that he disagreed with a "smear campaign designed to defame and discredit good and loyal Americans with whom we might not chance to agree . . . . We can be vigilant without being demagogic." The personal attacks on the Ole Miss faculty soon subsided, but the legislature did pass the anti-subversives bill.[38]

Winter's defense of Jim Silver and ODK from charges of communism represented a defiant stand against the prevailing sentiment of his legislative colleagues and probably many of his constituents. With anticommunist fears growing within the state and around the country, speaking out against the practice of red-baiting was a potentially risky proposition for a man with a budding political career. Winter's actions in this instance stand in marked contrast to his more muted dissent from the Dixiecrat attempt to halt all efforts at altering the racial status quo. Winter was not averse to taking a stand for what he thought was right, even if that position entailed potentially adverse political consequences. But for Winter and other racial moderates in 1948, including Senator Stennis, opposing the Dixiecrat approach in any substantive way was not worth the political risk. That calculation suggests the limitations of Winter's racial moderation in the late 1940s. World War II had challenged his thinking on race. He believed that some type of racial reform should be a part of the larger set of changes Mississippi needed to move forward. Yet, among Winter and other racial moderates, the support for adjustments to Mississippi's system of racial segregation and black disfranchisement dwindled in the face of the Dixiecrat clamor for all white Southerners to come to the defense of the South's longstanding arrangements in black-white relations from external attack.

5

MASSIVE RESISTANCE

In the fall of 1953, William Winter was halfway through a second term as a Mississippi state legislator. He also had a struggling law practice in Grenada, managed the Grenada County farm, taught as an adjunct for Ole Miss, and held a part-time job with the Grenada Chamber of Commerce. As part of Winter's Chamber duties, he helped organize Grenada County's second annual Harvest Festival, the town's first racially integrated community event. Weeks earlier, black citizens in Grenada had started their own Chamber of Commerce organization. Winter suggested that a representative from this new black Chamber join the Harvest Festival program. Less than a week before the event, his white Chamber colleagues agreed, and the head of the new black organization, Dr. Claude Walston, spoke on the same program as Senator John Stennis, the featured guest of the day. The November 21 event, which drew a racially mixed crowd of fifteen hundred, included a program of music, awards for the biggest cotton crops, and speeches, with Winter serving as master of ceremonies. The festivities concluded with a free barbeque. When Stennis addressed the crowd, he commended the community for their plan to expand cotton production "with the cooperation and understanding of both races." Walston followed and praised the senator for "his efforts in helping to solve the race problems of the South." All in all, the event represented for Winter the possibility that, despite segregation, blacks and whites could work together for the betterment of both races. He still believed in the need for racial segregation and thought it would remain intact in many areas of life for the foreseeable future. As he had for many years, however, Winter thought that gradual improvements in race relations were possible

83

and believed that efforts, such as the integrated Harvest Festival, should be made to break down racial barriers whenever possible.[1]

Within six months, however, even such a minor breach in the segregated arrangements of Mississippi—inviting a black leader to speak at a public event organized by the white community—became an impossible position for a white politician to advance. Once the U.S. Supreme Court issued its May 1954 decision in *Brown v. Board of Education*, which declared segregated schools inherently unconstitutional, whites in Mississippi closed ranks in an effort to halt racial change. State leaders, including most of Winter's legislative colleagues, embraced a strategy of massive resistance against federal pronouncements to end racial segregation and the increasingly active black civil rights movement, emboldened by the *Brown* decree. Any thoughts about promoting gradual adjustments in the South's racial arrangements essentially evaporated in the post-*Brown* environment. Winter, however, continued to favor a moderate approach of gradual racial change and believed that massive resistance was a misguided strategy. Similar to his stance during the Dixiecrat legislative session of 1948, Winter dissented from massive resistance at times but did so in a way that prevented him from becoming a political pariah. He also tried to work within the system to bring a more moderate political leadership to power in Mississippi.

After his first term in the Mississippi Legislature, Winter did not know if he would seek a second term. He looked forward to the opportunity to work with Senator Stennis, a Mississippi politician who shared more of his moderate sensibilities, and he went to Washington, D.C., unsure about his future plans. Winter began his new job in the spring of 1950 by working in Mississippi to help the senator prepare for his 1952 reelection campaign. Stennis sent Winter on a two-month trek around the state to "contact some of our friends there, make new contacts and size up the general situation." In general, the senator wanted Winter to meet with a broad cross-section of the population, establishing relationships with "forward-looking men who have faith in the future, not men who are looking backward and who are extreme reactionaries." Finally, Stennis advised Winter to pay particular attention to young people, "those who share the view points which are special to your generation." Winter arrived in Washington in July 1950 with a large notebook full of details about Mississippians and their political views. Stennis rightly recognized that the trip not only collected valuable intelligence for his upcoming campaign, but also gave Winter the opportunity to "make new friends over the State that will doubtless be helpful to you professionally and otherwise."[2]

Taking over as Stennis's legislative assistant with the 1950 session already underway, Winter had to hit the ground running. The U.S. Congress would have customarily concluded its work by the time Winter arrived in the nation's capital, but the beginning of the Korean War in June required the Congress to remain in Washington. The day after Winter's arrival, he watched the U.S. Senate in session. Enthralled to meet national political leaders, he excitedly recounted, in his first letter home, the senators he had met on his first day in the Senate chamber. Winter lived in a D.C. hotel and typically worked long hours as the Senate wrestled with matters such as a tax increase bill, a defense production measure, a consideration of statehood for Alaska and Hawaii, and legislation to check communist subversion at home. Winter also had writing of his own to do, as he had agreed to produce an article about the 1950 legislative session for the *Mississippi Law Journal*, which meant that during parts of September he worked late into the night. After two months in Washington, Winter began to recognize how slowly the Senate proceeded by observing "that the time of that great deliberative body is taken up with much irrelevant and inconsequential debate." Indeed, Congress resolved few issues during the first two months Winter worked for Stennis, and congressional leaders recessed for two months as the 1950 elections approached.[3]

As members of the U.S. Congress headed home to campaign, Winter returned to Mississippi to marry Elise. The couple had dated for almost four years and had already delayed the wedding date by several months. They had originally planned to get married soon after the conclusion of the 1950 legislative session, but because of the demands of Winter's new job with Stennis, including the long trip around the state, William and Elise decided to postpone the wedding. Once Winter was settled in Washington during the summer of 1950, a date for the wedding was set, October 10, and the ceremony took place at the Methodist church in Elise's hometown of Senatobia. Aylmer Winter could not attend the wedding, as he was receiving treatment for prostate cancer in Hot Springs, Arkansas. Stennis, however, did attend. The senator greatly approved of his assistant's choice of mate. He told Winter after first meeting Elise two years earlier that few could "equal, much less exceed, [her] in beauty, brains and charm." Thus began a successful and enduring marriage (the Winters celebrated their sixtieth wedding anniversary in 2010) and the start of a tight-knit family that would eventually include three daughters: Anne, born in 1952; Elise—known as Lele—born in 1955; and Eleanor, born in 1960.[4]

When Congress reconvened on November 27, the most pressing issue for Senator Stennis, and consequently William Winter, was the admission of Alaska and Hawaii as states. Before the session began, Winter conducted background research at the Library of Congress on the statehood measures. The Alaska statehood bill, which had passed the House prior to the congressional recess, came up first, and Senator Stennis "violently opposed" it, a position Winter agreed with—as did many white Southerners—since new states would "further dissipate the voting strength of the South in the Senate," thereby weakening the region's ability to block legislation, such as civil rights bills. This southern opposition, along with Republican concerns that new Alaskan and Hawaiian delegations would be Democratic, perhaps even "leftist," killed the statehood bills in the 1950 Congress.[5] The Senate battle over Alaskan and Hawaiian statehood showed that even white racial moderates, such as Stennis and Winter, although they might favor gradual changes in racial arrangements, wanted southern leaders to remain in control to determine the pace of any adjustments.

By Christmas 1950, Winter had decided to resume his career in state politics rather than pursue a long-term career as a Senate staffer. He began to make plans to stand for reelection to the Mississippi House the following summer, but in June 1951, he received orders, because of the Korean War, to return to active military duty on July 12 at Fort Jackson, South Carolina. Senator Stennis, who valued his legislative assistant and would have gladly made him a permanent member of his staff, suggested that Winter apply for a legislative exemption or arrange for a Pentagon appointment. Winter, however, felt obligated to fulfill his military duty to his country. As he noted at the time, "Somebody has to give up something if this country is going to survive. It is little enough for me to give up a few months, if thereby I can assist in some small measure in the strengthening of this country's defenses in an hour of peril." Winter's orders designated that he serve as an infantry replacement training officer in the Eighth Infantry Division, the same job he had at Fort McClellan during World War II. Since he was now a lawyer, he would also likely be assigned to do some court-martial work. Winter received a one-month delay in reporting for duty, which allowed him to return to Mississippi and vote in the first primary of the 1951 elections. He had no opposition in his legislative race, and rather than campaigning during his time back in Grenada, Winter merely visited some of his supporters to offer his thanks.[6]

Two days after his uncontested victory, Winter arrived at Fort Jackson and began readjusting to army life. He and Elise lived off-base. The training was intense, as the army was rapidly expanding. Winter spent two days a week working court-martials, with the rest of his time training a regiment of support personnel, such as radiomen, mechanics, and drivers. Most of his fellow officers had already served in Korea, and Winter heard directly about the fighting from these men. It had only been five years since Winter had been on active duty, but he noticed a number of differences about this second tour of service. For one thing, people outside the base barely seemed to notice that the country was at war. Winter noted that on the streets of nearby Columbia, South Carolina, life "went on essentially as usual." Such a disconnect between civilian life and the military world had not existed during World War II, and for Winter, such "public apathy and lack of interest" made it "mighty hard to gear my mind to making the sacrifices that I have felt were necessary if the country is going to make it through the present crisis."[7]

Another major difference, of course, was the newly integrated military. The mixing of black and white soldiers, which Winter had been one of a selective few to experience during the 1940s, was now official U.S. Army policy. Winter's Eighth Infantry Division was completely desegregated, though segregation still existed at Fort Jackson. The other major unit at the base was the Thirty-First Infantry Division, the Dixie Division, created primarily from National Guard units in Mississippi and Alabama. Since these were state troops in federal service, the army's desegregation orders were not enforced, and the division remained all-white. Indeed, despite the changes in the U.S. Army, the National Guard remained a primarily white institution, even beyond the South. At Fort Jackson, the Thirty-First lived in a separate enclave, and a Confederate flag flew over the division's headquarters. Winter took a fair amount of ribbing from his fellow Mississippians in the Thirty-First, who said Winter served in the "Checkerboard Division." For the most part, however, the all-white Thirty-First did not disrupt the generally successful integration of the base, although racial animosity sometimes flared.[8]

Winter received an early discharge from active duty because of his father's rapidly declining health, which also allowed him to return to Mississippi in time to make the beginning of the legislative session in January 1952. Back in Mississippi, Winter faced a host of responsibilities and concerns in addition to his political duties. Because of his father's health problems, Winter took over as the primary manager of the farm. He commuted regularly to Jackson to attend to his legislative duties, often with his high school friend and fellow attorney, Billy Semmes, who had also been elected to the House in 1951. The two shared a room at the Edwards Hotel during the session, but Winter returned to Grenada at every opportunity. By the middle of February, Aylmer Winter's condition worsened dramatically, and he passed away on March 12. William Winter lost not only his father but also the man he admired above all others.[9]

Winter's second stint in the legislature began much as his first had, with Governor Fielding Wright rallying lawmakers to the states' rights cause. Wright, in his outgoing speech to the legislature, told the assembled leaders that the Dixiecrat cause was not a lost one: "Our efforts in 1948 provided the groundwork that will be the foundation of an even greater fight in 1952." A few weeks later, the new governor, Hugh White, in his inaugural address, decried the "usurpation of the Federal Government of the powers reserved to the states." Many Mississippi leaders wanted to continue the fight to halt national Democratic support for black civil rights, and they, along with other Southerners, proposed to mount another challenge to national Democratic leadership at the 1952 convention. Compromise, however, short-circuited that effort. The national party watered down its civil rights plank, and the presidential candidate, Adlai Stevenson, chose a Southerner, Senator John Sparkman of Alabama, as his running mate. When the Mississippi Democratic convention convened in August, it agreed to support the Stevenson/Sparkman ticket. Dixiecrats believed state Democrats "double-crossed" them, and they created a Democrats-for-Eisenhower organization with an independent slate of presidential electors. Winter campaigned for the Stevenson ticket, and in the end, the more moderate position prevailed in Mississippi in 1952, as Stevenson won 60 percent of the state vote.[10]

Despite continuing concerns over black civil rights, racial fears did not dominate legislative deliberations as they had in 1948. Winter suggested something about the more mundane nature of the 1952 proceedings when he told Senator Stennis a month into the session "that the State is now having its biennial case of legislativitis, but it is expected that the patient will recover." Sillers named Winter chair of the House Agriculture Committee, but that body dealt largely with routine matters. However, it did promote one important piece of legislation, the Livestock, Poultry, and Egg Production Assistance Act of 1952. The law created a fund of $2 million to provide loans to farmers wanting to diversify by expanding their livestock and poultry operations, a strategy Aylmer Winter had employed successfully on the Winter farm. Few in the legislature had much enthusiasm for bold initiatives, such as Winter's proposals to reform state government. He introduced two pieces of legislation designed to modernize the judicial system, but the House declined to support either bill. The House also failed to act on any of the changes suggested by the state reorganization study committee Winter had helped create during the 1950 session.[11]

At the close of the rather uneventful session, Winter returned to Grenada County, where he focused his attention on running the farm and building his law practice. Winter supplemented his income by teaching extension classes for the University of Mississippi two nights a week in Grenada and Winona. In 1953, he joined the Dixie Division of the Mississippi National Guard, and the weekend military duties brought in additional income. In January 1954, when the completion of a dam on the Yalobusha River created Grenada Lake northeast of Grenada, Winter and Bill Semmes purchased forty acres adjacent to the lake, subdivided the property, and sold the lots to prospective homeowners. In 1953 and 1954, Winter also had a part-time job managing the Grenada Chamber of Commerce. Many of his Chamber duties involved handling routine activities of the organization, although much of the job focused on helping the Chamber attract new industry to Grenada. Like other Mississippi communities, Grenada had embraced the Balance Agriculture with Industry (BAWI) program, created in the 1930s to allow local communities to approve bond sales to pay for land acquisition and plant construction for new industrial concerns. During his year and a half with the Grenada Chamber, Winter played a key role in attracting a major manufacturer from Minnesota to Grenada, the McQuay Manufacturing Company, which produced air conditioning and heating equipment. County citizens approved a $1.1 million bond issue in 1954 to lure the company, which created over four hundred jobs and had a $1 million annual payroll.[12]

Beginning in the fall of 1953, the Mississippi legislature turned its attention once again to the looming challenge to racial segregation. For the next year and a half, the legislature remained in almost constant session in an effort to craft a plan to resist school integration. In early November 1953, Governor Hugh White called legislators into special session to consider a comprehensive educational equalization program, which would improve the state's segregated school system, especially black schools, and serve to silence critics within the state and outside the South, who noted that the state's separate schools remained far from equal. State leaders hoped the equalization strategy would influence the pending decision in the *Brown* case. The Mississippi solons eventually passed a comprehensive education measure, known as the Minimum Foundation Program, which planned for a significant infusion of funds both to equalize expenditures between the black and white school systems and to make the kind of significant investment in public education the state had long failed to provide. The legislators, however, deferred funding the measure, precisely because uncertainty existed about whether or not the federal government would soon outlaw school segregation.[13]

At the same time, the Mississippi House made sure to clarify that its support of educational equalization represented no abandonment of segregation. A resolution declaring Mississippi's intention to maintain separate white and black schools passed with no negative votes. Although Winter voted for this resolution, he refused to endorse a more drastic demonstration of devotion to Jim Crow, a proposed constitutional amendment to abolish the public schools, should the federal government force integration. Winter confided his doubts about the amendment to Senator Stennis, who agreed that efforts to abolish the public schools would "prove to be a backward step to our white children." Like Winter, Stennis also thought that the equalization strategy would discourage blacks from pressing too hard for integrated schools: "common sense and local opinion would prevail," likely delaying school integration for years. Winter argued at the time that the "pressure for change" would lose much of its force "when the desirability for change is not so apparent." He also emphasized that the equalization efforts of the state "should have our attention not only because it is expedient but because it is right."[14]

Winter promoted equalization as a solution to potential racial problems in areas beyond the public schools. He and Semmes, with support from the Grenada business community, proposed in the 1954 session—just months before the *Brown* decision—the creation of two new state parks on the newly created Grenada Lake, one for whites and one for blacks. At that time, no state park existed in the entire state for black Mississippians. Some legislators grumbled about providing recreational facilities for blacks, but Winter convinced his colleagues that if blacks were to be enticed to support equalization as an alternative to integration, then the policy would have to encompass more than just the public schools. Two years later, Grenada Lake had two state parks on its shores, Hugh White State Park, on the more accessible south side of the lake, for whites; and Carver Point State Park, on the more isolated north shore of the lake, for blacks.[15] Although the two park facilities were not exactly "equal," Winter's effort did create a new type of state-funded service for blacks, which gave the equalization campaign additional credibility.

At the legislature's regular session of 1954, which began just weeks after the 1953 special session concluded, lawmakers once again took up the question of funding the Minimum Foundation Program. They initially rejected all financing measures but eventually agreed to provide limited monies for one year, an extra $9 million for the education budget. The bulk of money needed for the school equalization program, however, would have to wait until after the anticipated U.S. Supreme Court decision. At the same time, the legislature reiterated its support for racial segregation and made plans for an unfavorable court ruling against the practice. Winter was one of the sponsors of a resolution that, once again, declared that state policy mandated the segregation of the white and "colored" races, in case anyone still had any doubts about this fundamental truism of official white Mississippi. Winter supported some but not all of the efforts to prepare for the expected court ruling. He backed the establishment of the Legal Education Advisory Committee (LEAC), charged with finding ways to circumvent the law should the court rule against Jim Crow. Only four House members opposed this measure. On the other hand, Winter abstained when lawmakers passed a pupil placement law, designed to manage the assignment of school children in a way to avoid school desegregation. Winter believed such a law would not survive a legal challenge since, as he argued in a *Mississippi Law Journal* article written later in 1954, "the broad effect of its application was to maintain a pattern of segregation." Winter also continued to oppose the efforts to abolish the public school system in the event of forced integration. As in the special session, the House passed a school abolition amendment but it failed to get Senate support.[16]

After the *Brown* ruling in May 1954, the dominant reaction among Mississippi whites was to fight vigorously any attempt by the federal government to alter the racial status quo. Many of Mississippi's political leaders clamored to outdo each other in their promises to ensure massive resistance to the court's mandate for ending segregated schools. Senator Jim Eastland, up for reelection in 1954, proclaimed, "The South will not abide by nor obey this legislative decision by a political court." Winter reluctantly supported the candidacy of the man he had traveled the state with twelve years earlier. Eastland's opponent in 1954 was Carroll Gartin, who also opposed the *Brown* decision, though not in the same animated and defiant tones as Eastland. Winter told Senator Stennis in 1954 that he actually favored Gartin, as his "political philosophy and my own [are] more nearly alike than Jim's and mine." Winter, however, voted for Eastland because of "certain immutable ties of friendship," although he declined to be "in the forefront of the flag-wavers" for Eastland.[17]

Winter's lukewarm support for Eastland's politics in 1954, despite the loyalty he felt for one of his early political mentors, can be attributed to the fact that Winter had little interest in actively advocating for massive resistance. At the same time, he had no inclination to embrace the black civil rights movement. Racial moderates like Winter believed in gradual change in southern race relations, but these modifications should only occur, as Winter told one correspondent a couple of years later, as part of "an orderly but maybe time-consuming process that would diminish the confrontation and diminish the dislocation of society." The speed at which white moderates sought to make adjustments to existing racial arrangements was both too slow and too limited for black activists and too fast for committed white segregationists. Given a choice, Winter would have preferred to limit the focus on the race issue in the interest of addressing some of Mississippi's considerable economic and educational problems.[18]

In the wake of the *Brown* decision, that position became untenable, especially for public officials. State legislators faced intense pressure from hard-core white segregationists to toe the party line of not yielding an inch to efforts to dismantle the system of racial apartheid. As a segregationist, although one who favored gradual changes in race relations, Winter did not oppose the legislative effort to forestall the assault on segregation. What he objected to primarily was the nature of the resistance. Winter was a commonsense lawyer who recognized that any opposition to *Brown* would have to appeal to recognizable constitutional principles, rather than flimsy subterfuges such as the recently adopted pupil placement law. Writing in the *Mississippi Law Journal* in 1954, Winter examined the viability of one possible resistance strategy. He explored whether Mississippi might utilize the police powers reserved to the states by the Tenth Amendment to oppose *Brown*. He wondered whether Mississippi might claim the need to preserve segregation as "the means of promoting the public safety of members of both races and the maintenance of peace and order," as each state had a duty "to do all that is reasonably prudent to maintain order." Yet Winter concluded that the U.S. Supreme Court would be unlikely to accept such reasoning, and he believed that the search for a constitutional argument against *Brown* was "a task [that] is not a simple one. Perhaps, it would be more frank to regard it as an impossible one."[19] Much of the legislature disagreed with this assessment and resolved to try any tactic, however unrealistic, in the ongoing massive resistance campaign.

When the legislature returned for a three-week special session in September 1954, "a series of irate speeches bashing the United States Supreme Court" punctuated the gathering. The main item on the agenda was consideration of a school abolition amendment to the state constitution, which would eliminate the constitutional requirement to maintain free public schools and allow the legislature to abolish local school systems with a two-thirds vote of legislators. Supporters of the amendment tolerated little dissent to the measure. Delos Burks, a representative from Pearl River County who opposed the amendment, claimed that the "deliberations" after the bill's first reading "had the effect of a 'steamroller.'" Burks, Winter, and several others offered amendments that would raise the bar before the legislature could actually abolish any public school, by inserting language requiring a vote of two-thirds, three-fifths, or even a simple majority of all legislators elected—rather than simply those present at any given session—to shut down a public school. The majority quickly rejected all these proposals. Although Winter had voted against the school abolition measure in the 1953 special session and at the 1954 regular session, during the 1954 special session he joined the majority of legislators in approving the proposal and sending it to the voters for a verdict. Winter struggled over this decision but shifted his vote because hardliners had pledged to block the funding of the recently passed Minimum Foundation Program—the first comprehensive funding plan for education in the state's history—until the power to abolish schools, if necessary, was in place.[20]

Having secured voter approval in December 1954 for the school abolition constitutional amendment—by a three-to-one majority—the legislature returned for another special session in early 1955 to approve funding for the equalization program. Legislators also continued to bolster the state's system of racial apartheid and to monitor any breaches to the white solidarity perceived as absolutely necessary to preserve that system. A bill passed by the House for another constitutional amendment made a slight but important change in the wording of the constitution's literacy requirement for voter registration. Instead of requiring that voters either read *or* interpret the Mississippi Constitution as a prerequisite to registering to vote, potential voters would now be required to read *and* interpret a section of the constitution. This adjustment ensured that registrars would always use the disfranchising mechanism of the "understanding clause," a change clearly designed to further stymie black efforts to exercise the franchise. No legislators opposed the new provision, although Winter and twenty-six other House members abstained on this vote. Opponents of massive resistance often used abstention as a strategy designed to prevent the "ayes" from prevailing without recording a potentially damaging public stand against the defenders of Mississippi's racial status quo. Toward the end of the 1955 session, a resolution was offered to censure newspaper editor Hodding Carter for an article he wrote in *Look* magazine in 1954 condemning the newly formed White Citizens' Council, a private group dedicated to using their economic power and social status to intimidate anyone who dared challenge racial segregation. Winter and seventeen other House members voted against the censure resolution. As Winter later recalled, while he sometimes went along with massive resistance proposals out of political necessity, "there were bills in the legislature that were introduced that were so offensive that I couldn't support them." The censure resolution against Carter was one such measure.[21]

Winter himself never joined the White Citizens' Council, though many other legislators did. Winter had, however, unknowingly attended one of the early organizational meetings of the group during the summer of

1954. Held at Greenwood City Hall to discuss the response to the *Brown* decision, many in the crowd talked about fears of a black uprising and of blacks clamoring to register to vote. Others talked about the necessity for white people to stick together and about all the possible methods to get around the recent court decision. As part of the discussion, Winter cautiously rose to address the assembled crowd and, as he recalled years later, told them "the precedents are clear that the courts are not going to let us do anything indirectly that they would not let us do directly." In a careful way, Winter suggested that the kinds of defiance being proposed would not likely work, an analysis similar to the one he offered in the pages of the *Mississippi Law Journal*. Winter's comments elicited silence. As he left the meeting, only one person offered any support for his position, Means Johnston, a respected older lawyer, who told Winter that he had presented a sensible objection to the proposed resistance efforts. Although Winter's questioning of the tactics proclaimed by what he realized later was the embryonic White Citizen's Council had raised eyebrows, his thoughtful critique did not cause the excited segregationists to ride Winter out on a rail. Indeed, at least one observer at the meeting, fellow legislator David Womack, believed that Winter's very presence at the meeting indicated he would join the group. Winter, however, refused to sign up, even as the new group became a primary topic of conversation during the September special session of the legislature. When a local Citizens' Council chapter formed in Grenada County, one of the organizers of the group, John Lake, the manager of a local hosiery mill and a longtime friend of Winter, asked him to join the organization. Winter told Lake that he understood the group's objectives, but he did not want to get "officially identified, because I don't know where this is going to lead." Lake accepted the explanation.[22]

Winter's rebuff of the Citizens' Council came with potential risks. At the time, he was still trying to establish his law practice in Grenada. He and Billy Semmes had recently constructed a building in downtown Grenada, around the corner from the courthouse, to house their respective law offices. Opposing the emerging massive resistance consensus in even a limited way did not represent perhaps the best choice for a lawyer trying to build his practice. In the midst of the tumultuous summer of 1954, Senator Stennis presented Winter with a possible exit from the growing insanity of Mississippi politics, by offering him the position of the senator's administrative assistant. He and Elise debated for days the possibility of moving back to Washington. Although his income would increase significantly, the move might mean a permanent commitment to Washington and government administration. Winter, however, really wanted his own career as an elected official in his home state. As the couple talked over the matter on the banks of the pond on the Grenada farm, they agreed to stay in Mississippi.[23]

Although Winter wanted a political career in Mississippi, after the 1955 special session, he considered once again leaving the legislature. He later recalled that at the time he "was somewhat disillusioned with the legislative process . . . . I saw as a result of the supreme court decision, several years of being involved in a bitter no-win contest with the federal government." Because of the need to address the civil rights challenge, legislative service had become considerably more than a part-time job during his second term in the House. The constant sessions to craft resistance to school integration made establishing his law practice and attending to his other responsibilities difficult. Winter explored other political options, and during the summer of 1955, he considered a race for district attorney. After testing the waters, however, he decided he could not unseat the incumbent. So, when no other candidates announced for Winter's legislative seat, Winter signed on for another term, two days before the filing deadline.[24]

Winter's failure to embrace massive resistance did not damage his standing in the eyes of state political leaders or his local constituents. Two gubernatorial candidates in 1955, J. P. Coleman, another relative moderate on matters of race, and Fielding Wright, the states' rights champion of 1948, asked Winter to manage their campaigns, but he declined both offers. Although some of the legislative leadership, including Speaker Sillers, did not consider Winter totally "safe" on the race issue, he also had not done anything that had completely undermined his political reputation, even among the most outspoken opponents of racial change, men like Governor Wright. In Grenada County, when Winter returned from the 1955 special session, a local leader of the Citizens' Council asked him why he voted against denouncing Hodding Carter. Winter explained that he did not think it was the legislature's business to censure newspaper editors. As the two men talked, the Council supporter said he would like to hear Carter for himself and asked if Winter could invite the editor to speak to the Grenada Rotary Club, to which both men belonged.

Winter agreed, and Carter, who had not received many invitations to speak to civic clubs because of his outspoken criticism of Mississippi politicians, gladly accepted. Carter gave a speech that was well received by most of the Rotarians. If nothing else, most political leaders and the hometown folks understood that Winter did not advocate anything radical, like racial integration. He urged moderation by questioning the plan to abolish public schools and the demands to censure newspaper editors and, as he explained later, tried "to keep us from looking too foolish in the process of opposing integration." While many of his fellow politicians and constituents disagreed with some of his positions, they also seemed to admire his independence of thought and action. As fellow legislator Joel Blass remembered, there was "something about William that engendered respect."[25]

Racial moderates such as Winter saw J. P. Coleman's 1955 gubernatorial race as a chance to move away from the massive resistance frenzy that had begun to grip the state. Before the election, Winter told Stennis that he would look forward to returning to the legislature if Coleman won the top spot, but "would be less enthusiastic" if Coleman lost the race. Although Winter declined to run Coleman's campaign, he actively stumped for the candidate. Coleman won the election, and although he had a more moderate stance on race than other leaders at the time, Coleman also did not advocate for radical changes in race relations. He disagreed with the *Brown* decision and thought it "represents an unwarranted invasion of the rights and powers of the states." Coleman simply thought, as Winter did, that Mississippi did not need to take on the federal government over the race issue.[26]

The moderates offered a cautious and risk-averse approach in an atmosphere where events increasingly sharpened the moral drama unfolding in Mississippi and across the South. Soon after the August 1955 state elections in Mississippi, Roy Bryant and J. W. Milam murdered a fourteen-year-old black boy, Emmett Till, in Tallahatchie County for allegedly whistling at a white woman. Many white Mississippians believed that the killing of the young Chicago boy was justified for his violation of the state's racial code; Bryant and Milam had merely carried out the suggestion of the Citizens' Council to tolerate no attempts to alter racial mores. At the same time, the brutal killing of Till and the subsequent acquittal of his murderers, who later confessed the crime to journalist Bradford Huie, mobilized a

generation of activists, both black and white, to fight against the injustice
of the South's racial arrangements. For William Winter, Governor Coleman, and other racial moderates within the state, the Till murder and the
acquittal of Bryant and Milam were appalling, but the case did not spur
them to lead the charge in challenging racial segregation. Some moderates
thought that the attention focused on Mississippi by the events surrounding the murder of Emmett Till represented a setback to the gradualist
approach to racial improvement and blamed the national media for sensa-
tionalizing the killing and the resulting trial. Winter noted seven months
after the killing that "there have been many other cases, both before and
since, that were more flagrant in their misapplication of justice." At the
same time, he believed "that a great deal more progress in solving the
difficult race question is being made than is generally thought," and he
worried that the passions inflamed by the Till murder and subsequent
trial concealed that fact. He continued to maintain that a solution to
racial issues would require "the continued application of patient and wise
understanding for a long period of time."[27]

While the moderate stance seemed increasingly irrelevant in the battle
brewing between civil rights supporters and bitter-end segregationists, the
candidacy of J. P. Coleman in 1955 had emboldened Winter and other
moderates in the House. They thought the time might be right to challenge the rule of the powerful and conservative Speaker of the House,
Walter Sillers. The legislative sessions from 1952 to 1955 confirmed the
belief among many of the dissidents in the House that the Speaker's "attitudes on national affairs were too negative" and that the frequent special
sessions to fashion massive resistance legislation accomplished little and
took time away from other important matters that demanded attention.
Others disliked how tightly Sillers held his power and kept most of the
leadership positions in the hands of an old guard that hailed largely from
the Mississippi Delta. During the special session of 1955, a group of legislators, including Winter, Joe Wroten of Greenville, and George Rogers of
Vicksburg, started talking about the possibility of new leadership in the
House, with Winter as the likely candidate. Word of the plotting soon
leaked out. Early in the 1955 gubernatorial campaign, Coleman made a
campaign stop in Grenada. After his speech on the town square, he and
Winter met in Winter's law office. Coleman had heard about the plans to
challenge Sillers and said he would favor a Speaker who shared more of

his own views. Although he did not totally commit himself to the effort to unseat Sillers, he encouraged Winter to explore what kind of backing he could marshal. Coleman also dropped hints, in conversations with Winter and others, such as George Rogers, that if elected governor, he would support Winter's bid for House Speaker. In part based on the somewhat vague expressions of support by Coleman, Winter publicly announced his intentions in mid-June. Some of Winter's friends responded to the news by noting that the thirty-two-year-old legislator was throwing away what had seemed a promising political career.[28]

Sillers outmaneuvered Winter before the campaign for the Speaker's slot had even begun. After Coleman defeated Paul Johnson Jr. in the second Democratic primary in August to win the governor's race (Mississippi still had no competitive Republican Party at the time), Winter, Rogers, and a few other Winter backers went to Ackerman—Coleman's hometown—to seek the governor-elect's open support, but he was not yet ready to commit. In the meantime, Sillers and his lieutenants began to line up commitments among the House members. Knowing he had the necessary votes, Sillers also went to Ackerman. Presenting Coleman with the evidence of more than enough votes for his candidacy, Sillers told Coleman that he would support the incoming governor's legislative agenda, if Coleman would not intervene in the Speaker's contest. Coleman agreed. Shortly thereafter, Coleman met with newly elected legislators at the Greenwood courthouse. After the meeting, Coleman tried to convince Winter to withdraw from the Speaker's race. In the privacy of a nearby anteroom, Coleman told his young protégé that he did not think he could win and expressed concern that a contentious battle for the Speaker's position might jeopardize the governor's legislative program. [29]

Winter met with his core group of fifteen to twenty supporters, and they all urged him to see the contest through, despite Coleman's refusal to back his cause, in order to demonstrate opposition to Sillers's regime. With this nucleus of support, Winter set out on yet another tour of the state, this time to talk to as many legislators as he could, especially those he knew supported a change or at least had not publicly committed to Sillers. Almost all of those who promised to back Winter came from northeast and south Mississippi, areas where voters had expressed doubt about the most extreme proposals for massive resistance, such as the school abolition amendment. Members from these sections had also

long chafed at the domination exercised by the economically conservative Delta planters in the legislature, of which Walter Sillers was the most
obvious embodiment. Only two of the Winter supporters came from the
Delta area, Joe Wroten and George Rogers. At the end of his tour, Winter
thought he had perhaps fifty-five votes, including "maybes"; a win would
require seventy votes. Winter continued his campaign into the fall, even
after Coleman publicly stated in September that he would remain neutral
in the battle. Meanwhile, Sillers and his lieutenants pressured individual
members to declare publicly their support for the Speaker. In December,
Winter tried to undermine the Speaker's credibility by suggesting he was
a closet Republican, a serious charge in the virtual one-party Democratic
state. Sillers admitted he had not voted for a Democratic presidential candidate since Al Smith in 1928, but he responded to Winter's charge by telling Kenneth Toler, the Jackson bureau chief for the *Memphis Commercial
Appeal*, "I am not a Republican and no one knows that better than William
Winter . . . . I am a Jeffersonian States' Rights Mississippi Democrat."[30]

When the legislature convened in January, the Winter forces first tried
to alter Speaker Sillers's control of the all-important Rules Committee.
Although the Speaker typically chaired the committee and named all its
members, an amendment offered by Joe Wroten proposed to have the
membership of the Rules Committee elected by the House, two members from each of the state's six congressional districts, with the Speaker
still serving as chair. Winter and thirty-three other members supported
this change, not enough to pass the proposal. Soon thereafter, the House
voted for their leader. Sillers prevailed by a count of ninety-four to forty.
In addition to the thirty-three members who voted for Wroten's amendment to change the Rules Committee, an additional seven members supported Winter in the roll-call vote for Speaker. Afterwards, as expected,
Sillers marginalized Winter and his supporters when he made his committee assignments. No Winter partisans were named to the all-important
Appropriations Committee, which had thirty-three members. Although
Sillers appointed Winter and Joel Blass, a Winter supporter, to the equally
strategic Ways and Means Committee, no other Winter followers joined
the committee, which also had thirty-three members. Winter remained
on the Agriculture Committee but lost his chairmanship.[31]

With Sillers still in control of the House, and with Coleman committed
to working with the Speaker, the preservation of segregation became the

major issue on the legislative agenda during the 1956 session. Winter and his fellow moderates mustered only limited opposition to the vast array of massive resistance measures put before the 1956 House. A month before the legislature met, the LEAC drafted a series of proposals it deemed necessary to maintain segregation. The Jackson Citizens' Council endorsed the measures and called on the legislature to pass the laws quickly. Sillers moved those items to the top of legislative agenda, and six of the bills came up for a vote early in the session. Winter voted yes on four of the items. One bill to abolish common law marriages seemingly had little to do with defending segregation, but it was designed to highlight this common form of family arrangements among Mississippi blacks as proof of the race's moral "inferiority." Another measure prohibited the "fomenting and agitation of litigation," in an effort to prevent third parties, like the NAACP, from encouraging blacks to file lawsuits to enforce the *Brown* decision. A third bill, aimed at preventing civil rights protests, prohibited "any person from creating disturbance in any public place or business." The law defined disturbance broadly: "loud or offensive talk, the making of threats or attempting to intimidate, or any conduct which causes a disturbance or breach of the peace or threatened breach of the peace." The fourth measure gave individuals or businesses the right to "choose customers or clients." This law touted a "right of association" as trumping any requirement for equal access. The bill's provisions included penalties for anyone "who refuses to vacate a public place when ordered to do so by the owner or an employee thereof." On the other two pieces of massive resistance legislation, one to abolish the state's compulsory education law and one that made it unlawful to advocate "disobedience of state laws," Winter did not vote. A number of legislators joined Winter in abstaining on some or all of these six bills, but House members cast only a total of eight negative votes against the six measures.[32]

One additional measure, the state's interposition resolution, asserted that individual states had the right to declare federal laws unconstitutional; this legislation represented the clearest expression of Mississippi's refusal to recognize the validity of federal law expressed in the *Brown* decision. When this item came up for a vote, Winter and seven other House members offered an amendment stating, "We expressly reject the doctrine of nullification"—in other words, rejecting the essence of the interposition mechanism—but they failed to muster support for this position.

Having registered their objection but unwilling to record publically their opposition to massive resistance, Winter and the other dissenters then joined their House colleagues in unanimously approving final passage of the interposition resolution. One of the most contentious issues that arose during the 1956 session involved the creation of the State Sovereignty Commission, initially presented as a public relations measure to advocate for constitutional government. Although Winter and all but two representatives originally voted for the commission, he joined a group of twenty-three legislators who voted for a failed motion to reconsider the first vote, after it became clear that the White Citizens' Council actually sponsored the bill. Section six of the legislation authorized the commission to cooperate and even "pool" funds with other groups working to preserve segregation. Only three representatives voted against funding the spy agency, but Winter, along with thirty other members, abstained from voting on the Sovereignty Commission funding bill. Abstentions on appropriation bills had even more significance than on regular legislation, since a majority of the *elected* members were necessary to pass any appropriation measure, while other legislation required only a majority of those voting. Winter and others withheld their vote out of concerns that the Citizens' Council would dominate the operations of the new agency, a situation that indeed came to pass during the administration of Governor Ross Barnett in the early 1960s.[33]

Winter refused to blindly support legislative efforts to implement massive resistance to the *Brown* decision, and he did not join the White Citizens' Council. In the end, he managed to stake out a position in which he sometimes opposed massive resistance while not crossing the line in a way that he became completely ostracized in a political culture where massive resistance had become a litmus test of one's suitability for legislative service. Winter did not question the right of Mississippi politicians to try to preserve segregation, for he himself did not clamor for radical alteration in social relations, but he believed that Mississippi needed to follow federal law, which now included the *Brown* decision. Writing in the *Mississippi Law Journal* in the aftermath of the 1956 legislative session, Winter said, "It seems realistic to believe that the application of any statute that has the effect of continuing a pattern of mandatory segregation will be invalidated." Winter believed greater attention to equalization solutions represented one possible way to diminish black demands for an end to "mandatory segregation," which would in turn obviate the need for massive resistance.

Winter's careful balancing act in the legislature did not bode well for his future in that body. With the legislature obsessed with maintaining racial segregation against all attacks, both external and internal, Winter's progressive ideas about the possibilities of government to move Mississippi forward in other areas would likely receive a limited hearing. In addition, the legislative leadership, after Winter's failed attempt to unseat Speaker Sillers, viewed him as a potential renegade.[34] Fortunately for Winter, at the end of the 1956 session, Governor Coleman presented him a way to stay involved in state politics, yet leave the legislature.

6

STATE POLITICS
AND CIVIL RIGHTS

On Saturday, March 31, 1956, the Mississippi House was in the last week of its session, one that had focused considerable attention on maintaining racial segregation. As William Winter and his colleagues attended to end-of-session duties, word arrived that the state tax collector, Nellah Bailey, had died suddenly. Mrs. Thomas L. Bailey, as she was more generally known, was the widow of Thomas L. Bailey, Mississippi's governor from 1944 to 1946, who died in office. The first woman to win statewide office, she had been elected three times to the post of state tax collector. The news of Mrs. Bailey's death aroused substantial speculation in the House chamber about whom Governor Coleman would name as her successor, in large part because the position was a lucrative one. The office of state tax collector retained 10 percent of all taxes collected by that office. Under Mrs. Bailey the office had brought in around a million dollars a year. Even after paying out salaries and administrative expenses, the tax collector stood to earn significantly more than any other elected official in a state where the governor received an annual salary of $15,000. One House member noted that for that kind of money, the governor might want to resign and have the lieutenant governor move up and name Coleman to the post.[1]

Winter turned out to be the lucky recipient of this plum position; Coleman selected him largely as atonement for failing to support the legislator in his challenge to House Speaker Walter Sillers. The job allowed Winter the opportunity to stay involved in state government yet disentangle himself from the intense racial politics then consuming the legislature.

The post also provided a major boost to his income, which gave him a certain amount of financial independence as he moved forward in his public career.

Winter's new job in 1956, as state tax collector, was seen as frivolous by some, as immoral by others. The position had assumed new, controversial duties during World War II after the passage in 1944 of a law to collect a "black market tax," a 10 percent levy on the sale of any personal property prohibited by law. The legislature had ostensibly enacted the measure to exact revenue from wartime black market trafficking in commodities in short supply, such as sugar, tires, and cigarettes. Its main purpose, however, as almost everyone recognized (including the legislators who passed the measure), was to tax illegal liquor sales. After the war, efforts to repeal the black market tax had failed. Aylmer Winter, a member of the Mississippi House between 1944 and 1948, both supported passage of the original black market tax and fought against its repeal. During the 1946 session, Aylmer Winter told his son that he opposed repeal because the law "has brought a million dollars into the state treasury that otherwise would have been kept by the bootleggers." William Winter agreed at the time that the law would "enable us to reap as much financial good from the selling of the foul stuff as we possibly can." He believed "the present tax bill—inconsistent as it appears and ridiculed by journalistic jokers—is still a down-to-earth approach to the problem."[2]

Although Winter's new job primarily involved collecting taxes on illegal liquor in one of the nation's last officially "dry" states, he abstained from drinking himself. He told *Jackson Daily News* reporter Phil Stroupe a few days after assuming the job that "I wish we could abolish the use of the stuff in Mississippi. It has led to more crime, trouble and problems than any other one thing in our society." At the same time, Winter recognized that prohibition was not universally popular, and he told Stroupe that "as a practical matter, it seems almost impossible to stamp it out in certain areas of the state." In fact, in 1957, the putatively dry state had almost one thousand federally licensed wholesale and retail liquor dealers in fifty-one of its eighty-two counties, with the bulk of the establishments concentrated in three areas: the Gulf Coast, the Mississippi River counties, and Rankin County, across the Pearl River from the capital in Jackson. Harrison County on the Gulf Coast alone had 292 retail and 6 wholesale liquor outlets. In the areas where liquor flowed freely, local law enforcement officials generally declined to enforce the prohibition measures, although bootleggers, even in the drinking parts of the state, sometimes faced arbitrary enforcement of the liquor laws when local administrations changed. One savvy liquor dealer in the Mississippi Delta built his store straddling the county line between Washington County and Bolivar County, giving him ready insurance against a change in local sentiment. If one county suddenly decided to enforce prohibition, the store owner would simply move all his wares to the side of the store in the other county. In essence, Mississippi had a de facto local option for liquor sales. One tax commission official claimed this arrangement satisfied all parties at the time: "the drys had the law, the wets had the whiskey, and the state got the money." Winter himself favored statutory local option, which had been proposed and defeated in the legislature for many years, including in 1948, when Winter had voted for the proposal.[3]

To operate his office, Winter had a staff of seven deputy tax collectors, a secretary, and a bookkeeper. The collection of the tax was a relatively simple matter. Most of the alcohol coming into Mississippi entered from Louisiana, since the neighboring state allowed Mississippi dealers who had a federal license issued by the U.S. Treasury Department to purchase their products without paying Louisiana tax. Since Louisiana was the main source of supply, the Mississippi state tax collector's office had worked out an arrangement years earlier to help pay for the salaries of two employees in the Louisiana Department of Revenue. In return, Louisiana delivered daily reports of the liquor purchases made by Mississippi dealers to the Mississippi state tax collector's office. Then, the deputy tax collectors simply visited the dealers and collected the fees. To simplify calculations, the state applied a standard rate of taxation: $0.75 for each case of illegal wine and $4.20 for each case of contraband liquor, regardless of the actual cost of the alcohol. Most of the bootleggers paid their taxes without complaint, although some tried to take their operations underground and avoid paying the black market tax.[4]

Just because a bootlegger received certification from Winter's office that he had paid the black market tax, that official stamp of approval did not make the commerce any more legal. In fact, the tax receipts in the collector's office could be used as evidence to prosecute violators of the dry laws, and in keeping with state statute, Winter's office supplied these receipts to local law enforcement whenever requested. A Coleman administration crackdown in May 1956, the month after Winter took over as state tax collector, led a number of Delta distributors to shut down temporarily because "of dwindling inventories." At times, a liquor dealer might pay his tax and then have his bottles seized by lawmen before the wine or liquor could be sold to thirsty customers. For example, soon after a Lauderdale County bootlegger received a $20,000 shipment of alcohol in 1959, local law enforcement raided, confiscating and destroying the liquor dealer's entire collection of booze. The owner of the liquor asked Winter for a refund of his black market tax, which he had already paid. Winter replied as he always did in such situations: "That is just one of the hazards of the occupation you are in."[5]

As everyone knew, Winter was paid well as state tax collector. In 1958, his office collected a record amount of tax revenue, almost $1.3 million. Ten percent of all the monies received, $130,000, went to the tax collector's office. Out of this amount, Winter had to cover the salaries of his nine employees and most of his office expenses, all of which averaged roughly $67,000. Even after paying for these operating costs, the young politician still received a sizeable salary. Over the seven and a half years that Winter held the position of state tax collector, he collected approximately $11 million in taxes, earning him a $1.1 million commission over that period. That translated into almost $600,000 in salary for Winter. His annual pay averaged between $60,000 and $80,000 a year, depending on a particular year's collections. In 1960, a year with one of the highest amount of taxes gathered, Winter cleared more than $81,000. That was a huge payday in the late 1950s and early 1960s, especially for a public servant. A *Life Magazine* feature on the Mississippi tax collector in 1962 noted that Winter was the second highest paid elected official in the country, right behind President John F. Kennedy, who earned $100,000 annually.[6]

Throughout the rest of Winter's political career, his opponents would often charge that he became a millionaire because of his tenure as state tax collector. While technically true, at least half of that million dollars Winter earned went to pay the expenses of his office during his years of service. The remainder went to support his growing family during the many years he could not maintain a full-time law practice because of his political duties. Winter put some of the money into investments; a 1974 financial report showed that he owned not only the family farm in Grenada County but also another 240 acres in south Mississippi, a rental house in

Grenada, and almost $100,000 in various stocks and bonds.[7] He also contributed over $100,000 directly to his later political campaigns. The tax collector salary ensured a comfortable existence for Winter and his family, but it did not make him the wealthy tycoon his detractors later claimed.

At the time of his appointment to the tax position, Winter pledged to work for the abolition of the office. As a legislator, he had lobbied for more efficient government, and he recognized that his new position was an unnecessary one. Since the state had failed to adopt a true local option system for the sale of liquor, Winter reasoned that the black market tax, because of the important revenue it generated, should be retained as long as official prohibition remained. He believed, however, that a more efficient method of collecting the tax existed: abolish the tax collector's office and merge its duties with those of the Mississippi State Tax Commission. Winter made his recommendations about eliminating his office known to his former legislative colleagues, but they took no action during the 1958 session, in part because the head of the state tax commission, Noel Monaghan, who disliked the black market tax and wanted nothing to do with collecting the funds, lobbied against Winter's proposal. Although a number of key legislators, including Hilton Waits, head of the powerful House Ways and Means Committee, favored Winter's cost-saving suggestion, they were concerned that debates about more efficient methods of collecting tax money on illegal liquor might easily lead to broader questions about why such a tax should exist in the first place. Religious groups regularly implored politicians both to resist all attempts to repeal prohibition and to eliminate the black market tax, which "gives a quasi-legal standing to the sale of liquor." In addition, according to House member George Rogers, some legislative leaders, including Speaker Sillers, may have opposed the legislation simply because they did not want Winter to get credit for abolishing his own lucrative public office in the interest of government efficiency, a stance that would undoubtedly earn him a great deal of public admiration.[8]

When the legislature failed to abolish the tax collector's office, Winter decided to seek election to the position in the 1959 elections. His campaign got off to a rocky start. In late January 1959, Winter spoke at the Jones County Chitterling Eaters Convention. The next morning, he awoke to a headline in the *Jackson Clarion-Ledger*, "Judge Charges Winter Violating Whiskey Law." As he read the article, Winter discovered that a circuit judge in south Mississippi, Sebe Dale, had asked the Lamar County grand jury to indict Winter for conspiracy to violate the prohibition laws. Dale, an ardent defender of prohibition, believed that Winter's arrangement with Louisiana to collect the tax added up to a felony conspiracy charge. The Lamar County grand jury failed to return an indictment, but Dale promised to make the same charge to the grand juries in three other counties of his circuit in the coming months. The next court was scheduled for Lawrence County later in February. Winter decided to make an appearance at the proceedings. Arriving undetected as Judge Dale presented the case against the state tax collector to the grand jury, Winter stood up when Dale finished and said, "Judge, I have just heard your charge to the grand jury. I would like to speak to them before they begin their deliberations." Dale denied the request, but soon after the jury had retired, the local prosecutor came out and told Dale, "The jurors want to hear from the state tax collector." When they returned, Winter gave them a twenty-minute lesson in how the collection of the black market tax worked. He explained that he only carried out the duties the legislature had charged him to perform and added, "Your state treasury now has more funds for hospitals and schools because of what I have been able to do. Instead of indicting me, I hope all of you will vote for me for reelection." The Lawrence County grand jury refused to charge Winter and ended Judge Dale's crusade against the tax collector.[9]

Not surprisingly, given the high pay associated with the office of state tax collector, Winter's 1959 race attracted a field of nine challengers. Many of Winter's opponents emphasized the unfairness of allowing Winter to continue in his position. He had already had his turn; it was time to pass the well-paid position around. Most of Winter's opponents, however, had little name recognition, while Winter had been actively engaged in state politics for over a decade. Because of the salary he had earned over the previous three years, he was able to draw on $50,000 of his own money to finance his campaign, using part of the funds on early forms of television ads. He would show up at a local station, buy five or ten minutes of air time, and present his live pitch as the cameras rolled. Elise Winter also played a role in her husband's campaign. She had little experience with public speaking but proved to be an effective ambassador for her husband's cause. She made speeches around the state when the appearances did not conflict with her child-rearing responsibilities.[10]

Each of the other aspirants for the job had his own local base of support, and Winter failed to win a majority in the first primary. His runoff opponent in the second primary was John Whitfield Birdsong, who carried the politically fortunate names of both a former governor (Whitfield) and the head of the state highway patrol (Birdsong). Winter managed to survive and win reelection, however, largely because of his statewide name recognition.[11]

The state tax collector position allowed Winter time to pursue other interests. He continued to oversee the farming operations of the numerous tenants still working the Grenada farm. In April 1957, he was appointed to the Board of Trustees of the Mississippi Department of Archives and History, a task he would devote much time to over more than fifty years of service and leadership on the board. In the late 1950s, Winter also became active in the Mississippi Association for Mental Health; he was chosen as president of the association in 1962 and served for many years on the board of directors of the group. One of Winter's continuing passions, of course, was politics. He remained an important ally of Governor Coleman and his administration during the late 1950s. He also kept a busy schedule of public appearances and made speeches to a variety of groups throughout the state.[12]

Because Winter remained visible as a public figure, he still had to respond to the civil rights movement and massive resistance. Unlike many Mississippi politicians at the time, he did not seek political power by condemning blacks and their white allies pressing for racial change. As one friend of his correctly realized in 1957, Winter would "never seek to debase another race in order to ride into office on the crest of an emotional wave of hate." At the same time, Winter remained a segregationist himself. Although he believed that Mississippi should move toward cautious and moderate change in the area of race relations, largely in the interest of solving more "critical" problems, the exact nature or timing of any racial adjustments remained unclear. Avoiding conflict over race, if possible, was an important part of this approach. In early 1957, Winter lauded Governor Coleman's leadership in keeping the racial peace when he told one correspondent, "He has discouraged intemperate actions on every hand and consequently Mississippi is the only state in the South that has not had a great deal of unfavorable publicity last year."[13]

    With the civil rights movement in Mississippi largely quiescent throughout the late 1950s, white extremists represented the main threat to racial peace. Winter worked with white leaders within and outside of state government who made some limited efforts to check the extremism of the White Citizens' Council crowd. In 1957, he and other moderates organized the Young Democrats, a group "pledged to progressive action, rather than to useless 'crying in our beer.'" The Young Democrats maintained that the Democratic Party was "the only true political friend of Mississippi and the South" and "had traditionally advanced progressive programs to eliminate poverty and make a better life for ALL the people." Whatever differences existed among Democrats from around the country "should be settled within the party." The Young Democrats included men such as Charles Deaton, a staffer of moderate Mississippi congressman Frank Smith; former legislative colleague George Rogers; and moderate newspapermen Paul Pittman of *The Tylertown Times* and Hal DeCell of the *Deer Creek Pilot* in Rolling Fork, among others. Governor Coleman, though not an active member of the group, encouraged the gathering of young moderates. One of the national heroes of the Young Democrats, and a leader for whom Winter had already developed an abiding admiration, was John F. Kennedy. At the first event sponsored by the Young Democrats, in the fall of 1957, Kennedy addressed a crowd of two thousand in Jackson. Many of those in attendance were "young people," who, Congressman Smith observed, "thought of themselves as a new force in Mississippi politics." Kennedy's address focused primarily on foreign policy, but he did refer to the *Brown* decision as the law of the land, a statement that received a warm and enthusiastic response from the moderate crowd. Kennedy himself accepted the gradualist approach to black civil rights at the time. The previous summer, he had endorsed southern amendments that helped dilute the 1957 Civil Rights Act.[14]

The Young Democrats never really developed as an effective counterweight to the Citizens' Council, and for the most part, Winter did not risk his political future by publicly opposing the well-organized massive resistance forces. Instead, he tried to avoid the race issue whenever possible. In public appearances, Winter would often tell his audiences that he was an Eastland-Stennis Democrat, which identified him as a follower of the state's two U.S. senators, and by implication, as someone safe on the issue of protecting Jim Crow and black disfranchisement. Winter was one of the few politicians in the state who could actually claim a history of close relationships with both men. Eastland, of course, had been a longtime friend of the Winter family and had provided Winter with his first introduction to statewide politics in the summer of 1942. Although Winter continued to support Eastland publicly (though not very actively), including during his 1960 reelection campaign, Winter had grown uncomfortable with the senior senator's increasingly scathing condemnations of the civil rights movement. Winter, however, never burned any political bridges. While his relationship with Eastland remained cordial, it was based more on a personal friendship than agreement on political philosophy. On the other hand, Winter remained extremely close to Stennis and frequently turned to him for advice. Stennis also had misgivings about the strategy of massive resistance and preferred quiet delay rather than outright defiance on the issue of racial change, a stance that Winter also generally embraced at the time. When Stennis helped in the summer of 1957 to water down the first civil rights measure considered by the U.S. Congress since Reconstruction, Winter expressed support for the southern delegation's "reasoned point of view . . . in opposing the extreme features of this Legislation."[15]

By the end of the 1950s, the approach of encouraging moderate and gradual change became more and more difficult to sustain as the civil rights movement increasingly mobilized. In 1959, Dr. Gilbert Mason and others staged the state's first direct-action protest, a wade-in on the Gulf Coast, and protests in other communities soon followed. Rising civil rights demands only added to hysterical white fears about broaching any change in social relations. The state elections of 1959 demonstrated the power of the massive resistance forces to capitalize on these white fears. Ross Barnett, who had lost two previous races for governor running as a racial moderate, entered the 1959 campaign for the top office as the Citizens' Council candidate. He won on a pledge to preserve segregation at all costs and to resist the federal government's efforts to force school integration.[16]

Part of Barnett's resistance included continuing to challenge the national Democratic Party. Soon after his inauguration in January 1960, he and others in the massive resistance faction indicated that they would bolt the party at the 1960 convention in Los Angeles rather than accede to a candidate or platform that challenged racial segregation. Winter, Congressman Smith, and U.S. Senators Stennis and Eastland favored the nomination of Lyndon Johnson for president. Most of the Mississippi delegation, however, including the other five congressmen, prevailed with a failed plan to support Ross Barnett himself for the presidency at the convention. Soon after the national meeting, the state Democratic Party endorsed the effort to challenge the national party and backed a lineup of unpledged electors in the 1960 presidential contest. Consequently, the race in Mississippi became a three-way battle among the small but growing group of Republicans, Barnett's unpledged slate of electors, and the Democratic John F. Kennedy–Lyndon Johnson ticket. Despite the fact that the Democratic Party platform in 1960 had a strong civil rights plank, the party's standard bearers did not yet have the civil rights credentials they would later acquire. Kennedy's record on racial issues going into the fall campaign was lackluster at best; in Mississippi, the most serious obstacle to his candidacy was probably religion, not race. Senators Stennis and Eastland signed on to support the national Democratic ticket in 1960 largely because Kennedy's running mate, Lyndon Johnson, was their Senate colleague and majority leader.[17]

By October 1960, Winter found himself at the center of the presidential campaign in Mississippi. He helped set up a Kennedy-Johnson headquarters, and Elise chaired a committee that hosted a reception in Jackson for JFK's mother. In late October, Winter gamely debated Barnett backer Charles Sullivan in the Delta community of Marks. The flier announcing the clash described Winter as representing "those supporting the *platform* of the national Democratic Party," in other words the side of civil rights for blacks. The advertisement described Sullivan as "that incomparable orator and statesman from Clarksdale—Mississippi's next governor," three years before the next statewide election. The announcement emphasized that Sullivan would show "the vital importance to the South of the unpledged Democratic electors in the big fight to maintain our way of life." Winter received a respectful hearing from the crowd, but few in the audience supported his point of view. He and Elise also joined the LBJ Special on its whistle-stop tour through Mississippi in October. Seeking to bolster Kennedy's candidacy in the South, Lyndon Johnson and his family boarded a train in Virginia and headed toward New Orleans, making stops at southern communities along the way to stump for JFK. At Meridian, the Winters boarded the LBJ Special, along with Stennis, Eastland, Coleman, Gartin, attorney general Joe Patterson, and others. Stopping in Laurel, Hattiesburg, and Picayune, the train attracted big crowds, and Johnson's speeches were fairly well received. Although neither Kennedy nor Johnson was that controversial racially in 1960—unlike the party's platform—the White Citizens' Council made sure to record the names of all those who rode the train with Johnson that fall. In the years to come, as both Kennedy and Johnson began to offer more support for the cause of black civil rights, the Citizens' Council would tag Winter and some of the other politicians on the LBJ Special as Kennedy-Johnson racial liberals. In the end, Winter's efforts on behalf of the national Democratic ticket in Mississippi failed. He told Senator Stennis in August, "I just can't see any substantial segment of our people voting for the independent electors," but the Barnett ticket carried the state in a close election, and the unpledged electors eventually cast their ballots for Virginian Harry Byrd.[18]

In the ongoing showdown over the issue of black civil rights, the herd mentality of white supremists often reached absurd heights. A good example is the flap that developed during 1961 surrounding the election for the editor of the student newspaper at Ole Miss, *The Mississippian*. One of the candidates, Billy C. Barton, had worked during the summer of 1960 as an intern at the *Atlanta Journal*, where he covered an Atlanta sit-in protest. A member of the Georgia Citizens' Council notified Mississippi Citizens' Council leader William J. Simmons about Barton's supposed activities. Largely based on this snapshot of Barton's summer job and the reasoning that the Ole Miss student was a "close friend" of P. D. East, a racially moderate newspaper editor in Petal, as well as the fact that Barton also apparently knew history professor Jim Silver at Ole Miss, Simmons convinced the State Sovereignty Commission that "Barton is well regarded in left-wing circles as a promising young man." The Commission began to spread rumors that Barton was a civil rights activist and member of the National Association for the Advancement of Colored People (NAACP).[19]

As these events unfolded, Silver conducted his own investigation. He talked to Barton and secured a signed statement. He wrote East, who responded that "he had never heard of Barton." Silver also had a copy of a letter that Barton had written to Governor Barnett, in which Barton proclaimed his innocence and asked for the governor's help in clearing his name. Rightly convinced that the Sovereignty Commission had launched a smear campaign against Barton, Silver sent Winter the documents he had assembled. Silver realized that if the attack on the Commission came from him it would have limited effect, given the professor's longstanding reputation as an outspoken critic of Mississippi's efforts to limit open discussion of controversial issues. Silver urged Winter to turn over the information to sympathetic newspapermen. Winter declined, but Silver remained convinced that the information should be made public. He thought the exposure "would have a healthy effect in calming down the Sovereignty boys. This is a big mistake they have made and the opposition as well as the State ought to be able to find a way to profit by it." Silver, however, agreed to accept Winter's judgment, although he dubbed the politician, "Will—the non-militant." Winter's failure to expose the Commission's tactics in the Barton affair sprang from his own fear that, as a public figure, he would also become a target of extremists determined to brook no compromise on the issue of civil rights. Although Winter avoided inserting himself into the controversy, Ole Miss students helped expose what Silver had correctly identified as the Sovereignty Commission's "big mistake." Two months after Silver sought Winter's assistance in outing the Commission's attack on Barton, the story did break in the press, leading segments of the white press, leaders of the Ole Miss student body, and at least one legislator to criticize the "Gestapo" tactics of the Sovereignty Commission. Although the Barton incident clearly showed the State Sovereignty Commission capable of gross fabrications and crossing the line of decency, white Mississippians still supported its overall objectives. Advocates of massive resistance had, with only the smallest of setbacks, succeeded in their program to prevent any racial desegregation in Mississippi.[20]

In this toxic atmosphere, racial moderates, especially those in political office, were reduced to staying under the radar. When Benjamin Muse visited the state several times in 1961 on behalf of the Southern Regional Council, an Atlanta-based group that advocated racial justice in the South, he noted that the state had "many more moderates" than he anticipated. He estimated that perhaps a majority of "educated Mississippians are silently or privately moderate on the race issue. That is, they are prepared to accept the inevitable without disorder." Among public officials, Muse singled out Winter, Mississippi Supreme Court justice William N. Ethridge Jr., former governor Coleman (who was then a member of the legislature), and at least eighteen other members of the legislature. Muse noted the difficulty faced by these public officials: "even the most marginal public approach," advocating anything less than absolute resistance to racial change, "requires courage."[21]

As civil rights tensions rose and moderates became increasingly immo-
bilized, the idea that some kind of limited compromise might be found
on the civil rights issue seemed more and more unrealistic. In the spring
of 1962, Erle Johnston, public-relations director for the State Sovereignty
Commission, and like Winter, a Grenada County native, gave a commencement speech at Grenada High School entitled, "The Practical
Way to Maintain a Separate School System in Mississippi." Winter, who
attended the address, heard Johnston tell the crowd that since blacks had
"the federal government and federal courts ready to support them," it
might be wiser "to give up an inch" than "to give up a mile." Johnston
proposed a full school equalization program, one that would need support
from black educators and other black leaders. He counseled that "extremists on both ends," in the civil rights movement and in the White Citizens'
Council/Sovereignty Commission apparatus, needed to show restraint
to allow this black/white cooperation to occur. Asked by a reporter his
opinion of Johnston's speech, Winter judged it "a very realistic and frank
analysis of the situation" and an outline of "the only approach which will
save us from serious trouble." By 1962, however, advocating that racial segregation might be preserved in an improved form no longer represented
a palatable solution for either civil rights advocates or their massive resistance opponents. Citizens' Council leader William J. Simmons criticized
Johnston's speech in Grenada as a call for whites to surrender the fight
and argued that such an approach pointed "the way to integration." As
a result, Johnston had to fight to keep his Sovereignty Commission job.
At the same time, Medgar Evers, state field secretary of the NAACP, was
similarly unimpressed with Johnston's suggestions. Evers noted that the
NAACP would continue "to work for democracy in Mississippi."[22]

James Meredith's admission to Ole Miss in the fall of 1962 proved to
be a turning point for white moderates in Mississippi. After Meredith
attempted to enroll at Ole Miss in 1961, his challenge ended up in a legal
fight in the federal courts. In September 1962, federal district judge Sidney Mize ruled against the university, issuing an injunction at the behest
of the U.S. Supreme Court that required Ole Miss to desist from further
efforts to block Meredith's enrollment at the school. Governor Barnett
called for total resistance to the court orders, leading to a campus showdown in which the Kennedy administration sent in federal troops to support Meredith. A riot ensued in which two people died and more than

150 were injured, but Meredith did enroll at Ole Miss.[23] After successfully preventing change for many years, the massive resisters finally lost a battle in Mississippi to the civil rights movement and the federal government.

In the aftermath of the events at Ole Miss, Winter saw the possibility for political change. A week after Meredith's enrollment at the school, Winter wrote to his cousin in California, Jimmy Hall, that the violence surrounding the desegregation of Ole Miss occurred because "many Mississippians have been victimized by the deliberate efforts on the part of some to inflame their passions." Winter told another correspondent that he believed most "thinking Mississippians" could not "earnestly and sincerely condone what has happened." While deploring the violence caused by Meredith's desegregation effort, Winter thought an event like the Ole Miss melee necessary "to cause some people here to be willing to go to more reasonable methods of resolving our problems." He hoped the Ole Miss events would lead to "a more moderate approach adopted by our state, in the pattern of most of the other Southern states, which have already experienced some of these adjustments." Although Winter discerned that the voices of white moderation remained "relatively weak," he was certain that "men who previously kept their silence now are beginning to face facts and to say some things that it was impossible to say before."[24]

A number of moderate economic, community, and political leaders did began to speak out for a more reasonable approach to solving the race issue, and Winter was the most prominent state official urging change. He began to meet privately with other moderates across the state and in Jackson. Jim Silver attended one such dinner in Jackson in February 1963 at the home of Rabbi Perry Nussbaum, which included a number of religious, educational, and business leaders in the capital city "trying to do something about Barnett." At another meeting of thirty or so Jackson-area moderates, one person commented sardonically that "if a bomb drops here, that'll get every liberal in the state of Mississippi." Winter, in his public appearances, honed his message of turning away from massive resistance. Addressing the Mississippi Library Convention in Greenville at their annual meeting in late October 1962, Winter portrayed the recent actions of the state as wrong-headed and urged Mississippi to move forward rather than continue to look back. Winter described the choice as one of self-interest—concern for economic and educational advancement—rather than a moral issue. When he addressed an audience at All

Saints' Junior College in Vicksburg in March 1963, Winter called for political leadership that would "appeal to the best that is in us—not the worst; to our higher selves not our baser instincts. Only in this way can our section diminish some of the tensions that have already caused us so much grief and even now threaten more. This is no time to be drinking from the wells of bitterness and recrimination." Winter pressed the need for a leader "who can successfully turn his people from a preoccupation with the race issue and the supercharged emotions of anxiety, fear, and hate which that issue suggests." Instead, according to Winter, the focus should be the economic development of the South and Mississippi, which required "an effective educational system," public institutions that would provide opportunities "to all of the bright young men and women and not just to the chosen few." Elise Winter also contributed to the effort to encourage a more moderate response to the civil rights movement. She was "quietly active" in the Mississippians for Public Education, a group of 150 white women in Jackson who began meeting in the aftermath of the Ole Miss crisis and sought to encourage a peaceful transition to the inevitable next step: desegregated public elementary and secondary schools.[25]

In the midst of these developments, Winter's immediate political future remained unclear. Soon after his 1959 victory, he had resumed his initiative to have his office eliminated. The new chairman of the Mississippi State Tax Commission, J. Dexter Barr, was more amenable than his predecessor to taking over the responsibility for collecting the black market tax. The resentment of those legislators who had opposed Winter's reform simply because he suggested it dissipated with the realization that preserving the office only allowed Winter to amass a huge war chest. A 1962 bill adopted Winter's original recommendation to abolish the state tax collector's position and merge its duties with those of the state tax commission. The proposed change would take effect at the end of Winter's term, in January 1964. After the legislature completed its work, Winter praised the measure "as a forward step in state administration," one that would initially save about $250,000 per year. *Newsweek* magazine marveled, "One of the best-paying—and strangest—state jobs in the U.S. has just been abolished—at the request of the man who holds the job." Having successfully eliminated his office, Winter considered becoming a full-time lawyer, but he preferred to extend his fourteen years in Mississippi politics. While he had frequently been mentioned by political observers as a future governor, Winter decided 1963 was too soon for that campaign. Instead, he sought the office of state treasurer, which would continue to give him some statewide visibility. Since every part of government interacted with the treasurer's office, the position would also allow Winter an opportunity to learn even more about how the state operated.[26]

The 1963 campaign was one of the last in Mississippi that depended primarily on stump speeches to reach voters, and Winter spent the three months before the August primary campaigning hard. He visited every county in the state, generally accompanied by his young driver, James "Jeep" Peden, who had just completed his freshman year at Ole Miss. The two set out from Jackson at least three days a week, sometimes spending the night out on the campaign trail. Following a hectic schedule reminiscent of Winter's 1942 road trip with Eastland, Winter typically appeared at political events staged for other state or local candidates. Despite sometimes small crowds, Winter attended as many political gatherings as possible, having Peden or Elise speak on his behalf when he could not make an appearance. The 1963 treasurer's race required little money and cost Winter only about $7,000, all from his own funds.[27]

Unlike his 1959 race, Winter only had two opponents in 1963, B. G. "Bob" Jones and Charlie Mosby, both virtually unknown politically. Mosby, a farmer from Meridian who always referred to Winter as the "black market collector," had run in the 1959 state tax collector's race and finished fifth in the first primary. Winter's opponents eventually injected the issue of race into the campaign. About ten days before the first primary, Winter spent the night at his mother's house in Grenada where he got a call from Carroll Gartin, then running for reelection as lieutenant governor. Gartin reported that at a campaign rally earlier that day Bob Jones had "jumped on you for being on that Lyndon Johnson train in 1960." The next day, at a campaign event in Calhoun City, Winter appeared with Jones, who hammered home the point that Winter had backed Kennedy and had ridden on the LBJ Special. As Winter later recalled, "He had me as engineer on the train." Winter followed Jones at the podium and simply ignored the attack. In most instances, Winter did not respond to such tirades but focused attention on his spotless and distinguished record during fifteen years of "elective public service." People also took note of the fact that Winter had worked to abolish the last elective position he held, a job that everyone knew paid him handsomely. Many voters saw a candidate who, while perhaps more moderate on race than most, did not advocate anything radical in this area and was certainly a proven, honest and efficient public servant. Winter received almost 60 percent of the vote in the first primary and won eighty-one of eighty-two counties.[28]

The duties of the state treasurer were almost as routine as those of the state tax collector. The state treasurer oversaw the flow of money into the treasury and its distribution to the various operations of state government in accordance with the directives of the legislature. Winter also managed the selling of bond issues to help finance state government, a job that had become more difficult in the 1960s because of the bad reputation the state acquired nationally as it continued to resist civil rights changes. On one of Winter's first trips to New York as treasurer, to market school bonds, he found that Mississippi bonds carried about a whole percentage point more than similarly rated bonds from other states. When Winter protested this inequity, the banker replied, "Have you ever tried to sell Mississippi school bonds up here in this part of the country?" Winter found that all bond sales faced similar penalties during much of his tenure as state treasurer. At times, bond issues had no takers, because of the stigma attached to the state name. One bond issue floated on Wall Street in 1965 was cancelled when no bidders came forward. At other times, the offers on Mississippi bonds were so low that Winter rejected the bids, such as those made on a $13.6 million offering in 1966 designed to fund school construction projects.[29]

Although the race issue played a minor role in Winter's campaign, the question dominated a number of other races in 1963, including the governor's race, which devolved into an extremely racist campaign. The winner of that contest was Paul B. Johnson Jr., lieutenant governor during the Barnett years. Johnson ran on the slogan "Stand Tall with Paul," an allusion to his having once substituted for Barnett and physically blocked Meredith's admission to Ole Miss. With Johnson's election, Winter's optimism about the possibilities for change flagged, and he thought the state was doomed to four more years of state-sponsored racial conflict and resistance to the federal government. Johnson, however, despite his heated campaign rhetoric, proved a more moderate governor than his predecessor.[30]

One bright spot at the time was the effort made by Winter's home church in Jackson, Fondren Presbyterian, to integrate its congregation. In

1960, after the Winters had moved permanently to Jackson, they joined Fondren. Both William and Elise Winter eventually served as elders in the Jackson church, and they remained active participants in the life of the congregation. Although William Winter was a leader in his church, he did not wear his religion on his sleeve, and he never focused on the issue of his faith in his political campaigns. Winter's commitment to Christianity helped shape both his personality and his political philosophy and provided for his "own personal, emotional security . . . the support and strength that I think all of us need." At the same time, he never believed that religion could provide the answers for specific problems of a temporal nature. As he later reflected, he could not always know what "the Christian answer" was to every problem: "Some folks will say, 'I've prayed about this, I've found the answer, and this is it.' It's been a lot more complex than that for me." Instead, Winter ultimately believed that "my faith gave me a feeling about myself that recognized that I didn't have all the answers, and I was probably making mistakes along the way," although at the same time, his "religious background provided that ethical, moral, emotional support that keeps you reasonably on course."[31]

Martin Luther King, Jr., had famously observed in a 1956 sermon that 11:00 a.m. on Sunday morning was "the most segregated hour of Christian America," and this was especially true in Jackson in the early 1960s. However, in June 1963, civil rights protestors from Tougaloo College began making attempts to be seated at white churches in the capital city, as part of the larger effort underway in Jackson to desegregate community organizations and facilities. White churchgoers repeatedly turned away the black students at churches throughout the city, including initially at Fondren. As the church visits increased in the fall of 1963, local law enforcement moved in to enforce the state's segregation laws. At that point, in October 1963, the Fondren congregation, led by Winter, businessman Warren Hood, and the church's pastor, Moody McDill, agreed to open its doors to all who wished to worship there, becoming one of the earliest churches in the city to integrate its services.[32]

The battle to desegregate Jackson's churches was part of a broader struggle throughout the South, as segregationists and white moderates in various denominations and individual congregations grappled with how to respond to the civil rights movement. Winter recognized what a significant step his congregation had taken, for he knew from direct experience that religious belief and racial toleration did not necessarily go hand-in-hand. Earlier that year, in June 1963, Winter traveled to Memphis for a meeting of the Presbyterian Synod of Mississippi scheduled for the following day. That night, Byron De La Beckwith assassinated Mississippi civil rights leader Medgar Evers. Winter learned about the killing when he awoke the following morning. As Winter ate breakfast with one of the respected elders of the Mississippi Presbyterian church, the man told Winter, "The nigger got what he deserved." Winter sat in shocked silence, appalled that a self-declared religious man could make such an assertion.[33]

A month after the Fondren congregation opened its doors to black worshippers, Winter was in Washington, D.C., visiting Senator Stennis. Winter had just had lunch with Stennis's administrative assistant, Eph Creswell, and when they returned to the office, they heard the news that President John F. Kennedy had been shot. Winter was overcome with "a sense of just very dark feelings about the future." This despair turned to anger when he heard reports from Mississippi about the expressions of joy from segregationist leaders and their followers. Stories circulated that schoolchildren had applauded in their classrooms on hearing the news. Returning to Mississippi and addressing a small group in Jackson on the Sunday after Kennedy's death, Winter deplored "this personal hatred of people that has been expressed here in this city of Jackson by people who cheer the murder of the president of the United States." Over the next few weeks, however, expressions of sorrow and affection for the dead president from many Mississippians led Winter to conclude that a sense of "basic decency" existed among his fellow citizens. JFK's assassination bolstered his determination to speak out against the forces of white racial extremism.[34] If the 1962 Ole Miss crisis had initially sparked Winter to advocate more forcefully for the moderate white position on race, JFK's assassination further prodded him to take a bolder stand in the days ahead.

The civil rights cauldron brewing in the state seriously tested Winter's resolve. Civil rights protests intensified in 1963 and 1964 and culminated with the massive Freedom Summer campaign in 1964, which brought northern white volunteers to the state to assist local blacks in registering voters and challenging racial segregation. Mississippi segregationists responded to the increased activism with violence and intimidation. In fact, by early 1964, the Ku Klux Klan, largely dormant for decades in the state, reappeared and began a campaign of terror directed at those who sought racial change. Winter proceeded cautiously without giving in to the often-hysterical calls for all whites to man the barricades in the fight to defend racial segregation. Frank Smith in his autobiography, *Congressman from Mississippi*, published in early 1964, clearly expressed Winter's dilemma. Smith wrote that while serving as a Delta congressman (1950–1962), he had advocated progress in the state while avoiding the constant pandering "to the state's obsession with race." Even so, "As a condition to holding my office, I made obeisance to 'the Southern way of life,'" which meant speaking out against black civil rights when necessary. Smith hoped that Mississippi politicians in the future would do better and encourage "all citizens to join in the effort to assure all Mississippians their rights as Americans." Winter, who had known Smith for many years, responded to the former congressman's book by telling him, "I don't believe that I have ever read a book that has more meaning for me than this one. You have put in such clear perspective the cloudy thoughts that have moved back and forth through the minds of many of us that now I feel that at last I have a true picture of what I believe in and where I stand."[35]

Although Smith's book helped Winter better understand the predicament he faced, he continued to encounter the difficulties Congressman Smith had experienced. Fully embracing the enlightened position the former congressman supported did not seem like a realistic option for a Mississippi politician in 1964. In fact, Winter believed that merely being identified as a moderate on race could spell doom for his future political prospects. James Silver's book *Mississippi: The Closed Society*, which also appeared in early 1964, described the racial atmosphere in the state and explained how white supremacy had survived essentially unchallenged for more than a century. Winter's former professor had originally included an account in his book of the gathering of moderates at Rabbi Perry Nussbaum's house in 1963, listing Winter as one of the attendees. After Winter read a draft of the book, he told Silver that he planned to run for governor some day and if Silver identified Winter in this way, his political career could suffer. Silver kept the account in the book, but replaced the names of some of those attending with blanks lines.[36]

When Winter gave the keynote address at the Hinds County Democratic Convention in the summer of 1964, he spoke to an audience greatly distressed by the arrival of "outside agitators" as part of the Freedom Summer project. Winter's speech at the county courthouse, made two days after three civil rights workers disappeared under suspicious circumstances in Neshoba County, offered no calls to defend segregation or states' rights. Rather, he urged the audience to take the high road in the brewing storm. He encouraged the delegates "to try to insure the swift and safe passing of our great state and nation through the perilous times in which we live" and "to make certain that our particular contributions to this journey will be calculated to keep the train on the track and not derail it into the sloughs of defeat and hopelessness and despair. Let us, therefore, cross our bridges as we come to them and by all means let us burn none behind us." Winter received a cold reception from the delegates. He returned to his office "very depressed," as he realized that the delegates had expected a "fighting speech." After Winter's talk, as he told Benjamin Muse at the time, the delegates set aside their county chairman and secretary, "who were merely segregationists, and elected ultra, ultra segregationists to succeed them."[37]

Even as some whites remained committed to using any means, including violence, to halt racial change, their actions actually bolstered the cause of white moderation in the state. Increasing numbers of white Mississippians began to favor a more reasoned approach, some type of accommodation to the new realities being forged by the civil rights movement. Not surprisingly, many of this growing white moderate group looked to William Winter as their champion. When Benjamin Muse visited Mississippi in 1964, he found that white moderates, from newspaper editors and professors to business leaders like Billy Mounger and labor leaders such as Claude Ramsey all "talked about Winter with wistful admiration: 'There's the man who could save the state! If we could get him elected! In 1967 maybe?'" As Muse noted, Winter had shown a particular facility for getting elected and maintaining his standing as a political leader "without sacrificing his convictions on the race issue (or getting into the controversy)." He also remarked that Winter's "character and intelligence inspire universal respect."[38]

By the beginning of 1965, Winter was speaking out frequently and forcefully against continued resistance to federal law, specifically the recently passed Civil Rights Act of 1964, which outlawed racial segregation in places of public accommodation. In January 1965, he spoke to the Catholic Youth Organization at one of the first integrated meetings held in downtown Jackson. Winter told the integrated gathering of young people that Mississippi had to stop trying to defend the last one hundred years and get ready to face the next one hundred years. To move forward would require the state "to lay aside old slogans and myths." Winter noted that improved education, economic development, and "domestic tranquility" were the necessary ingredients for Mississippi's future prosperity. At a February talk at Ole Miss sponsored by the Mississippi Students for Responsible Citizenship, Winter told an assembly of students and faculty that contempt of the law only harmed their state and reminded them that "this campus is just now recovering from its experiment in defiance." He added that the state's political leadership knew that a better solution to racial problems existed, but they "don't act better."[39]

In the summer of 1965, Winter made his annual pilgrimage to the Neshoba County Fair. After listening to a string of politicians, including Governor Johnson, disparage the Civil Rights Act of 1964 and the Voting Rights Act of 1965 that President Johnson would sign into law the next day, Winter took the podium and presented a strikingly different message. He criticized the "rash and reckless defiance by a political leadership that would invite bloodshed and the destruction of our institutions." He told the fair goers that "It's our job, yours and mine, to see to it that more of our people understand that good citizenship in the times in which we live demand the very best qualities we have, not our worst qualities. Our state needs as never before the constructive leader who will find the solution, who will find the way, not the despairing critic who knows only the voice of alarm." While not everyone in the crowd appreciated such remarks, the state treasurer's message galvanized others. One of those in the audience that day was a fifteen-year-old boy from Neshoba County, Dick Molpus, who would become one of Winter's most important political supporters and protégés. Over the next year, Winter continued to speak out as a voice for racial conciliation in a state still plagued by conflict, sometimes violent, over the transition to a post–Jim Crow society.[40]

Winter's position as a prominent moderate white voice in Mississippi attracted notice outside the state. After reading a national press report of Winter's February 1965 address at Ole Miss, a Kansas City woman wrote the state treasurer to say that his talk was "the first sane speech that I have heard from any Mississippi politician." In April 1965, Jules Loh's story for the Associated Press discussed the changes in white attitudes occurring in Mississippi in the aftermath of the 1964 Civil Rights Act. The story, which ran in papers around the country, highlighted William Winter as the most notable advocate for "a new Mississippi" and identified him as a likely gubernatorial choice in 1967. Winter explained to the reporter a big part of the problems in the past: "Mississippians have been confused and frustrated by a lot of people who have been telling them things that just weren't true. For example, they told them that practically everybody in the country was on our side. Well, they found out in the last presidential election what the truth was." Winter said that he and other politicians needed to tell the citizens of the state "what our image can be if we get over this preoccupation with defiance of our nation's laws."[41]

Because Winter forthrightly suggested that Mississippi should accept the accomplished fact of civil rights legislation, in 1965 he was mentioned as a possible appointee to the Fifth Circuit Court of Appeals. One of the court's conservative jurists, Ben Cameron of Mississippi, had died in 1964, and another Mississippian would take the "Mississippi position" on the appellate court. It was Senator Stennis's turn to make the choice, but despite his close relationship with Winter, the senator did not support Winter. Stennis favored Claude Clayton, a federal district judge from Tupelo, for the job, but Clayton's opposition to the civil rights movement made his confirmation impossible. Former congressman Frank Smith suggested Winter to the U.S. Justice Department as an appointee who would be a committed racial moderate on the Fifth Circuit. Smith reported that the American Bar Association would give Winter its "very best recommendation possible." When U.S. Attorney General Nicholas Katzenbach offered Winter's name to Stennis, however, the senator inquired if the Justice Department was going to try to make him accept a "liberal" candidate. In the end, Stennis agreed to nominate former governor J. P. Coleman for the appellate slot, a racial moderate less outspoken than William Winter.[42]

In the decade between 1956 and 1966, Winter's moderate views on civil rights were muted in the interests of political survival, but events steadily pushed him to affirm racial moderation in more open and strident terms. Heading into the 1967 elections, Winter seemed the logical standard-bearer for those white Mississippians ready to accept that the recent federal civil rights laws had already begun to transform social relations and could no longer be successfully resisted. The question remained, however, exactly how many white Mississippians had come to such conclusions by 1967.

7

THE 1967 GOVERNOR'S RACE

The 1967 statewide elections in Mississippi represented an uncertain moment of political transition in the state. In the first contests held after passage of the federal Voting Rights Act of 1965, almost two hundred thousand potential new black voters joined the electorate. The end of black disfranchisement promised to alter the state's political landscape, but the pace and shape of that transformation remained unclear in 1967. For one thing, although the law changed, white attitudes about sharing political power with black citizens did not shift overnight. For William Winter, an almost twenty-year veteran of state politics with a reputation as a racial moderate, the possibility of mounting a successful run for governor in 1967 remained uncertain.

Winter supporters and local political observers sensed the potential difficulties for a Winter candidacy. His Grenada friend, Larry Noble, who had left Mississippi years earlier, found it "hard to believe that a state that voted 85% for Barry [Goldwater] in 64 is ready for Mr. Winter and his ideas in 67." Noble told Winter that he could not "expect to win the highest office in the closed society in 1967." Kenneth Toler of the *Memphis Commercial Appeal* mused in 1966 that Winter should try for the lieutenant governor's job in 1967 rather than the governor's seat, although Toler believed Winter "is definitely pegged for governor when the majority position in certain areas catches up with realities." Winter also recognized the possible pitfalls to launching a gubernatorial campaign in 1967. In the spring of 1966, he told Jim Silver that his gubernatorial candidacy in 1967 remained a long shot. Winter pointed to a recent poll that "indicates still a massive resentment and that the sure way to win is to cuss LBJ and the Feds." Winter knew that the poll findings presented "a real dilemma" for his potential candidacy, but he told Silver, "If I can get the money, I may just bow my neck and plunge into the Governor's race." In the end, Winter gambled that white attitudes had changed enough that he could win the election and help lead Mississippi forward in the new post–Jim Crow world. He officially entered the Mississippi governor's contest in January 1967.[1]

By the time Winter joined the gubernatorial race, a number of contenders had already announced their intention to seek the office. Jimmy Swan, a staunch segregationist and radio personality from Hattiesburg, promised to create "FREE, private, SEGREGATED SCHOOLS for every white child in the State of Mississippi" within twelve months of taking office, or he would resign as governor. Former governor Ross Barnett, who had to sit out the race four years earlier because Mississippi did not allow its chief executive to succeed himself, entered the race and touted his reputation as the politician who had tried to save Mississippi's system of segregation in the face of federal coercion. Bill Waller, a racial moderate, though not as well known as Winter, had earlier attracted notice as the Hinds County district attorney who had twice prosecuted the killer of civil rights leader Medgar Evers (both cases ended in mistrials). Another candidate, Carroll Gartin, the moderate three-term lieutenant governor from Laurel, had thrown his hat in the ring during the fall of 1966 but had died suddenly of a heart attack the week before Christmas.[2]

After Winter entered the race, early polling showed him finishing a strong second, behind Ross Barnett. As expected, Winter's perceived liberalism on race posed his biggest liability. Believing Winter could not defeat Barnett, many whites who opposed a second term by Barnett, including a number of Winter's supporters, looked around for another candidate who might run better against the former governor. A number of moderates, including J. P. Coleman, a Fifth Circuit justice and former governor who had been one of Winter's political mentors, played a role in convincing Mississippi congressman John Bell Williams to enter the race. Williams had been an outspoken segregationist and longtime backer of the White Citizens' Council. The Democratic Party stripped him of his seniority in the U.S. House of Representatives after he openly campaigned for Republican Barry Goldwater in the 1964 presidential contest. The anti-Barnett crowd, however, even those with more moderate sensibilities, figured they needed someone with better segregationist credentials than Winter to beat the former governor, and Williams proved a popular candidate. His strong stance for Goldwater would not hurt him in a state that had given 87 percent of its vote to the Arizona senator. In addition, Williams was a rousing speaker, a good campaigner, and a wounded veteran of World War II. Campaigning in northeast Mississippi when he heard that Williams had announced for the race, Winter remembered, "I kind of felt my heart sink, because I knew he was going to be a strong candidate." A poll conducted for Winter shortly after Williams's announcement confirmed these fears and suggested that Williams might even win in the first primary. The election now seemed a battle between Barnett and Williams. Winter thought he might have miscalculated, but he decided to press on.[3]

As Winter entered the race, he stressed his deep roots in Mississippi and twenty years of experience in state government. He promised to run "a campaign based on a positive, affirmative program that will come to grips with the needs of the state." He campaigned hard by spending long hours visiting all parts of the state. He also started advertising early. The campaign placed billboards around the state with the slogan "Win with Winter" and showed some of the first professionally produced political television advertisements in the state's history. Winter hired Gene Triggs, director of the Mississippi Agricultural and Industrial Board and an ally of Governor Paul Johnson, to manage the campaign. Triggs resigned from his job in March to head the campaign and began to organize the state county-by-county. Winter's friend and fellow Fondren Presbyterian congregant, timber businessman Warren Hood, headed the campaign's finance operation and began to help raising funds. Overall, the Winter campaign would spend almost $1 million, a staggering figure at that time and one that dwarfed the total amount of money spent on all previous Winter races. The candidate focused his message on the need for better schools and better jobs, and the platform as well as the media blitz began to attract significant attention for his campaign. Much of his support came from people in the business and professional community, from other moderate-minded citizens in the state's more urban areas, and especially from young people. Although Governor Johnson had made no official endorsement in the race, rumors circulated that he also supported Winter "under-the-table." A poll by the Mississippi Broadcasters Association in late April showed that Winter's earlier weak support had blossomed into frontrunner status. Of those polled, 45 percent chose Winter. John Bell Williams trailed with 31 percent and Ross Barnett finished third, with only 8 percent saying they would vote for the former governor.[4]

During the early days of the campaign, Winter avoided the race issue as much as possible. Occasionally, someone in a crowd would call him a "nigger-lover." After one campaign stop in McComb, a group of "grim-looking men" approached Winter and said they had heard that he was friends with "that communist professor" who had been at Ole Miss, "John Silverman." Winter responded, "Never heard of him," and moved on through the crowd. At a Confederate Memorial Day speech in late April at Kosciusko, Winter did not use the memory of the Civil War to rail against the Second Reconstruction underway; rather, he told the audience that the "ideals of our forebears can best be preserved by meeting the problems of 1967 with courage, dignity, and integrity . . . . Our generation needs to keep the faith with the best ideals of the Old South. We can do this by rededicating ourselves to building a state in Mississippi that is second to none." Winter initially hoped to avoid a contest that relied on racial appeals. He wanted to focus on "bread-and-butter issues, not the old emotional ones—not racial issues." Yet, racial politics played a central role in the 1967 governor's race. While few at the time could predict the impact of the new black vote on the 1967 polling, none of the candidates, Winter included, planned to campaign openly for black votes. Given the racial animosities that lingered in the state, Winter did not believe that such a strategy represented a formula for success. At the same time, he did not have total confidence that enough whites shared his moderate approach to racial change for him to secure election on that platform.[5]

Aware of these political realities, Winter soon found himself appealing to white segregationists more than he ever had before in a political race. When the Jackson Citizens' Council held a governor's candidate forum in mid-May, Winter attended along with the other men vying for the chief executive's spot. In advance, the Council posed to each of the candidates six questions on a variety of topics, including how the 1962 James Meredith "affair" should have been handled, the "impending crisis of massive integration of the public schools this fall," the 1968 presidential election, and the "remedy for the infringement . . . by the federal government of the right of state control of voting requirements." When the Meredith question came up, John Bell Williams charged Ross Barnett with making secret deals with the Kennedys. Barnett followed Williams and vehemently denied these charges. Winter responded that he found the question difficult to answer without knowing what really had happened in 1962. In an obvious reference to Williams's claim that Barnett was making secret deals with President Kennedy while claiming to do everything to prevent Meredith's enrollment, Winter noted, "We've never gotten the straight story . . . I would have handled it in a way that would not have resulted in violence and bloodshed and the people of Mississippi would have been told the truth, the whole truth and nothing but the truth." Responding to the question on school integration, Winter maintained, "The overwhelming majority of Mississippians don't like the chaos that is being forced on our schools by the HEW." He promised to address this "serious problem . . . as courageously as any man anywhere in Mississippi. I have three little girls and I am not going to forsake them to the HEW social planners and bleeding heart liberals as long as there is a breath in my body."[6]

The final inquiry spoke directly to the Citizens' Council's fear of becoming increasingly marginalized in political affairs: "Why haven't our ideals of state's rights and racial integrity been featured in this campaign as in the past?" Winter began his answer to this question by drawing attention to the heritage he shared with many white Mississippians: "As a fifth generation Mississippian whose grandfather rode with Forrest, I was born a segregationist and raised a segregationist." He continued by claiming, "I have always defended that position. I defend it now." Winter actually had a comparatively limited record he could point to as a defender of segregation, and he did not offer any further evidence on this point. He turned much of the remainder of his answer into an attack on his opponents. Noting that the real battle against civil rights took place at the federal level, Winter pointed out that one of the candidates was a member of the congressional delegation, "but lately he hasn't been up there on the firing line." In addition, Winter said, another candidate "had presided over the affairs of this state at a time when the most sweeping integration measures in the history of Mississippi were being put into effect." Winter closed out his answer by warning that it would be "the greatest disservice" for the issue of race to become "a political football" in the campaign. He claimed that Mississippians "know that loud talk and arm waving mean nothing. The people are tired of this do-nothing kind of leadership. The people of Mississippi want a man who will maintain law and order. They want a man who is not afraid to fight . . . but one who has common sense enough to win. They are tired of losers . . . they want winners." The last part of his answer produced a new slogan for the campaign. In addition to "Win with Winter," campaign literature also began to include the phrase, "Fight to Win for Mississippi."[7]

Hoping that he had said enough at the Citizens's Council Forum to alleviate the racial fears of whites, Winter turned his attention to developing a detailed platform that addressed what he considered more substantive issues. The first "Winter Plan," as his position papers were called, was "The Winter Plan for Better Schools." Issued a week after the Council forum, the document declared that "the schools of Mississippi face a dilemma today of near crisis proportions." Winter was not referring to the perceived horrors of HEW enforcement of school integration mandates, mentioned in his statement the week before. The real cause for alarm was the fact that "Mississippi is last in the nation in nearly every index of support to education." To solve this problem, the Winter education plan called for an array of measures: decreasing class sizes and increasing teacher pay; providing "additional opportunities, subjects and services to each child"; raising the salaries of nonprofessional staff, such as custodians, lunchroom workers, and secretaries; boosting the limit on local tax rates for education; providing additional support for all other levels of education, from vocational schools to junior colleges, from universities to facilities for the deaf, blind, and handicapped; and creating a state educational TV network. In short, Winter promised to "make education the top, critical priority of state government."[8]

Soon thereafter, Winter released "The Winter Plan for Better Paying Jobs," which addressed the state's other great need, economic development. To promote industrial development, the jobs statement outlined twelve specific ideas, all designed to "increase the opportunities in the state for good paying jobs and development of under-developed areas of the state." The plan also promised that Winter would nurture existing industries and create new markets for "locally produced products."[9]

Winter's opponents, however, had no intention of letting questions about Winter's attitude toward white supremacy fade away. Both Barnett and Williams during the first primary campaign continually labeled Winter a "liberal," which at the time stood just above "communist" in the pantheon of state enemies. When Barnett officially kicked off his campaign at Pontotoc in early June, he spent a good part of his speech denouncing his old foe, Robert Kennedy. Barnett tried to tie Winter to Kennedy by claiming that the New York senator financed the gubernatorial campaign of a "weak-kneed liberal," whom Barnett later identified as Winter. Soon thereafter, Williams charged Winter with the "crime" of liberalism. In Williams's favorite line, Winter was a "dedicated, demonstrated liberal," and, at various times, the congressman suggested specific evidence of Winter's liberalism: Winter had campaigned for JFK in 1960; Winter was the favorite of civil rights supporters; Winter approved of LBJ's Great Society; and Winter was a national leader in the mental health cause. Winter generally ignored the attacks, although he would occasionally deviate from his well-designed message to counter the liberal tag Barnett and Williams tried to hang on him.[10]

By 1967 advertising, especially through television, played an increasingly important role in statewide races, and Winter proved by far the most astute candidate at using this medium. Even so, the 1967 governor's race still featured a full slate of political rallies, some of which more than one candidate would attend. During these events, the candidates, especially Barnett and Williams, would delight their supporters with extravagant rhetoric denouncing their opponents. Barnett and Williams not only regularly attacked Winter as a liberal, but they also tried to convince voters that he was the candidate of the rich. Barnett noted that "the bootleggers made [Winter] a millionaire." Although many gave Winter credit for helping to abolish his own wasteful, yet lucrative, office, an act that they thought demonstrated his "honesty and sincerity," Barnett reminded the many teetotalers in the state that Winter had been "involved" in the illegal liquor trade and had profited nicely from this work. Just as often, Barnett and Williams would address their negative messages at each other.[11]

Despite the continuities with the past, this contest differed from Winter's previous statewide races. For one thing, the campaign was more mobile, with Winter often flying between destinations in private airplanes provided by supporters rather than traveling every highway and back road as he had done since 1942. The improved transportation meant that Winter could spend more nights at home during the contest and also allowed Elise to accompany her husband more often than would have otherwise been possible. In many ways, Elise remained Winter's closest advisor, and though naturally reserved and soft-spoken, she proved a valuable asset to the campaign by charming voters wherever she went. At one campaign stop, as she handed out Winter's card at the local courthouse, one man inquired if she was the candidate's wife. When Elise replied in the affirmative, the man, shaking his head, said, "Well, I guess if you can stand him, we can." On some days, Mrs. Winter traveled by plane to a different locale from her husband to speak on his behalf and thereby doubled the Winter message. At many of Winter's campaign stops, a gospel singing group, such as The Crownsmen or the Smitty Gatlin Trio, performed. The campaign even developed its own song, "Win with Winter," sung to the tune of "Hello, Ma Baby," a ragtime classic. In addition to the numerous personal appearances, TV and newspaper ads for Winter blanketed the state. The campaign also developed a fourteen-page comic book, which highlighted the candidate's background and laid out his positions on everything from education and economic development to racial segregation (a repeat of the Citizens' Council Forum statement about being a fifth-generation Mississippian who had always "defended" segregation).[12]

Paul Pittman, editor of the *Tylertown Times* and a good friend of the Winters, directed the public relations efforts from the campaign's state headquarters in Jackson. A host of young volunteers worked under Pittman's direction. "Jeep" Peden and Jesse White, both recent Ole Miss graduates doing postgraduate work abroad, came back to Mississippi for the summer of 1967 to work on the Winter campaign. Although they sometimes traveled with the Winters, Peden and White spent most of their time in the Jackson headquarters. They produced daily press releases detailing the candidate's campaign stops and developed additional Winter Plans: "The Winter Plan for the Aged and Economically Indigent," "The Winter Plan for Agriculture," "The Winter Plan for Waterway and Natural Resource Development," among others. Each Winter Plan—fifteen in all—gave a detailed explanation of the existing problems and proposed a variety of solutions. Eventually a "Winter Plan for Home Rule and State's Rights," one of the shortest ones, described Winter's "fifth-generation" Mississippi credentials, his connections to both Senators Eastland and Stennis, his dedication to law and order, and his "will-to-win leadership."[13]

The young people who turned out in force to help the candidate identified with Winter's message of progress and change. Jesse White recalled, "For people like me he was literally the difference between hope and despair, to see a young political leader . . . try to stand up for the right things was huge." Many of the youth were college students or even high school students, a number of them not yet twenty-one and therefore ineligible to vote. One underclassman from the University of Southern Mississippi claimed he worked in the campaign for a candidate he could not yet vote for out of "a conviction that an opportunity was being presented Mississippi that she might begin to overcome her prejudices, economic problems, social hindrances, etc. which obviously affect her." Many of the young people supporting the 1967 Winter campaign would later constitute Mississippi's white moderate and progressive political faction. Future Democratic gubernatorial candidate Dick Molpus, a high school student in Neshoba County, worked as one of Winter's youth coordinators by passing out leaflets and fliers and putting up posters in the county where the three civil rights workers had been murdered three summers earlier. Molpus saw in Winter a person "who looks and talks like the people I have grown up with, but he is actually saying something." Future Democratic governor Ray Mabus was a student at Ole Miss in 1967. After hearing a speech by Winter, he volunteered to help out with the campaign. Thad Cochran, a Jackson lawyer, who a decade later would replace Jim Eastland in the U.S. Senate and become the first Republican elected to a statewide office in Mississippi in over a century, supported the Winter campaign, even though his parents were friends with John Bell Williams and his Ole Miss fraternity brother, Brad Dye, was Williams's campaign manager. Pressed by Dye to join Williams's operation, Cochran declined. He saw Williams "taking us down the same road of dividing the state," while Winter was the candidate trying to help Mississippi "move ahead into the modern world."[14]

While Winter's candidacy clearly energized a segment of the white electorate, that contingent did not represent a majority and could not guarantee victory. To broaden his base of support, Winter sought to secure the support of black voters indirectly while also holding on to the allegiance of as many white voters as possible. *Washington Post* columnists Rowland Evans and Robert Novak explained Winter's dilemma: he needed black votes to prevail in the first primary, but any suggestion that he was the "black candidate" would doom his chances to attract additional white voters in the second primary. At the same time, Winter could not depend on securing the enthusiastic approval—and votes—of the nearly two hundred thousand potential black voters, precisely because he had to give at least a nod to the lingering white sentiment for racial segregation.[15]

Black Mississippians understood that any public expression of black support would damage a white candidate in the eyes of many white voters. As a result, although various black leaders supported Winter's gubernatorial bid, they typically did not make their intentions known until the last moment. In late April 1967, a Sovereignty Commission informant claimed that the Hinds County Mississippi Freedom Democratic Party (MFDP) and the Hinds County Community Council met jointly and determined to support Winter in the upcoming contest through "a whispering campaign so they will not hurt Winter's chances." Another Sovereignty Commission spy in June detailed a meeting conducted by two NAACP leaders, Charles Evers (Medgar Evers's brother) and Reverend Allen Johnson of Laurel. According to the account of the gathering, those present "decided to start a very quiet whisper campaign for William Winters [sic] in the Governor's race and on or about July 8 will pass the word to all negroes to vote for Winters [sic]." Evers later confirmed the accuracy of the report and explained that Winter "was the only one who wasn't calling us niggers at that time. He did everything but that, but at least he didn't call us niggers." Evers also favored and urged support for another candidate in the race, Bill Waller, who had prosecuted his brother's killer. Just prior to the election, Evers helped convince the Mississippi Voters League, a group launched in June 1967 by NAACP leaders as an alternative to the MFDP, to endorse Waller. In a series of statewide interviews conducted with black and white voters by the *Greenville Delta Democrat-Times* in July, the paper reported that all the major candidates except Jimmy Swan had some black support. Winter, however, garnered the most enthusiasm among black voters, a fact attributable, according to a number of unnamed black leaders, to "his moderation." The journalists also noted that the state's civil rights groups and local voters' leagues would likely make endorsements for the governor's race only by word-of-mouth, issued in the final week of the campaign, or even the night before the first primary.[16]

To secure his share of the white vote beyond those enthusiastic about Winter's moderate stance, the candidate had an additional calculus to figure: how to prove acceptable to the large number of white Mississippians still firmly devoted to white supremacy. Part of Winter's legitimacy with these white voters included the fact that he had remained firmly within the regular Democratic Party and had not joined recent attempts to forge a biracial alliance among Democratic voters, such as those pursued by the Mississippi Democratic Conference and the Mississippi Young Democrats. In his campaign appearances, Winter signaled his continuing devotion to the regular Democratic Party by noting that he was a "Jim Eastland–John Stennis Democrat." Connecting that association to his campaign slogan, "Fight to Win for Mississippi," Winter declared, "These are the men I have been fighting and winning with." Though unstated, this assertion implied that Winter was part of the effort by the regular Democratic Party to limit the impact of civil rights changes.[17]

Winter utilized other tactics to shore up support among whites. He frequently talked about the need to maintain law and order. Winter had long advocated that Mississippians must obey the law, most notably civil rights laws. He tweaked this message during the 1967 campaign, which coincided with increasing militancy within the civil rights movement and a series of urban riots in Newark and other northern cities. He criticized Stokely Carmichael and H. Rap Brown, two Black Panther leaders, as men "who pervert the laws of our land to espouse widespread anarchy, vandalism, and hooliganism." Winter pledged that under his leadership, "We are not going to permit inside or outside agitators to break our laws and bring the resulting violence which follows. . . . We will not permit crime in the streets." At the same time, consistent with his earlier calls for law and order, Winter also emphasized that he believed that Mississippians had to obey all laws—not just the ones they liked—and that he would "not fan the fires with loud threats, phony headlines, or [in a not-so-subtle attack on Barnett] behind the scenes scheming." Winter also distanced himself from civil rights groups still working in Mississippi perceived by many, even some white moderates and middle-class blacks, as "radical," such as the Delta Ministry, which had worked for many years to improve the economic, social, and political fortunes of impoverished blacks in the Mississippi Delta. When the Presbyterian Church decided to continue supporting the controversial organization in the spring of 1967—a move Winter had argued against in 1965 as a commissioner to the General Assembly of the denomination—Winter issued a statement that called the Delta Ministry "a great detriment to the people of both races in Mississippi," one which "has broken down channels of communication and understanding among our people."[18]

Despite Winter's efforts to alleviate white fears, most committed segregationists saw him as the least suitable choice for governor and roundly condemned him and his candidacy. The *Southern Review*, a newspaper produced by hardline segregationist Elmore Greaves, a farmer and lawyer from Madison County, devoted most of its July 15, 1967, issue to spurious attacks on Winter. One article falsely charged that Winter had made a 1966 speech at Howard University in Washington, D.C., described as an "all negro, radical, socialist hotbed." The piece suggested that an unnamed source held film footage of the talk and would be willing to sell it to one of Winter's opponents for a mere $100,000. Another article claimed Winter had a secret meeting with Robert Kennedy when he came to Mississippi in the spring of 1966, "got drunk, and investigated 'poverty.'" Also present at the meeting, according to the paper, were "Charles Evers, the black insurrectionist" and "Dr. James Silver, the socialist ex-professor who was run out of Ole Miss." A picture of blacks standing in a line in front of a building carried the caption, "A typical bloc-voting, negro-dominated precinct in south Mississippi," and an accompanying article claimed that the Winter campaign counted on "this massed, bloc vote of savage Africans" to "win for Winter while he fools white voters with expensive 'Win with Winter' billboards and 'segregation image' in North Mississippi." The *Southern Review*'s writers seemed particularly upset about Winter's subtle attempts to navigate the complex racial terrain of 1967. Greaves editorialized that Winter "pretends to believe in States' Rights and yet he would revolutionize Mississippi; he tries to give the impression that Mississippi should handle her own affairs and yet he is in constant contact with the most rabid socialist centralizers; he gives lip service to some of Mississippi's traditions and yet he conspires with negro insurrectionists; he appeals to the youth and yet under his administration the very white youth he appeals to would be thrust forth into the degeneracy of mixed schools." One preposterous story tagged Winter as the Fiji Mermaid, an allusion to a popular nineteenth-century attraction of showman P. T. Barnum, in which a taxidermist seamlessly joined two animals, a monkey and a fish, to form what looked like one actual hideous monster.[19]

As much as possible Winter focused both his advertising and his public speeches on the issues and his own personal biography. He explained the Winter Plans, which he described correctly as "the most imaginative and comprehensive program of progress ever put before the voters of Mississippi." He emphasized his many accomplishments, as a student, as a World War II veteran, and as a political figure over the preceding twenty years. Winter's campaign material reminded voters, "His honesty and integrity are a matter of record. He doesn't smoke or drink and he's a regular church goer. At 44 he's in excellent health." He also made people aware of his lovely family. In one campaign ad that appeared days before the first primary, the entire group—William, Elise, and their three daughters—were shown striding across the lawn of the Winter home and looking into the camera, all smiling. The tag line for the ad read, "Four Reasons Why WILLIAM WINTER Is Fighting to Win for Mississippi!" Winter generally remained true to his pledge to avoid the mudslinging. About the worst he said about his opponents, typically without referring to them by name, was that Mississippi was tired of losers (Barnett) and quitters (Williams).[20]

The August 8 balloting brought out the largest turnout ever in a Mississippi primary election. An increase of more than 200,000 voters since the 1963 statewide election reflected the increase in black voter registration after the Voting Rights Act of 1965. Fifteen of the nineteen counties with the most significant increase in voters in 1967 had black majorities. Overall, nearly 74 percent of all registered voters and 70 percent of registered black voters cast a ballot in the first primary election. The final tally had Winter leading with 222,001 votes, while John Bell Williams trailed close behind, with 197,778 ballots. Jimmy Swan bested Ross Barnett for third place by a margin of almost 50,000 votes, and Bill Waller came in fifth, receiving only 15,000 fewer votes than Barnett. Winter finished first in forty-five of eighty-two counties, his greatest strength coming from the Delta, north Mississippi, and the Gulf Coast. The runoff, to be held three weeks later, would pit Winter against Williams.[21]

Winter won a large share of the black vote in the first primary, although both Williams and Waller also received significant black support. One area with a sizeable number of new black voters in which Winter did not fare well was southwest Mississippi. This area was the home base of Charles Evers and included several counties that had a majority black population. Rumors later circulated that Evers had urged blacks in Jefferson and Claiborne Counties to vote for Williams or Waller, to deflect the anticipated criticism from segregationists that Winter had polled well in every area with large numbers of black voters. The fact that these two counties were the only ones Winter won in the second primary that he did not lead in the first primary adds credence to the stories. It is also true, however, that Evers had indicated support for Waller during the campaign and that Williams had name recognition in the area since it was part of his congressional district. Statewide, over one hundred black candidates had run for a variety of offices. Fifteen won their races outright in the first primary, most to minor posts such as justice of the peace. An additional twenty-two made it to the second primary runoff. Only one reported incident of racial violence marred the victories. In Jefferson County, two days after the election, a white farmer, apparently upset by the local results, shot one of his black farmhands. He told the other black workers, "I oughta kill all of you," before driving into town and turning himself in to the authorities.[22] While things were certainly changing in Mississippi—blacks were voting and even winning elective office and the white farmer knew he could no longer kill a black man with impunity—racial peace did not exist everywhere.

The day after the first primary, Winter met with his campaign advisors Gene Triggs, Warren Hood, and Paul Pittman, and his pollster, Gene Newsome. As they looked at the numbers from the election, they all came to the same conclusion. The only place to get additional votes in the second primary was from Barnett voters, and especially from those who had favored Swan. Winter and his team decided that the candidate would have to slant his message in the coming weeks to appeal to the arch-segregationist Swan and Barnett voters. At the same time, he would portray Williams as an ineffective defender of segregation. For a candidate who had long been identified as a racial moderate, going hard after segregationist votes would be a difficult task, yet if Winter wanted to have any chance of winning in the second primary, everyone agreed no other feasible strategy existed.[23]

Winter emerged from the first primary sounding more like a firebrand segregationist than he ever had. In the first couple of days after his primary victory, when speaking to the press, he sought to quell any worries about his moderation. He presented himself as one who understood the concerns of the white voters who had supported Swan and Barnett in the first primary. He "blasted" the Lyndon Johnson administration and vowed that "one of his prime objectives would be a fight to prevent [the] renomination and re-election of President Johnson." Winter also proclaimed his desire to eliminate the HEW's school desegregation guidelines and restore local control to the public schools. In addition, he praised George Wallace of Alabama and indicated he might support the segregationist in the 1968 presidential contest or ally the state's Democrats with the forces of Republican Ronald Reagan, as a way "to preserve conservative government in this country." Winter's adoption of a strong segregationist stance disillusioned some of his white moderate supporters, but he hoped that most of his long-time allies recognized his new strategy as a change "in approach rather than principle." As he noted a couple of years later, "A political race is no place for a dogmatist." Most Winter partisans did understand that Winter's tactic was a matter of "expediency," although some believed their candidate had let them down.[24]

Winter, however, quickly discovered he had neither the stomach nor the acting skills to pose as an unreconstructed segregationist. By the time he returned to the campaign trail on the Saturday after his first primary victory, he quickly abandoned his new strategy. Winter remembered standing before a group in Pontotoc trying to read a prepared text of defiant segregationist clichés and nearly choking on the words. On the way to the next appearance he told Elise, "I can't do that anymore." Instead of the overheated rhetoric Winter had fed newspaper reporters in the immediate aftermath of the first primary, he returned largely to the message he had honed in the first primary. During appearances in north Mississippi, Winter told audiences, "The choice in the governor's race is between a man with twenty years' experience in state government and with a positive program for the state and the man who has no plans, no program, and no experience in state government." Although he continued to face pressure from some of his advisors, contributors, and friends to be more aggressive in his appeals to the segregationist vote, he chose not to do so. In the two weeks of campaigning before the second primary, whenever Winter talked about race, he turned to his standard muted statements about being a fifth-generation Mississippian, one who had always defended segregation. Other than obliquely declaring fealty to segregation, and taking an occasional swipe at LBJ, Winter spent most of the time in his public appearances and advertisements addressing how his administration would solve numerous problems and reiterating that he would be a more effective governor than Williams.[25]

Winter's initial hard-line segregationist strategy in the second primary campaign, however brief, provided an opening for Williams and others to attack Winter as insincere. The *Meridian Star* noted that Winter, "the liberal candidate," only tried to pose as a conservative after the votes from the first primary were counted; he "suddenly 'got religion' as the old farmer puts it and started trumpeting how strong he is for George Wallace." A political cartoon in the *Jackson Daily News* titled "A New Image" showed Winter in a barber chair. On the back of the barber's coat were the words, "Political Make-Up Artist," and a talk bubble shows Winter saying, "I've got to look like George Wallace—Quick!" During a statewide television address on August 17, Williams said that after Winter "has read the results of the first primary, suddenly he has become an arch-conservative, putting himself to the right of the John Birch Society. This man has tried to change his spots by hiding his liberal record behind a Confederate flag and under a George Wallace hat, but this is not going to fool the people of Mississippi." A cartoon produced by the Williams campaign depicted Winter as a leopard with spots labeled Charles Evers, Hodding Carter, Great Society, Aaron Henry, Bobby Kennedy, and LBJ. Nearby were containers identified as spot remover, soap, lye, and kerosene. The smiling leopard vigorously scrubbed the spots.[26]

In his effort to secure the votes of the losers in the first primary, Winter employed other tactics as well. He played up an unexpected endorsement he received from Ross Barnett. The former governor threw his support to Winter, not because he best represented the segregationist position Barnett had championed but because Barnett disliked Williams's attacks on him during the first primary contest. In one Winter ad, a former Barnett supporter testified, "It is inconceivable to me that any voter who respects Ross Barnett could fail to vote for William Winter." The endorsement had limited usefulness, however, as most Barnett supporters had more interest in electing a governor who would represent Barnett's values than vindicating Barnett's honor. Winter appealed to the Swan vote by adopting the Hattiesburg candidate's first primary abstinence pledge, "as long as I'm governor, no liquor will be served in the governor's mansion." Mississippi legalized liquor only the year before, much to the chagrin of the sizeable anti-liquor contingent in the state. Winter was himself a teetotaler, but he had focused little attention on this fact early in the campaign and had never been a strong advocate of prohibition throughout his political career. He now promised to keep the mansion dry if elected. This bit of strategy, however, might have cost him as many votes in strong Winter areas, like the Gulf Coast and the Delta, as any Swan votes he picked up by catering to the dry forces.[27]

Winter still made no effort to appeal publicly to black voters, an approach that at least some black leaders continued to understand. Although Winter's strident segregationist tone in the days after the first primary undoubtedly led many blacks to question whether much difference actually existed between the two white candidates, most black leaders still viewed Winter as a better alternative than Williams. They recognized that Winter made his segregationist statements "for self-protection." In the end, most black leaders recommended that black voters choose Winter as "the lesser of two evils." As in the first primary, those endorsements would come only at the last minute. Charles Evers indicated his support for Winter the night before the election. In most cases, on the eve of the election, black activists distributed to black voters sample ballots listing Winter as the preferred choice.[28]

Williams could also count votes, and he pursued the Swan vote by promising to work for the passage of a federal constitutional amendment that would guarantee state control over the public schools. Williams knew that to win in the second primary he had to make Winter unacceptable to the Swan and Barnett voters. A typical Williams political rally during the second primary campaign consisted of a string of attacks on Winter. One Winter supporter calculated that, in one forty-two minute speech, Williams spent twenty-three minutes attacking Winter. The lines of attack included some that were familiar, some that were particularly racist, and others that were somewhat bizarre. Emphasizing the oft-repeated charges concerning Winter and the 1960 presidential election, Williams rhetorically asked the audience what Winter was doing in 1960 while Williams "was opposing the Kennedy-Johnson attempt to socialize our great nation?" Answering his own question and ignoring his own Democratic Party affiliation, Williams replied that "his holiness, William Winter, was out drumming up votes for the Democratic ticket and apologizing for Mississippi." Williams also attacked Winter's claim to be a fifth-generation Mississippian, explaining that "we checked into that and we could only go back three generations. We were afraid to go back any further because we were afraid we might find some of his forebears swinging in the trees!" Finally, alluding to Winter's service as state tax collector and state treasurer, Williams asserted that "the only jobs William Winter has held in state government were girls' jobs."[29]

To make sure that white voters knew the true defender of segregation in the governor's contest, Williams portrayed Winter as the candidate favored by black Mississippians. At one of Winter's political rallies outside the courthouse in Charleston, attended by both blacks and whites, a photographer from the *Memphis Commercial Appeal* took a photo from behind Winter of the crowd listening to the candidate. The angle of the photo showed a predominantly black crowd seated before the candidate with a smaller group of whites standing farther back on the lawn. The Williams campaign made copies of the photograph and distributed them at rallies, under the headline, "Awake White Mississippi." According to the flyer, "For the first time in our history we are faced with a large NEGRO MINORITY BLOC VOTE—William Winter's election will insure negro domination of Mississippi elections for generations to come."[30]

The Williams camp also circulated a handbill entitled, "How the Black Bloc Voted For Governor." The sheet claimed that Winter received 83.6 percent of the black vote in the first primary, though it never explained how that figure was calculated. The publication, however, did provide some examples from four precincts where the "voting boxes are as high as 90 percent or even more negro." One of the examples was Diamond Precinct in Wayne County, in south Mississippi. The flyer claimed that this voting district had eighty-four registered black voters and sixteen registered white voters; Winter had received sixty-nine votes here, and all the other candidates had polled sixteen, or "exactly the number of the white voters registered!" The handbill urged voters to go to the polls; otherwise, "IF WILLIAM WINTER IS ELECTED GOVERNOR then politicians in Mississippi in the future will think they have to court the negroes to get elected, and *THE NEGROES WILL RUN MISSISSIPPI.*" Winter made little effort to counter Williams charges.[31]

By the last week of the campaign, Winter seemed to be picking up votes, even in the heart of Jimmy Swan territory in south Mississippi. At a rally in Laurel a week before the election, an enthusiastic crowd greeted Winter and seemed receptive to his plans for the future. The biggest applause from the crowd came when Winter talked about the need for better schools: "I say we can't afford not to have quality education in the State of Mississippi, and we're going to get it in the Winter Administration." Winter spent several days during the last week of the campaign working the counties in south Mississippi where Swan had prevailed. One poll conducted during the final week showed Winter and Williams almost dead even, with 12 percent of voters still undecided. The success Winter had by focusing on the issues even caused Williams to put out advertisements attacking Winter's voting record on such matters as old-age assistance, school teacher pay, and vocational rehabilitation rather than focusing on his lack of commitment to the cause of white supremacy.[32]

As Winter seemed to draw even with Williams in the waning days of the campaign, hardcore white segregationists became concerned. The Saturday before the election, Gene Triggs received a collect call from an unnamed man who said he had important information for the campaign. Triggs accepted the call and, sensing something unusual, decided to tape the exchange. The man started off by saying, "Your man's in extreme danger." Triggs asked what had happened, and the voice replied, "There was a meeting today, and your man has been marked." The caller seemed rattled by what he knew and struggled to convey his message: "It's fanatical. I mean extremely fanatical. And the man that's set up for it is—I don't know how to describe him. I don't get any pleasure out of this kind of stuff. He's not gonna serve. I'll put it to you bluntly. And that he's just not gonna serve—even if he's elected. And this thing—I can't be a part of it. I'm not going to be a part of it. And I had to call you to tell you . . . . but even after the man is elected, he's not going to serve. Because it's just fanatical. Death threat in purpose and in intent—that he don't serve." The man said he was from Alabama and had attended a seven-hour meeting that had broken up earlier that morning. Triggs asked about the group that met, but the man would not name it and claimed that if his identity became known, "My life wouldn't be worth a bit more than William Winter." The caller also explained, "This thing has been festering ever since [the] first primary. And it came to a head last night." The informant urged Triggs to take the message seriously and reiterated that the people plotting against Winter were "an insane bunch of idiotic fanatics."[33]

Winter was traveling that day through south Mississippi, accompanied by White and Peden. The three were scheduled to meet a plane in Magee late in the afternoon, which would take the two staffers back to Jackson and pick up Elise to fly to a 9:00 p.m. rally at the local football stadium in Biloxi. When Winter arrived at the Magee airport, he noticed both of the plane's engines already running. Someone quickly hurried the candidate to the plane, and it took off immediately. In the air, Winter learned about the death threat. At the Jackson airport, Winter huddled with his aides and Elise. As they listened to the chilling tape recording, some of Winter's advisers urged him to cancel the Biloxi rally. Winter told them, "Well, I'm sorry, but we've got to be there." Elise agreed and said if William went, she would also make the trip. Triggs arranged for two plainclothes highway patrolmen to accompany the Winters to Biloxi. On the Gulf Coast, some of Winter's supporters had been alerted to the death threat, and a number of them came to the rally that night heavily armed. These silent bodyguards stood around the edges of the crowd of some three thousand people, ready to provide protection for Winter if needed. Fortunately for all concerned, Winter spoke from the fifty-yard line to an enthusiastic audience without incident. Elise Winter sat calmly on the platform during the presentation.[34]

The death threat cast a pall over the final days of the campaign. Not taking any chances, the Winters moved out of their Jackson home. The girls stayed with the families of their friends. William and Elise moved into the Heidelberg Hotel. No attempt was ever made on Winter's life, but these precautions were absolutely necessary. The fanatics the anonymous caller had talked of were not a fantasy. Later that fall, the Ku Klux Klan unleashed a series of attacks against white moderates in Jackson. The Klan bombed the Jewish Temple Beth Israel, as well as the home of Perry Nussbaum, the rabbi of Beth Israel and Winter's friend and neighbor. Other Klan bombs targeted a Tougaloo College administrator and a Jackson businessman. As Winter closed out the campaign, concerned about his own safety and that of his family, he found it hard to believe that he could win on August 29.[35]

In the end, Winter lost to Williams in the second primary by a count of 371,815 to 310,527. Winter won only twenty-one counties, with victories concentrated in the Delta, north Mississippi, the Gulf Coast, and the two southwest Mississippi counties (Jefferson and Claiborne) with black majorities that had previously voted for Williams in the first primary. The overall number of voters in the second primary declined only slightly from three weeks earlier, although the percentage of eligible black voters declined to around 50 percent. All twenty-two black candidates vying for positions in the second primary lost, although seven other black candidates, six running as independents, would win during the general election in November. As expected, Winter received the vast majority of the ballots cast by black voters in the governor's race; if the black turnout had been as good or better than in the first primary, the race would have been closer, although probably not close enough for a Winter victory. Part of the declining participation of black voters likely resulted from white intimidation. An unsuccessful candidate for sheriff in southwest Mississippi noted that someone burned a black church there the week before the election and scrawled the letters "KKK" on the campaign signs of black candidates. In Simpson County, which had no blacks running for office, some residents claimed that in one precinct the votes were taken by voice vote in a white man's dining room. Other more subtle forms of racial intimidation, not reported, undoubtedly also occurred. One young white educator from Moorhead told Winter that in the Delta, "where the Negro is so reliant on white power for a livelihood," he was certain that some blacks "were directed by farmers to go in and vote for John Bell Williams and I am sure also that few dared do other than as instructed."[36]

The day after the election, Larry Noble pointed out the considerable obstacles Winter had failed to overcome in 1967: "the liberalism label really hurt you—plus your sane background—and your education and civilized manner. In other words, your record! You just didn't have the image for those Swan people—too different from them—despite what you said." In the days and weeks following the election, Winter received letters from many around the state who praised him for the campaign he had run. The common thread running through this correspondence noted that Winter had inspired many white Mississippians, and in the process, he and his family had created a dignified image for the state.[37]

In Mississippi's 1967 gubernatorial election, Winter attempted to run as a racial moderate, as an early incarnation of the New South governors who would win election across the South a few years later. Winter's timing, however, was not good. The race issue remained alive and well in Mississippi in 1967, and the governor's contest proved the state's last overtly racist election. Even though political ambition and a practical calculation about the route to victory had led Winter to make some uncharacteristic pronouncements during the 1967 governor's race, his campaign actually represented the possibility for a new type of political leadership in Mississippi, one that sought to move beyond an emotional defense of white supremacy. Unfortunately for Winter, a majority of white Mississippians were not yet ready to take that path to the future.

8

RIGHT MAN, WRONG JOB

After the grueling campaign of 1967, William and Elise Winter took a short vacation to upstate New York. Driving along the Hudson River in October, Winter was greatly relieved that he was no longer spending his days walking the fine line between Mississippi's past and the reluctant New Mississippi. He did not know what his next move would be or whether he would make another run for governor. Yet in spite of the disappointments of his campaign, Winter remained confident that Mississippi would succeed in moving beyond the racial divisions that had held it back for so long. As he prepared to leave state politics after nearly twenty years of continuous service, he chose for the family's 1968 New Year's Day card a passage from a letter General Robert E. Lee wrote to his aide de camp Charles Marshall shortly after the end of the Civil War. The quote offered telling insight into Winter's mind set at the time:

> My experience of men has neither disposed me to think worse of them nor indisposed me to serve them; nor, in spite of failures which I lament, or errors which I now see and acknowledge, or of the present aspect of affairs, do I despair of the future. The truth is this: The march of Providence is so slow and our desires so impatient; the work of progress is so immense and our means of aiding it so feeble; the life of humanity is so long, that of the individual so brief, that we often see only the ebb of the advancing wave and are thus discouraged. It is history that teaches us to hope.[1]

When Winter turned over the state treasurer's office to Evelyn Gandy in early 1968, he had several job offers to consider. One of the major banks in the state had tendered an officer's position, which Winter turned down. He had also been suggested once again for a federal judgeship, and despite Senator John Stennis's backing this time, Winter declined to pursue that opportunity, choosing to practice law instead. The field of law he planned to focus on developed out of his work as treasurer. During the height of the 1967 campaign, Governor Paul Johnson proposed a massive bond issue to support the expansion of Litton Industries' Ingalls Shipbuilding division at the port in Pascagoula and called the legislature into a special July session to approve the plan. Realizing that his proposal might become a political football in the governor's race, Johnson invited all the gubernatorial candidates to the governor's mansion and secured their agreement to support his monumental bond effort. The legislature approved the plan, and in the fall, Winter, acting in his role as treasurer, oversaw the sale of the $130 million bond issue, at that point the largest sale of tax-exempt bonds designed to assist a single industry in Mississippi. To assist with the bond sale, the state engaged the Wall Street firm of Nixon, Mudge, Rose, Guthrie, and Alexander, whose senior partners included former Vice-President Richard Nixon and John Mitchell, a municipal bond attorney and future U.S. attorney general. Winter made several trips to New York in connection with the sale, working primarily with Mitchell. On the day the purchase was finalized, the New York law firm hosted a dinner at the 21 Club to celebrate the successful bond sale. During dinner Mitchell complimented Winter on his work and asked about his plans when he left office. When Winter replied that he had not decided, Mitchell noted that Mississippi remained one of the few states that farmed out the legal work for its bond sales to out-of-state lawyers and suggested that Winter should consider establishing a bond practice in the state.[2]

When Winter returned to Mississippi, he broached the subject of such a specialty with members of Watkins, Pyle, Edwards and Ludlam, one of Jackson's oldest and most respected law firms, formed at the turn of the century. The organization's senior partner, Vaughan Watkins, had previously talked with Winter about the possibility of joining the firm after he left the treasurer's job, and another partner there, John Hampton Stennis, son of Senator Stennis, also encouraged Winter to come to Watkins,

Pyle. Watkins expressed enthusiasm about Winter's proposal to develop a bond practice and agreed to work with him on it. In April 1968 Winter joined Watkins, Pyle as a partner, and the following year, the name of the firm became Watkins, Pyle, Ludlam, Winter and Stennis. Winter and Stennis immediately began making contacts with major security dealers and banks in New York City, Memphis, and New Orleans. They also traveled around Mississippi to develop their new practice. Winter's many local contacts proved useful, and within a couple of years, the bond approval business at the Jackson law firm began to thrive. The nature of Winter's specialty helped him maintain contact with political leaders. In the summer of 1968, he wrote to Jim Silver that the bond work allowed him to keep "in close touch with the local county officials, where I am afraid I was largely undone last summer."[3]

As Winter worked on building up his law practice, the racial divisions that had dictated the tone of the 1967 gubernatorial campaign did not dissipate. In 1968, Governor John Bell Williams led a successful effort to continue the exclusion of blacks from the regular state Democratic Party. After being officially shut out of the so-called Regular Democrats at the state convention, black Mississippians—including members of the Mississippi Freedom Democratic Party (MFDP)—and white moderates formed a competing Democratic organization, the Loyalist Democratic Party of Mississippi. Winter did not participate in the activities of either group and steered clear of the Democratic Party factionalism. As he later recalled, the Regular Democrats were controlled by Governor Williams, and the Loyalist Democrats were associated with the perceived radicalism of the MFDP, and "I didn't have a dog in that fight. I didn't see that my participation would make any difference one way or the other, and it was just a way to get scarred up, in terms of any future races I might make." The national Democratic Party convention, which Winter did not attend, chose to seat the Loyalists instead of the Regulars. Winter personally supported Humphrey in the 1968 presidential race, though he did not openly campaign for the Democratic nominee. On election day, Mississippi gave over 63 percent of its vote to the independent candidate from neighboring Alabama, segregationist George Wallace; Humphrey finished second with only 23 percent of the ballots. Republican Richard Nixon, who received only 14 percent of Mississippi votes, won the presidency. As Mississippi Democrats struggled to create a party hospitable to both whites and newly enfranchised black voters, the emerging Republican Party in the state sought to attract converts from the ranks of white Democrats. Prominent politicians who did not openly embrace the biracial Loyalist organization, such as William Winter, were considered candidates for defection to the Republican Party. Although a number of white Democrats switched parties in the late 1960s and 1970s, Winter never considered such a move.[4]

Another racial issue that remained alive was the battle over the integration of the public schools. Following the U.S. Supreme Court's decision in *Alexander v. Holmes* in October 1969, which required all Mississippi school districts to integrate fully by the fall of 1970 (some districts, such as Jackson, began compliance in mid-year), Governor Williams urged Mississippians to keep fighting for the preservation of freedom-of-choice school desegregation plans, which had resulted in only token school integration. He also prodded the legislature to provide public support for private school efforts. Most tellingly, although Williams never publicly promoted abandonment of the public schools, his own children attended the White Citizens' Council segregation academies in Jackson rather than the integrated public schools. More than 40 percent of whites in Jackson followed the governor's lead and left the public schools in Jackson during 1970. Senator Stennis also did what he could to topple or seriously derail the massive integration orders for Mississippi, most notably by his frequent calls that the U.S. government do something about de facto school segregation in the North and West, a calculated effort to encourage a nationwide backlash against federally mandated school integration. At a presentation in Jackson in mid-January 1970, Stennis indicated that his plan might take "a long time" but eventually the courts would back off and "we will have control of our schools again." Stennis emphasized that he did not "want to say anything that looks like the whites are being encouraged not to go to the public schools," but he did add that parents should "continue lawful protest of integration" if they opposed it.[5]

In the meantime, Winter stated that he planned to keep his children in the public schools and also worked to encourage other white parents to do the same. Winter missed Stennis's January speech in Jackson because he was attending another meeting: a gathering of white parents "concerned about maintaining adequate support for the public school system here in Jackson." While Winter told Stennis that he had heard "favorable comments" about the senator's remarks in Jackson, Winter did not plan to join the white resistance to integrated schools. He declared, "I am fully committed to doing all that I can to maintain the public school system, and that includes keeping my children in it if at all possible. I think that we're going to be able to make it here in Jackson, but it is going to take calm, sensible, and dedicated people to do it." While Winter sometimes disagreed with Senator Stennis on policy matters, the two men retained the close, personal ties they had first established in 1947.[6]

When school integration began in Jackson in February 1970, the Winters' oldest daughter, Anne, scheduled to graduate in May, remained at the same high school, now integrated. The two younger Winter girls, however, became part of the massive reshuffling of students in the city's school system. Lele, a ninth-grader, was bussed to a new junior high school, a formerly all-black school in a black neighborhood. Only a handful of her white friends joined her at the new school. There were disruptions, but she adjusted well and three years later, she graduated from majority-black Murrah High School. The youngest daughter, Eleanor, had a more difficult experience. A fifth-grader in 1970, she was bussed in mid-year across the city to a formerly all-black elementary school. When Eleanor started seventh grade, she moved closer to home, to Bailey Junior High School, but white flight had continued, and very few other white girls attended Bailey with Eleanor that year. She had a rough year. In gym class, several black students harassed and threatened her. By chance, William Winter diminished the ranks of Eleanor's tormentors. Traveling home one afternoon, he saw a woman on the side of the road struggling to change a flat tire, and he stopped to help her. Unbeknown to Winter, the woman was the mother of one of the black girls harassing Eleanor in gym class. The girl never bothered Eleanor again. Even so, the abuse took its toll, and the following year, she transferred to St. Andrew's Episcopal School, one of the few private schools in Mississippi that predated the *Brown* decision and one of the few that operated on a desegregated basis. She completed high school at St. Andrews.[7]

Winter did what he could to promote the preservation of a strong public school system in Jackson and throughout Mississippi. During the early 1970s, he championed groups across the state, such as the Friends of Public Schools, that worked to maintain white support for public education during the transition period. Most whites in Jackson, however, never rallied to support the public schools in the city after massive integration began, and the school system struggled for a number of years as it lost a sizeable part of its constituency. When the Jackson school system and black parents sought to revise the city's school integration plan in 1975 to limit the continuing exit of white students and to increase the resources spent on the most needy black-majority schools, Winter worked with the attorneys and helped bring about a compromise agreement.[8]

The controversy over school integration played a role in Winter's decision about his political future. Considering whether or not to run in the 1971 governor's race, Winter had concerns about how important racial issues would be in the contest. The Winters and other prominent whites in Jackson who supported the public schools after integration had received postcards with the message, "You are being watched." The communiqués caused enough concern that for a time local law enforcement posted a guard near the Winter home. Winter knew for certain that he did not want to participate in another campaign like 1967, one where race dominated the contest. There were also other factors to consider. Charles Sullivan, then lieutenant governor and twice previously a gubernatorial candidate, was an unannounced candidate in the upcoming governor's contest, and he seemed to be a strong frontrunner. By early 1971, Sullivan had convinced many of Winter's supporters from 1967—including Warren Hood—that he had the best chance to become governor. A poll Winter commissioned confirmed that a Sullivan-Winter contest would be a close affair, and Winter did not want to make another race he could not win. Besides, Winter was still paying off a $50,000 debt from the 1967 campaign, and his private law practice had just begun to flourish. There was a final concern. Although Senator Jim Eastland had promoted Charles Sullivan as a gubernatorial candidate in 1959, the two later had a falling out, so Eastland and former governor Paul Johnson, a strong political ally of Eastland, urged Winter to enter the 1971 governor's race against Sullivan. While an Eastland-Johnson endorsement would help any gubernatorial candidate, Winter did not embrace the more conservative political philosophy of the Eastland-Johnson faction of Mississippi politics and worried what "commitments" he might have to make to secure such support.[9]

Because of all the potential negatives, Winter decided to seek the office of lieutenant governor instead. That race would cost less money than another gubernatorial run, and Winter felt confident he could win, as no major candidates had lined up to enter that race. Since the lieutenant governor's position was a part-time job, he could maintain his new and successful law practice. At the same time, as lieutenant governor, he would keep his name in the public eye in anticipation of a run at the top seat in 1975. Winter announced his candidacy for the lieutenant governor's race in late April, a decision that opened the door for the gubernatorial candidacy of another racial moderate, Bill Waller.[10]

Winter, however, underestimated his chances for success in the 1971 governor's contest. Most important, he misjudged the extent of racial adjustment in the state. Although racial conflict still simmered—as demonstrated by the continuing battle over school integration—by 1971 even Mississippi, it seemed, was ready for the kind of New South leadership that had recently triumphed all over the region: a politics freed of the old obsession with preserving white supremacy. Race remained an issue in the 1971 elections, but it was decidedly more muted than four years earlier. Jimmy Swan, who ran again as an unabashed opponent of racial change, finished a distant third in the first primary, though he still polled more than 125,000 votes. The continuing impact of the 1965 Voting Rights Act, however, diminished the use of overt racial appeals in the 1971 governor's race. By that year, more than 300,000 black voters had registered in the state, nearly 30 percent of the electorate. Those numbers did not necessarily translate into huge victories for black political candidates in 1971, as only 50 of the 309 who ran were elected. Even so, it was no longer possible for a white candidate in a Democratic primary to win a statewide election without courting black voters. The two candidates who made it to the second primary, Sullivan and Waller, might have railed against school busing, confirmed the importance of private schools, and issued vague calls for "law and order," but they both also promised to appoint blacks to state jobs if elected. As the black press noted, the second primary "was virtually devoid of anti-Negro tirades," and the two candidates "not only respect, but fear the huge Mississippi black vote because it is breathing down their necks." Indeed, with white voters fairly evenly divided between Waller and Sullivan, the black vote became a decisive factor in the second primary victory of Waller, the candidate with the stronger credentials as a racial moderate.[11]

In the lieutenant governor's contest, Winter faced two challengers: Cliff Finch, a district attorney from Batesville, and Elmore Greaves, the dedicated segregationist and die-hard member of the White Citizens' Council from Madison County. Winter's campaign focused on the same issues he had emphasized in 1967: education, economic development, stewardship of natural resources, an improved highway system, and the other programs enumerated in the Winter Plans. The Winter campaign also paid particular attention to organizing young voters. A county youth campaign, organized by Danny Keyes and Bill Cole, mobilized young people to pass out Winter bumper stickers and organize letter-writing efforts in their communities. Winter's campaign ads highlighted three reasons that he was the best choice for lieutenant governor: "extensive experience in state government, a will and a dedication to serve—and, most of all, a sincere faith in Mississippi and in the ability and the desire of all Mississippians to work for a better tomorrow." Part of the Winter pitch also included a suggestion that as lieutenant governor Winter could help Mississippi improve its image in the eyes of the nation. Although Winter campaigned actively, the 1971 operation, a low-key effort, cost only about $40,000. Many of those who had worked in the 1967 campaign returned for the 1971 race; Elise and the two younger Winter daughters also pitched in to help.[12]

Similar to the governor's contest, race played only a minimal role in the lieutenant governor's election. Winter skated over the recent controversy surrounding school integration by blandly noting that both private and public schools played an important role in educating the children of Mississippi—a nod to the 10 percent of white families statewide who had abandoned public education after 1970. Elmore Greaves's platform featured a promise to restore the southern Confederacy, and he tried to use the old tactic of direct racial appeals during the campaign, but with little success. He called Winter "the candidate for both the liberals and black loyalists," a reference to the biracial Loyalist Democrats. The charges, however, generated little attention, and Winter ignored Greaves and his attacks. Winter won the race in the first primary on August 3 with almost 60 percent of the vote, and he received more than 150,000 more votes than his closest challenger, Cliff Finch (Greaves garnered only 5 percent of the vote). In addition to Winter's statewide name recognition and a rather issueless campaign, his effort to attract the support of young people paid off, especially since that group expanded significantly when the Twenty-Sixth Amendment to the Constitution, lowering the voting age to eighteen, was ratified just weeks before the 1971 primary election.[13]

Although Winter achieved what the *New York Times* called a "significant comeback" by winning his contest, almost immediately after announcing for the lieutenant governor's race, he began to second-guess his decision not to try for the top spot. Winter had long been the standard-bearer for the politics of racial moderation in Mississippi, but now, Bill Waller was poised to take the governor's spot. After Waller easily defeated independent candidate Charles Evers in November (there was no Republican nominee), Winter became depressed about the outcome. Worrying "that I had forfeited forever my opportunity to be elected governor of Mississippi," Winter discussed his disappointment with his former Ole Miss political science professor, H. B. Howerton. The teacher told Winter he might have won the governor's race, but only "if you had been willing to be the *flunky* for Jim Eastland, Ross Barnett and others. But thank the Lord you were and are not." Howerton also reminded Winter of a Shakespeare quote, one his father had also frequently cited: "To thine own self be true, and it must follow, as the night the day, thou canst not then be false to any man." Winter promised his old professor that "I am going to do my best to be my own man" and to "serve as effectively as I know how" in the lieutenant governor's position.[14]

Despite Winter's dissatisfaction, the lieutenant governor occupied perhaps the most powerful political position in Mississippi. The lieutenant governor led the state Senate, appointed all Senate committees and committee chairmen, chaired the Senate Rules Committee, presided over the Senate sessions, broke tie votes in the Senate, and appointed senators to a variety of state boards. By virtue of the office, the lieutenant governor also served as a member of a number of important state boards, including the Commission of Budget and Accounting and the Agricultural and Industrial (A & I) Board. Unlike the governor, the lieutenant governor could also serve multiple consecutive terms, so the possibility existed to establish a significant base of power and shape legislative priorities. Of course, in Winter's case, most assumed that, because of his gubernatorial ambitions, he was almost certainly a one-term lieutenant governor. By comparison, the governor exercised far less legislative power, although that job carried more prestige. Winter knew that a lieutenant governor had to "recognize that you are not the number one official, that when the governor comes along folks are going to stand up for him, and they're not going to pay much attention to you." In spite of the lieutenant governor's power, the office remained a part-time position with minimal pay—only $8,500 a year. Since the legislative sessions lasted three or four months, Winter could maintain his law practice, although he spent considerable time, frequently half his days, on legislative business, even when the Senate was adjourned.[15]

As a former member of the Mississippi House of Representatives, Winter had ample legislative experience when he assumed his position as lieutenant governor. Well aware of "the frustrations and inefficiency of the legislative process," he also knew that legislative success often depended on the personalities of the members. That factor had added importance in the state Senate, which had only fifty-two members, about one-third of the House membership. When Winter began his term as the head of the Senate, Ellis Bodron, a longtime senator from Vicksburg, offered this advice: "You'll get along all right, as long as you remember that there are fifty-two prima donnas in the Mississippi State Senate." Two members in particular challenged Winter's leadership: Bodron himself and Bill Burgin from Columbus. Both had attended Ole Miss with Winter, and both had first won election to the Senate in 1952, serving almost continuously since then. Burgin had been a fellow Coleman supporter in the late 1950s. Between them, Burgin and Bodron controlled the Senate's two major money committees. By the time of Winter's election, Burgin, a tall man with a booming voice, had become the influential chairman of the Senate Appropriations Committee. Bodron chaired the Senate Finance Committee. Fellow legislators widely respected Bodron, who had been blind since childhood, for his brilliant mind, his eidetic memory, his debating skills, and his sense of humor. Although the Senate did not officially have a seniority system, the lieutenant governor customarily reappointed committee chairmen unless they had done a particularly poor job under the previous administration. As a man who honored the legislature's protocols, Winter reappointed both Burgin and Bodron. Burgin, however, almost from the beginning of Winter's term, led the opposition to his leadership of the Senate. Bodron, an extremely conservative, "low-tax, low public service supporter," fought many of the reforms that Winter hoped the Senate would enact. Winter, of course, did have strong allies in the Senate, including freshmen senators John Corlew of Pascagoula and Carroll Ingram of Hattiesburg, and more established members like Herman DeCell of Yazoo City, Perrin Purvis of Tupelo, and Fred Rogers of Meridian.[16]

As lieutenant governor, Winter did not try to dominate the Senate in the manner of Walter Sillers. Winter's style tended more toward seeking consensus than demanding obedience. Winter did, however, try to shape and secure passage of legislation he thought important. He had private meetings with committee chairmen in an attempt to persuade them to bring certain measures to the floor for consideration. Winter also used the powers of his office when necessary, which often provoked the ire of powerful senators stymied by the lieutenant governor's maneuvers. One of the most important tools at the disposal of the lieutenant governor was his ability to control the bill assignment process, which could be used to promote or derail legislation.[17]

During the 1974 session, Winter had an altercation with Burgin over the committee assignment of a new sixteenth-section land reform bill that Winter favored and Burgin opposed. When the U.S. Congress set up procedures in the early nineteenth century for the sale of public lands, it provided that the sixteenth section of every township (out of a total of thirty-six) should go to the states to support education. Although the sixteenth sections belonged to Mississippi, it leased them to private individuals or corporations. In the 1970s, the county supervisors oversaw the renting of these lands. Burgin had a particular interest in sixteenth-section land matters since the county he represented, Lowndes, included the city of Columbus, which lay in large part on sixteenth-section land. In 1974, the House passed a bill to give local school boards veto power over the sixteenth-section leases made by county supervisors, who often had little concern for local public education. When the reform legislation arrived in the Senate, Winter did not send the bill to the Senate Education Committee—where such matters were usually placed—because Burgin was a member and always derailed reform efforts. Instead, Winter put the matter before the Senate Judiciary Committee, chaired by Bill Alexander, a Delta senator who had no vested interest in sixteenth-section lands and who had agreed to ensure that the measure made it to the Senate floor. Burgin, angered at Winter over this maneuver, rushed up to the presiding officer's platform during the floor debate and yelled at Winter, "You'll never get another vote from Lowndes County." The sergeant-at-arms intervened to restore order. But Winter's strategy worked. The Senate passed the sixteenth-section reform bill, and it subsequently became law. The new measure helped generate additional income for public schools and represented the beginning of a thorough reorganization of the state's administration of sixteenth-section lands, which culminated with the 16th Section Reform Act of 1978.[18]

Winter also used his power as head of the Senate Rules Committee to affect the outcome of legislative deliberations. In 1972, 1973, and 1974, the legislature considered bills to simplify and modernize, to the consumer's benefit, the regulation of small loan, auto loan, and credit card businesses. In 1974, the House passed a small loan reform bill and sent it to the Senate. Gulf Coast senator Ben Stone, chair of the Senate Banks and Banking Committee, pronounced the measure "completely unworkable" and offered an alternative version, which one senator said "couldn't be more perfect for the small loan dealers if it had been written by the Association of Small Loan Dealers." After the Senate passed Stone's version of the small loan legislation, the matter went to a conference committee. Stone served as one of the six conferees, but Winter also named John Corlew to the conference committee, to help ensure that a solid reform measure emerged. The compromise bill eventually agreed upon largely adopted the House version of the small loan legislation. Stone refused to endorse the amended measure and declined to bring it up before the full Senate. When Stone balked, Winter called on the vice-chair of the Banks and Banking Committee, Con Maloney, to present the measure. Stone and Burgin protested that Winter had violated Senate rules by calling on the vice-chairman and accepting a report with "technical errors." Winter pointed out the validating regulation allowing a bill to be called up by either the chair or vice-chair of a committee and ruled that a conference committee "had wide discretion" in writing its report. As Stone blasted away at Winter on the floor of the Senate, the lieutenant governor listened attentively and then thanked him for his comments. The small loan bill went on to passage.[19]

Although Winter and Governor Waller shared a common political heritage—both early advocates of racial moderation during the 1960s—and they had a similar vision for Mississippi, the two clearly did not work together as a team. Jesse White, whom Winter had appointed as secretary of the Senate, judged the interactions between Winter and Waller as functional, but noted in 1974 that it "has not been a close, cordial relationship." Newspaperman Bill Minor called it a "non-relationship." One sign of the lack of communication between the two leaders was that Waller seldom notified Winter when leaving the state, sometimes for as long as ten days. Winter, typically finding out that he was "acting" governor when he read the newspapers, had not been briefed on any possible important issues that might arise. In part, the uneasy relations between the two leaders sprang from Waller's limited legislative experience. Unlike previous governors who had such a background, Waller did not seek to build alliances with legislative leaders. He did not ask for Winter's counsel or assistance, and Winter did not press the matter with the governor. There was nothing personal about this lack of consultation, as Waller also made little effort to garner support for his legislative program with the Speaker of the House, John Junkin.[20]

At the same time, Winter's own political ambitions shaped the interactions between the governor and lieutenant governor. As Winter's friend and newspaper editor, Paul Pittman, observed in 1972, the lieutenant governor's position had "historically been a burying ground for ambitious politicians." By the end of the first session of the legislature, Winter had already decided that he would run for governor in 1975, and his advisors urged him to separate himself as much as possible from the governor's agenda. Winter's friend Tom Bourdeaux told him in 1973 that his "identification with the establishment is a negative factor. I believe that you can and should stake out some positions separate and apart from the present administration."[21]

During Winter's term as lieutenant governor, he pressed for legislation in areas he had long identified as important to the state's future. He successfully shepherded legislation for improved social services and preservation of the state's natural resources. He also supported passage of the federal Equal Rights Amendment for women, although Mississippi never ratified the measure. The issue that remained a top priority for Winter, however, was public education. Support for public schools had diminished significantly because of racial integration, as many whites had moved their children to private schools, especially in the Delta and a number of larger cities, like Jackson. Among the measures advocated by Winter and other public education supporters, including Governor Waller, were funding for public kindergartens and the restoration of Mississippi's compulsory school attendance law abolished in the wake of the *Brown* decision. Various legislators filed public kindergarten proposals in every session of Waller's term, and Winter strongly promoted the measures. The full Senate, however, never got the chance to act on any of these proposals, even the optional kindergarten bill passed by the House in 1975, as all the measures died in the Senate Education Committee. Likewise, six compulsory education measures introduced in the Senate (three in 1973 and three in 1975) all failed to emerge from the Senate Education Committee. The chair of that committee, Jack Tucker, hailed from Tunica County, a Delta location where a white minority had moved completely to private schools and left an increasingly underfunded public school system in the hands of the black majority. Many public education supporters doubted Tucker's enthusiasm for creating a strong system of state-funded elementary and secondary institutions.[22]

Another perennial public education issue was teacher compensation. Mississippi consistently ranked at or near the bottom of the national salary scale for public school teachers. As one Wayne County teacher told Winter in 1974, he and his colleagues were "the lowest paid professional people in this country." Winter sympathized with the teachers' pleas and favored bringing their salaries up to the average of the southeastern states, but not everyone agreed. During the 1973 session, the House approved a bill granting public school teachers an average raise of 12 percent. Senate Education Committee chair Tucker favored a more modest cost-of-living raise. Winter advocated adoption of the more substantial teacher pay raise passed by the House, and eventually, the two chambers compromised on a 10.5 percent raise for 1973 and 6 percent raises for both 1974 and 1975, an action that temporarily moved Mississippi up to forty-ninth on the national list of teacher salaries. Inflation skyrocketed to 11 percent in 1974, however, and the 6 percent increase became, in effect, a pay cut. The House passed a supplemental salary measure for teachers, but Senator Tucker appointed himself chair of the Education subcommittee considering the House bill, and he refused to bring the measure up for consideration before the full Senate Education Committee, a move that effectively killed the attempt to provide additional monies for teachers and pushed them back to the bottom of the national teacher salary pay scale. A Gulf Coast teacher complained to Winter "that it is unfair and unjust for the public schools all over the state to be strangulated because of personal opinions." A number of Mississippians had real concerns about the many shortcomings of the public education system, and many of these citizens saw Winter as a prominent champion of improving public education.[23]

Although the Waller administration signaled the beginnings of a post–Jim Crow society in Mississippi, the largely ineffectual efforts to bolster the public schools during the early 1970s illustrate that racial concerns remained alive. For one thing, the transition to a biracial political system continued to be fraught with difficulties. As the 1972 presidential election approached, both Waller and Winter encouraged the Regular and Loyalist factions of the state Democratic Party to come together under one banner, but they failed to resolve their differences, and at the national Democratic convention in Miami, the party's credentials committee endorsed the Loyalist Democrats. In an odd turn of events, neither of the state's top two political officeholders attended the Miami convention as a delegate. When the Democratic Party nominated George McGovern as its standard-bearer, Winter believed it was "an impossible assignment in Mississippi," as few whites would support such a liberal Democrat. Winter did not actively campaign for either McGovern or Nixon, though at one point, he did publicly claim that he would vote for Nixon, an act that one critical observer calculated "stood somewhere near zero on the scale of political bravery in Mississippi." In the end, Winter cast his ballot for McGovern, a fact he did not publicize.[24]

Although Winter did not publically support the Democratic standard-bearer, he quietly continued to work for a reuniting of the state's Democratic Party. After the 1972 election, Wilson Golden, a Winter staffer, regularly attended meetings of the Loyalist Democrats as Winter's representative. Aaron Henry, head of the Loyalists and leader of the state conference of the National Association for the Advancement of Colored People, applauded Winter's efforts at reconciliation by telling him that "it just might be through your genuine concern and efforts together with ours that we may be able to bring this total Democratic Party together, which is a dream that both you and I have had for a long time." Other Loyalist Democrats expressed more frustration with Winter's cautious approach to mending Democratic Party factionalism. Patt Derian complained in 1973 that Winter "seems to be a Democrat. He has a good working relationship with the legislature. It's just that nobody knows where he stands, not only with political affiliation but on a number of other key issues."[25]

Race continued to influence politics in other ways as well. In the early 1970s, the Mississippi legislature still promoted strategies designed to dilute black voting strength. In 1966, in the wake of the Voting Rights

Act of 1965, Mississippi had reapportioned its legislative seats to create multimember districts, to gerrymander black-majority areas into larger voting districts that contained a white majority. Lawsuits in the late 1960s and early 1970s successfully established the discriminatory nature of this tactic, but the legislature delayed changing the size of its districts as long as possible. As the 1975 elections approached, Mississippi was the only Deep South state that still had multimember legislative districts. During debate in the Senate over legislative reapportionment, Charles Evers led a delegation of black leaders to the Capitol to press for a new redistricting plan. When Senator Troy Watkins of Natchez asked the Senate to suspend its rules to allow Evers to address the all-white chamber, a voice vote loudly defeated his motion. Evers headed to the podium anyway, noting, "You suspend the rules for everyone else. I have a right to speak." Bill Burgin called for the sergeant-at-arms, who removed Evers from the room. Winter was absent from the Senate that morning, but when he returned that afternoon, he arranged for Evers to meet with him and the Senate Elections Committee the following day, which resulted in a "cordial and productive" meeting on the reapportionment issue. A few weeks later, however, the Senate decided to do nothing about legislative reapportionment, with only four senators dissenting from the decision: John Corlew, Carroll Ingram, Theodore Smith of Corinth, and James Molpus of Clarksdale. Eventually, the Senate compromised on its position by approving a House measure that eliminated multimember districts in three of the state's most populous counties: Hinds, where Jackson is located, and the Gulf Coast counties of Harrison and Jackson. The federal courts approved this extended delay in the state's other counties and put off the complete elimination of the multimember districts until 1976, thereby diminishing the full impact of black voting on legislative elections until the next statewide contests in 1979.[26]

Beyond politics, Winter's Presbyterian faith also faced ongoing strife over adjustment to a post–Jim Crow society. In 1973, the southern Presbyterian church split into two groups. Although a number of theological issues played a role in the division, racial concerns were part of the equation. Many white Southerners perceived the Presbyterian Church in the U.S. (PCUS), the "southern branch" of Presbyterianism, as too liberal on a range of fronts, including its acceptance of racial integration. The new Presbyterian Church of America (PCA) attracted congregations across the South, with the largest number of defecting groups coming from Mississippi: 60 of the state's 128 Presbyterian churches. Many of Jackson's Presbyterians ultimately joined the PCA, but Winter's church, Fondren Presbyterian, which had a long history of racial moderation and had made its peace with the black civil rights movement a decade earlier, stayed with the PCUS. Just as some white Mississippians were dismayed over Winter's support for school integration, Winter also lost political allies among Mississippi Presbyterians who saw his continuing membership in a PCUS congregation as "identifying with what were perceived to be liberal trends in the church."[27]

Despite the ongoing struggles to create a post–civil rights polity in Mississippi, the state gradually entered a new era. One relic of the old days, the State Sovereignty Commission, remained intact in the early 1970s. Although the agency had monitored the conflicts over school integration in 1970 and 1971, the commission had little real business by the time the Waller administration took office. Winter had opposed the agency since the time of its creation in 1956. After the 1971 elections, both Waller and Winter delayed and then reluctantly named their required appointees to the agency. The governor and lieutenant governor had ex-officio membership on the commission, but neither of them attended the scheduled monthly meetings, though both sent representatives. In 1973, after the legislature once again approved funding for the Commission, Governor Waller vetoed the bill. In June 1973, Winter attended his first meeting of the Sovereignty Commission so he could confirm the governor's veto of its funds and acknowledge the end of the spy agency. The Sovereignty Commission closed its doors later that month, but the legislature did not officially abolish the agency until 1977.[28]

By the time the Sovereignty Commission ceased to operate, Winter's racially moderate views, a mark of wild radicalism to many white Mississippians a decade earlier, no longer attracted much notice. Winter welcomed the changing racial attitudes he saw and believed that the future of black-white relations in the state held great promise. Addressing a convention of community action groups sponsored by the federal Office of Economic Opportunity in August 1974, Winter noted that, until quite recently, most whites in the state "had been kidding themselves about the hopes and aspirations of the black community," yet he took heart in the realization that cooperation between blacks and whites "has come a long way." Winter knew as well that Mississippi still had a long way to go toward creating a real biracial society, as the continuing battles over black political power, school integration, and integrated religious practice made painfully clear.[29]

ౝ

The years of Winter's term as lieutenant governor coincided with a growing citizen distrust of politicians and government at all levels. Such cynicism intensified as facts of the Watergate burglary and cover-up emerged and dominated the national headlines in 1973 and 1974. Throughout Winter's long public career, most Mississippians had regarded him as an honest politician, a public servant with impeccable integrity. In 1972, he had pushed through the Senate Rules Committee a requirement that Senate proceedings remain open, an act that earned him the Margaret Dixon Freedom of Information Award from the Louisiana-Mississippi Associated Press. Yet even William Winter would face questions about his ethics. The skepticism about Winter's integrity demonstrated how low the esteem of all politicians had plunged by the early 1970s and how standards of public ethics were shifting. Winter responded to his critics with typical equanimity, while he worked to secure passage of measures designed to restore trust in Mississippi politicians and state government.

Questions about Winter's public ethics arose in 1973 after the legislature took action to strengthen the General Legislative Investigating Committee (GLIC), which oversaw the operation of state agencies and state personnel. Created in 1946, in its first two decades, the GLIC used its broad powers to investigate charges of communism lodged against state employees, such as Winter's former professor Jim Silver, and to probe civil rights incidents, such as the melee surrounding James Meredith's admission to Ole Miss. By the early 1970s, the GLIC, composed of three representatives and three senators, had become, according to one press account, "little more than a touring group of legislators." One noteworthy exception was the enthusiastic determination by one of its members, Senator Theodore Smith, to root out corruption and inefficiency in state government. In 1972, Winter renamed Smith to the GLIC, even though a number of people, especially county supervisors, urged Winter to leave Smith off the list. Brusque and demanding, Smith typically annoyed his fellow senators as much as the objects of his official investigations.[30]

Because of the general ineffectiveness of the GLIC, the legislature created the Joint Legislative Committee on Performance Evaluation and Expenditure Review (PEER) in 1973 to replace the older agency. In addition to its legislative members, five from each chamber, PEER had a professional staff. Winter, who would select the Senate's members, immediately became embroiled in a controversy when Senator Smith asked Winter to appoint him to the new committee. The legislation creating PEER, for good reason, prohibited the appointment of any legislator who also served in any other capacity for a state agency. As chair of the Senate Public Health and Welfare Committee, Smith automatically had a seat on the Mississippi Medicaid Commission. Smith volunteered to resign from the Medicaid commission, but according to the rules, Smith would have to resign his committee chairmanship to forgo the Medicaid commission position. Since Smith did not offer to make that move, the lieutenant governor did not include him on his list of nominees. Given Smith's vigorous work on the GLIC attacking county supervisors, Winter's decision not to appoint him to PEER appeared to some an indication that the lieutenant governor did not want a bulldog on the committee, and the *Greenville Delta Democrat-Times* editorialized that Winter was "a man anxious to appease every single pressure group in the state."[31]

A few months later an offhand remark renewed questions about the motive behind Winter's appointments. In a speech to the Mississippi Association of Supervisors, Winter talked about the need for reform of county government—a position Smith favored and most supervisors opposed. However, Winter also offered customary words of kindness for the head of the supervisors' organization, Edward Khayat, an old friend who had pled no contest earlier in the year to charges of federal tax evasion. Criticism of Winter soon followed, including from the Mississippi Coast Crime Commission, which had called for Khayat's resignation. Theodore Smith also chimed in, charging that Winter was "going to bed with the supervisors." Winter was surprised at the negative portrayals of his comments, but the uproar became so loud that he had to deny publicly that he had "sold out" to the supervisors.[32]

Later that summer, at the annual Neshoba County Fair, Winter offered a possible solution to the widespread concern about unethical government officials: open meetings legislation. He had pushed for open government meetings as far back as 1956, and he had proposed such a measure in his opening remarks to the legislature in 1972. Although Senator Corbet Patridge introduced a bill that year, it never gained any traction in the session and died in committee. When the legislature reconvened in January 1974, both the House and Senate proposed open meetings and records legislation, and Winter offered strong support for the measures. However, the legislature did not pass an open meetings bill until 1975, a less-than-comprehensive law that still allowed for closed meetings of government bodies as long as they followed a set of established procedures.[33]

In the months preceding the 1975 session, a House subcommittee studying the question of ethics and open meetings legislation held a series of hearings. Senator Smith presented testimony and brought up an ethics charge against the lieutenant governor. Smith claimed that Winter, by virtue of his position, served on the A & I Board and that his law firm had earned hundreds of thousands of dollars in legal fees representing local governmental entities doing business with the Board. In short, Smith charged that Winter used his position in state government to advance his own personal financial interest. Questioned by reporters about the accusations, Winter called them "grossly overstated and inaccurate." He denied any conflict of interest: "I have been extremely careful not to involve myself or my law firm in that kind of situation." Winter also claimed that his firm had not handled any bonds "issued or approved by the State Bond Commission." A few weeks after the ethics hearings, Smith lodged another charge against Winter, that he made "excessive" use of state aircraft. Citing official records, the senator said Winter had made 120 flights in the previous thirteen months. The lieutenant governor did not challenge Smith's calculations but claimed that all the trips were made as part of his official duties. "I make no apologies," he told the press. While Winter's use of state planes did not violate any laws, questions about his prudence in using the state's limited tax revenues had added urgency since Winter had already unofficially launched his 1975 campaign for governor, which necessarily blurred the line between Winter's lieutenant governor duties and his campaign activities. Smith's attacks, though likely prompted in large part by the lieutenant governor's failure to appoint the senator to PEER, highlighted that the actions of all public officials would face greater scrutiny in the post-Watergate era—even for leaders like Winter with a solid record of honesty and trustworthiness. The mere appearance of impropriety could lead to serious questions.[34]

᎒Ꮬ

Although Winter managed to secure some of his legislative priorities while leading the Senate, the position of lieutenant governor was not his ideal job. At the end of 1972, Winter told his friend Larry Noble that the office was both "rewarding and frustrating." It allowed him to "keep my hand in state politics," but he regretted that the position did not give him "access to the center of [the] decision-making process." Of course, Winter underestimated the potential power he could have wielded as lieutenant governor, but he had no interest in serving the multiple consecutive terms necessary to achieve that level of influence. Winter's ambivalence about the position he held led some political observers to criticize him as a weak, ineffective, and overly cautious legislative leader; commentators attributed these faults to the fact that Winter wanted to avoid alienating future voters. By the middle of Winter's term as lieutenant governor, he was indeed actively preparing for another gubernatorial campaign. An internal memo written in 1973 by Wilson Golden, who increasingly worked on political matters for Winter, noted that the lieutenant governor had "steered clear of many controversial issues" and was "maintaining a low-profile." As lieutenant governor Winter provided the kind of leadership he had always offered Mississippians: honest, competent, forward-looking public service. He advocated forcefully for many positions he believed important and frequently used the tools at his disposal to help shape key legislation. However his critics had a point. Winter aspired to be governor.[35]

9

A TALE OF TWO CAMPAIGNS

William Winter made two more campaigns for the Mississippi governor's office in the 1970s. In 1975, he began as the clear favorite but lost because of a failure to appreciate the increasing importance of image in appealing to voters and because he could not capitalize fully on two of his most important qualities: his reputation as an honest and experienced politician and his history as a racial moderate. Winter almost abandoned politics after this defeat, but in 1979, at the eleventh hour, he decided to make another attempt to win the governor's chair. He defeated a female candidate in the Democratic primary and bested a fellow white racial moderate in the general election.

Soon after the 1972 legislature had concluded its work, Winter's preparations to run in the 1975 governor's race began. He and key members of his Senate staff—Jesse White, Bill Gartin, Wilson Golden, Ricky Fortenberry, James Peden—along with other important supporters like Warren Hood, began in the summer of 1972 to hold periodic political strategy sessions at Winter's Capitol office or at the Winter home. National political advisers occasionally stopped by to offer guidance, including Matt Reese, who had first worked on the John F. Kennedy campaign in 1960. One consultant, Roy Pfautch, of Civic Service Inc. in St. Louis, advised Winter in early 1973 that he needed to work on "long range image development," which was "continually increasing in today's political market place." In the fall of 1973, the campaign selected Peter Hart of Washington, D.C., to undertake polling and political analysis for the campaign. Winter's friend Tom Bourdeaux dubbed him the "fast gun from the East." Some of Winter's advisers thought the campaign should conceal Hart's involvement, since many Mississippians remained, if no longer advocates of a "closed society," at least somewhat suspicious of outsiders.[1]

Winter's potential opposition in the upcoming race did not seem very formidable. The polls Peter Hart conducted in late 1973 and 1974 showed Winter as the apparently unbeatable frontrunner. The main contender appeared to be one of his opponents for lieutenant governor in 1971, Cliff Finch. Since his defeat, Finch had continued to stump around the state, especially in the rural districts. Most political observers, however, did not take Finch seriously. The other major candidate to emerge by the beginning of 1975 was a former mayor of Columbia and south Mississippi district attorney, Maurice Dantin, who was backed by Governor Waller. When Hart conducted a new series of polls in early 1975, they confirmed the early results. Winter remained the choice of more than 65 percent of the voters. Finch and Dantin each pulled less than 10 percent of the vote.[2]

Although the polling numbers suggested that Winter could easily win in 1975, Hart's analysis of the data revealed some potential pitfalls. More than anything else, the surveys suggested that Mississippi voters, like those around the country in the wake of Watergate, wanted a candidate who "represents change." Hart's breakdown of the numbers showed that the campaign had a clear choice: "either to heed the voters' cry for change, or to hope that the candidate's present lead will be enough to sustain him." Whatever Winter did, he had to "avoid being seen as the candidate of the status quo" and "being supported by the big business interests." Hart advised that Winter should "personify the kind of leadership and responsiveness the voters are looking for." Campaign associates had already noted that Winter was "stiff" and "lacks warmth." A candidate of change would need to convey a more personable, down-to-earth image. According to the polling data, the specific qualities voters wanted in their next governor were "leadership, integrity, ability, and Christian compassion," all attributes Winter had in abundance. Experience in government, however, had less importance for voters (and perhaps could even be a detriment). Voters wanted a leader who had "the ability to get things done" and one "who understands and works for the average person." Hart suggested that Winter should emphasize his proven ability to deal with the legislature, without being controlled by it. In addition to Peter Hart's detailed analysis of the mood of Mississippi voters, which ran to forty-seven pages, Winter heard from supporters who sensed the same attitudes and saw them as a potential quagmire for the lieutenant governor. Bob Riser, a former mayor of Batesville, told Winter in February 1975 that he perceived "an attitude of the public that change is being sought; that there is generally a lot of dissatisfaction and unrest." Riser urged Winter not to enter the governor's race, but rather, to seek the next U.S. Senate seat that became available.[3]

For the most part, the Winter campaign rejected Hart's analysis and decided to follow a strategy that leaned heavily on Winter's record and experience, much as he had done in previous races. At Winter's kickoff for his campaign in June 1975 at the Mississippi Trade Mart in Jackson, the candidate reminded voters that he had prepared for the office his entire life, and that he could offer Mississippians "my training, my knowledge, my character." A Winter brochure proclaimed, "Winter is the only candidate in this Governor's race with the real experience and proven ability to do the job." Another Winter campaign brochure accurately described Winter's strengths, although they were not attributes that necessarily made the candidate seem an exciting man of the people or an agent of change: "The Quiet Man Nobody Owns, Everybody Respects. William Winter is one of those easy, quiet men you read about in the history books. But seldom in the headlines. Not a grand-stander or a glad-hander, William Winter has always had more faith in hard work than loud talk." Winter campaign ads often carried tag lines like "William Winter. The Difference is Know-How" and "Others Promise. Only William Winter Campaigns on Performance." At the same time, the campaign heeded some of Hart's suggestions. It tried to show Winter as more than a "pinstriped, fancy-pants, downtown bond attorney," or an establishment politician. The campaign made a concentrated effort "to de-formalize" Winter—dampen his polished, intellectual demeanor and make him appear more of a warm and friendly down-home guy. John Dittmer, a historian at Tougaloo College, expressed the attitude even some Winter supporters had about his image when the professor told Jim Silver that Winter "does all the right things, but lacks the charisma us Mississippians love." In an effort to create a new persona, in campaign ads and on the campaign trail, Winter would generally shed his suit jacket and loosen his tie. The campaign slogan became "Elect William Winter Governor. He's for real." A new, more laid-back and average-guy persona for Winter, however, rang hollow for many voters.[4]

In addition to emphasizing his experience, Winter hoped to stress in the 1975 campaign his well-earned reputation as an honest and principled public servant. Events, however, conspired against Winter's effort to capitalize fully on this key aspect of his political career. The flap created by the ill-timed Khayat remark in Biloxi and Theodore Smith's ethics charges muddied the potential of the message. In addition, Winter continued to underestimate how skeptical the public had become of all politicians. In late 1974 Senator Smith proposed a law mandating limits on spending in political campaigns. Governor Waller supported Smith's proposed bill, but Winter thought the law unnecessary, believing that as long as candidates made "full disclosure of sources of contributions," there was "no need for a maximum limitation." When Winter quickly dismissed Smith's proposal, the press criticized him for his opposition to campaign spending limits. Apprehensive that Winter was simply "not interested in making it easier for any would-be opponent in the gubernatorial race in 1975," the *Greenville Delta Democrat-Times* noted, "What is good for William Winter is not necessarily good for Mississippi." To emphasize his standing as an honest politician, prior to making an official announcement of his candidacy for governor, Winter released his personal financial records to the press, along with a statement reminding voters that he had always "strongly and vigorously fought for a policy of open meetings, honesty and integrity in government, and open-door access to public officials by the people."[5]

Another thread in Winter's long political career that the campaign thought might aid in his election was his history as a white politician who had avoided a hard-line segregationist stance during the civil rights battles. Racial concerns did not dominate the 1975 contest, but the issue had not entirely disappeared. Winter's moderate stance on race, however, had ceased to be an issue; as one political veteran observed, "Times have changed, and the Mississippi political climate has caught up with William Winter." A newspaper editor from south Mississippi put the matter more bluntly and used language that revealed the persistence of old attitudes: "This time they can't hang the nigger around William's neck like they did eight years ago. Race no longer controls the race." Yet, "down under the surface," some whites considered Winter "soft" on preserving whatever white privilege might still be salvaged in the post-civil rights era.[6]

With white racial attitudes in flux, Winter proceeded cautiously. Early on, the campaign planned to utilize young black leaders supportive of

Winter to canvass for votes in the black community. Concerned about lingering racial animosities, however, Winter hesitated to make any kind of bold public statement embracing the black constituency of the Democratic Party. In January 1975, Aaron Henry, head of the Loyalist faction that then controlled the state's Democratic machinery, invited Winter to give the opening remarks at a Democratic Party meeting and announce his desire for a unified Democratic Party. A month earlier, an integrated delegation of Mississippi Democrats had attended the party's mid-cycle mini-convention in Kansas City, and their hopes soared that the state Democratic Party would soon reunite. Wilson Golden thought Winter's attendance at the party meeting would "demonstrate the kind of leadership in party/political affairs which a large number of politically active blacks and progressive whites are looking for," but Winter declined the invitation. He believed that taking sides in the ongoing dispute within the party would cost him as many votes among the more "conservative elements" as any new supporters he might gain.[7]

For much of the first primary campaign, the Winter strategy seemed to be working. Polls showed that little of Winter's early support had evaporated; into the middle of July, the surveys still suggested that he could win in the first primary in early August with more than 55 percent of the vote. The campaign had allocated much of its primary budget of more than $500,000 to advertising (TV, radio, newspaper, billboards). Although Winter traveled around the state making speeches, political advertising played a much bigger role in 1975 than it had in 1967. The television ads produced, however, did not reach the standards of excellence and innovation of Winter's first gubernatorial campaign. Large sums of advertising money went to lengthy broadcasts. A thirty-minute campaign documentary aired on eleven network stations during early July, and on the night before the first primary vote, the campaign broadcast on TV outlets around the state a fifteen-minute replay of the June Kickoff Rally. These long television pieces seemed more appropriate for the political TV of the 1950s and early 1960s than to the faster-paced mid-1970s, when short, quick ads were proving the best way to get out a candidate's "message." In addition, critics widely mocked the campaign slogan. On one billboard near West Point, some prankster had altered the tag line to read, "Elect William Winter Governor. He's for rent." Despite these problems, many of the state's major newspapers, including the largest one, the *Jackson*

Clarion-Ledger, endorsed Winter before the first primary. The *Greenville Delta Democrat-Times*, reasoning that none of the three major candidates had distinguished himself in a "low-key, occasionally dull" campaign, endorsed Winter for exactly the reason the candidate had stressed: his experience, "a commodity which William Winter has in abundance." The paper also observed that Winter's career "has been marked by a thread of decency which was almost unique in Mississippi's politics of the 1950s and 1960s."[8]

If some in the press thought the 1975 governor's race a bit colorless, they had not paid attention to one of Winter's opponents: Cliff Finch ran an exciting campaign that attracted both black and white voters. Finch, a former district attorney and a successful damage-suit lawyer, had been a strong supporter of Ross Barnett and a vocal defender of massive resistance in the early 1960s. Although Finch's law practice probably brought in two to three times Winter's salary in 1975, he ran as the "working man's candidate." His campaign events consisted of performing various types of manual labor at locations around the state: driving a bulldozer at a Jackson construction site, running a dragline in the Delta, plowing a field in his home county of Panola, working on a shrimp boat off the Gulf Coast, bagging groceries in a Jackson supermarket, driving a truck down the Mississippi highways. The media covered all these actions, which became the center of Finch's advertising campaign. At speaking engagements, to further symbolize his working-class sympathies, Finch would place a big, black lunch box filled with bologna sandwiches on the podium while he talked. Most of Mississippi's political establishment, Winter included, dismissed Finch's actions as a "gimmick." But the "lunch-pail campaign" resonated with voters. In Winter's kickoff speech in June, he made an oblique reference to Finch's campaign tactics, "I am convinced the people do not want a clown or stuntman leading you for four years. I think you yearn for an authentic, genuine, and real Governor who will . . . represent you with feeling and dignity." Finch picked up on the remark and used it to cement his alliance with the common folk of Mississippi, telling voters that he did not think himself better than "anybody else who is working by the sweat of his brow. If they call them rednecks, clown, or whatever, then I'm proud to be one."[9]

Winter remained convinced that voters would eventually see through Finch's antics and choose experience over what seemed a superficial attempt to identify with the working class. The election may have played out that way, but an attack launched by Winter's other main opponent, Maurice Dantin, drastically changed the dynamics of the first primary race in the closing weeks. Deloss Walker of Memphis, who had assisted Bill Waller in his successful 1971 contest, directed Dantin's media campaign. The Dantin team thought they had a chance to win if they could get into the second primary with Winter. They looked for an issue to cut into Winter's big lead and solidify Dantin's second-place position. Early in the campaign, Dantin revived the charge that Winter had improperly directed state business to his bond law practice while serving as lieutenant governor. Dantin claimed Winter should have resigned from his law firm when he became lieutenant governor, hardly a reasonable proposition considering the post paid only a small, part-time salary. At first, the accusations garnered little notice, but the Dantin campaign had reserved the majority of its campaign funds for use in the final two weeks. Walker, emerging as a master among southern political consultants in using television in political races, helped craft an avalanche of thirty-second TV spots that hammered at the issue of Winter's "unethical" behavior.[10]

The Winter campaign at first ignored the charges, and then it responded by decrying the "desperate, deliberate falsehoods." Trying to explain, in a short rebuttal TV spot, the intricacies of state bond business to demonstrate that Winter had done nothing wrong proved almost impossible. When Dantin repeated his attack on Winter at the Neshoba County Fair, Winter claimed that some people would try anything to get elected governor, including using a "brand of pig pen politics you've heard here this afternoon." In an atmosphere where distrust of politicians had reached an all-time high, the Dantin offensive proved effective, despite the inaccuracies of the attacks. Winter told a Greenville audience that he did not believe Mississippians "are going to fall for the idea that suddenly after twenty-five years in public life William Winter can't be trusted." A telephone poll conducted by Hart the weekend after the first primary revealed, however, that a two-week barrage of well-designed television ads had seriously undermined Winter's longstanding reputation as an honorable and reputable politician.[11]

Although Dantin's strategy succeeded in slicing Winter's support below the 50 percent he needed to avoid a runoff, Dantin also undermined his own position. On election day, Winter's support dropped to just over 36 percent. Finch collected 32 percent of the vote to finish second and earn a runoff with Winter, while Dantin, who had been polling in second place behind Winter for much of the first primary race, dropped to third with less than 23 percent of the vote. Winter won in thirty-eight of eighty-two counties, polling particularly well in the majority-black Delta, the Gulf Coast, most of the Jackson metro area (except for Rankin County), and parts of north Mississippi. His support was the weakest in most of the white-majority areas of east and south Mississippi. In the south Mississippi counties of Lamar and Marion, Dantin's home territory, Winter received only 17 percent of the vote. As Winter's stock declined, support for Finch surged.[12]

In an effort to force Finch to engage in more than gimmicks, Winter challenged his second primary opponent to a debate. Winter believed that although Finch's working gigs "dramatized a position"—that Mississippi had a lot of working folks who needed a friend in the governor's chair—his actions did not suggest "solutions to the problems he's talking about." About the only concrete proposal Finch had ventured was his MIDAS program, the Mississippi Internal Development Assistance System, which as Winter pointed out, seemed little more than "a massive appropriation out of the state treasury, that comes from taxes of the working people of Mississippi." Claiming that "government is too important to be resolved by press agentry gimmicks," Winter urged Finch (and the voters) to "put us in the ring together, look us over, and see which one of us comes out the best." Finch declined Winter's offer by saying that Winter had turned down an offer for a debate in the 1971 lieutenant governor's race and that Finch was "too busy to give Winter a platform."[13]

The Winter campaign also tried to tarnish the Finch reputation by raising questions about a potential New Orleans Mafia connection to his campaign, a story first reported by Mississippi journalist Bill Minor in the *New Orleans Times-Picayune*. The upshot of the controversy was that a full-time worker in the Finch campaign, William Netterville, was a colleague of New Orleans mob boss Carlos Marcello and that significant financial contributions to Finch from the New Orleans area were possibly connected to Marcello. Finch, out shrimping in the Mississippi Sound the day Winter raised his questions about his opponent's New Orleans connection, called the charges "ridiculous," and nothing ever surfaced to confirm the Marcello ties to the Finch campaign.[14]

During the second primary campaign, Finch continued with his lunch-pail tour, and Winter resumed his strategy of highlighting his political experience and knowledge. A new slogan replaced the bland "He's for real" line: "Elect William Winter Governor. A statesman. Not a stunt man." The Finch approach, despite its apparent shortcomings as a real political platform, captivated more and more voters, a fact Winter became painfully aware of when he returned to the campaign trail. Shaking hands with workers at shift changes was a common tactic Winter had used without incident in the first primary race; he found that the same workers now refused to shake his hands, telling Winter, "You ain't one of us" or "We're for Finch! You come down here and work beside us like Finch does." Elise Winter, working a 5:00 a.m. shift change at the Ingalls Shipyard in Pascagoula, handed out her husband's card, only to see most of the workers promptly toss them on the ground.[15]

Winter tried to counter Finch's working-man appeal by continuing to highlight the problems the state needed to address, along with his own experience to get the job done. Those who knew Winter realized that he had as much or more in common with the working people as Cliff Finch. Winter reminded the voters of his own rural background, but he could not bring himself to claim that such a past carried more importance than his vast experience in state government. Speaking to reporters, Winter noted, "I have probably driven a tractor more than my opponent has, but I am not saying that driving a tractor would qualify me to be governor." At a campaign rally in Cleveland, attended by many from the working class, Winter offered too much honesty about what the governor could do to help citizens recover from the economic recession that plagued the state and the country. He warned the gathered crowd, "The key is not some MIDAS program. It's getting people better qualified to hold down more jobs." That effort would require "hard work" to improve education and to bring new industry to Mississippi. At the same time, Winter claimed no one could "wave a fairy wand and make jobs for everybody in Mississippi."[16]

Winter's logic may have been impeccable, but the message did not resonate with voters struggling to get by in a tough economy. Although Winter had the more thoughtful and reasonable message, Finch came across, in his personal appearances and in television ads (now more important than personal interactions with voters) as the true "friend" of the working people. After the election, Winter realized how important image had become in selecting political leaders. He told a friend that Finch succeeded because he could attract "a lot of people who are impressed with showmanship and gimmicks in the kind of media campaigns that now seem to be effective."[17]

Ironically, given the political background of the two candidates, Finch convinced significant numbers of black voters he could best be their champion. Although Winter had the credentials of a lifelong racial moderate and Finch had enthusiastically supported massive resistance, Finch portrayed the image of the true friend of black Mississippians. When Miss Jackson State, Helen Jean Ford of Hattiesburg, won the Miss Black America pageant during the second primary campaign, Finch met her at the Jackson airport on her return to Mississippi. The media captured the moment, and a photo of Finch hugging the black beauty queen beamed around the state. John Dittmer thought this one action garnered "a helluva lot of black votes" for Finch. A Finch television ad showed the candidate in front of his Batesville church talking about his experiences as a youth with a black man. The spot suggested a white man who liked black people, cared about them, and would be their friend if elected governor.[18]

While Winter secured the endorsement of Aaron Henry, state chairman of the National Association for the Advancement of Colored People (NAACP) and head of the Loyalist Democrats, it was not exactly a ringing affirmation. Henry claimed that Winter's record was "not as good as I would want it to be for our governor, but it is better than anyone else who is running for that office." At the same time, Charles Evers blasted Winter by claiming he was "part of the old establishment. He's sort of pretended he was for blacks, for equality for all of us, but he's never proven it." Although Evers claimed he had voted for Winter in past elections, he said, "He was the least of two evils before. This time, he's the evil one." Winter was both surprised and disappointed at the "defection" of a significant part of the black vote to Finch. Winter had long advocated that blacks and whites in Mississippi had to work together to move forward, and now Finch had actually succeeded in creating a successful alliance somewhat along those lines. The partnership Winter had envisioned, unlike Finch's, would include middle- and upper-class whites, a cross-class and biracial coalition of Mississippians who shared "progressive ideals."[19]

With almost 58 percent of the vote, Finch scored one of the largest victories ever over an opponent in a Mississippi gubernatorial primary runoff. Winter added fewer than fifty thousand additional votes to his first primary total, while Finch received almost two hundred thousand more votes in the second primary. Winter won only sixteen counties, with his best showings still in the Delta, on parts of the Gulf Coast (although he lost the most populous county there, Harrison), and in the more urban areas of the state. One of Winter's old friends correctly analyzed Winter's two gubernatorial losses. In 1967, many whites had considered Winter "too liberal" on race to be the governor. In 1975, many poorer, rural whites and large numbers of blacks thought Winter was "too conservative" on economic issues to enter the governor's mansion.[20]

After the election, Winter, then fifty-two, resolved to build a career beyond politics. As he prepared to leave the lieutenant governor's office, he chaired a joint session of the House and Senate, where he received a rousing ovation and thunderous applause. When asked about his future political plans, Winter told the press that "right now, it would be hard to conceive of getting back into politics," although he added that "I will let the future take care of itself." Reflecting on the 1975 race, Winter said he had no regrets or bitterness but many frustrations: "at a point when I think I possessed maximum ability to serve the people, I was unable to get this across to them." Many greeted Winter's apparent exit from politics with sadness. An editorial in the *Greenville Delta Democrat-Times* summarized these feelings and noted that Winter was leaving "public life, perhaps for good, and state government will be the poorer for his absence." The paper also offered an evaluation of Winter's political career: "He had deep, decent convictions about government, about democracy and about Mississippi in particular, and he held to them for more than 20 years as an elected official. There were times when he did not say all that he should have said, as we saw it, but few times indeed when he said or did that which he knew he should not."[21]

Even as Winter planned his exit from politics, he received an invitation in December 1975 to manage the Mississippi campaign for Jimmy Carter's 1976 presidential bid. The Georgia governor impressed Winter, but like almost everyone else at the time, he remained skeptical about Carter's chances to become president. In addition to his wariness about

becoming involved in another losing campaign, Winter declined the over-
ture from the Carter camp because he truly did need some time away
from the political scene and looked forward to returning to his law practice. Winter made a few speeches for Carter in the fall of 1976 and witnessed the reuniting of the state Democratic Party after a dozen years of
battle. Winter told Jim Silver that he "had to pinch myself at times to see
and believe the amalgam of people" that came together to support the
Carter candidacy. Winter welcomed "the *new* Mississippi politics which I
never thought I would see."[22]

For someone who had spent his entire adult life in politics, however,
completely forsaking public service proved difficult, if not impossible. In
June 1977 Winter asked Senator Stennis about the proposal to expand
the Fifth Circuit Court of Appeals or to split it into two districts. Either
option would mean new appeals court judges from Mississippi. Winter
told Stennis that he enjoyed working at his law firm, which was "doing
exceedingly well," but "my interests have lain in the area of governmental
service, and I have derived my greatest satisfaction from those efforts,
successful or not, that have been directed toward making our system of
government work as well as it can." Stennis agreed to recommend Winter if new judicial positions materialized. As it turned out, the effort to
transform the Fifth Circuit became bogged down in congressional politics
during the 1978 session, in part over concerns that Jim Eastland, chair of
the U.S. Senate Judiciary Committee, had pushed the change in order to
secure the nomination of more conservative judges in the Deep South.
Even if Congress had created new appellate judges in 1978, it is not clear
whether or not Eastland, who typically had a major say in new appointments, would have actually supported a Winter nomination. When Winter wrote to Eastland in March 1978 expressing his interest in one of the
potential new positions, Eastland responded to "Billy" with an exception-
ally brief response: "Your letter has been received. I will do my best in the
matter mentioned in your letter."[23]

On the other hand, Senator Eastland may have had less influence in
1978 than in the past over judicial appointments since he announced in
March that he would not seek a seventh term in the U.S. Senate. Bill
Waller had already declared that he would challenge Eastland in the
upcoming race, and after the senator decided to retire, three other familiar
candidates also decided to seek the Democratic nomination for Eastland's

seat: Maurice Dantin, Charles Sullivan, and Governor Cliff Finch. Winter could not help thinking the Senate race represented his opportunity to return to politics. As he observed at the time, "once you are indoctrinated with that political injection, like the old fire horse, you hear the bell ring and you want to break out and see where the fire is." He talked the matter over with friends and family but got "mixed reactions" from both, so he decided not to make the race. However, he still had the desire and ambition to seek public office. Another possibility was one more try for governor, especially since the Cliff Finch administration had become a disaster. Finch's leadership as governor proved as short on substance as his campaign, and corruption wracked his administration. As Winter watched the Finch administration unravel, he remembered the experience of his old political hero, Mike Conner, who won the governor's office in 1931 after two failed attempts. Winter also received a call on election night in 1978 from one of his old political mentors, J. P. Coleman, still a judge on the Fifth Circuit Court of Appeals, who expressed his opinion that Winter could win the governor's race in 1979. Winter, however, remained uncertain whether he should try again. Then, one afternoon in January 1979, he met Bill Cole on the streets of Jackson.[24]

Cole, an assistant attorney general, had worked for Winter during the 1967 race for governor while a student at Hinds Junior College and helped in subsequent Winter campaigns. In 1979, Cole was advising one of the lieutenant governor hopefuls, John Ed Ainsworth, and told Winter that the pollster Peter Hart was conducting a political preference survey for Ainsworth. The undertaking also included a poll for the governor's race. Cole asked Winter if they could include his name in the list of potential gubernatorial candidates. Three people had already entered the contest: Evelyn Gandy, the incumbent lieutenant governor and widely perceived frontrunner; John Arthur Eaves, a Jackson lawyer; and Jim Herring, former Madison County district attorney. Charlie Deaton, a legislator from Greenwood, and Richard Barrett, a lawyer and white supremacist from Hinds County, would later enter the race. Winter agreed to have his name entered in the survey, although he said he had no intentions of running. Several weeks later, Cole called to share the results: voters were seriously disillusioned with the Finch administration; most of the announced gubernatorial candidates generated little enthusiasm; and Winter was the only name on the list who had as much appeal as that of Gandy. To test the waters further, Winter sent out a letter in late March to several hundred of his long-time supporters asking for their opinions about whether he should run for governor again. One-quarter of the respondents told Winter that he should not run, an equal number expressed strong support for another Winter candidacy, and the remainder either failed to answer or remained unsure what Winter should do.[25]

With a lukewarm response from the people Winter considered his most loyal supporters, he was torn between fears of another defeat and his longtime political ambition of becoming Mississippi's governor. Continuing to weigh the decision, he sought further advice from Jesse White, then working in Senator Stennis's Washington, D.C., office, who suggested that Winter come up for a meeting with Peter Hart. Accompanied by Danny Cupit, a Jackson lawyer who had been active in the Young Democrats and in the reuniting of the two factions of the Democratic Party in 1976, Winter went to Washington. At the meeting, Hart was not encouraging, although he had great respect for Winter as one who represented "what is best in American politics." Upon his return to Jackson, Winter talked with Warren Hood, the finance chairman from his previous two gubernatorial runs, who indicated his willingness to make another race. Winter then sought the advice of another well-known political consultant, Bob Squier, who came to Jackson for a meeting. Squier asked Winter, "Why do you want to be governor of Mississippi?" Winter eagerly enumerated the reasons he had advocated throughout his political career: the state had not educated its people, it had not developed its economic or human resources, and it had adopted "a be-last position." One reason the state had fallen so far behind, Winter explained, was because of weak leadership at the top. Squier and Winter met with Hood, and they all agreed they could run an effective first primary campaign for about $250,000, with almost all of those funds dedicated to television advertising. On June 6, Winter announced his candidacy, in front of his family and about twenty skeptical supporters, at a press conference on the grounds of the state Capitol. It was two days before the filing deadline.[26]

The Winter primary campaign of 1979 was a "low-key" affair. As Winter began to plan his effort, he discovered that some of his old supporters had already signed on to work for other candidates. Winter, however, assembled a small but talented team. Jesse White became campaign manager, concentrating on strategy, polling, and media efforts. Bill Cole took a leave of absence from his assistant attorney general position and joined as campaign coordinator to run the day-to-day operations of the Winter organization. David Crews, who had just assumed a new position as editor of the *Winona Times*, left his job and became press director. Warren Hood would again serve as finance chairman. Peter Hart, despite his initial misgivings, agreed to conduct polling and provide analysis, and Bob Squier joined as media adviser. In Hart and Squier, Winter had perhaps the best talent of the day in identifying and understanding public opinion and in the effective use of political media.[27]

During the first primary campaign, Winter spent a good deal of time driving, rather than flying, around the state. His driver was Guy Gillespie, a Harvard graduate attending Ole Miss Law School who would later marry Winter's daughter Lele. Instead of arranging a series of political events at his destinations, Winter went to the home or office of a local supporter and called lists of Winter partisans and "prospective converts." He had a brief but personal message: he was in town and calling to ask for support in the upcoming race. Winter would frequently make a hundred calls over several hours. Next, he visited the local newspaper and radio station, which willingly provided some free publicity. Winter and Gillespie would sometimes cover two or three towns a day. The campaign had no billboard advertising and produced few signs and posters for distribution, as Hart's polling clearly showed that Winter already had a very high name recognition among voters.[28]

Unlike 1975, in the 1979 campaign, Winter's familiarity with state government and his long service as an honest and respected politician produced clear benefits. With the Finch administration plagued by ineffective leadership and scandal, Winter's early mantra became that he would "clean up the mess in Jackson." He offered voters a thoughtful six-point program to end corruption among public officials. A number of Squier's early television ads portrayed Winter as the "candidate ready to restore order and dignity to a state government in shambles." Instead of reading scripted copy in his political commercials, as he had done in the last race, Squier would go out with Winter and film hours of the candidate talking informally with voters and then pull out the "most authentic" and "most engaging nuggets" to use in the ads. Media developed later in the first primary race moved away a bit from the anti-Finch message and emphasized the issues that Winter had long advocated, including the need for better schools and more job opportunities.[29]

Most of the candidates in the first primary attracted black votes, confirming that the state had moved beyond the racially charged campaigns of earlier years. Winter, of course, reminded black voters of his long history of racial moderation, dating back to the massive resistance days of the late 1950s, but the basic message he delivered before all-black crowds did not differ from the one used for other audiences. Winter again secured the endorsement of Aaron Henry, head of the state NAACP, while the state's Black Mayors Conference officially backed Jim Herring, although some individual mayors favored Winter. Charles Evers, increasingly at odds with many black voters in the state, decided to support John Arthur Eaves, noting that "I just like plain old redneck crackers because when they tell you something, they mean it." When the votes were counted in the first primary election, Winter finished second, with 25 percent of the vote. Evelyn Gandy received 30 percent of the ballots; Eaves finished third with just under 20 percent.[30]

In the second primary, Winter faced off against Evelyn Gandy, who began her political career in the 1940s as an assistant to Senator Theodore Bilbo. Like Winter, her first elective office came as a member of the 1948 state legislature. The second woman ever elected to a statewide office in Mississippi, Gandy had served two terms as state treasurer, bracketing Winter's own stint in that office. She had also succeeded Winter as lieutenant governor. Hart's polling during the first primary campaign showed that in a head-to-head race with Winter, she would likely lose, in large part because of her gender. Winter and Hart agreed that they should avoid attacking Gandy directly. Voters would need to discover in other ways that, although they liked her personally, she might not have all the attributes required of the governor. Hart suggested "the importance of emphasizing that a governor must be tough, decisive, and a leader who is capable of saying no." Squier crafted a series of television ads to capitalize on Hart's perceptive analysis. In one key commercial, Winter was shown at the National Guard training facility in south Mississippi, Camp Shelby, standing on a tank and talking to some soldiers. The ad emphasized that the governor's job included serving as commander-in-chief of the Mississippi National Guard, a job most Mississippians at the time could hardly conceive a woman fulfilling. In a related ad featuring the National Guard,

Morrison Heights, Grenada, Mississippi, 2008. William H. Winter, great-grandfather of William F. Winter, purchased this house in the 1850s so that his children could receive an education in town, since no schools existed near his plantation more than ten miles away. Photograph by author.

William F. Winter on the knee of his grandfather, the Confederate veteran William B. Winter. The former Civil War soldier lived with William Winter and his parents until his death in 1929. Courtesy of Mississippi Department of Archives and History.

William Winter playing with the livestock on the Winter farm, late 1920s. Courtesy of Mississippi Department of Archives and History.

William Winter with his father, Aylmer Winter, a farmer and state legislator. In 1932, the nine-year-old boy spent three weeks attending the sessions of the Mississippi Senate with his father. Courtesy of Mississippi Department of Archives and History.

Jim Eastland and William Winter during the 1942 U.S. Senate campaign. Winter served as the driver for Eastland, who was making his first run for the U.S. Senate seat he would hold until 1978. Courtesy of Mississippi Department of Archives and History.

William Winter with his mother, Inez, during World War II, on the family farm in Grenada County. Courtesy of Mississippi Department of Archives and History.

Second Lieutenant William Winter at Fort McClellan, Alabama, 1945. Courtesy of Mississippi Department of Archives and History.

William Winter at the beginning of the 1948 legislative session. Elected to his first political office at the age of twenty-four while still at Ole Miss Law School, Winter served for nine years in the state legislature. Courtesy of Mississippi Department of Archives and History.

William Winter in the Philippines, 1946. In connection with his military duties, Winter traveled across the island of Luzon as an officer in the Eighty-Sixth Infantry Division. He is pictured here holding the spear of an Igorot tribesman in the mountains north of Baguio. Courtesy of Mississippi Department of Archives and History.

William Winter receiving his law degree at Ole Miss, May 1949. Courtesy of William F. Winter.

Chief Justice Robert Gillespie of the Mississippi Supreme Court swears William Winter in as state tax collector, 1956. Courtesy of Mississippi Department of Archives and History.

The state tax collector and his young family in 1960. Courtesy of Mississippi Department of Archives and History.

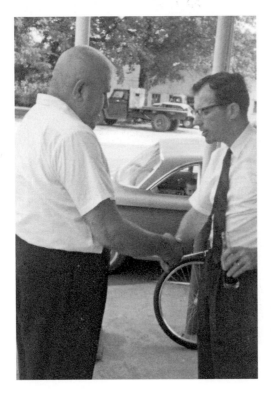

William Winter campaigning during the 1967 governor's race. Courtesy of Mississippi Department of Archives and History.

Handbill created during the second primary campaign of the 1967 election for governor, suggesting that black voters favored Winter in the contest. Though unattributed, supporters of John Bell Williams distributed the document during the campaign in an effort to diminish support for Winter's candidacy among white voters. Courtesy of William F. Winter.

This picture of the Winter family walking across the lawn of their Jackson home was used in campaign ads for the 1967 gubernatorial campaign. Pictured left to right are Eleanor, Anne, William Winter, Elise, and Lele. Courtesy of Mississippi Department of Archives and History.

Campaigning at the Neshoba County Fair during the 1971 lieutenant governor's contest. Courtesy of Mississippi Department of Archives and History.

Erle Johnston (left), Estelle Turner, and William Winter. Johnston and Winter, both from Grenada, gave a birthday party in 1973 for Turner, their favorite teacher from Grenada High School. Courtesy of Mississippi Department of Archives and History.

Elect William
WINTER
Governor

If you want a
public servant in the
Governor's office, not
a public relations
man . . .
If you want a
Governor who'll put
the people of
Mississippi above
his own ambitions . . .
If you want a man who has the real
experience, the real background and
ability to get things done, to move
Mississippi forward, then vote for
William Winter.

He's for real.

Campaign ad, 1975 governor's race.
The photo in the ad shows Winter with
a loosened tie, part of the effort during
the campaign to "de-formalize" his
public persona. Courtesy of Mississippi
Department of Archives and History.

Lieutenant Governor Winter on his
way to work at the Mississippi State
Capitol, 1975. Courtesy of Mississippi
Department of Archives and History.

William and Elise Winter talking to
a worker at the Ingalls Shipyard in
Pascagoula during the 1975 race for
governor. Winter lost the election to
Cliff Finch, who claimed the mantle
of the workingman's candidate during
the contest. Courtesy of Mississippi
Department of Archives and History.

William and Elise Winter wave to supporters early on what proved to be a disappointing election night, August 1975.

Inauguration Day, January 1980. Joining Governor and Elise Winter at the podium at the conclusion of the ceremony are Lieutenant Governor Brad Dye (left) and House Speaker Buddy Newman (right). Courtesy of Mississippi Department of Archives and History.

Governor-elect William Winter jogging, 1979, with three boys at the Chastain Junior High School track near his home. Courtesy of Mississippi Department of Archives and History.

Among the numerous Dinner at the Mansion events held during the Winter administration was one for Winter's friends from Grenada County. Here Winter poses with members of some of the families who had lived on the Winter farm. Courtesy of Mississippi Department of Archives and History.

William Winter at a 1982 Dinner at the Mansion for four distinguished Mississippi writers: Walker Percy, Margaret Walker Alexander, Eudora Welty, and Shelby Foote. Courtesy of William F. Winter.

William Winter and the family dog, Toby, 1980s. Courtesy of William F. Winter.

William Winter with the Boys of Spring at the time of the passage of the Education Reform Act, December 1982. Pictured from left to right are Andy Mullins, Dick Molpus, David Crews, Bill Gartin, John Henegan, William Winter, and Ray Mabus. Courtesy William F. Winter.

Governor William Winter with two of his political mentors, John Stennis (center) and J. P. Coleman (right), at the dedication ceremony for the remodeled Mississippi State Capitol, 1983. Courtesy of Mississippi Department of Archives and History.

Governor William Winter with journalist Bill Minor at the Neshoba County Fair, summer 1983. The sign in the background touts the candidacy of Dick Molpus for secretary of state, one of three Winter staffers to win statewide office in the 1983 election. Courtesy of Mississippi Department of Archives and History.

Caroline Kennedy presents William Winter with the 2008 Profile in Courage Award from the John F. Kennedy Presidential Library and Museum. Board Chairman Paul Kirk and Senator and Mrs. Ted Kennedy observe the presentation. Courtesy of William F. Winter.

President-elect Bill Clinton with William Winter, Renaissance Weekend, Hilton Head Island, South Carolina, December 1992. The two men became friends in 1980, when they served as governors of neighboring states. Courtesy of William F. Winter.

Elise and William Winter at their Jackson home, 2010. Courtesy of William F. Winter.

Statehood Day at the Old Capitol, December 9, 2011. Pictured from left to right: Kane Ditto, Jackson mayor (1989–1997) and president of the Board of Trustees of the Mississippi Department of Archives and History; William Winter; James Graves, Mississippi Supreme Court Justice (2001–2011), federal judge on the Fifth Circuit Court of Appeals (2011–); Reuben Anderson, Mississippi Supreme Court Justice (1985–1990). The address for the occasion was delivered by Judge Graves. Courtesy of William F. Winter.

Winter emphasized, "The Guard is the first line of national defense." Still other spots showed Winter taking target practice at a law enforcement firing range.[31]

The National Guard/firing range commercials had aired briefly during the first primary contest, but the Winter campaign pulled them over concerns that they would damage Gandy too much too soon. The Winter campaign strategy favored a runoff with Gandy. When the "macho" ads ran in the second primary campaign, they proved quite effective. Gandy's own commercials did not help the gender role perceptions, as some of her spots showed her talking to children or in a flower garden, the perfect images of a mother or a teacher, but not perhaps of the state's top leader. The slogan for the Winter campaign became, "William Winter for Governor, The Toughest Job in Mississippi," a phrase that emphasized the perceived advantages of a male candidate without mentioning Evelyn Gandy's gender. Winter, who sometimes referred to Gandy as "a fine, sweet lady" and questioned whether she would be able to provide "hard-nosed leadership," rejected suggestions that he played on gender fears and claimed he merely pointed out a difference in the leadership style of the two candidates. Squier, however, later admitted that he created a campaign message that "reinforced all the doubts voters would have about women," and the ads clearly worked to Winter's benefit.[32]

The Winter campaign emphasized that state government had to be "cleaned up," a job that would require "tough decisions." Winter's continued use of the floundering Finch administration as a foil remained a popular issue, and although Gandy offered similar promises, her association with the Finch regime (as lieutenant governor) harmed her, as well as reports that a number of leaders in the Finch administration favored Gandy over Winter because they thought they might keep their jobs if Gandy won the election. Winter claimed he would end "cronyism" in the appointments made to state boards and agencies. He also promised to eliminate the system of governor's colonels, an honorary staff of gubernatorial "advisers" appointed from every county. The colonels had originally developed to recognize a group of a governor's key supporters, and in the early days, the state actually issued them military uniforms. Over the years, a special coat replaced the uniform, and the number of colonels expanded significantly. Winter himself had served as a colonel during the J. P. Coleman administration. During the Finch administration, however, the colonel system had degenerated to a group of favored individuals who had paid a fee for the appointment and who primarily used their status to get out of traffic violations or other minor scrapes with the law by pointing to their government "credentials." Winter described the colonels as nothing more than "several hundred specially favored people in the state." He also connected his desire to straighten out state government with his larger vision for how to move forward: "The results of dishonesty and mismanagement are poor schools for our children, badly deteriorated roads on which we travel, and general neglect of the pressing needs of the people of our state."[33]

In the second primary campaign, Winter continued to receive support from areas where he had always done well, especially the state's more urban areas, but in 1979, even voters in the rural south and east Mississippi counties where he had done poorly in past elections, embraced his campaign. Dick Molpus, who had worked for Winter in the 1967 and 1975 campaigns, helped organize the 1979 effort in Neshoba County, where Winter had never done particularly well. Unlike those earlier contests, in 1979, Molpus had plenty of local residents who wanted to join the Winter campaign. Part of the new connection with rural and blue-collar white Mississippians undoubtedly resulted from Winter's "tough-guy" campaign but also reflected the different attitude Winter brought to this election contest. With two difficult campaigns for governor behind him and a small campaign organization in which he had complete confidence, Winter personally felt more relaxed and comfortable, and this disposition helped dispel the past complaints that Winter was "aloof" or "stiff," much more than a contrived image makeover (such as the loosened-tie look of 1975) could ever achieve.[34]

The Winter approach in 1979 proved a winning formula, and he triumphed over Gandy with almost 57 percent of the vote and finished first in all but fourteen counties. He prevailed in practically every south and east Mississippi county except Gandy's home county of Forrest, and he won a majority of the black vote, although Gandy made some of her best showings in several of the majority-black Delta counties that had earlier been among the most reliable parts of Winter country. When Winter appeared before his supporters at a Holiday Inn in Jackson that evening, he told them, "The clear message of tonight is our people want a change from the past and a commitment to the future."[35]

In the general election, Winter faced the Republican candidate Gil Carmichael, a businessman from Meridian who called himself a "progressive conservative" and who shared many of Winter's views about what Mississippi needed to do to move forward. In 1975, Carmichael, like Winter, had offered voters a record of intelligence and accomplishment but had also been vanquished by the Cliff Finch juggernaut. Carmichael entered 1979 with a strong organization and a sizeable campaign war chest, but a difficult Republican primary against conservative Delta cotton farmer Leon Bramlett, in the first contested Republican primary for governor in the state's history, diminished Carmichael's stature and his balance sheet. During the 1976 presidential primaries, Carmichael's support of Gerald Ford over Ronald Reagan had angered many of the more conservative political activists in the Mississippi Republican Party, as had his advocacy of gun control.[36]

Compared to Winter's summer campaign, the fall contest against Carmichael developed into a full-press effort. The paid campaign staff grew from five to ten. The candidate returned to flying around the state, in an effort to get himself and his message before the voters as much as possible. In addition to Winter's direct appeals to the voters, television advertising became especially important in the race against Carmichael. Overall, around 60 percent of the expenditures in the Winter campaign of 1979, which totaled more than $870,000, went to polling and television ads. The campaign saved most of the television commercials in the general election campaign for the last six weeks. Squier created a number of inventive and effective advertisements to counteract Carmichael's positions. For example, in response to Carmichael's suggestion that Mississippi could operate more effectively and frugally with fewer than eighty-two counties, a Winter TV spot showed a young boy playing with an eraser and a map of Mississippi and randomly erasing county lines; the ad implied that something only slightly less chaotic would occur if Carmichael became governor. The pitch worked. At a political event in Oxford, a woman from Harmontown, north of Oxford in Lafayette County, came up to Winter, and with a look of concern across her face, asked, "You're not going to put us over in Panola County, are you?" Winter wryly replied, "No, that's Mr. Carmichael."[37]

Carmichael, without much success, tried to sully Winter's standing as the frontrunner. In September, Carmichael reargued the "unethical bond lawyer" charges against Winter that had been raised in 1974 and 1975 by claiming that Winter had not done anything illegal but that his involvement in the local bond business created a conflict of interest. In addition to the bond practice charges, Carmichael tried to pin Winter down on the old matter of how much Winter had earned as state tax collector in the late 1950s and early 1960s. Carmichael claimed that Winter had used "public service for private gain" and would likely continue the practice as governor. Winter responded to Carmichael's innuendo by simply stating, "I never have and never will benefit improperly from any position of public office with which the voters entrust me." Even Carmichael admitted, "I don't doubt Mr. Winter has done everything in an honest way. I am sure it is all legitimate." Such an admission only made Carmichael's claims look like a desperate, baseless political attack. Even so, Carmichael continued to use the "unethical bond lawyer" charge in television ads and on the stump. Squier developed an effective response ad that showed someone pelting a map of Mississippi with blobs of mud. As the map disappeared, the voice-over simply said, "This is the kind of campaign that Mr. Carmichael is running; all he knows to do is throw mud at his opponent," and then the screen faded to black.[38]

Both candidates in the general election recognized the black vote as important to any winning strategy, and both sought to attract black voters by reference to their credentials as racial moderates. Carmichael had served on the advisory committee of the U.S. Commission on Civil Rights in the early 1970s and had made a strong appeal to black voters in his unsuccessful U.S. Senate race against Jim Eastland in 1972. Although Winter had an even more impressive history of racial moderation, during the campaign, Carmichael claimed he had the better record supporting black rights. The Republican candidate described Winter as a "parlor liberal." Carmichael noted that Winter worked at a large law firm that had no black workers, while he had long employed blacks in his car dealerships in east Mississippi. When the two candidates appeared at the state NAACP convention a week before the election, both men made their pitch as the best candidate for black voters, a far cry from the racial dynamics that had shaped Winter's first gubernatorial race twelve years earlier. Carmichael promised that as governor he would work to improve the economic situation for black citizens. Winter pointed to his long record as a racial moderate in a state that had vigorously fought against the black civil rights movement, reminding the NAACP delegates, "I spoke out for equal opportunity at a time when few public officials did so. Very frankly, those were costly positions for me. I probably would have been elected governor a long time ago if I hadn't put my neck on the line." Despite Carmichael's racially moderate credentials, his Republican Party label hurt him, as most blacks viewed Mississippi Republicans as a group seeking a "lily-white" alternative to the new biracial Democratic Party.[39]

On election day, November 6, Winter scored a decisive victory over Carmichael, winning 61 percent of the almost 700,000 votes cast. He won every county save three: Harrison and Jackson on the Gulf Coast, and Rankin, just across the Pearl River from Jackson. After Carmichael conceded, Winter addressed his supporters and told the crowd, "We will dedicate the next four years to righting the wrongs, providing the inspiration and the idealism that our people are looking for and to moving our state into a position of leadership in the sisterhood of states." The celebration continued well into the following morning, as a host of well-wishers offered Winter hearty congratulations. Looking ahead, Winter told one national reporter present, "Mississippi has wasted such energy fearing change and combating progress. Now we can do some things we should have been doing all along."[40]

The 1979 election also finally saw the beginning of the end of Mississippi's massive resistance to the Voting Rights Act of 1965. A federally imposed redistricting plan that resolved a fourteen-year lawsuit by civil rights groups against the state eliminated the use of multimember districts and resulted in the election of seventeen blacks to the state legislature (only five had served in the previous legislature). The *New York Times* editorialized that "generations of strife to bring democracy to Mississippi produced the election of many blacks to the legislature and a contest for governor free of racist appeals; William Winter won but all Americans can take pride in this truly national achievement."[41]

Winter had finally put together the kind of broad coalition he had long envisioned, one that embraced progressive change—improving Mississippi's educational system and providing better job opportunities for its citizens—and one that attracted black and white, poorer Mississippians, the middle-class, and business leaders. In many ways, Winter's message in 1979 mirrored the ones he had proposed in both 1967 and 1975. In 1967 the race issue sidetracked that message. In 1975 voters ignored Winter's

message altogether in the hope that a "working man" could magically produce economic salvation. On two occasions, Mississippians had rejected a
quiet voice of reason in favor of someone flashier but with less substance.
When George Street, public relations director at Ole Miss, who had first
met Winter when he attended law school, wrote to congratulate the governor-elect, Street also offered his appreciation of the Mississippi voters
"who moved at long last to the high plane of personal integrity where
William Winter has been waiting for such a long time." As Bill Minor
once noted, "Winter doesn't have the flashy personality, doesn't talk in
sound bites. There's just this dedication to public service, which, at any
given time, is appreciated by 48 percent of the people." In 1979, however,
a majority of Mississippi voters embraced his ideas and his leadership.
After thirty-two years in state politics, nine campaigns, and two defeats,
William Winter was the governor-elect of Mississippi.[42]

IO

GOVERNOR
WILLIAM WINTER

A New Image for Mississippi

The inaugural ceremonies for William Winter in January 1980 highlighted the intellectual and forward-looking approach the new governor
brought to his office and launched an administration that would help
transform the image of Mississippi in the eyes of her citizens and the rest
of the nation. Winter wanted an inaugural event that would be more
than "hoopla and parades." The day before the inauguration ceremony,
a symposium held at the Old Capitol—"Mississippi and the Nation in
the 1980s"—featured an impressive group of accomplished Mississippians: writers Eudora Welty and Margaret Walker Alexander, businessman
Doug Kenna, Catholic Bishop Bernard Law, noted physicist and University of Chicago vice-president Walter E. Massey, former University of
Alabama president Frank Rose, and *Time* magazine writer Frank Trip-
pett. Winter opened the proceedings by urging Mississippians to "not be
afraid to explore with the depths of our intellect . . . where we are and
where we have to go." The distinguished panel explained the dimensions
of what they saw as a largely hopeful road ahead. Alexander predicted
that Mississippi "stands on the threshold of a decade of destiny." Welty,
in her remarks, noted that Winter's election had "brought us hope: in our
lasting—I think everlasting—identity as Mississippians, and in the full
awareness and strength of that integrity, we assume, with you and your
leadership, our place in the nation as 1980 begins."[1]

The installation ceremony for governor normally would have occurred in front of the State Capitol, but since that building was undergoing renovations, the event moved to a location outside the Old Capitol building. Heavy rains, however, forced the ceremony inside, to the old House of Representatives chamber, where Mississippi had seceded from the Union almost 120 years before. As a large crowd of government officials and Winter supporters crowded into the small room on the second floor and hundreds more huddled in the first-floor rotunda to listen over a public address system, Leontyne Price opened the proceedings with a stirring rendition of the National Anthem. Mississippi had never really acknowledged Price, a Metropolitan Opera singer from Laurel, as one of the state's most accomplished artists, and before the inauguration, she had made few public appearances in Mississippi, simply because she was black.[2]

After taking the oath of office, Winter presented an inaugural address that laid out the high standards he would set for the government he would lead: "There will be no place in this administration for anyone who is not utterly and impeccably trustworthy in all of his affairs and relations and activities with the people of Mississippi, their property, and their possessions. There will be no place in this administration for bias or prejudice based on sectionalism or class or race or religion or anything else. There will be no place in this administration for mediocrity or shoddy performance or a half-done job." He then reiterated a theme he had long emphasized in his political campaigns—many of Mississippi's problems were self-inflicted: "We have wasted too much time. We have wasted too much of our substance. We have spent too many of our years, too much of our energy being against things we did not understand, being afraid of change, being suspicious of the intellectual, and being oblivious to our image and reputation." Yet, as he had throughout his political career, Winter suggested that the ship could be righted and that Mississippi had a bright future. Accomplishing this transformation would take hard work from all the state's citizens and would require that all Mississippians "stop selling ourselves short by not utilizing all of our people—our talented people—our creative and imaginative people. The old solutions will not do. Let us not be afraid to launch out into new areas. Let us not feel threatened by new ways of doing things."[3]

Winter concluded his speech by reading a part of the inaugural address he had heard Governor Mike Conner deliver in 1932: "And if in this hour we shall set the public welfare as the only goal of our ambition, if we shall make it the supreme object of our effort and dedicate to its achievement the best endowment of our lives, we need not fear for the results or our labors, nor for the future of the state." The statement highlighted what Winter hoped to bring to his tenure as governor and what his long career as a public servant had embodied—honest and effective government for the betterment of Mississippi. After his remarks, Winter asked the House Speaker, Buddy Newman, and the lieutenant governor, Brad Dye, to join him on the podium as a nineteen-gun salute outside signaled the start of the Winter administration. At the end of the ceremony, an old politico, who had only lukewarmly supported Winter's 1979 gubernatorial bid, told the new governor, "I knew your daddy and I knew Mike Conner. You made a good speech, but you got a lot of work to do to be as good as them." Winter politely agreed with the elderly man and promised to do his best.[4]

A major component of Winter's effort to improve Mississippi involved changing the operation of state government. As journalist Bill Minor explained, "Winter is going to try to make state government run on all cylinders, something it hasn't ever done." Part of this effort involved getting the best people possible to serve in state government. Winter started with his own staff. He named Janice Ammann, his personal secretary, as his special assistant and office manager. He assembled an impressive team of young men, a group that a critical legislator would later derisively call the "Boys of Spring." Bill Cole became chief of staff. David Crews, who had first met Winter while interning in the former lieutenant governor's office, continued as press secretary. Dick Molpus, manager of his family's timber business in Neshoba County, became director of federal-state programs, the area where many of the problems associated with the Finch administration were concentrated. Bill Gartin, who had served on Winter's staff during his term as lieutenant governor and who was the son of former lieutenant governor Carroll Gartin, took the job of administrative assistant and scheduler. Ray Mabus, a Harvard-educated lawyer Winter had met when the young man was an Ole Miss undergraduate, joined the staff in the summer of 1980 as legislative assistant and legal counsel. Andy Mullins, a history teacher and coach at St. Andrews Episcopal School, where Eleanor Winter had graduated, came on board in November 1980 to work primarily on education issues and became one of Winter's closest advisers. John Henegan replaced Cole as chief of staff in early 1981, once Winter named Cole state treasurer after John Dale died in office. The age of these staffers ranged from twenty-five to thirty-two. Most had first been drawn to Winter while in high school or college during one of the Winter campaigns between 1967 and 1975. For all of them, Winter stood as the most dynamic politician representing the possibilities of a new Mississippi. The young staffers were well educated, and most had studied the liberal arts, primarily history or English; three had earned law degrees. Ole Miss represented a common connection for the group. Four had earned degrees from the university, and David Crews grew up near the campus, where his father was an English professor.[5]

As a counterbalance to this youth brigade, Winter also had several experienced colleagues in his inner circle. Former congressman Frank Smith joined the Winter team as a special assistant. To help the new governor with legislative relations, Winter retained Herman Glazier, a former law partner of Fielding Wright who had worked for the previous five Mississippi governors, dating back to Ross Barnett. Although Glazier's personal politics were fairly conservative, he was always intensely loyal to every governor he served. Charlie Deaton, former chair of the House Appropriations Committee and also a candidate in the 1979 governor's race, joined the team as another legislative aide. Willie T. Allen, a Grenada educator and one of the city's first black city council members, came on board to work on education and health and human service issues. Finally, Warren Hood, who had served as Winter's finance chairman in all three of his gubernatorial contests, continued to be an informal yet influential Winter adviser.[6]

Winter typically met with his staff on weekday mornings whenever he was in town, and they proved an effective sounding board for the governor. Winter had what Mullins called a quiet leadership style. The governor was not looking for "yes" men; he believed vigorous debate would spark new ideas. Winter typically listened intently as the staff argued options and approaches for addressing policy issues and legislative matters. Winter urged his staff to not let politics dictate their actions and not "to weigh political considerations too heavily" when formulating policy or giving him advice. He told the staffers that "the best politics is to do the best job we can." After the staff debate, Winter would make a determination on the matter, and because of their loyalty and respect—especially among the young advisers—the staff would typically accept the decision. Although a staff hierarchy existed, it was not a rigid organization. Cole (and then Henegan) served as chief of staff, but all members of the inner circle had direct access to the governor.[7]

In addition to his own staff, Winter sought out, as he indicated in his inaugural address, honest, dedicated people to fill various appointments in executive branch agencies. Because of his long tenure as a public servant, Winter had a vast knowledge of capable people and their strengths and weaknesses. Bolstered with such understanding and unfettered by any campaign promises on the matter of government appointments, in many cases Winter identified qualified officials and put them in place. At other times, Winter made a careful search of potential appointees before naming his selections. For example, among the most sought-after appointments were the five members to the Board of Trustees of the State Institutions of Higher Learning. In 1944, this citizen board received constitutional authority to oversee the state's colleges and universities, to prevent a replay of an earlier incident where Governor Theodore Bilbo had personally hired and fired college personnel, which led to the loss of accreditation of several Mississippi colleges. As a result, the members of this board, who served twelve-year terms, exercised a substantial amount of power over higher education in the state. After assuming office, Winter received hundreds of letters and phone calls from people interested in securing a slot on the state college board. To help with his selections, the governor commissioned the Hardin Foundation, a nonprofit group located in Meridian that focused on educational issues, to develop a list of prospective college board members from which Winter could make his selection. Tom Wacaster and Tom Ward of the foundation created a roster by consulting black and white sources around the state. They devoted particular attention to compiling information on potential black appointees, a list that included Reuben Anderson, a county court judge in Hinds County; and Claire Collins Harvey, a businesswoman from Jackson. Winter selected another of those profiled, George Watson, an assistant superintendent of education for the Pass Christian Public Schools. The Hardin report described Watson as "a fair man who could withstand pressure from extreme black militants but who would also challenge white racist attitudes he might encounter on the Board."[8]

Once Winter made his selections for state positions, he generally let his appointees do their jobs and did not micromanage the affairs of their agencies. When Winter received inquiries about specific personnel or policy matters within the purview of one of his executive agencies, he would emphasize that he delegated the responsibility for such decisions to his appointed representative; this procedure represented a major step toward removing the cronyism that had plagued the Finch administration. For example, when one of Winter's supporters asked for the governor's help in having the regional Welfare Department office located in a building the man owned, Winter replied that he would forward the information to his newly appointed director of the agency, Donald Roark, who made such decisions. Winter thanked the man for his support and explained that he wanted "to ensure an honest and efficient administration as free of politics and political interference as I can possibly make it. I do not know how to operate on any other basis and trust that as a consequence of this we can eliminate some of the waste and inefficiency in state government." Unless required by statute, Winter also resisted the longstanding practice of appointing legislators to various boards within the state's executive branch. The Building Commission, which approved all state construction projects, had traditionally been staffed almost exclusively with legislators, but Winter did not appoint any lawmakers to serve on this key group.[9]

Although the governor did not intervene in the day-to-day operations of the numerous agencies within the executive branch, he maintained regular contact with their leaders by holding a monthly breakfast with the appointed heads of the major state agencies. These gatherings allowed the agency leaders to keep Winter abreast of the issues facing their slice of government and also helped Winter coordinate administration policy among the various agencies. Winter had a separate breakfast each month with the elected leaders of other state departments, which led to fruitful discussions across all agencies and helped the entire executive branch work together as a single unit.[10]

Winter's effort to professionalize the staffing of state government received a major boost with the first bill he signed from the 1980 legislature. The Uniform Personnel Act, a measure Winter strongly supported, created a state personnel board that established a set of standards for the hiring of twenty-seven thousand state employees. The law protected workers from excessive political interference, and one clear benefit was to ensure equal access to state jobs for black citizens. Although Winter favored a process completely free of political input, the law still provided for legislative service on the new state personnel board. Even so, the unprecedented procedures represented a progressive step by removing decision-making from the good-old-boy system of political favoritism. When Winter discovered that the state employment form still required that an applicant indicate whether they were "White" or "Colored," he issued an executive order removing the designation. In a further move to eliminate political favoritism in the executive branch, Winter, as he promised in the campaign, ended the system of governor's colonels.[11]

Winter also sought to reshape state government through a major reorganization of parts of the executive branch. Aided by legislation passed during the 1980 session, the changes both promoted more efficient public service and rooted out corrupt government officials; after government reorganization, Winter had the opportunity to name new officials to the affected state boards or commissions. A number of offices underwent major changes. During the Finch administration, numerous problems and scandals surrounded the Department of Motor Vehicles, which collected gas taxes, issued truck permits, and regulated vehicles using the state's highways. Unscrupulous truckers had reportedly paid off employees of the department to ignore weight limits; the office had also been used to dispense jobs to political supporters of the Finch administration. New legislation allowed Winter to abolish the department and transfer its functions to the State Tax Commission. The Department of Banking Supervision represented another problem area during the Finch administration; the state Bank Comptroller, James Means, would later be convicted for mail and wire fraud committed while in office. Winter secured legislation that completely reorganized bank regulation agencies. Most important, Winter received legislative approval to reshape the Division of Federal and State Programs, in order to coordinate the work of fifteen different state agencies employing 377 people, a situation that had developed over the previous decades as new federal programs brought money into the state. Winter appointed Molpus to oversee the consolidation of the programs into one agency and then to become the director of the new agency. The reorganization eliminated duplication of support services such as accounting and trimmed one hundred jobs, including all the directors and deputy directors under the old structure. The new organization also released more federal money for actual programs, and the governor's office gained more discretion over how to allocate the funds. In addition, an office of audit and investigation within the new agency guarded against the mismanagement of federal dollars, which had run rampant during the Finch administration.[12]

Winter also oversaw the reorganization of the state's economic development agency. The 1979 legislature had authorized the replacement of the Agricultural and Industrial (A & I) Board with a Department of Economic Development (DED). The board overseeing the new agency had seven citizen members (in addition to the governor, lieutenant governor, Speaker, and legislative appointees). Winter chose some of the state's leading economic figures for positions on the board. Although the head of the A & I organization had traditionally been a political appointee, the new economic development board formed a search committee to find the most qualified director. In May 1980, Bill Hackett, a Mississippian who headed the Louisiana Department of Economic Development, returned to Mississippi and assumed the directorship of the agency. The new DED completely reordered the state's economic development operation and focused on employing people with economic development experience or training.[13]

Winter made his appointments to the DED board based on his belief that well-connected economic leaders could best direct the efforts to attract new industry to the state. His appointment of an all-white, all-male board for the agency, however, was roundly criticized. Ada Reid of Long Beach claimed she was "not a Woman's Libber," but she "was disappointed that you did not consider even one woman, from all over our state, capable of serving on the Economic Development Board." The displeasure coming from the black community was more sustained and strident. Matthew Page, a black doctor from Greenville, told Winter, "Your rhetoric of a new Mississippi involving all Mississippians in government is turning out simply to be rhetoric from the very beginning." Fred Banks, a black lawyer in Jackson and a Winter supporter, went to see the governor and informed him, "It is essential that your administration be fair and equitable in both appearance and substance. This will require an affirmative effort to include black people in the decision-making processes at every level and in every area," including the important DED board. When Winter met with the executive committee of the state NAACP shortly thereafter, he agreed to create a Minority Economic Development Task Force to address economic development issues of particular interest to minority businesses in Mississippi, a move that helped quiet some of the anger over Winter's appointments to the economic development board.[14]

Despite the flap over Winter's selections for the DED board, he generally upheld the commitment he made after his election to have blacks play a meaningful role in his administration. By the end of June 1980, Winter had made 406 appointments; of those, 91 (22 percent) were black, and blacks assumed seats on practically every major state board or commission except for the DED. By comparison, only 7 percent of Cliff Finch's appointments during his first year in office had gone to black men or women. Winter believed that anyone who looked at his overall pattern of appointments "has got to be basically satisfied that they are fair and they are made without regard to any racially prejudiced motives." Even so, some critics complained that Winter had not adequately consulted with black leaders around the state in selecting his black nominees. Winter's record on appointing women to state positions was not quite as impressive, as they made up only approximately 15 percent of Winter's appointments to state boards and commissions during the early part of his administration.[15]

Winter's efforts to improve the operation of state government extended to the judiciary as well. Although Mississippi elected all its judges, the governor had the power to appoint jurists to fill unexpired terms that came open between elections. This appointive power of the governor had been used over the years primarily to elevate political friends to the bench. Winter, however, created a nineteen-member judicial nominating commission to vet potential judicial nominees when an opening occurred and suggest three names for each circuit or chancery opening and five names for a state supreme court vacancy. Winter continued to receive personal recommendations for judicial openings, but he referred those to the nominating commission. During his administration, Winter used this process to appoint more than fifteen judges to fill vacancies on the state's courts. His appointments included Lenore Prather of Columbus, the first woman to serve on the Mississippi Supreme Court, and Reuben Anderson, appointed to a state circuit court judgeship in 1981, the first black Mississippian to hold such a position.[16]

In addition to Winter's success in reorganizing and restoring confidence in state government, his actions as governor also altered some of the negative perceptions of Mississippi that existed nationally. In many ways, the governor's personal demeanor helped generate a new image for the state. At the time of Winter's inauguration, Bill Minor had compared the event to John F. Kennedy's inauguration and had suggested that the Winter administration represented the beginning of a Mississippi Camelot. Winter's call for selfless public service from those in state government enhanced these comparisons. Although Winter was older than Kennedy when he arrived at the White House, Winter also exuded the kind of physical vitality that had contributed so much to the Kennedy charm in the early 1960s. For instance, throughout his term as governor, Winter continued his longtime practice of jogging, sometimes starting his day with an early morning run or taking a late afternoon break for a few laps at the Chastain Junior High School track. Even when traveling, the governor's daily routine included jogging. Highway Patrol officer Jimmy Simmons, who worked security for Winter and often traveled with him, noted that "you pack your jogging shorts and shoes before your toothbrush." In addition to jogging, Winter loved nothing better than to organize a pickup football or softball game among his staff or with the Jackson residents who worked out at Chastain. Word of the governor's love of athletic competition soon spread, and by the spring of 1981, the governor's office received several calls a week from groups wanting to challenge the governor and his staff to a softball contest. On weekends, when the Winters had nothing particular planned, local residents might see the couple walking around downtown Jackson. At times, returning to the Governor's Mansion and seeing tourists outside the gates admiring the house, Winter would invite the shocked strangers inside for a closer look.[17]

When Winter appeared in national forums, he did not strike the typical negative image many observers associated with Mississippi or her citizens. Winter played an active role in the National Governor's Association (NGA). He also worked vigorously on behalf of the Southern Growth Policies Board (SGPB), a group organized by southern leaders to promote the economic fortunes of the region; he served as chair of the SGPB in 1981–1982. Addressing meetings of these organizations, Winter impressed officials from other states, their staffs, and the press who covered these conferences as an articulate, knowledgeable voice from a state long viewed as an ignorant backwater. Mullins, who often traveled with Winter to these meetings, remembered people coming up to him after Winter's speeches and saying, "My God, do the people of Mississippi realize what they have here?" Reuben Anderson recalled attending a NGA meeting where some of the other governors treated Winter "like a rock star because of the contrast between his intelligence and fairness and those of many of the governors who had preceded him as members of that group."[18]

One of the most important contributors to Mississippi's image make-over during Winter's gubernatorial term was the regular series of events that became known as Dinner at the Mansion. Even before they moved into the house, the Winters had decided to host a series of events with Mississippians and other notable guests. As Winter explained, he and Elise hoped the events would "bring Mississippi to the attention of prominent and influential people the world over, and to help present a sampling of the views and ideas of national and world leaders to a cross-section of the people of Mississippi." Mississippians or former Mississippians who had distinguished themselves in some field were invited for dinner at the Governor's Mansion, along with as many as sixty guests, including Mississippians who knew the honored guest, or supporters of Winter, many of whom had never had an opportunity to come to the Mansion. At other times, people with no Mississippi connections were invited for these special events. The Winters, along with Frank Smith, planned the dinners and compiled the guest lists. The meals were typically followed by a salon-type conversation and sometimes by performances of the honorees. The Mansion events both recognized the homegrown talent of Mississippi, often reconnecting the state's expatriates to their native state, and provided visitors from outside the state with a glimpse of a Mississippi they had never imagined. In the process, the dinners attracted publicity and polished the image of the state both at home and abroad. The First Family itself became a big part of the favorable impressions conveyed. One reporter thought that visitors to the Mansion got a "marvelous impression of Mississippi . . . after having been exposed to a couple as civilized and gracious as the Winters."[19]

The guests chosen for the Mansion occasions represented an eclectic mix, one that reflected the wide-ranging interests of the governor himself. The honorees included numerous writers, including Margaret Walker Alexander, Walker Percy, Elizabeth Spencer, Shelby Foote, Tom Wicker, and William Styron; political figures such as former Secretary of State Dean Rusk, President Jimmy Carter, and the Mexican ambassador Hugo Margain; and Mississippi entertainers, such as Jerry Clower. Business leaders such as Steve Forbes and Kenneth Durr, at the time the president of Chevron Oil, also were honored guests. Because of Winter's lifelong interest in sports, a number of famous stars from that world received invitations as the special guest for a Mansion dinner, including such notables as Mickey Mantle and Hank Aaron. A special event also honored Winter's fellow Grenada Countians, including members of the black families Winter had grown up with there. One 1983 Dinner at the Mansion feted Myrlie Evers, the widow of Mississippi civil rights leader Medgar Evers, and Charles Evers, brother of the slain civil rights champion. After dinner, Winter began the conversation by telling Myrlie Evers, "we white folks owe your martyred husband as much as black folks do, for he helped free us, too."[20]

The activities that occurred after the dinners represented part of what Bill Minor described as Winter's effort to bring a "degree of intellectualism" to "the upper reaches of state government." When Leontyne Price, Eudora Welty, Willie Morris, and Bill Ferris were honored in April 1981 at one of the Mansion dinners, the conversation afterwards centered on the South as a place that "inspired and created art and celebrated place." Ferris, a folklorist and founding director of the Center for the Study of Southern Culture at Ole Miss, demonstrated Mississippi's rich musical heritage by bringing out a guitar and playing songs by Elvis Presley, B.B. King, Muddy Waters, and Jimmie Rodgers. Price then performed an a capella version of "God Bless America." After her performance, the appreciative gathering broke into applause, followed by a long, reflective silence. Following a Mansion dinner for Muddy Waters, Winter told the famous singer that Mississippi is "a better state than it was when you left here." He also thanked Waters for being "an ambassador for this state. I think we have a lot of friends over this country that we wouldn't have had but for you." During the conversation, which developed into a skillful interview by the governor with a man who admitted he was "not much of a talker," but "I'm a pretty good singer," Waters described his life before moving to Chicago in 1943 as "choppin' cotton, pickin' cotton, drivin' a tractor, doing anything you're supposed to be doing on a plantation."[21]

Winter found numerous other ways to promote a positive image of Mississippi. Only a month after he assumed office he went to New York to meet with national print and broadcast journalists. To encourage a more accurate and more favorable perception of the state and stimulate coverage, the new governor talked with them about changes the state had made since the 1960s and about his own forward-thinking plans for his term. Winter also encouraged the pride many expatriate Mississippians had in their state by supporting the annual Mississippi Picnic in New York's Central Park. Begun in 1979 by a group of homesick Mississippians, who wanted to connect with fellow home state natives, the picnic received a boost during Winter's first year in office when he provided official state support and financial backing for the event. Winter also attended the Mississippi Picnic and, according to one observer, "displayed to the doubters of the North that we are a people with grace, charm, and intelligence." The picnic became a yearly celebration of Mississippi culture, food, and community in the heart of New York City and generated favorable publicity about the state in an area where images of the 1960s still dominated public perceptions.[22]

Most Mississippians welcomed the governor's efforts to improve the image of their state. Howard Scarborough, a Jackson preacher, expressed his approval for Winter's administration by noting that the governor had "brought a high degree of dignity and prestige to the office of Governor and to the state which were long overdue." As Winter neared the end of his four-year term, one woman told him, "Your intelligence, kindness, and appreciation of culture and education were evident each time you made an appearance, and it was because of you and the image you and your whole family portrayed that I was, at long last, proud to be from Mississippi." In 1983, a columnist for the *Jackson Clarion-Ledger* summed up the feeling many Mississippians had about Winter's efforts to reshape the state's image: "he has helped to move us into the mainstream of the Southern and American consciousness. And, by his words and actions, he showed the rest of America that this state has more to offer than clown-like politicians, good ole boys, syrup-mouthed women in crinoline, and moonlight and magnolias."[23]

The new image for Mississippi rested in part on the fact that it had moved beyond the racial battles that defined it in the 1950s and 1960s, when white Mississippians had vigorously opposed the efforts of black Mississippians to end segregation and gain the right to vote. By the early 1980s, race no longer played such an overt part in the public life of the state, although racial animosity had not disappeared either. White resentment over black advances still lingered in some quarters, as demonstrated in the letter that a white woman from Jackson wrote Winter in the spring of 1980. She complained, "Caucasians rarely stand up or push for *anything* they believe in anymore, therefore the blacks have succeeded in getting most of the things they desire. They've moved into lovely white neighborhoods, and the majority of them are now ruined . . . . They are at least 50 % it seems in every office and business you enter. A *majority* of the time when you call trying to get information from some place of business you get a black voice, and the knowledge of a 10 year old."[24]

True believers in absolute white supremacy also still prowled the landscape, but their influence had dwindled considerably. In the spring of 1981, the Ku Klux Klan mobilized in Winter's hometown of Grenada, handing out racist literature on the downtown streets. A big difference now was that the Klan no longer really intimidated blacks, as a local black leader made clear. The head of the Grenada chapter of the NAACP, Jasper Neely, responded to the local Klan presence by announcing that blacks in Grenada would not tolerate any shows of violence from white supremacists; rather, "the Black Community will counter and defend themselves against any attacks of violence: the Black Community will not be intimidated by anyone."[25]

The election of Winter as governor, a man with a long history of racial moderation, had strengthened the notion that the racial attitudes of white Mississippians had changed. In addition, the Winter administration expanded the effort begun by the two previous administrations to bring black Mississippians into state government. Early in his tenure, however, Winter's concerns about the future of the state's Democratic Party actually heightened racial tensions. When the two factions of Mississippi's Democratic Party reunited in 1976, they agreed to a joint chairmanship for the party (one black leader, one white one). In 1978, the party made plans to abandon this leadership structure in favor of a single chairman, beginning two years later. In the spring of 1980, Winter urged the party to make the scheduled change in the interest of party unity and suggested a young white lawyer, Danny Cupit, for the new chairmanship; Cupit had been involved with the Loyalist Democrats and was well-respected by black Democrats as treasurer of the state party. Black Democrats, however, wanted to know why a white man had to hold the chair's position in the new party structure. They found it hard to see why the current black co-chair, Aaron Henry, should step aside under Winter's new leadership proposal. Henry had led both the Loyalist Democrats and the reunited state Democratic Party for a number of years, and he was one of the new black legislators elected in 1979.[26]

Reacting to Winter's comments, a number of black Democrats proclaimed their opposition to the end of the dual chairmanship, and a group of party leaders organized to work out a compromise on the issue. When the Democratic Party's executive committee met in May 1980, a month after Winter made his proposal, whites and blacks had reached an agreement, after some intense negotiations, to make the change to a single chair. When Winter spoke to the committee before it voted, however, he reignited the controversy in his explanation of why he thought the executive committee should choose Cupit for the new position. Winter argued that in order to stanch the defection of white Democrats from the party, "I think at this time what we need to lead this party is a white chairman." That statement may have accurately reflected the reality at the time, but it ignored the recent history of white efforts to exclude blacks from positions of political power. It also rested on a faulty assumption that, despite racial progress, racial considerations could be suddenly ignored and discounted in policy decisions. Finally, Winter's proposal was at odds with his frequent suggestions that the qualifications for leadership and public service involved much more than race. The executive committee, composed of a 60 percent white majority, selected Cupit in a vote that divided strictly along racial lines. Afterwards, black members of the committee walked out of the meeting, which ended the planned election for the remaining slate of party leaders. Henry told the press that Winter's comments represented "an affront to the total black community."[27]

Soon after the executive committee meeting, Henry wrote Winter and reminded him of the state's long opposition to black voters and public officials, including its sustained resistance to the 1965 Voting Rights Act. After all that, Henry noted, "Now the request is to relinquish our present ability to be involved in the top leadership of the Democratic Party of the State of Mississippi with a promise of its return in two to four years. There are no takers for this duplicity!" The Hinds County Democratic Executive Committee approved a resolution in the aftermath of Cupit's election condemning Winter's remarks as causing "many Mississippians concern about the racism and sexism inherent in such a statement" and calling on Winter to apologize for his remarks. Winter offered no response or explanation to his critics. The anger directed at Winter over his Cupit comment continued to build over the next month. At the state NAACP meeting in Jackson in mid-June, the organization passed a resolution denouncing Winter "for this act of racism and sexism." The resolution also claimed that the governor "has with callous sophistication used the Black Voter for his own political purposes, until he was elected Governor and now takes a position that he has no further desire or use for Black folks until his next political escapade."[28]

Black members of the state Democratic Party, led by Henry, threatened a formal challenge with the national Democratic organization. Before that effort went very far, however, black and white Democrats, all mindful that the internal dispute would only weaken the party, reached what Henry called a "delicate truce." At the scheduled executive committee meeting of June 21, the Democrats approved a revised form of the previous power-sharing arrangement. The political organization added the post of executive vice chair, to be held by a person of the opposite race than the chair. Ed Cole, the first black person to work on the staff of Senator James Eastland, assumed this new post. In addition, Henry, who was running for Democratic national committeeman for Mississippi against Jack Harper, a white chancery clerk from Indianola, was named to the national post.[29]

Despite the clash over the leadership structure of the state's Democratic Party, it emerged from the controversy more unified than before. At the 1980 national Democratic convention in New York, some southern delegations were divided between Carter supporters and backers of Edward Kennedy. Mississippi Democrats, however, displayed impressive unanimity and spoke with one voice on almost every matter presented to the delegates, including the renomination of Jimmy Carter as the party standard-bearer. Winter gave a speech at the national convention, and he stood on the podium with Carter when he accepted the Democratic nomination. Winter became the first governor since J. P. Coleman in 1956 to take a leading role at a national convention in supporting the Democratic Party's presidential nominee. After the convention, Aaron Henry called the event "Mississippi's finest hour," although some black Democrats in Mississippi—specifically those leaders in the Hinds County party who had criticized Winter—continued to charge that they were "being systematically excluded from all party functions in the state."[30]

Following the convention, Winter actively participated in the Carter campaign, at a time when many southern Democrats sought to distance themselves from the president, who had won in 1976 in part because of almost solid support from the South. Winter spoke on Labor Day in Tuscumbia, Alabama, at the event officially opening Carter's campaign, and urged the crowd to not turn its back "on one of our own." One of the branches of the Ku Klux Klan had its headquarters in Tuscumbia, and the Republican Party candidate, Ronald Reagan, criticized Carter for formally launching his presidential bid in such a community. Winter helped organize a statement by seven southern governors, which denounced Reagan's remarks as a "callous and opportunistic slap at the South" and for injecting race into the 1980 presidential campaign. Actually, the racial issue had already reared its head a month earlier at the Neshoba County Fair, when Ronald Reagan, during his opening campaign appearance, made a veiled racial appeal, announcing that "I believe in states' rights." During the fall, Winter attended Democratic Party rallies around the state, made some appearances on Carter's behalf in several southern states along with South Carolina Governor Dick Riley and Georgia Senator Sam Nunn, and hosted Carter's visit to the state on the Friday before the election.[31]

Unlike 1976, Carter did not carry Mississippi, narrowly losing the state with 48 percent of the vote. Some white Mississippians, including a number of Winter supporters, disliked Winter's active campaigning for Carter. One Winter backer asked him, "Why would you want to jeopardize your own personal political life to join up or board a Sinking Ship with Carter," and added that "there is concern among your supporters of your present stance." A Mississippi Republican who had backed Winter in the 1979 campaign and was a good friend of the governor understood that Winter had to assist his party's presidential nominee but pleaded with the governor "not to do any more than is absolutely necessary on behalf of what I consider to be the worst president that I can remember during my lifetime."[32]

Although Winter received criticism for his role in the leadership conflict of the state's Democratic Party, he personally demonstrated his support for a political system in which blacks shared power with whites when he campaigned energetically for Robert Clark's election to the U.S. House of Representatives in 1982 to represent the Second Congressional District. The Mississippi Delta district had recently been restored, after the 1966 legislature had split it among three separate congressional districts to dilute the black vote. Robert Clark had won election to the

Mississippi House in 1967, the first black person selected for the legislature in the twentieth century, and he remained the lone black legislator until 1975. Running in the majority-black Second District (though the area still had a majority of white registered voters), Clark faced three white opponents in the Democratic primary. Winter did not endorse any of the Democrats in the primary, which he considered the proper position for the state party leader.[33]

After Clark won the primary, however, Winter pledged his "unqualified support" of the Democratic nominee and announced that he would "rally a united Democratic Party behind him." In the general election, Clark confronted Republican Webb Franklin, a white lawyer from Greenwood. In an area that had always voted Democratic, many observers thought Clark could win if he could carry even a small fraction of the district's increasingly Republican white vote. At a Democratic rally in Washington, D.C., for Clark, Winter described the candidate as "a self-made man who understands the problems of the people of his area, the black people and the white people." Clark told the assembled Democrats that politics in Mississippi had reached a point where "we can put race behind us." Race, however, still mattered. Franklin labeled Clark as a "liberal," a tag that one Democrat judged as absurd as "calling William Winter a liberal. He just is not." Clark, in fact, was more a moderate in the Winter mold. Franklin also inserted subtle racial appeals into the campaign, such as peppering his ads with photos of his opponent—to remind viewers of Clark's race—and appearing in one TV spot in front of Greenwood's Confederate monument while talking about the importance of Mississippi's "traditions." The tag line of one Franklin commercial was "Elect Webb Franklin to Congress. He's one of us." In support of Clark, Winter appeared in frequent television commercials promoting the black legislator's candidacy. Winter also wrote officeholders in the district and reminded them that Clark's election offered the opportunity for Mississippi "to show the nation that a new day has dawned in our state politics." While Winter did his part, some observers felt that white Democrats in the Delta did not work very hard for a Clark victory. Some whites in the district undoubtedly voted for Clark, but many more of them voted for Franklin simply because he was white, and when the votes were counted, Clark lost narrowly to Franklin. As one white Delta farmer explained, "It comes down to the race issue."[34] The 1982 congressional election in Mississippi's Second District suggested that the new day of race relations Winter had hoped for had not yet fully arrived.

Despite the defeat, Winter's support for Clark's congressional bid was particularly noteworthy, because for the first time, a white governor in Mississippi had supported a black candidate running against a white one. Winter's stance angered a number of whites in the Second District. For example, one Holmes County man told Winter that many of the governor's "friends" in the area resented "very much people from outside our district telling us who is best qualified to represent us in the Congress." The correspondent questioned why Winter would "want to impose on this district a black to satisfy some philosophical whim of yours about laying to rest racist politics." Black Mississippians, on the other hand, applauded Winter's support of Clark. Willie and Cornelia Dillard of Greenwood offered their thanks to Winter "for working so hard and openly for our Candidate, Robert Clark. I have never seen a man of your race and position to work openly for a Black."[35]

❧

Halfway through Winter's term as governor, few would have denied that Winter had done a great deal to rehabilitate Mississippi's battered image, yet his success in securing legislative victories had been fairly limited. Winter had substantial legislative experience and worked hard to build solid relationships with legislative leaders. House Speaker Buddy Newman and Lieutenant Governor Brad Dye had both been on the other side of the political fence from Winter throughout their careers. Newman had first been elected to the legislature in 1947, the same year as Winter, and their fathers had served together in the legislature before them. A protégé of Speaker Walter Sillers, Newman had assumed the Speaker's chair in 1976 after thirty years in the House. Dye, a native of Winter's hometown of Grenada, had managed John Bell Williams's successful race against Winter in 1967. Despite past political differences with both men, Winter made a conscious effort to keep the lines of communication open. Every Tuesday morning while the legislature was in session, Winter invited the two legislative leaders to the Mansion for breakfast. Joined by Herman Glazier and Charlie Deaton, the small group would discuss upcoming legislative matters. Winter also frequently included Newman and Dye in the various functions held at the Mansion and recognized the need to adjust his own personal preferences to cement his dealings with them. For instance, the Winters had originally resolved to follow an alcohol policy at the Mansion similar to the one that prevailed at their home: no liquor but occasional wine or beer with dinner (although Winter had been a teetotaler for much of his life, by the early 1970s, that stance had softened somewhat). The Winter approach on the alcohol question remained almost indistinguishable to prohibition to a number of leaders. Winter noted, "Some of my friends in the legislature were absolutely dismayed when I had them over for a meal, and we served tomato juice." The Winter alcohol policy especially perturbed Speaker Newman, as he liked to drink whiskey. Over time, Deaton successfully impressed on the Winters the necessity of lifting their liquor ban in the interest of helping to advance the governor's legislative priorities.[36]

Winter's efforts, however, paid few dividends. In addition to the legislation secured to reorganize state government, Winter had convinced the legislature to create a low-interest mortgage fund for Mississippians who needed help purchasing a home, had prodded lawmakers to pass small pay raises for teachers, and had won approval for a number of other minor pieces of legislation. More substantive proposals, such as an open records law and an array of education reform measures, had failed to garner legislative approval. Bill Minor encapsulated the concerns of many in May 1982 when he noted, "Winter has not been able to, or has declined to, really grab the helm of the ship of state to put it on a definite new course. Oh yes, honesty and decency and sincerity are plentiful around the administration, and that means SOMETHING." But, he added, "Winter has gotten virtually nothing of major consequence through the Legislature." Another journalist admired Winter's "class and intelligence" but judged him a "caretaker governor." Critics of Winter believed his relationships with legislators were too cozy, which made the governor reluctant to challenge important legislators on key matters. For instance, when Attorney General Bill Allain filed a lawsuit in 1982 against state legislators to end the practice of lawmakers serving on executive boards and commissions, Winter refused to endorse the attorney general's action, even though Winter had advocated for such a change before he became governor. Part of the problem Winter faced was exactly the situation Allain's lawsuit sought to address. In Mississippi, the legislature still held most of the power in state government, and an "Old Guard" maintained control over the legislative body. Mississippi had elected a governor interested in progressive change, but many in the legislature did not share his enthusiasm for reform.[37]

Budget problems also stymied many of Winter's initiatives. Those difficulties stemmed in part from declining tax collections as a result of the 1979 legislature's $83-million tax cut. Legislators approved the tax reduction because in the summer of 1978 Mississippi had a $100 million-dollar surplus (much of it generated because of high inflation rates) at the same time that California's Proposition 13 had created a tax-cutting craze nationwide. In January 1980, soon after taking office, Winter approached legislative leaders about rolling back some of the 1979 tax cut. Other than Lieutenant Governor Dye, however, key lawmakers rejected that proposal. In addition to the tax cut, state revenues had declined because the economic recession had diminished receipts from the sales tax, the state's main source of income. Also, by 1982, federal aid to Mississippi had dropped significantly as a result of President Reagan's new federalism.[38]

These economic realities hamstrung the Winter administration for four years with continual deficits. For example, the 1981 legislature passed a budget that included appropriations for state operations based on unrealistic revenue projections, especially given the continued weakness of the national and state economies and the reduced revenues available. Almost immediately after the legislature adjourned, Winter had to come up with more than $70 million of cuts to the budget just approved. Winter ordered budget reductions across the board—except for elementary and secondary education—and delayed the start of some programs and building projects approved by the legislature. Winter continued to look for efficiencies in state government that would reduce expenses, but he also realized that budget cuts could only go so far and that the legislature might need to consider additional revenue sources "to maintain the competitive position of this state."[39]

Adding to the state's economic woes, Mississippi continued to lag behind other southern states in attracting industrial concerns to the state. Mississippi had been one of the first southern states to launch the search for new industry with its Balance Agriculture with Industry program of the 1930s. Like other southern states scrambling to find jobs for citizens increasingly unable to survive through farming, Mississippi had long touted to business owners fleeing the northern Rust Belt the state's advantages: cheap land, cheap labor, and low or no taxes. Winter had done as much when he worked for the Grenada Chamber of Commerce in the 1950s. This strategy produced new jobs, but primarily low-wage positions in companies that often stayed only as long as their tax exemptions lasted. In the 1960s, Mississippi had fallen far behind in this race to attract the bottom-feeders of industry to the South because of the state's strident and sustained resistance to the black civil rights movement. Bill Hackett, head of Winter's new DED, recognized that part of the sales campaign to outside industry in the early 1980s still had to counter the state's "backward" image, to convince the country that "we're not barefooted and that alligators don't eat our toes."[40]

The low-wage industries Mississippi had managed to attract had eased some of the pain in the transition from an agricultural economy, but increasingly, those companies that had been coming to the South for the promise of nonunionized workers and tax relief bypassed the region for Latin America and Asia, locales with even lower wages. Winter recognized that in this shifting economic landscape Mississippi would have to compete in an increasingly global economy for more skilled positions in manufacturing companies producing products like computers and precision instruments. Winter learned early on in his administration that the state faced a disadvantage in this competition as well. In the spring of 1980, a major electronics company from Chicago wanted to relocate to south Mississippi, a move that promised hundreds of high-wage, skilled jobs. Two months later, however, the company went to South Carolina instead. Afterward, Winter met with company executives in Chicago, who told him that they liked Mississippi, but the state did not have an education system strong enough to produce the skilled workers the company needed. This conversation further bolstered Winter's longstanding belief that improving Mississippi's educational system represented the essential first step in ensuring economic progress for the state. At a joint session of the legislature on the opening day of the 1982 session, the governor told the assembled lawmakers, "In our quest for industry and for new jobs . . . the concern I hear expressed by industrialists more than any other has to do with the skill level of our workers and our capacity to train workers for specific skills."[41]

ᘓ

William Winter's term as governor restored faith in state government. The governor appointed qualified people to state offices, reorganized state government on a number of fronts, and skillfully asserted the limited powers of the governor. In a larger sense, Winter helped alter the state's negative image acquired during the civil rights era. He took action to try to help the state continue to move forward in a world no longer defined by Jim Crow. Winter's intellect and his personal demeanor did much to challenge settled opinion of the Magnolia State, and the regular Dinners at the Mansion highlighted the achievements of Mississippians for both the state's citizens and those beyond her borders. Journalist Orley Hood accurately described the Winter administration as one of "common sense, forward thinking, cultural heights and genteel ambiance [that] transformed the sadly comedic governor's mansion of Cliff Finch into a house of responsibility and respect and achievement."[42] Despite the successful efforts to rebuild trust in state government and reshape Mississippi's image, economic problems and legislative inertia made policy victories difficult for the Winter administration for most of his term. Even so, Winter persisted in prodding the legislature to approve what he considered his most important legislative proposal: education reform, an ambitious series of proposals that carried a hefty price tag.

II

EDUCATION REFORM

The Christmas Miracle

William Winter had long believed that Mississippi could not move forward with a second-rate public education system. He had benefited from an early childhood environment where his parents instilled reading and education as essential values for a better life. He had also broadened his horizons intellectually while an undergraduate at Ole Miss in the 1940s. Throughout his long political career, Winter had argued that better public schools and a more educated citizenry were necessary prerequisites for creating a stronger state economy. It is not surprising that education reform became the top legislative priority of the Winter administration. Huge obstacles, however, existed during the early 1980s to achieving any meaningful reform in this area. Economic problems limited the possibilities for costly new initiatives of any kind, and legislative support for public education had diminished since school integration began in earnest in 1970. Winter, however, overcame these intractable problems to achieve one of the greatest legislative victories of the twentieth century in Mississippi, the Education Reform Act of 1982, through a combination of skillfully working with legislators and ably mobilizing public opinion.

Mississippi's educational system had substantial shortcomings. In the early 1980s, Mississippi was the only state in the country that did not provide any funding for kindergartens. Despite the wide acceptance of the early grade nationwide, many Mississippians objected to state funding for kindergartens. According to Representative Jim Simpson from the Gulf Coast, some white opponents, including several in the legislature, believed that kindergartens would be little more than a babysitting service for blacks. Others opposed early childhood education on religious grounds and argued that families should provide such instruction. The state was forty-fifth among the fifty states in per capita spending on education and forty-ninth in spending per pupil. The illiteracy rate remained more than double the national average. In practically every other statistical measure, Mississippi's educational system could be found on the wrong end of the scale: tied for the lowest median school years completed by its population, lowest teacher salaries in the country, and the highest rejection rate for any state's citizens seeking entry into the military based on its mental aptitude tests. Winter often emphasized the connection between these deficiencies and another glaring statistic—Mississippi was last in the nation in per capita income. The reason for the state's economic woes, according to Winter, was "because we have too many underproductive people—too many unskilled people—too many undereducated people. And we are going to be last until we do something about that problem."[1]

When Winter became governor, he had a definite plan on how to accomplish his goal to improve education. At the start of the 1980 session, Winter asked the legislature to create a study commission to make recommendations for future enactment. The Blue Ribbon Committee on Education, as it was known, included eight citizens appointed by the governor, twelve legislators (six from each chamber), and the state superintendent of education. Among the individuals appointed by Winter were Claude Ramsey, head of the Mississippi AFL-CIO; Jack Reed, a prominent businessman from Tupelo; and Robert Walker, executive director of the state NAACP. Reed served as chair of the committee, and Andy Mullins provided support from Winter's staff.[2]

In December 1980, after six months of intensive study and fifty meetings, the Blue Ribbon Committee presented twenty-three proposals for upgrading education. The most important suggestions called for the creation of statewide public kindergartens; a lay board of education, which promised to focus more on improving public education than the existing board composed of the attorney general, the secretary of state, and the statewide elected superintendent of education; and a strengthened compulsory education law. The legislature had abolished its compulsory education law in 1956 in response to the *Brown* decision. The state had enacted a new compulsory education statute in 1977, though it provided no funds to hire attendance counselors to enforce the measure. Additional proposals made by the education committee included equalization of financing for public schools, tougher teacher certification standards, and teacher and administrator salary increases. The committee's report also suggested ways to fund these new initiatives: repeal the remaining phase of the 1979 tax cut; increase tobacco, alcohol, and soft drink taxes; boost corporate income taxes; and raise the oil and gas severance tax.[3]

All of the education proposals died early in the 1981 session, in various House or Senate subcommittees. Jack Reed reasoned at the time that the legislature "really does not consider the improvement of public education to be a priority of state government" and claimed that lawmakers' reluctance could be traced to the three Rs: "resentment of federal interference," "reluctance" of private school supporters to tax themselves for public education, and "racism." Winter, however, had not expected the education proposals to get very far in 1981. The Blue Ribbon Committee's report had been released only weeks before the session began, and lawmakers had little time to digest them. Soon after the 1981 legislature adjourned, Winter began to build support for passage of the education package at the 1982 session.[4]

Winter took his case directly to the people of Mississippi, believing that mobilizing pubic opinion in favor of education reform could lead to legislative success. When Mullins complained after a hard day of talking with legislators during the 1981 session that the legislative attitude on education surely did not represent public opinion, Winter told Mullins, "Yes, it does. If you don't remember anything else, remember this: it is a direct mirror image of Mississippi and how Mississippians feel." Winter set out to transform public sentiment on the education question. During the second half of 1981, he met with business people, civic clubs, and teachers' organizations. He also visited schools to get a firsthand look at their operations. Elise Winter and members of the governor's staff made speeches to a variety of groups and also visited schools to talk with education officials. When Mrs. Winter visited schools, she often invited local legislators to join her and some admitted that they had never actually been inside the educational institutions in their districts.[5]

As part of his plea to his fellow citizens, Winter offered what he thought was a sensible method to pay for the reforms he proposed. Since legislative leaders had already pledged that they would not raise the income or sales taxes they had cut in 1979, Winter emphasized one of the other suggestions of the Blue Ribbon Commission: an increased oil and gas severance tax. Winter thought this tax might be a good source of additional revenues, especially with oil production on the rise in the state. The price of oil approached an all-time high of $40 a barrel, which created what Bill Minor dubbed "redneck millionaires" in the south Mississippi countryside. The severance tax, paid by those who received royalties on the removal of oil and gas from the ground, had not changed since first enacted in 1944. The Mississippi tax fell in the middle range of similar taxes in other states. Winter reasoned that since oil and gas were finite resources, the state should receive some benefit from these irreplaceable assets. Winter talked to friends in the industry, who indicated that a small increase in the severance tax would have a negligible effect on fuel production. Winter suggested that the tax rise from 6 to 9 percent, and that the revenues generated be put in an education trust fund; the interest from the account would support new education initiatives. Opponents of this tax hike, however, had begun to speak out almost from the time the Blue Ribbon Commission floated the idea. One disgruntled man from south Mississippi complained that it would hurt the "hardworking people in the oil and gas industry. . . . When lights go out, homes go cold, and cars go dead, parents with kindergarten-age children will still go to the polls and give votes to ignorant lawmakers who produce nothing, nothing at all."[6]

Despite the opposition to Winter's suggested funding mechanism, the effort to mobilize public opinion proved largely successful. At least forty state organizations endorsed Winter's education plans, including the Mississippi Economic Council, the League of Women Voters, the NAACP, the Children's Defense Fund, and practically every education group. A poll conducted by the Political Science Department at Mississippi State University in late 1981 indicated that 61 percent of the state's residents favored state-funded kindergartens and 91 percent wanted an effective compulsory school attendance law. By the beginning of the 1982 session, an active network of citizen lobbyists had joined the Winter administration in the campaign for education improvements. For instance, Tom Dulin, superintendent of the Winona Public Schools, wrote two hundred letters during the 1982 session urging support for the education trust fund and spoke to several groups urging adoption of the lay board of education.[7]

Heading into the 1982 legislative session, Winter was optimistic that lawmakers, though unprepared for bold action in 1981, would join the chorus of voices he had assembled clamoring for change. Some senators, however, had a different idea for reforming education. Fifteen minutes after the 1982 session began, Senator Emerson Stringer of Columbia introduced a bill providing for the teaching of creationism in the public schools. One hour later, the Senate, bypassing the typical committee deliberations and acting as a committee of the whole, passed the measure by a vote of 48 to 4. Many legislators feared voting against religion, even if they were troubled by or unaware of the details of the law. After passage, one senator commented that Governor Winter did not need to worry about improving education anymore, because the Senate had "just passed the most significant education bill in the South." When the legislation was sent to the Education Committee in the House, the chair, Robert Clark, announced that his committee did not feel that the legislature should dictate the curriculum for the public schools. Governor Winter agreed that the creationism bill was not a proper exercise of government authority, and he knew that the legislation would only create controversy and distract lawmakers from more substantive education matters. The creationism bill never made it out of Clark's committee.[8]

Despite Winter's hopes, his education reform package fared only slightly better in the 1982 session than it had in 1981. The most important proposal, public kindergartens, passed a couple of key committees in the House but never got further. The House bill for state-funded kindergartens faced a midnight deadline on February 11 for consideration by the full House but remained low on the calendar of bills to be considered. The chief sponsor of the bill, Jim Simpson, knew that many in the House, including Speaker Newman, opposed kindergartens; he also knew that in a voice vote many of the opponents would approve the bill because of its strong constituent support, especially from blacks and educators. According to House rules, if the bill were considered before deadline day, it could win with a simple majority, which its sponsors believed was possible; passage after deadline day would require a two-thirds vote, a virtual impossibility. Despite Simpson's support for kindergartens, he did not think the calendar of bills should be altered or the rules suspended. On the morning of February 10, Simpson and other House leaders agreed with the Speaker that adjournment would occur at 5:30 p.m.; the agreement was common knowledge among the House membership. At the appointed time, Simpson moved for adjournment, and Newman approved the motion to adjourn on a voice vote, although an audible sentiment opposed the motion. Just before the adjournment motion, Newman failed to recognize the chair of the Education Committee, Robert Clark, and his vice-chair, Tommy Walman, who both sought to have the kindergarten bill moved up to the top of the calendar for immediate consideration. Newman walked off the floor after he rapped his gavel to end the day's session, which effectively killed Winter's kindergarten plan in the 1982 session.[9]

Most of the other education proposals faced a similar, if less dramatic, fate. Several bills seeking to enact a new compulsory attendance law never advanced beyond the committee stage. Funding an education trust fund with an increased severance tax for oil and gas also failed to gain traction. The industry's lobby, the Mid-Continent Oil & Gas Association, adamantly opposed any increase in the levy. Just before the 1982 legislative session opened, the governor invited a group of industry leaders to the Mansion for lunch to discuss the possibility of raising the severance tax, and he was met "with some of the most hostile response that I can possibly describe." Soon after, the oil and gas lobby organized a protest that involved drilling rigs and oil trucks driving in circles around the Capitol, which snarled traffic in much of the downtown. Even without the protests, however, the tax increase had little chance of passage, especially in the House. After Winter's opening speech to the 1982 legislature argued for an increase in the severance tax, Speaker Buddy Newman, who had close ties to the oil and gas lobby, countered with the firm declaration that "there will not be a tax increase." Sonny Merideth, chair of the House Ways and Means Committee, also opposed tax increases, but believed if new revenues were raised, they should go to support existing programs, rather than new ones, such as public kindergartens. The legislature's rejection of oil and gas severance taxes as the way to fund education improvements, however, proved fortunate, as the world price of oil soon dropped precipitously, meaning that even with a higher tax rate, there would have been far too little additional revenue to fund the new education program in the years ahead.[10]

The only part of the education package passed by the 1982 legislature was the constitutional amendment for a lay board of education and an appointed state superintendent of education. The bill had been bottled up in debate over competing versions of the proposal for much of the session and received approval just prior to final adjournment. If ratified by Mississippians in a November vote, the amendment would transform the state Board of Education from a committee of three elected officials to a nine-member lay board, which would hire the state superintendent of education.[11]

After considering Governor Winter's education proposals in 1981 and 1982, the legislature had, in effect, dismissed them. From the governor's perspective, "both of those sessions were fiascos as far as education was concerned." After the 1982 session ended, the governor received a good deal of criticism. Political observers judged Winter a "well-meaning but not very politically effective leader." Norma Fields, capitol correspondent for the *Northeast Mississippi (Tupelo) Daily Journal*, wrote that the governor had succeeded in cleaning up state government, but "he has not accomplished the great things almost everyone expected of him, particularly in the field of education." Winter's advisers thought the governor should "play hardball" with the legislature and "adopt a take no prisoners approach to his enemies." But that method had never been Winter's style. Having fought many political battles, and having lost a number of those, Winter advised patience, maintaining the lines of communication, and better preparation for the next engagement. He told his staffers "there would almost certainly be another fight."[12]

Despite the detractors who thought Winter had failed to bend the legislature to his will, most people identified lawmakers as the chief obstacles to education reform. While Norma Fields expressed disappointment in Winter, she claimed, "The Mississippi House is dominated by a power clique headed by Buddy Newman and the Senate is dominated by a bunch of brainless dunderheads." She noted that this state of affairs might suffice "as long as a turkey's in power in the governor's mansion, . . . But then when you get a good governor for a change, you realize just how awful the legislature truly is." Buddy Newman received the most criticism for killing Winter's education package, especially after the ABC news magazine *20/20* aired a piece in August that dramatized Newman's abrupt adjournment on deadline day as the downfall of Mississippi's education reform efforts. The network's portrayal of the events of February 10, while somewhat simplistic, generated a good deal of anger within Mississippi toward the Speaker, and it increased the perception that Winter's proposals had not received a fair hearing because of the parliamentary shenanigans of one man. To counter criticism that legislators had blocked education reform, both the House and the Senate created ad hoc education committees to recommend action in the future, although neither committee embraced public kindergartens. Newman went on a speaking tour in the fall to offer a narrative touting "the 1982 session's stellar performance."[13]

For the next round of the education reform battle, Winter decided to take his cause directly to the people of Mississippi on a much larger scale than he had done in 1981. To help with the endeavor, his administration hired State Research Associates (SRA), educational consultants from Kentucky. The group proved a good choice, as it had worked with the Mississippi legislature on vocational education and had credibility among lawmakers. Based on SRA recommendations, the administration organized its public relations effort much like a political campaign, putting in a sophisticated and disciplined operation. From the summer of 1982 until the end of the year, 90 percent of the staff's attention centered on the education issue. Key members of the staff—David Crews, Dick Molpus, Ray Mabus, John Henegan, and Andy Mullins—met on the weekends at Molpus's isolated east Mississippi cabin to plan strategy for the education drive. They established a Speakers' Bureau, known as PACK (Public Awareness, Compulsory Education, and Kindergartens), and organizations throughout the state received speaker request forms. A series of speaker workshops prepared staff members to participate in the Speakers' Bureau. Those attending the workshops received a sample speech, fact sheets, and directions on how to record public opinion of those attending one of their talks. Between June and October 1982, the staff made almost 250 speeches statewide; Molpus led the way with more than thirty-five talks. Elise Winter had at least forty-one speaking engagements. The governor made even more presentations; he gave his education reform pitch to any gathering that would stand still long enough to listen. Particularly targeted were locales with legislators opposed to education reform. At every stop, someone collected lists of supporters who were subsequently asked to talk to their lawmakers about the need to vote for education reform. The campaign developed a media strategy, complete with radio spots and television and newspaper ads. Funding came from donations from the business community, which had organized as a nonprofit support group, Mississippians for Quality Education. A local public relations firm offered assistance pro bono.[14]

Nine public forums, billed as town meetings, took place around the state. Winter chaired these assemblies, intended to attract not only area legislators and educators to the events but also business people, local politicians, and the press, especially those who could be counted on to offer vocal support. Winter would speak and, if time permitted, take questions. Then he would hold a private meeting with legislators, while the staff and Elise Winter led small group sessions. The first forum was scheduled for Oxford at the local high school on the Tuesday evening after Labor Day. That evening, as the Winters and members of his staff flew over Oxford on the way to the airport, the governor could see from the air that the streets were jammed with traffic. The scene looked like a football Saturday when the Ole Miss Rebels were in town. Two to three thousand citizens jammed the high school, far too many for the auditorium; public address systems were set up in other parts of the school to accommodate all the listeners. After the event, Winter told Molpus that perhaps there was "a feeling out there that was stronger than any of us could have envisioned." After the Oxford forum, Winter became "convinced that the people of Mississippi were really interested in education reform and that we could get it passed."[15]

In the days and weeks ahead, similarly large and supportive turnouts greeted the Winter education caravan in Meridian, Columbus, and the Gulf Coast. Not every event, however, was an unqualified success. At Greenville, an overwhelmingly black crowd of about eight hundred, enthusiastic supporters of the governor's efforts, dominated the public forum, but the legislative meeting that followed deteriorated into a contentious affair in which backers and opponents of education reform engaged in a shouting match. In Laurel, the center of the Mississippi oil industry, negative statements in the local press and a bomb threat preceded the event. A large number of oil industry workers who thought the proposed oil and gas severance tax would cost them their jobs turned out for the meeting. Despite a potentially hostile crowd, the audience listened to Winter's remarks attentively in what most observers thought was his best speech of the nine forums. After Winter concluded his talk, however, a number of the workers came up to him and denounced his planned tax. One shouted in anger, "You're one-sided in everything you've done. It's rigged." The least successful of the nine forums was in Jackson. Although a large crowd turned out at the event, Winter found that most of the capital city lawmakers opposed education reform and that public opinion bordered on apathetic.[16]

The education forums during the fall of 1982 had shown a great deal of public support for reforming public education, and Winter had to decide how best to get the legislature to respond to this public groundswell. One key question was whether to call a special session or to wait for the regular 1983 session. During the public forums, most legislators who attended, even those who supported education reform, favored waiting for the regular session. Forcing the legislature to deal with the issue in a special session, however, offered some real advantages. Unlike the regular session when the legislature had to juggle many different issues and the education measures could get lost in the shuffle, in a special session, legislators had "no stumps to hide behind." They would have to take a stand. One indicator to the governor of whether to issue a call for a special session was the outcome of the lay education board constitutional amendment. In a close November vote, the reform passed with 52 percent of the electorate approving the change. Winter took the result as a sign that the people of Mississippi favored further education reforms. Most of those whom Winter consulted, however, thought an extra session would accomplish nothing, since the regular session was due to begin in less than two months. Even one of Winter's strongest advocates in the House, Jim Simpson, told the governor, "I don't think a damn thing is going to happen" but urged Winter to give it a try anyway. Only a few advisers, including Elise, thought Winter could capitalize on the public momentum by bringing the legislature back to Jackson as soon as possible.[17]

In mid-November, Winter issued the call for a special session to begin on December 6; the sole item on the agenda was education reform. As expected, the legislative response was generally negative, with important lawmakers claiming that they would do little to encourage passage of any legislation. Sonny Merideth wrote legislators and urged them to come to Jackson on December 6, pass a resolution thanking the governor for his interest in education, indicate that lawmakers would deal with these matters in its regular session, and then adjourn. Ellis Bodron, chair of the Senate Finance Committee, claimed he would not call a meeting of his committee, a move that would block all efforts to fund any education proposals that passed. He also claimed that "95 percent" of lawmakers opposed the special session. An important sign of support came from

House Speaker Buddy Newman—sensitive to his recent demonization as the primary stumbling block to education reform—who said Winter's plans deserved a full and fair hearing by legislators during the special session. Winter responded to the negative comments of key legislative leaders by continuing to talk to them about his proposals and their importance. In a meeting with Bodron and Merideth, chairs of the money committees in the Senate and House respectively, Winter made a key concession: if lawmakers opposed the oil and gas severance tax, they could propose another revenue source to fund education reform, and the governor would consider whatever they suggested.[18]

Although a number of legislative leaders remained reluctant to consider education legislation in the special session, Winter and his staff continued to work on mobilizing public opinion. Those efforts received a boost from the coverage of the education issue by the state's largest newspaper, the *Jackson Clarion-Ledger*. Under the leadership of executive editor Charles Overby, the paper had run numerous stories and editorials supporting educational change in the months leading up to the special session. In the week before the special session, reporters Fred Anklam Jr. and Nancy Weaver produced an eight-part series that detailed the team's six-month investigation into Mississippi's public schools. The first line of the series summed up the conclusion of the lengthy report: "Mississippi public schools aren't making the grade."[19]

Unlike the regular legislative sessions throughout Winter's gubernatorial term, which met in Jackson's old Central High School, the special session of December 1982 would take place in the newly renovated Capitol. In preparation for its reopening, Winter placed his own stamp on what the building should symbolize for the new Mississippi. Before the renovation, one of the first things visitors saw as they entered the Capitol, in the rotunda of the first floor, was a life-size statue of former Mississippi senator, Theodore Bilbo. The bronze statute had come to the Capitol soon after Bilbo's death in the late 1940s because of the efforts of the longtime secretary of state and Bilbo protégé from Pearl River County, Heber Ladner. The Bilbo monument had originally resided along the wall in the east wing of the first floor, where the portraits of all the former governors hung. In 1954, someone moved the statue to the central spot in the rotunda, where it became a rallying point for segregationists who applauded Bilbo's often outrageous racism and later for civil rights groups pressing for racial change. During the renovation, Winter arranged for the statue to be reinstalled in its original location in the east wing. In early November 1983, soon before the reopening date, Winter was taking a Saturday morning jog and stopped in at the Capitol to observe the final preparations. He was surprised to see the Bilbo statue being placed in its old spot in the rotunda. He called the head of the State Building Commission and the interior decorator for the Capitol and instructed them to have the statue moved back to its original location along the east hall. On his way to the Ole Miss-Tennessee football game later that afternoon, Winter stopped by the Capitol once again, only to find the statue located in the east hall but placed in the center of the hallway rather than along the wall. Winter ordered the workers to move the statute once again, and the next day, the story of the statute's travels was front-page news, as one of the workers, a Bilbo fan, had tipped off the press to a redecorating detail that Winter considered important but that he hoped to accomplish quietly.[20]

When legislators assembled for the special session a month later, Winter opened the proceedings with a paean to the newly appointed Capitol and told lawmakers they had a "special responsibility to make our action here worthy of this building." As he always did, Winter emphasized the economic benefits of education reform. He then discussed the need for the full range of changes bandied around over the preceding two years, including state-funded kindergartens, teacher aides for the first three grades, an effective compulsory school attendance law, better teacher training, and increased salaries for teachers.[21]

Acting first, the Senate quickly passed a bill that contained more education reform than the chamber had ever embraced but far less than Winter had requested. The Senate bill authorized reading aides for the first three grades, an improved compulsory attendance law, and new teacher certification and school accreditation standards. Bodron's Finance Committee, however, produced no corresponding legislation to fund the education proposals. The House, meanwhile, had crafted a more substantive proposal, one that eventually included all the Senate provisions and also had a kindergarten measure and a raise for teachers. To pay for the package, the same bill also contained $95 million in various "special interest" tax measures, including an increase in the oil and gas severance tax. Winter initially did not favor a bill combining the enabling legislation with the funding mechanisms, since a three-fifths vote would be needed on any bills that included revenue provisions, instead of a simple majority. Winter told Charlie Deaton, who directed staff legislative efforts during the special session, that he thought legislators had combined the proposals merely to kill education reform. Jim Simpson, however, convinced the governor that this maneuver would actually prevent the potential situation of lawmakers voting for reform measures and then failing to pass the revenue bill necessary to make those changes possible. The combined bill, known as the Education Reform Act, also satisfied Merideth, who wanted Mississippians made fully aware of what education reform would cost.[22]

Mississippi citizens and journalists helped keep legislators focused on passing an education reform program. During the session, people from around the state filled the Capitol to express their support for the governor's plans. The Winter administration urged citizens back home to keep the pressure on reform opponents by making daily calls to their legislators. The huge mobilization of public support got legislators' attention. As Ray Mabus noted, if a lawmaker got two phone calls about an issue, that was serious. If three calls came in, it was "a full-fledged emergency." Many legislators received as many as a hundred calls a day. The *Clarion-Ledger* and other newspapers in the state, such as the *Northeast Mississippi (Tupelo) Daily Journal* and the *Biloxi Sun-Herald*, covered the proceedings with a level of detail usually reserved for the major college football contests, and the editorial positions of many of the state's papers left little doubt that Governor Winter coached the favored home team. During the session, the *Clarion-Ledger* even included box scores listing those legislators voting against reform in a Hall of Shame column. Elise Winter also applied her own subtle form of pressure. As she had done frequently during the 1982 regular session, she attended a number of the proceedings during the special session. Education reform opponents would point her out in the gallery: "I see the First Lady up there trying to check on us and see how we're going to vote today."[23]

When the bill reached the floor of the House on Saturday, December 11, debate raged for eight hours. When one trio of representatives offered a substitute amendment that was little more than a thinly disguised version of the Senate bill passed earlier in the week, Simpson passionately denounced the attempt to substitute all the hard work of the House with the Senate's hastily drawn alternative, and legislators roundly defeated the proposed amendment. On the final vote, the House approved the Education Reform Act by a count of eighty to thirty-eight, well above the 60 percent needed for passage. Outside the House chamber after the vote, Winter shook hands with representatives. When he reached out to congratulate one lawmaker on his affirmative vote, the man refused to offer his hand; he said he opposed the plan, "But you got these folks [his constituents] to make me do it."[24]

House passage of the education bill increased the pressure on the Senate. Lieutenant Governor Brad Dye had listened to the House debate on the legislation. Although he had not started out as a strong supporter of education reform, Dye resolved after the House acted that the Senate needed to pass an education bill that included public kindergartens. Dye knew that Ellis Bodron remained a potentially fatal obstacle. Since the House bill would need to go to both the Senate Education Committee and Bodron's Finance Committee, Bodron had the power to block the bill from ever getting to the full Senate. Dye called Bodron and asked for assurances that the House bill would emerge from the Finance Committee. The following Monday, Winter held a private meeting with Bodron. During a lunch at the Mansion, Bodron continued to argue against both the need for and the expense of education reform. Winter asked his former Ole Miss classmate and Senate colleague at least to let the bill come to the Senate floor for a fair hearing and a vote.[25]

Bodron did as Winter and Dye asked: he ensured that a version of the House bill made it out of his Finance Committee. At a crucial moment, he even broke a tie vote in the committee to block a motion to table the bill. Bodron's committee, however, made substantial amendments to the measure. Instead of the broad range of "special interest" taxes, the Finance Committee substituted a 1 percent raise in the sales tax, which would generate more revenue than proposed by the House—a total of as much as $150 million. The House, however, did not favor a sales tax boost. Robert Clark and other black members of the legislature disliked increasing the sales tax because that levy fell disproportionately on the state's poorest citizens. Winter also disliked the regressive nature of additional sales taxes. In addition, the Senate Finance Committee took kindergartens out of the bill by a close vote of eleven to nine. Bodron commented before the committee vote, "The governor and some other people have taken the position that you can't do anything for education without kindergarten," but, he added, "We're not concerned with building a monument to the governor." The Senate Education Committee approved the Finance Committee's amended bill, but only because Dye had asked Senate Education chair Jack Gordon to approve it and send it to the Senate floor, where Dye had arranged for Senator Perrin Purvis to offer a floor amendment to reinsert the kindergarten program.[26]

When the full Senate considered the legislation, Purvis offered the kindergarten amendment, which led to an intense debate. The chamber remained evenly divided on the matter, but the kindergarten amendment survived by a vote of twenty-six to twenty-five, after Charles Ray Nix of Batesville, a vocal opponent of kindergartens, left the chamber, according to some accounts, to answer an important phone call. The night before, Dick Molpus had organized a cadre of four hundred of Nix's constituents to mount a calling campaign pressuring the senator to vote for the amendment. It is unlikely that Nix left the Senate chamber at such a crucial moment to take one of these calls, but he may have been reluctant to cast a negative vote against kindergartens after the flurry of messages he had recently received from pro-education voters back home. On the other hand, Nix had a close friendship with Lieutenant Governor Dye and may have "taken a walk" to spare Dye from having to cast a vote to break the tie, although Dye later indicated that he would have voted in the affirmative. With kindergartens back in the Senate bill, it passed by a vote of forty-three to nine.[27]

Since the House and Senate versions of the education bill differed, especially on their revenue provisions, a conference committee began deliberations over the weekend of December 18. The six-member committee (three from each chamber) included Robert Clark, Sonny Merideth, and Mike Nipper from the House, and Jack Gordon, John Frasier, and Ellis Bodron from the Senate. Merideth, Nipper, and Bodron were not supporters of education reform. The conference committee elected Clark chair, and the committee members began their deliberations by indicating what they did and did not want in the bill. Clark indicated his strong opposition to using the sales tax as a revenue source, which Bodron seized on as a way to kill the bill, by demanding that any funding for the education program include an increase in the sales tax. Bodron argued that the primary beneficiaries of education improvements would be people too poor to put their children in private schools, so the tax burden of the changes should in part fall to these folks. Following two days of negotiations, and after discussions with both the Speaker and with Winter, Clark agreed to a one-half percent increase in the sales tax as part of a larger revenue package. Clark realized that if he did not agree to some increase in the sales tax, he would only hurt "these little, poor children that I'd been fighting for, for years." He and Winter persuaded the legislative black caucus to agree to the wisdom of that position. The conference report worked out the funding differences but also included what many in the Winter administration thought was a killing amendment backed by Bodron, one that provided for a study that could potentially lead to further consolidation of school districts in the state. Although additional school consolidation offered efficiency and cost-savings, Winter had intentionally left out the controversial matter because it always encountered opposition. Winter decided not to fight the amendment and to take his chances with the conference bill as presented.[28]

The final bill approved by five of the six conferees (Nipper refused to sign the agreement) had essentially everything Winter had wanted included in the Education Reform Act: kindergartens, which would become mandatory in 1986; reading aides, a program to be implemented over a three-year period; a new compulsory attendance law; a teacher pay raise; and new mandates for teacher certification. The only major piece missing was the education trust fund, a far-reaching idea, but a small omission considering all the other reforms approved. The bill included Bodron's provision for a study of further school consolidation. To pay for the package, in addition to the sales tax increase, the bill provided for increases in corporate and personal income tax, as well as additional levies on alcohol, tobacco, and soft drinks. Altogether, the new taxes totaled $110 million, the largest tax hike in state history. With state elections less than a year away, lawmakers deferred the sales tax increase until January 1984, two months after a new legislature would be chosen. Limited debate on the conference bill in both chambers included some grumbling about the sales tax and school consolidation provisions, but the House approved the bill by a vote of ninety-six to twenty-five, and Senate concurrence followed by a count of thirty-seven to thirteen. Much like Winter's attempt to become governor, the third time was the charm for education reform. Reporters called it a "Christmas Miracle."[29]

Passage of the Education Reform Act represented a major victory for Winter. He praised legislators for passing "the most monumental education-tax program—the most monumental economic development program this state has ever seen in my lifetime." Others agreed about the legislation's importance. Frank Smith told Winter soon after the vote, "I believe you have just about accomplished the greatest legislative victory of a Governor since Mike Conner passed the sales tax"—high praise for one who had witnessed Conner's victory fifty years earlier. Nationally syndicated columnist Carl Rowan called the Education Reform Act, "The greatest piece of civil rights, national security and economic recovery legislation enacted" in 1982. Democrats around the nation took note of Winter's victory and touted him as a potential member of a future Democratic administration in Washington, D.C. Walter Mondale, at the time the frontrunner among potential Democratic presidential candidates in 1984, said, "Any President who would not consider him [Winter] for a high position is missing a big opportunity. Bill Winter is as good a governor as there is in the nation. At a time most states are pulling back and retrenching, he has dealt with the problems of the present and the demands of the future. He is an able, courageous, honest, substantial leader. This guy is class." Hamilton Jordan, Jimmy Carter's former chief of staff, believed that Winter's administration represented a good model for national Democrats seeking the White House. Jordan described Winter as a "progressive," but one who knows "how to put together an electoral and governing coalition that addresses the human needs of our people while also recognizing and accepting the limits of government and government resources."[30]

The passage of the Education Reform Act of 1982 may have raised the national profile of William Winter, but its true impact was much more profound. A major achievement for Mississippi, it was the most important education law in the state's history, and its passage represented a racial turning point for the state as well. For decades, the state legislature had slighted public education because many lawmakers resisted providing resources for black schools. Passage of the Education Reform Act of 1982, as the *Memphis Commercial Appeal* noted, demonstrated an acknowledgment "of the special needs of the state's black residents" and a "recognition that the progress of white Mississippians is bound to that of its black citizens." Black Mississippians realized the significance of the new legislation.

L. C. Dorsey, a former sharecropper who worked on a broad range of civil rights issues in the Delta, told Winter's friend Larry Noble that the governor's education initiatives would ensure that her grandchildren received a better education than the one she had been able to get. Winter's signal victory in his long crusade for educational improvement in his native state advanced the cause of racial reconciliation, which Winter's political career had helped promote. The education reform bill also demonstrated the power of an informed electorate to arrest the oligarchic lethargy of the Mississippi legislature. As Dick Molpus later observed, passage of the act "brought for the first time, maybe since Reconstruction, democracy to the state capital."[31]

12

POST-GOVERNOR BLUES

The Christmas Miracle of 1982 not only boosted William Winter's popularity but also transformed the political landscape of Mississippi. The 1983 state elections demonstrated strong public support for the education reform cause, and numerous individuals with close ties to the governor were elevated to political office. As journalist Bill Minor noted, the governor succeeded in "Winterizing" state government.[1] At the same time, Winter, who was still only sixty years old in 1983, lamented the end of his four years as governor. He would have liked to have served another four years and likely could have easily won reelection, but the Mississippi Constitution prohibited gubernatorial succession.

The momentum that produced the Education Reform Act of 1982 carried over into the last year of Winter's administration. Mississippi governors usually accomplished little in their last year in office, but when the legislature convened in early 1983, just a few short weeks after ratifying the Education Reform Act, lawmakers acted on a number of Winter priorities. The legislature approved the Public Utilities Reform Act, the first overhaul of Mississippi's utilities law since 1956. Winter aide Herman Glazier helped draft the new model law, which provided extra staff for the Public Service Commission and required public oversight of both utility construction projects and contractual agreements between utility affiliates. The legislature also approved an open records bill that the governor had pressed for since he took office. The law granted the public the right to examine most records generated by Mississippi government at all levels and advanced a key Winter objective: maintaining citizen faith in government by encouraging transparency and accountability on the part of elected and appointed public officials. In addition, prison reform initiatives supported by Winter, which the 1982 legislature had rejected, were reintroduced in 1983, this time with greater success.[2]

After the close of the 1983 legislative session, a number of matters occupied the governor's attention. At the beginning of June, the dedication ceremony for the remodeled Capitol was held. A crowd of two thousand attended to hear speeches by J. P. Coleman and William Winter. Coleman recounted the history of the construction of the New Capitol at the turn of the twentieth century. He recalled that twenty-two years earlier he had spoken at the dedication of another newly restored structure, the Old Capitol Building, a project Winter had helped win legislative support for in the 1950s. While Coleman paid homage to Mississippi's official architecture, Winter used the occasion to talk about the future for Mississippians. He said that the state's residents had a "reasonable anticipation that the majesty of the building would be matched by the performances of those who serve here. Nothing could be more detrimental to our system of government and its ideals than to have this architectural triumph be the scene of political mediocrity." Winter noted that the 1982 special session and the 1983 regular session had been a fine beginning, but, he said, Mississippi needed "an increased commitment to do much more if we are going to claim our rightful place among the leading states of the region." Winter restated his longstanding belief that great things were possible now that Mississippi had moved beyond the racial divisions that had dimmed its progress for so long: "I am convinced that there is a unique quality to this fascinating mix of human beings that claim to be Mississippians. It is a quality that lay unrecognized for so many years under the inhibitions of a social system that generated for itself too many fears. Now with those fears dissipated and laid to rest, we can truly be ourselves and enjoy what so many other people in this country may have forgotten how to enjoy, and that is our common humanity."[3]

Throughout the summer of 1983, Winter faced an impassioned debate in the state over a difficult human-rights issue: the resumption of capital punishment. After almost two decades in which lawsuits challenging the legality of capital punishment had halted the execution of Mississippi criminals, in May 1983 the Mississippi Supreme Court set a July date for the execution of Jimmy Lee Gray. In 1976, Gray had kidnapped, brutally raped, and murdered a three-year-old girl in south Mississippi. Less than a year earlier, Gray had been released on parole from an Arizona prison after serving seven years for murder. A jury convicted Gray of the Mississippi crimes in 1976 and condemned him to death in the gas chamber, but years of appeals delayed the sentence. As the July execution date approached, opponents of the death penalty, including Winter's minister from Fondren Presbyterian, urged him to commute Gray's sentence. At the same time, a majority of Mississippians supported capital punishment and urged Winter not to do so. Winter's own beliefs on capital punishment were as measured as his approach to almost every other issue. He was not a strong supporter of capital punishment, and he recognized the "inequities" that existed within the criminal justice system, which sometimes wrongly convicted the innocent. At the same time, Winter believed, as he told his friend Larry Noble earlier in 1983, "There are some unfortunate human beings who have perpetrated crimes so atrocious as to cancel out any responsibility on society to maintain them until they die of natural causes." For Winter, Gray's case fit that standard. Even Gray's mother had gone on record saying that the state should execute her son. After reviewing the case, with the assistance of his chief of staff John Henegan, Winter decided Gray did not deserve clemency. Although "I had hoped it would not become my lot to make a call on another person's life," Winter told reporters, "I feel I've done the right thing."[4]

Gray's July execution date, however, was delayed once again but then reset for early September; this time, all appeals were exhausted. As the new execution date loomed, numerous groups and individuals continued to try to convince Winter to stop the action. The night before the execution, protesters held a candlelight vigil outside the Governor's Mansion. Somewhat ominously, lightning struck the Mansion that night. Winter had heard all the arguments against capital punishment but remained unconvinced, at least in the case of Jimmy Lee Gray. He told Lieutenant Governor Dye shortly before Gray was put to death that "execution might not be a deterrent to other folks but Gray wasn't going to kill anybody else." Gray based his last appeal to the U.S. Supreme Court on the claim that execution by use of the Mississippi gas chamber was unconstitutional and violated the bar against "cruel and unusual punishment." That assertion seemed justified when Mississippi finally carried out Gray's execution. After the fatal gas entered the death chamber at Parchman, witnesses claimed Gray choked for at least eight minutes, while his head banged violently against a metal pole behind the chair that held him down. The following year, the state legislature abandoned the gas chamber and adopted lethal injection as the method of state execution.[5]

While the capital punishment debate raged in Mississippi, Winter dealt with the state's seemingly unending financial problems. For the first two months of the new fiscal year, which began in July, expected tax revenues fell below projections, and in September, Winter ordered budget cuts of 5 percent. Although the rest of the country was emerging from economic recession, the recovery had not yet reached the Magnolia State. As the money woes continued into October, with tax collections already more than $52 million below projections, Winter knew that he could slash the budget only so much without doing a "grave disservice to the people of Mississippi through an inability to deliver the essential services that they have a right to expect." Despite the spending cuts, the state still faced a $120 million deficit for the new budget year. As Winter told a *Time* magazine reporter, "We've cut all the fat we can. Now we're talking about cutting out arms and legs." Winter favored a tax increase to deal with the remaining deficit. He worried that lawmakers, in order to avoid dealing with the problem without seeking new revenues, might shift some of the large tax increase passed for education to cover general fund obligations. Winter strongly believed such an action would be "breaking faith" with Mississippi citizens. The governor also felt he had a responsibility to solve the state's financial crisis before a new administration took over.[6]

In November, after the state elections, Winter called the legislature into special session to address the budget shortfall. He proposed temporarily raising the sales tax an extra half cent and placing a temporary surtax on individual and corporate income taxes. Most legislators agreed that the solution to the budget problems required new taxes rather than additional budget cuts. The legislators quickly approved the temporary tax increase, to expire after seven months, which put the state's finances back in the black for the next administration and preserved the revenues slated for education improvements. The special session, which the *Greenwood Commonwealth* described as "a heartening demonstration of how our system of state government can respond to unanticipated problems responsibly, harmoniously and speedily," offered further proof of how much clout Winter had earned with the legislature as a result of his success in the education reform fight.[7]

ℰ✧

Winter could not run for a second term as governor, but he nevertheless had a major impact on the 1983 state elections and on the operation of Mississippi government for years thereafter. Ray Mabus, who served as one of Winter's legislative assistants and as his legal counsel, ran for state auditor. Winter expected Mabus to have a tough race, since insiders had typically held the office. Although the longtime auditor, Hamp King, was retiring, one of King's aides planned to succeed his boss. Mabus, however, ran a savvy campaign and won the primary election. Mabus had no Republican opponent in the general election, but King threatened to run as an independent because he thought Mabus had besmirched his office during the primary campaign. Winter successfully discouraged this independent candidacy when he met with King and advised him that voters would view that action as "sour grapes," and it would sully his twenty-year career in public service. As state auditor, Mabus worked with the FBI on a high-profile campaign, Operation Pretense, to clean up county government, which led to the indictment of sixty local officials. This anticorruption stand, and his support for continued education reform, helped get him elected to the governor's office in 1987. He has since served as ambassador to Saudi Arabia and as Secretary of the Navy.[8]

Dick Molpus, who directed Winter's Office of Federal-State Programs and was a key strategist in the education reform effort, was elected in 1983 to the first of three terms as secretary of state. During his tenure, Molpus earned a reputation as a reformer. He led the fight to place stricter restrictions on lobbyists, urged the adoption of the initiative and referendum, and oversaw the rebidding of leases for the state's sixteenth-section lands in order to generate additional funds for local school districts. In 1995, Molpus won the Democratic nomination for governor but lost a hard-fought battle to incumbent Republican Kirk Fordice in the general election.

Bill Cole, Winter's first chief of staff, who was appointed by Winter as state treasurer, won election to the position in his own right in 1983. The fact that three Winter staffers won election to major statewide offices in 1983 was unprecedented and demonstrated the approval voters had for the Winter administration. In addition to these major victories, Cy Rosenblatt, an administrative assistant for health policy in the Winter administration, won a seat in the Mississippi Senate. After the victories of his political associates, Winter congratulated them, saying, "They won on the basis of their individual efforts." He praised voters for making "the same decision I made—that is, that state government can run only on the basis of having capable, concerned, talented people." Other Winter aides would have successful political careers of their own in the years ahead. Marshall Bennett—a Winter legislative assistant before the governor appointed him to head the state's Workmen's Compensation Commission—was elected state treasurer for four terms beginning in 1987. Steve Patterson, who served as a special assistant overseeing intergovernmental relations in the Winter administration, won two terms as state auditor. Elected in 1991 and 1995, Patterson was forced to resign in 1996 over legal problems related to unpaid taxes, and in 2009, in an unrelated case, he pled guilty to federal bribery charges and served almost two years in prison.[9]

The 1983 elections clearly demonstrated the popular support voters gave Winter's education reforms. Mississippi First, a biracial citizen group that organized in 1982 to help promote education reform, recruited new pro-education reform candidates in many districts with entrenched incumbents who had opposed Winter's education program. A number of these legislators went down to defeat in 1983, most notably longtime Senate Finance Committee chairman, Ellis Bodron. A few successful House candidates campaigned on their opposition to the Speaker, Buddy Newman, still widely regarded as a symbol of legislative resistance to education reform, despite his acquiescing in the passage of the Education Reform Act at the 1982 special session. That opposition persisted in the years that followed and culminated with a substantial reduction in the House Speaker's powers during the 1987 session, which led Newman to retire from legislative service. The impact of Winter's education reforms continued to reverberate during the 1987 election cycle as well. Candidates from governor down to legislator pledged their dedication to maintaining and increasing state support for public education.[10]

Winter also played a crucial role in the selection of his successor in 1983. The race for the Democratic nomination for the top spot came down to a battle among three major contenders: Attorney General Bill Allain, Winter's 1979 opponent Evelyn Gandy, and Delta farmer and hotelier Mike Sturdivant. As had been his practice in other races while serving as governor, Winter did not take sides in the primary. Allain emerged as the Democratic nominee, in large part because of the highly visible positions he took as attorney general: opposing sharp rate increases by utility companies, punishing violations of the state's open meetings law, and most notably, suing to prevent legislators from serving on state executive boards (the case was decided in Allain's favor a few weeks after the general election in November). Leon Bramlett, who had lost to Gil Carmichael in the 1979 Republican primary, was the unopposed nominee of his party. Every candidate in the governor's race supported education reform, a further indicator of how effectively the Winter administration had reshaped the political debate.[11]

Although the primary campaign had not generated much interest, that all changed in late October, just weeks before the general election. A group of Republicans, led by Jackson oilman Billy Mounger, claimed they had evidence that Allain was a homosexual who regularly had sexual encounters with black male transvestites. The chief witnesses about this activity were the male prostitutes allegedly involved with Allain. Bramlett distanced himself from the investigation into Allain's background, but Mounger and others aggressively publicized the allegations. Allain denied the innuendo, and the state Democratic Party rallied to his defense, led by William Winter, who denounced the claims as "the most scurrilous kind of political activity." Although Winter and Allain had never been political allies, Winter strongly defended Allain's candidacy in the wake of the Republican bombshell. When some Democrats suggested replacing Allain as the Democratic nominee two weeks before the election, Winter responded by hitting the campaign trail hard for Allain. That effort by the popular sitting governor in the waning days of the contest played a pivotal role in Allain winning the contest with 55 percent of the vote. Shortly before Allain's inauguration, the male prostitutes recanted their stories and admitted they had been paid to lie about the affairs.[12]

While Winter helped others get elected to office as his term wound down, he also contemplated his own future. One possibility was involvement in the 1984 campaign of one of the Democratic presidential hopefuls. A number of potential candidates had visited Mississippi in 1982 and 1983, including Walter Mondale, John Glenn, Gary Hart, Ernest Hollings, and Reuben Askew, although Winter did not endorse any of them. Mondale in particular sought out Winter's support and tried to get him to accept a major position in his campaign. Winter continued to talk with Mondale about that possibility into the summer of 1983, but

Mondale wanted Winter to devote a significant amount of time to the campaign beginning in the fall of 1983, so Winter declined. He did not want to accept such a time-consuming job before his term ended, because it would interfere with his remaining gubernatorial obligations.[13]

Another possibility arose in 1983 after the Ole Miss chancellor, Porter Fortune, announced his retirement. A number of Winter's friends, including Warren Hood and Tom Bourdeaux, a member of the higher education board of trustees, urged Winter to seek the position. After all, Winter dearly loved Ole Miss. After the state's higher education board began its national search for Fortune's replacement, a petition signed in September 1983 by more than 70 percent of the tenured faculty on campus urged the board of trustees to name Winter to the post. Faculty members believed Winter might replicate the career of progressive North Carolina governor Terry Sanford, who followed up his gubernatorial term with a long and successful career as president of Duke University. Winter initially hesitated to indicate any interest in the position. He hoped to put off a decision about his future until after his term as governor ended, but with the search for a new chancellor rapidly coming to a close, in late October, Winter sent a brief letter to the board chairman, John Lovelace, expressing his interest in the position. Although a good deal of sentiment existed in favor of Winter's candidacy, not everyone approved of the move. In late November, a group of Ole Miss alumni came to see the governor and told him they thought his becoming chancellor would be a mistake. They argued that the move would appear politically motivated, since Winter had appointed five of the thirteen members of the board of trustees. Winter also recognized that problem and expressed similar concerns to a number of people. Others questioned Winter's suitability since he did not have the usual academic credentials or any higher education experience.[14]

The higher education board of trustees remained divided on the Winter nomination. As expected, the five Winter appointees supported the governor. The four Finch trustees reportedly all initially opposed the appointment, while the four Waller board members were split. [15] A seven-person subcommittee of the board of the trustees served as the search committee and interviewed Winter in early December as one of the finalists for the job. The search committee actually voted four to three against offering Winter the position, but the full board overturned that recommendation, by a count of eight to five. The eight positive votes came from the five Winter board members, one Finch appointee, and two of the Waller trustees. After the board's endorsement of Winter on December 14, Lovelace called Winter, who was in Williamsburg, Virginia, giving a speech. Winter initially agreed to take the job, but shortly thereafter, he called Tom Bourdeaux and indicated that he wanted to talk things over with the board the following morning before making a final decision. Winter returned to Mississippi that night and talked to a number of his supporters. The next day he told the board of trustees that he would accept their offer to become the next Ole Miss chancellor.[16]

Winter "spent a miserable weekend" agonizing over whether he had made the right decision. On Monday morning he told Elise that he had changed his mind about accepting the chancellorship. Later that morning, Winter announced his new decision to reporters at his weekly press conference. Those present noted that the governor seemed visibly relieved about his change of plans. He could not get over the fact that his selection smacked of the kind of political favoritism he had long abhorred. He admitted to "a continuing concern about the precedent that would be set by an incumbent governor being selected by a relatively narrow majority made possible by his own appointees." He did not want his selection as chancellor to in any way be perceived as a return to the days when state politicians, like Theodore Bilbo, micromanaged the universities. In the end, Winter decided "that the University would be better [off] if they went out and sought somebody who did not have any political connections." Winter also worried about the University's financial situation and believed that the "resources are just not available for me to do the kind of job that would satisfy me and the university." He thought that much of his time would be spent fundraising, not the kind of work he particularly liked to do. Winter's vacillation on the chancellorship offer "puzzled" some of his supporters and lent credence to Winter's critics, who said the governor had trouble making decisions. Winter, however, told reporters, "Only foolish people never change their mind." Members of Winter's inner circle tried to talk to him after his surprise announcement, but for one of the few times during his gubernatorial administration, he had no interest in a spirited debate with his subordinates.[17]

Winter would later second-guess his decision to refuse the Ole Miss chancellorship, but he was considering another opportunity at the same time, which may have played a role in his decision to reject the Ole Miss job. In the summer of 1983, national Democrats searched for candidates to challenge Republicans in the U.S. Senate up for reelection in 1984. Thad Cochran of Mississippi, just completing his first term in the upper chamber, seemed like a possible target, and Winter represented a strong potential challenger. One national Democrat called Winter the "wonderchild of the Democratic Senate possibilities." Some within the Democratic Party thought Winter had a promising future on the national stage, perhaps as a future presidential or vice-presidential candidate.[18]

In June 1983, while attending a meeting of the Appalachian Regional Commission in Washington, D. C., Winter had a breakfast meeting with a dozen Democratic Senate leaders, including Robert Byrd and Lloyd Bentsen, chairman of the Democratic Senatorial Campaign Committee. Byrd and Bentsen gave Winter the "hard sell" about challenging Cochran. The Senate leaders promised financial support for a Senate bid and also reminded Winter that if the Democrats could regain control of the Senate his old friend John Stennis would rise to the position of President Pro Tempore and would assume the chair of the Senate Appropriations Committee. Winter made two additional trips to the nation's capital in the fall, one to meet with the Democratic Senatorial Campaign Committee, where he received further reassurances of "financial and technical" assistance in a Winter campaign for Senate, and another visit to consult with national Democratic constituencies—including labor leaders and officials from the National Education Association and the American Israeli Public Affairs Committee—and to reconnect with the two national political consultants from his 1979 race: Peter Hart and Bob Squier. As Winter considered reversing his decision to accept the Ole Miss chancellorship over the weekend of December 17, Senator Bentsen called again and urged the governor to make the race against Cochran.[19]

A Hart poll conducted in October 1983 reflected Winter's popularity and suggested that he had a ten-point lead over Cochran in a U.S. Senate race, although Republican polls disputed Winter's advantage. Hart told Winter that he could win against Cochran but his victory would not be easy. Winter would need nearly all the black votes in a large turnout and at least one in three of the white votes in order to win. Winter remained unsure about his chances. He also did not particularly want to relocate to Washington, D.C. After one of his fall visits to the nation's capital, Winter and Andy Mullins became snarled in a major traffic jam on the way to the airport. Winter confided to Mullins, "I don't want to come up here." Despite Winter's personal preferences, other forces pulled him toward entering the race. Most important, he felt a certain obligation to assist the Democratic Party in general, and his longtime friend, John Stennis, in particular by regaining Cochran's seat for the party. His closest advisers differed in their guidance. Some worried that he could not convince voters of a "compelling reason for the people of Mississippi to replace Thad Cochran." Others, however, urged Winter to make the race, not only because they thought he could win, but also because they thought the contest would help him get through an especially difficult time for him personally: he was saddened about leaving the governor's office, a job he had enjoyed immensely.[20]

Defeating Cochran would not be as easy as some Democrats assumed. The Republican senator had emerged as a popular and effective politician. Originally from north Mississippi, Cochran grew up near Jackson. He attended Ole Miss as an undergraduate, served in the Navy as a lieutenant, and then returned to Ole Miss for law school. He joined a Jackson law firm after graduation and first entered Republican politics in 1968, when he served as head of the Mississippi Citizens for Nixon-Agnew. In the 1970s, he was elected to the House of Representatives three times from a congressional district that was 40 percent black; he then won the 1978 U.S. Senate contest and became the first Republican senator from Mississippi since Reconstruction.[21]

Winter struggled to make a decision about entering the Senate race for several months. For weeks after he left office in January 1984, he continued to weigh whether his widely acknowledged popularity within Mississippi could translate into a U.S. Senate victory. One factor in his uncertainty was another poll conducted by Hart in late January 1984, which showed that Winter's support in a race against Cochran had declined. After being ten points ahead of the senator in October, Winter had dropped to a five-point underdog just weeks after leaving the governor's office. His indecision about the Ole Miss position had apparently tarnished his image, even among Democrats, and certainly played a role in diminishing public sentiment for Winter in a race against Cochran.[22]

On the day of Winter's scheduled press conference to announce his intentions, no one really knew his final decision. The event was delayed almost a half hour as Winter consulted with Elise and Lele Winter and his minister, Emett Barfield, up to the last minute. Even Winter still remained unsure what he would say as he approached the podium. His opening remarks, about the high cost of a senatorial campaign and the difficulties of moving to Washington, D.C., should he win, suggested that Winter would decline to run against Cochran. After hearing the first part of the speech, Cochran's aides relayed a message to the senator that Winter was not going entering the race. When those same aides returned to hear the rest of the speech, Winter was still weighing the pros and cons of making the race. Then, he announced his candidacy for the U.S. Senate. The assembled crowd erupted in applause, lifting Winter's spirits about his decision, at least temporarily. The Republican leadership in Mississippi immediately attacked him for his indecisiveness about whether to run against Cochran (and his earlier uncertainty about accepting the Ole Miss chancellorship). Republican leader Mike Retzer quipped, "We [will] all wait three days for a cooling off period and see if he is real serious about running. Then we are going to get busy and reelect our senator."[23]

In the days ahead, some may have indeed thought that Winter had changed his mind about running against Cochran, as the former governor did little to advance his candidacy until after the April qualifying deadline, and then, he did not campaign much before the primary vote on June 5. When Winter began raising funds in the state, he soon discovered that many of his former supporters, especially among the "business and professional establishment," had already decided to back Cochran. Some of them were Democrats who had crossed party lines to vote for the moderate Cochran in his previous races. Others were simply "prudent business people," hesitant about funding a challenge to an incumbent senator who remained in a position to help them. Winter secured a significant amount of financing from outside the state, as promised by the Democratic Senatorial Campaign Committee, which helped make up for the loss of in-state support, but Cochran still had a better-financed campaign than Winter. In the end, Cochran raised four times more than the Winter campaign generated. Winter assembled a campaign organization headed by Guy Land, who had served as a staffer in Senator Stennis's office. Jan Garrick, a lawyer and former newspaper reporter from Quitman, worked as press secretary, and Beverly Coleman, who had served as comptroller for the Winter administration's Office of Federal-State Programs, coordinated the fundraising efforts. Peter Hart and Bob Squier signed on again as political and media consultants, and Squier provided a boost to the fundraising efforts, "by talking up the campaign around the country." As in previous Winter campaigns, his family also provided essential campaign support, especially in the latter stages of the race.[24]

The strategy for the Winter campaign, which Land outlined in late April, acknowledged that many former Winter supporters could not be counted on for this race and emphasized that Winter would need to appeal to a coalition of "blacks, traditional Democrats, the education establishment, labor, working-class whites, and a residue of old-line Winter supporters." To win these votes, Land urged Winter "to run a more populist race than he has in the past." He would need to attack Cochran's record in Congress aggressively, especially his votes for Reagan policies that harmed poorer Mississippians and for his lack of concrete achievements during his first term in the U.S. Senate. Because voters liked Cochran personally, Land suggested Winter portray the senator as "the nice guy who just hasn't produced." Winter correctly concluded he did not need to campaign energetically to win the Democratic primary; he won 70 percent of the vote over three little-known challengers. His lack of activity during the primary campaign, however, which the *New York Times* described as "languid," stood in marked contrast to Cochran's vigorous activities early in the race.[25]

Early on, Winter's closest advisers recognized that, unlike his nine previous political races, he never had his heart in the Senate campaign. The man who had always been a great campaigner seemed to be merely going through the motions. Winter was disheartened. Many of his longtime supporters were not with him this time, like his friend Warren Hood, who had been a key Winter stalwart and fundraiser in his three gubernatorial contests. When Hood and other close associates told Winter they believed Cochran was going to be reelected, and they could not get involved in the Winter campaign, or that they could not risk challenging an incumbent senator, much of Winter's usual drive and the joy of campaigning began to slip away. Winter, ever the history student, also realized that few in his position had won such a campaign. Since 1900 there had been twenty Mississippi governors: three died in office; fifteen of the remaining seventeen subsequently ran for another major political office, as governor, as lieutenant governor, or U.S. Senator, and only three of those won. In addition, only three incumbent U.S. senators from Mississippi had failed to be reelected in the twentieth century. Polls continued to confirm Winter's doubts about his chances. A May survey by Peter Hart showed that Winter trailed Cochran by 57 to 34 percent, with only 9 percent still undecided. As Hart noted, since Winter had announced his entry in the race, "this election has changed from a competitive contest to a lopsided one favoring Thad Cochran." To salvage the race, the consultant said, "William Winter must begin flat-out campaigning and change both the pace and style of his campaign."[26]

Winter did become a more active campaigner, but he found Thad Cochran a formidable opponent. The senator was personally popular, and he had made few enemies. When the candidates first appeared together in late June 1984, at the Mississippi Press Association candidate forum, Winter chided Cochran for his support of Reagan's policies, which had led to record federal deficits. Although Cochran had backed many of the proposals of the Reagan administration, the Mississippi Republican had also supported policies that endeared him to traditionally Democratic constituencies: school lunch and food-stamp programs, measures to aid historically black colleges, the Martin Luther King Jr. holiday, the extension of the Voting Rights Act, and loan programs for small farmers. At the same event, Cochran claimed that Winter was forced into the race by the national Democratic establishment merely to advance the interests of the national party. That charge was true, though its implication that Winter embraced the entire Democratic Party platform was inaccurate. In truth, Cochran was not a hard-line Reagan Republican, and Winter was not a liberal Democrat in the mold of Ted Kennedy.[27]

The Winter strategy depended on securing nearly all of the state's black vote, but Cochran made a strong bid to attract significant support from this constituency. Cochran campaigned hard in black neighborhoods, had a solid record on civil rights issues, and hired blacks to work on his Washington staff. His efforts to attract black votes made it impossible for Winter to assume that he had these traditional Democrats completely in his camp. Even so, most black Mississippians favored Winter as someone who would represent their interests in the U.S. Senate. Although it did not help woo some white voters, Winter embraced the cause of racial reconciliation. At a Panola County Democratic meeting, Winter told the crowd that he wanted Mississippians not just to "live better," but to "live together better."[28]

Winter also had to contend with the possibility of an independent black candidacy in the Senate contest, similar to the bid by Charles Evers in 1978, which had helped send Cochran to the U.S. Senate in the first place. Johnnie Walls, a black lawyer from Greenwood, openly discussed making the race for several weeks in late August and early September; Walls claimed that black Democrats did not "receive the same support we give whites." Black Mississippians had a concrete example of that in the actions of Senator Stennis, who endorsed Winter but refused to back Robert Clark in his rematch with Webb Franklin for a congressional seat. In a move that staved off potential disaster for the Winter campaign, national black Democratic leader Jesse Jackson helped convince Walls that his independent bid for the Senate would only harm the national Democratic cause. The sentiment that animated the Walls challenge, however, likely diminished the enthusiasm of some black voters for the Winter candidacy.[29]

Winter had the misfortune of running in a year when a popular Republican incumbent, Ronald Reagan, headed the national ticket. At the same time, many Mississippi voters regarded the Democratic standard bearers, Walter Mondale and Geraldine Ferraro, as too liberal. In early August, Mondale and Ferraro began their national campaign with a rally in Jackson, in front of the Governor's Mansion. Some of Winter's advisers thought he should find an excuse to miss the event, but Winter believed he needed to attend, along with Robert Clark and the other Democratic candidates, to demonstrate support for a unified party. At the rally, Mondale proclaimed that after "Geraldine Ferraro is elected vice president and William Winter is elected to the U.S. Senate, she will only recognize Sen. Winter until all the business of Mississippi is taken care of." Not enough Mississippians, however, saw the importance of how a Democratic administration might provide more benefits to a state like Mississippi that depended greatly on federal dollars. A month before the election, polls showed that the national Republican ticket would win the state with at least 60 percent of the vote.[30]

By early October, little had changed in Mississippi's U.S. Senate race since the beginning of the summer. Polls showed Cochran still led with 57 percent of the vote. Winter had increased his total slightly, to 37 percent, with 6 percent still undecided. About 80 percent of black voters (somewhat less than anticipated) favored Winter, and he polled only about one-fifth of the white vote, far short of the one-third he was thought to need.[31]

In the end, Cochran won the race with 61 percent of the vote. Despite the decisive defeat, Winter remained upbeat. He told his disappointed supporters on election night, "I want the Democratic Party to come out of this election more determined than ever that it will create a renewed spirit, a renewed faith that it will attract the majority of Mississippians and the majority of Americans." He also told *New York Times* journalist Tom Wicker that he remained "hopeful that reasonable people from both the white and black community actually constitute a majority in Mississippi, and given a normal political climate (without a Reagan or a popular incumbent running) will continue to work together to maintain an effective Democratic Party."[32]

Whatever the implications of the 1984 U.S. Senate race for the future of state politics, the contest had pitted two Mississippi moderates against each other. Winter had an impressive record as a distinguished Mississippi politician. Unfortunately for Winter, Thad Cochran also had done a laudable job as a member of the state's congressional delegation. As Winter later recalled, he never found a way to make the case that "Thad Cochran should be replaced by William Winter." With little to distinguish the candidates, the vote became something of a popularity contest, and Mississippians chose the well-liked incumbent Republican at the same time that they offered strong support for the reelection of a popular Republican president. Erle Johnston, who also hailed from Grenada but at the time served as mayor of Forest, told Winter shortly after the election that he had campaigned for Winter in Grenada. He sensed that many longtime Winter supporters there "had nothing against Cochran and thought he deserved a second term. At the same time, they told me they had not changed their warm feeling for you."[33]

At his concession speech, Winter did not completely eliminate the possibility that he might make another political race in the future, although he had no immediate political plans or prospects. For almost a year, Winter had searched for a leadership position as a follow-up to his successful term as governor. He would have preferred to serve another term as governor, but the law precluded that possibility. William Winter soon came to realize, however, that he did not have to hold an office to continue his lifelong vocation of public service. The next twenty-five years of Winter's life would offer ample proof of that.[34]

13

FIGHTING FOR THE NEW MISSISSIPPI

Winter's defeat in the U.S. Senate race in 1984 left him disheartened. He felt he had essentially wasted a year on a fruitless effort, one that he had never really totally embraced. Winter, however, quickly turned his attention to other matters. Harvard University's Institute of Politics named him one of its six fellows for the spring 1985 semester. Winter taught a seminar entitled, "The South and the Nation," which covered topics such as "New Versus Old Politics in the South," "Southern Growth: Blessing or Bugaboo?" "New Emphasis on Education," and "Southern Writers: Their Impact on the Region." As part of the course, Winter brought some of the Boys of Spring to campus to serve as guest lecturers: Jesse White, Andy Mullins, Ray Mabus, and Bill Cole all made appearances. Elise Winter and John Wilson, executive director of the Southern Governors Association, also participated in specific sessions. Winter attended the various dinners and luncheons sponsored by the Institute and ventured out on his own to make presentations about the South or the Democratic Party to gatherings in Portland, Maine, and South Boston, to classrooms in Waltham and Bridgewater, Massachusetts, and to public forums at the John F. Kennedy Library and Boston University.[1]

In the months after the election, Winter also had a chance to serve as a guest commentator on Jackson TV station, WJTV. Walter Sadler, a news anchor at the station who had worked on media for Winter's 1984 Senate campaign, asked Winter to offer brief comments two to three times a week on the station's news show. Winter, of course, had experience as a journalist during his Ole Miss days, and even briefly during his World War

II tour, and he welcomed the opportunity to present for a Jackson television audience what he promised would be "non-profound observations on our state of affairs." He also resolved to steer his remarks clear of partisan matters, since no Republicans would be hosting a similar segment. Winter recorded a number of the pieces before he left for Harvard in late January 1985 and taped additional installments throughout the year. The commentaries, which aired throughout 1985, covered Winter's personal observations about Mississippi history, current affairs, and other miscellaneous topics, ranging from his dog Toby to Boston Red Sox pitcher and Mississippi native, "Oil Can" Boyd.[2] Winter's stint teaching at Harvard and serving as a commentator on WJTV suggested that, although his political career had come to an end, he had no plans to retire completely to private life. When Winter returned from Harvard, he rejoined his old law firm as a senior partner, but he also remained extremely active as a private citizen with the effort to help Mississippi move forward in a world no longer defined by Jim Crow and plantation agriculture.

જી

Winter's engagement with the broad policy questions concerning economic development and public education in Mississippi and the South resumed soon after the end of his political career. In 1985, Jesse White, at that time the executive director of the Southern Growth Policies Board (SGPB), introduced Winter to George Autry, who headed a North Carolina organization, the Manpower Development Corporation (MDC), founded in 1967 as an anti-poverty group. MDC had started out dealing primarily with workforce retraining, especially in rural areas where southern agriculture had declined. Autry asked Winter to chair a blue-ribbon panel examining the issue of rural economic development in the South. In May 1986, the group's report, *Shadows in the Sunbelt*, revealed that the region had increasingly become "two Souths." While southern cities such as Atlanta and Charlotte had experienced rapid growth, those changes "masked the growing difficulties of the rural South," characterized by high rates of illiteracy and high-school drop-outs, as well as declining land values, farm assets, and per capita income. Drawing on an insight Winter had recognized while serving as governor, the report recommended that instead of just recruiting northern industry, southern states should focus more on local initiatives that supported rural development and state-level measures to ease the crisis facing southern agriculturalists. The report emphasized education as a key solution to the ills of the rural South. For southern people to get jobs in the new economy, they would need better education, and adult illiteracy should "be attacked as a matter of economic urgency."[3]

By the time the MDC issued its report, Winter had begun work on another major committee assignment, whose findings would carry even more weight with southern policymakers. In December 1985, Arkansas governor Bill Clinton, the incoming chair of the SGPB, selected Winter to chair the organization's Commission on the Future of the South, which met throughout 1986 and issued its report in November of that year. In naming Winter to this post, Clinton remarked that he "is a scholar of Southern history and is as committed as anyone I know to the development of our region and our people." Clinton, who attended almost all of the commission's meetings, suggested a name for the report that emerged from the commission's deliberations: *Halfway Home and a Long Way to Go*. The purpose of the report, Winter said, was to recognize and urge the preservation of the best attributes of the South, such as its relatively unspoiled natural environment and its "reverence for strong personal relationships and family values," while moving beyond "old mistakes and problems." *Halfway Home* echoed the conclusions of the earlier MDC report: "The sunshine on the Sunbelt has proved to be a narrow beam of light, brightening futures along the Atlantic Seaboard, and in large cities, but skipping over many small towns and rural areas." To guide the South's future actions, *Halfway Home* offered ten recommendations, including creating a nationally competitive education system, ending adult functional illiteracy, preparing a "flexible, globally competitive work force," creating more economic development strategies for assisting "home-grown business and industry," and developing ways to improve citizen participation in the public affairs of the South.[4]

Over the next several years, Winter traveled across the South to publicize the findings of the commission's report. He and Jesse White spoke to a joint session of the Mississippi legislature in 1989, where Winter told the lawmakers that the *Halfway Home* study offered a "game plan for the South." He described the report's suggestions as both "visionary and attainable," and he urged legislators to work toward fulfilling the proposals and to acknowledge not "southern independence but southern interde-pendence." Winter also made presentations to joint sessions of lawmakers in both Alabama and North Carolina. He talked with smaller groups of legislators in other southern states and numerous other public and pri-vate organizations to try to convince them all to embrace *Halfway Home*'s recommendations as a set of new priorities for the South. He also gave countless interviews and wrote articles for newspapers and journals across the region. Observing all this activity, George Autry of MDC called Win-ter a cross between a "roving ambassador for the South and a traveling preacher." The message delivered by the minister-diplomat emphasized that the South had "been selling the wrong things . . . cheap labor, cheap land, and low taxes. And we got exactly what we paid for." He continued to detail the emergence of "two Souths which are rapidly growing further apart" and highlighted the dangers of this trend: "Just as our nation found more than a century ago that it could not endure half-slave and half-free, so our region cannot stand, much less move ahead, if we are permanently divided into two groups of people—one thriving, prospering, enjoying the good life that comes from education and social privilege and prefer-ment—the other struggling to survive, locked into an existence limited by ignorance, disease, poverty, and misery."[5]

Winter knew of the two-South phenomenon because of his own famil-iarity with conditions in Mississippi. While working on the MDC report, he told Alabama journalist Brandt Ayers that Mississippi faced its biggest problem in "the serious decline of the rural areas." While the state's urban centers had generally prospering economies, a rural county like Greene, in south Mississippi, had "to rely almost entirely on social security checks. The only factory in that county has gone to Taiwan or some other such place to make underwear. The timber companies own the land." To address these problems, Winter told policymakers and anyone else who would lis-ten to heed the *Halfway Home* recommendations, to do more to cultivate home-grown industry, and to develop the region's human capital.[6]

The *Halfway Home* study influenced the public policy debate in the South in much the same way that the 1983 report, *A Nation at Risk*, had altered the national conversation about education. In both cases, not every recommendation was followed, but the analyses clearly delineated the problems and prodded both discussion and action. In the first year after the SGPB released *Halfway Home*, legislators and governors in a number

of states—Arkansas, Florida, Mississippi, North Carolina, and Oklahoma—began to take action to shift economic development strategies
and to bolster investments in their natural, cultural, and human resources.
Despite some initial positive achievements, however, change came slowly.
At the twentieth annual meeting of the SGPB, six years after it issued
the *Halfway Home* report, Winter gave one of the keynote addresses and
focused his remarks on explaining that the South still remained little more
than halfway home and still had quite a long way to go. Winter's talk
began with an explanation of the many paradoxes of southern history,
one of the most significant being that "for over a hundred years we Southerners have been speaking glowingly of a so-called New South," yet "the
prospect for a New South foundered on the fears inherited from the Old
South." Despite some important adjustments, Winter warned: "there is
so much left to be done before we can claim that our region has arrived.
As long as there are still so many poor children and ill-housed families
and uncompleted educations and misguided and misplaced lives, the New
South still has not arrived . . . . We must now learn from our history and
decide once and for all what we want this New South to be." [7]

Winter remained actively involved in implementing the recommendations contained in the *Halfway Home* report long after others had filed the
document away with other studies from past years. For example, he played
a key role in developing a foundation in his own backyard to solve some
of the problems he had pointed out to his fellow Southerners. One day
in 1988, Ed Lupberger, the new chief executive of Middle South Utilities
(later the Entergy Corporation) came to see Winter. Lupberger, who had
moved from North Carolina, had been reading some of the things Winter
had been writing about the *Halfway Home* report. The utility executive
said he thought he had seen poverty in North Carolina, but nothing compared to the down-and-out people he saw in the Mississippi and Arkansas Deltas and the bayou country of Louisiana, the three states where
the utility operated. Lupberger, a practical businessman, recognized that
impoverished people would struggle to pay their light bills, and he asked
Winter what could be done to improve the "quality of life and the economy" of these areas. By the end of a two-hour conversation, Winter and
Lupberger had agreed to work together to create the nation's first regional
community foundation. Lupberger pledged to raise $1 million from Loui-
siana sources for the creation of a nonprofit foundation if Winter would

help raise $1 million each from Mississippi and Arkansas; the organization would be called the Foundation for the MidSouth (FMS). Winter called on Arkansas governor Bill Clinton to help with the Arkansas fundraising, and business leaders like Sam Walton and Don Munro eventually provided much of the $1 million from that state. In Mississippi, Jim Campbell, owner of a successful office and school supply company; Billy Percy, a Delta farmer and civic leader of the well-known Percy family from Greenville; and Ted Kendall, prominent banker and farmer, played major roles in helping Winter secure support from Mississippi. At about the same time, a formal three-state compact also formed, when the governors of the three states (Ray Mabus from Mississippi, Buddy Roemer of Louisiana, and Bill Clinton of Arkansas) met on a barge in the Mississippi River near Rosedale, Mississippi, and agreed to work together to address some of the problems their states shared. Winter also persuaded George Penick, a nationally respected foundation executive, to accept the position of CEO of the fledgling organization.[8]

With the original $3 million in place, by the summer of 1990, the FMS began operations. Winter's law firm provided office space for the new foundation. In its first eight years of operation, the foundation raised an additional $25 million, from citizens and corporations in the three states and from national foundations, such as the Pew Charitable Trust and the W. K. Kellogg Foundation. The FMS provided financial support to non-profit organizations working in the three states on projects to improve education, to enhance local economic development, and to assist poor families and children in the region, with an overarching objective of "breaking the cycle of poverty which has prevented this region from realizing its full potential." In addition to boosting the economic fortunes of the South's poorest sub-region, the FMS also sought to develop a sense of community and to foster racial harmony in the three states. A major FMS project was the creation of Workforce Alliance communities across the region. Each of the locales for this program received almost $500,000 to create programs to retrain local workforces and develop job opportunities for area residents. The FMS also spun off another entity, the Enterprise Corporation of the Delta, which became a $200 million conglomerate that provided financing for small businesses, low-income home buyers, and community development groups throughout the Mississippi, Louisiana, and Arkansas Delta.[9]

As Winter continued to advocate education and economic reform in Mississippi and across the South, he always linked the two concerns. In public appearances, he frequently reminded audiences that "the only road out of poverty and economic dependency runs by the school house." Winter hoped that Mississippi might continue to lead the way in improving public education, and he applauded the Mississippi legislature when it passed the Mississippi Adequate Education Program (MAEP) in 1997, a potentially far-reaching program that set minimal educational achievement targets for school districts to achieve and provided for a minimum level of funding for every child in the state. The idea behind the second part of the program was to bring the funding of the poorest school districts at least up to the "average" level of outlays in the state's more affluent areas. Although MAEP passed in 1997, the legislature did not provide full funding for the first time until 2003. The next year, when the legislature came up $79 million short of the money needed to fund the program, Winter spearheaded an effort to rally public support for Mississippi education, more than two decades after his education reform campaign of 1982. Working with Tupelo businessman Jack Reed and the Coalition for Children and Public Education, Winter participated in eight coalition-sponsored public forums around the state, in which he and Reed called on citizens and the 2005 legislature to make funding of the MAEP its top concern. When the legislature met in January 2005, Winter, Reed, and a thousand others assembled on the steps of the Mississippi Capitol to urge the legislature to provide the money necessary for the MAEP. The Coalition also provided legislators with a petition signed by more than 140,000 registered voters who supported full funding of the education program. Despite the show of public support, neither the legislature nor Governor Haley Barbour sought the new revenue sources needed to fulfill the promise of the MAEP.[10]

℘

By the mid-1980s, although Winter had no thoughts of running for elective office, he remained interested and active in the state Democratic Party. The Boys of Spring who had served on Winter's gubernatorial staff had assumed leadership positions as Democrats in the late 1980s and early 1990s, but Winter remained concerned about the long-term health of the party. It had not become the force in the state he envisioned. Winter had supported the Democratic Party all his life because he thought that its policies would be the most likely to benefit Mississippians. That belief had motivated him to embrace the promise of national Democrats like Adlai Stevenson and John F. Kennedy when many other white Southern-ers focused more on the failures of the national party to preserve racial segregation and black disfranchisement. Winter hoped the Mississippi Democratic Party, once it accepted the changes forced by the civil rights movement, might unite poorer blacks and whites in a political alliance with those compassionate and progressive individuals from the middle and upper classes. He underestimated, however, how often lingering racial considerations pushed economic concerns into the background and how effectively the Republican Party took "root based to a very large extent on attitudes where race was concerned." As Winter's former Senate colleague and sometime antagonist Theodore Smith told the former governor in 1990, "Right or wrong, the impression among the white population of Mississippi is that the Democratic Party has been taken over by and for the black people." Poor blacks and whites remained more divided by race than united by economic plight, and as the gap between the haves and have-nots widened in the 1980s and 1990s, Mississippi seemed less will-ing to address the needs of those left behind, to recognize, as the *Half-way Home* report had suggested, that continued prosperity depended on ensuring a minimum set of educational and economic standards for all.[11]

Despite his disappointments about these political trends, Winter remained involved in the Democratic Party and tried to help build a bira-cial organization that would attract large numbers of Mississippians to its banner. In 1990, he assumed the position of chair of the state party's Finance Committee, a move that bolstered the standing of the organiza-tion among some would-be Democrats. The party, however, remained far from united, and in 1991 Mississippi elected its first Republican governor since Reconstruction, as well as a Republican lieutenant governor. At the same time, the Democratic majority in the state legislature wrangled over legislative reapportionment in the early 1990s, a struggle in which race dominated the deliberations. The state party also faced other serious prob-lems; in early 1992, Lisa Walker, the party's executive director, reporte that "the state party funding situation is out of hand" and that the sta headquarters had only "one functioning computer."[12]

As Winter worked to mend racial rifts and reverse sagging bank balances in the state party, he also became involved in a coalition formed to emphasize the moderate credentials of the national party: the Democratic Leadership Council (DLC), begun in 1985 following the Reagan-Bush landslide in 1984. The DLC sought to move the Democratic Party toward a more centrist position and away from 1960s liberalism, which proved an albatross in recent presidential elections. For instance, the DLC talked about the need to "restructure" government, rather than expand government, as a way to achieve progress. Winter helped found a Mississippi chapter of the DLC in 1990, along with a number of others with long-standing political ties to Winter, including Governor Ray Mabus, Secretary of State Dick Molpus, Wilson Golden, Marshall Bennett, David Crews, and Mike Espy (U.S. congressman from Mississippi's Second District and the first black person elected to Congress from the state in more than one hundred years). One of the national stars to arise from the ranks of the DLC was Bill Clinton, a man Winter had watched emerge as one of the South's most skillful politicians. Winter and Clinton had established close ties in the early 1980s when they served as governors of neighboring states, and Winter co-chaired Clinton's Mississippi presidential campaigns in both 1992 and 1996.[13]

Winter's efforts to build a biracial Democratic Party in Mississippi represented but one part of his effort to advance the larger cause of racial reconciliation. In March 1986, while working on both the *Shadows in the Sunbelt* and the *Halfway Home* reports, Winter had an unexpected encounter with a childhood friend, which reminded him of both the momentous changes that had already occurred in the South and the work that remained to be done in the area of race relations. In Chattanooga to make a speech at the Visions '86 conference, Winter received word that a local official who had known him as a boy wanted to see him. At a breakfast meeting the following morning, Winter was surprised and delighted to see Roy Noel, one of the black children who had grown up with Winter. Like his white counterpart from Grenada County, Noel had left Mississippi to serve in the army during World War II. Noel, however, never returned to the state. Instead, he became a schoolteacher in Chattanooga, served as an administrative assistant to the mayor of the city, and then directed Chattanooga's Equal Opportunity and Fair Housing agency. At breakfast, the two men swapped stories about their shared childhood and talked about respective family members. When the conversation turned toward the changes in the South since those bygone days, Noel observed that the region had "changed for you and me almost as much as it once changed for our granddaddies." He reminded Winter, "Our families go back a long way. We came off the same place. My granddaddy was a slave boy on your great graddaddy's farm, and he and your granddaddy grew up together just like you and I did." The two men sat in silence for a while thereafter, both pondering their shared and separate pasts. In his speech later that day, Winter described his thought-provoking encounter with his old friend. By chance, the author Alex Haley was in the audience, and after Winter's talk, Haley told him, "That's what *Roots* is all about."[14]

Reflecting on his encounter with Roy Noel, Winter contemplated anew how profoundly slavery and segregation had diminished the lives of both blacks and whites in the South: a quarter century after the advances of the civil rights movement, and more than a century after slavery ended, everyone in the region continued to live with that "burden." The fact that whites had largely accepted the end of Jim Crow and black disfranchisement did not fully heal the racial wounds inflicted by generations of slavery and segregation. What black and white Southerners needed, Winter believed, was a continued dialogue, much like his conversation with Noel. That conversation had demonstrated to Winter "that intertwined in the miracle of our living were the elements of pain and separation and alienation but also of kindness and generosity and compassion that formed the basis of our common humanity." Winter also recognized that, after racial segregation and black disfranchisement ended, the "burden" had shifted. No longer did most white Mississippians actively oppose racial integration; many whites, in fact, had embraced the equality of blacks and the improved race relations in the state. Among a number of his white friends, however, the prevailing attitude was now "that we have eliminated legal segregation . . . we've accomplished all that we need to do." Winter knew otherwise: "We all know that there is still a barrier—an unstated, unseen, invisible, subtle barrier between the races."[15]

Winter received an opportunity during the second Clinton administration to work on the cause of advancing racial reconciliation on a national level. In June 1997, the president announced the creation of One America in the 21st Century: The President's Initiative on Race. Clinton appointed the distinguished black historian John Hope Franklin to chair the board and named Winter as one of the seven members of the group. The main objectives of the race advisory board were to gather information, to take the pulse of existing race relations in the country, to examine existing programs or activities designed to eliminate racism, and to make recommendations to the president. At the initial meeting of the race board, Clinton told the seven members that he hoped the group would "spark a serious dialogue on race," and that this conversation and the board's other findings would lead to suggestions about what the government and private citizens could do to solve the problem. The board held hearings and meetings around the country. In the fifteen months of the board's existence, members participated in 275 events and an additional 38 town hall meetings, including one held at Ole Miss in March 1998. Although Winter did not attend all of these activities, he was present for many of them, and he personally visited twenty-six states during the tour.[16]

As Clinton's race board cataloged the condition of race relations around the country, it found how greatly racial interactions varied from place to place. Some locales had "recognized their responsibility to create structures that would minimize racial strife," while others "were literally fighting every day." The board discovered that some of the best race relations in the country existed in parts of the rural South, where people, though once officially segregated by race, had always lived in close proximity to one another and knew each other on a personal basis. For example, Winter introduced the board to a loosely structured organization in Kosciusko, Mississippi, called The Club, a monthly supper meeting of local black and white men of an equal number, with no officers and no agenda. The Club merely provided a forum where people could hear about the concerns of each other and find ways to work together. The race board collected a number of similar practices from around the country in a publication released by the White House in 1999, *Pathways to One America in the 21st Century: Promising Practices for Racial Reconciliation*. Board member Angela Oh, a Korean-American lawyer from Los Angeles, described the "promising practices" as ones that "represent the kind of leadership that envisions a future in which racial and ethnic divides can be overcome in the pursuit of leading our Nation closer to its highest aspirations."[17]

The board received criticism from the national media and civil rights groups who complained that the group generated considerable discussion but did not seem to be accomplishing anything concrete. Winter disagreed. He told Clinton in November 1997 that the group had "already accomplished one of our initial purposes, and that is to raise the subject of race to the level of genuine reflection, conversation, and inquiry. Every newspaper columnist, skeptical or not, has been writing about the Initiative." Winter viewed the race board as playing a function similar to that of John F. Kennedy's Council on Physical Fitness. Just as that committee had examined the country's physical health and described an unhealthy situation, which led to a broad-based movement of physical fitness initiatives, the race board would help create "a sense of urgency toward an environment where racism and racist speech and acts will be found to be unacceptable." The board's chair, John Hope Franklin, also thought that critics misunderstood the purpose of the race board. As he later reflected, Clinton created the board to examine an "immense and entrenched" problem, and "a constructive dialogue was our foremost goal, rather than formulating some programmatic solution."[18]

The race board made recommendations to President Clinton throughout the fifteen-month process and delivered its final report in September 1988. One of the major suggestions called for the creation of a President's Council for One America. Though never established, Winter envisioned that the council would "lead a sustained public awareness campaign" highlighting the "common values" shared by Americans, pointing to continued "racial inequities and the need to eliminate them," and offering advice about how to "spark racial healing activities in all sectors of society." The race board also made suggestions concerning civil rights enforcement and affirmative action, education, economic opportunity, health care, and the criminal justice system. The board's final report, however, received little attention, because it appeared just as Republicans began to initiate impeachment proceedings against Clinton over the Monica Lewinsky affair. A week before the board issued its final report on race, independent counsel Kenneth Starr released his explicit account of the president's alleged misdeeds, a document that outlined eleven possible grounds for removing the president from office. Because of Clinton's troubles, he did not formally address the race board's report until his last message to Congress, in January 2001, when he offered a series of proposals to solve what he labeled, "The Unfinished Work of Building One America." That initiative arrived too late to be addressed during the Clinton presidency, and the new Bush administration did not embrace it.[19]

Winter thought that much good came out of the race board's fifteen months of meetings and deliberations, despite disappointment that a high-level political squabble over the president's private life derailed much of the momentum established by the committee. Winter's service on the race board bolstered his own personal understanding of race relations in America and the continuing problems in this area. He appreciated the many examples of racial reconciliation he saw underway in communities all over America. At the same time, he became intimately aware of "how wide the gap still is between the races despite all the progress that we have made." While individuals remained divided over what Winter saw as superficial differences surrounding ethnicity, he believed that people all over the country essentially wanted the same things: a good education for their children, "a fair shot at a job that will sustain them and their family," "to live in a decent house on a safe street," access to "reasonably adequate health care," and "to be treated with dignity and respect." Winter's service on the national race board suggested to him that public policy should focus on achieving these results and promote a "national recommitment to community-building," which would lead to "a more unified and more prosperous country." Winter recognized that such an effort would necessarily require a massive effort on the part of government—something on the scale of the New Deal—to address adequately the persistent economic inequalities. Not surprisingly, he continued to believe that the starting point remained raising the education level of all citizens.[20]

As a group, the race board examined the nation's racial problems, surveyed the possible solutions, began a dialogue on the issue in many forums, and made wide-ranging recommendations to the president. Yet Winter came to understand that no matter how grand a program the federal government might develop—and such programs remained important—racial reconciliation depended on the decisions made by countless individuals and communities. As he told a Memphis audience, solving the country's racial problems would "require each one of us, black and white, making a personal commitment to do what we can to eliminate racial prejudice and misunderstanding and mistrust. We must work together across racial lines to build communities that recognize our common humanity and our common destiny. That duty particularly applies to some of our political leaders from both races who unfortunately continue to play the race card in subtle but divisive ways." Winter began to carry with him a copy of the Birmingham Pledge, created by a Birmingham, Alabama, attorney in 1997. The Pledge embodied Winter's belief that racial reconciliation would only succeed if enough individuals followed its principles:

> **I believe** that every person has worth as an individual.
>
> **I believe** that every person is entitled to dignity and respect, regardless of race or color.
>
> **I believe** that every thought and every act of racial prejudice is harmful; if it is my thought or act, then it is harmful to me as well as to others.
>
> **Therefore**, from this day forward I will strive daily to eliminate racial prejudice from my thoughts and actions.
>
> **I will** discourage racial prejudice by others at every opportunity.
>
> **I will** treat all people with dignity and respect; and I will strive daily to honor this pledge, knowing that the world will be a better place because of my effort.[21]

The dialogue started by the race board continued in many forums around the country, including Mississippi. Following the public forum at Ole Miss in March 1998, the University, at the suggestion of Winter and Mississippi federal judge Charles W. Pickering, and with support from Chancellor Robert Khayat, created a permanent Institute for Racial Reconciliation to continue the conversation and to search for ways to solve the racial rifts that continued to divide Mississippians and other Americans. Susan Glisson, who helped organize the Oxford forum in 1998, became director of the new Institute for Racial Reconciliation. In 2003, as part of a series of events honoring Winter on his eightieth birthday, the Institute was named for him, a fitting tribute to the man who had become the most visible symbol of the racial reconciliation efforts underway in Mississippi. Speaking at the renaming ceremony at the Old Capitol, Winter told the crowd, "The fault line of race is the paramount factor in keeping us from realizing our full potential as a state and as a nation." He urged the Institute to focus its work on "the elimination of the areas of racial injustice that remain, the improvement of social, educational and economic conditions that contribute to unequal opportunities, and the creation of a point of view that places racial prejudice and racist speech and acts outside the bounds of acceptable behavior."[22]

Winter received confirmation about the continuing importance of racial reconciliation when controversy erupted in 2000 over one of the state's symbols. For many years, the state flag, originally adopted in 1894, had generated controversy because the flag's canton—the upper left corner of the flag—replicated the battle flag of the Confederacy, a symbol utilized since the 1950s by hate groups, such as the Ku Klux Klan, and others that opposed the black civil rights movement. Winter had argued that the state should adopt a new symbol, precisely because the Confederate flag over the years had become tainted with negative connotations. The National Association for the Advancement of Colored People (NAACP) filed suit in 1993 to bar the state flag on constitutional grounds as a violation of equal protection guarantees. The Mississippi Supreme Court ruled in May 2000 against the NAACP's claims, but it also cited a long forgotten or ignored fact: that Mississippi did not actually have an official flag or an official coat of arms. In 1906, when the state issued a new codification of laws, it had failed to incorporate the earlier provisions pertaining to these state symbols into the new code.[23]

When the Mississippi Supreme Court announced its decision, the legislature had already adjourned for the year. Governor Ronnie Musgrove decided to create the Advisory Commission on the State Flag and the Coat of Arms, which would gather information and recommend a course of action to the legislature before it met in January 2001. The seventeen-member commission included six legislators and ten members appointed by Musgrove, primarily business people and educators. Musgrove asked Winter to chair the commission. Notwithstanding Winter's stated opposition to the old flag, he was the best choice for this task: senior statesman, student of Mississippi history, member of the Sons of Confederate Veterans, grandson of a Civil War veteran and named for a Confederate general, and a former governor whose long political career demonstrated he could handle antagonism with grace. Winter accepted the thankless job Musgrove asked him to do, and then, "took a deep breath, because I knew there would be a lot of hostility" to any effort to alter the flag.[24]

At the suggestion of commission member Ed Blackmon, a black legislator from Canton, the flag commission decided to hold five public hearings—one in each congressional district—to assess public opinion. The first meeting was in Tupelo, typically considered a bastion of progressivism, and supporters of the existing flag dominated the meeting. Winter could not attend this hearing, and commission member and Tupelo businessman Jack Reed chaired the meeting. Loud heckling from the large number of flag supporters drowned out the one white man who argued for changing the flag. A group of black citizens at the meeting quietly left once they saw the mood of the crowd. The second forum, held in Meridian, brought a more open debate, but flag supporters still clearly outnumbered those who ventured out to ask for change. Blacks who spoke at the meeting favored a new flag but seemed resigned to the futility of the process. One black man despaired that the hearings would not change any opinions. He also recognized that in a popular vote the white majority would prevail in keeping the existing flag, although he noted that such a vote would not make the Mississippi flag "right." Those who spoke in favor of the Rebel symbol denied any racist motives, and they claimed only a desire to protect their southern heritage. A man in a Confederate hat said the Confederacy's battle flag was a symbol of freedom, not hate. Another white flag supporter noted that he took the position he did to honor his ancestors, while "these scalawags" (referring to the commission members) wanted "to spit on the graves of his ancestors."[25]

At the third public forum, in the Delta town of Moorhead, the intensity of the discussion increased substantially. Supporters of the flag outnumbered any advocates of change by a sizeable margin. One organizer of the Rebel-flag forces in the state, Jim Giles, told the commission, "Our state flag represents grits, guts, and cohunes. Our state flag represents pride, principle, and reputation." He then directed his remarks at the chair of the commission: "Mr. Winter, now listen, you are despicable; you are anathema. You are anathema to what is honorable in this state. You have been nothing but a parasite your entire career. You're a sorry lawyer, you're gutless. You are worthy of being tarred and feathered and run out of this state." As the Moorhead crowd cheered and Giles left the room, Winter shot back: "I have been heckled by better men than you," which was as riled up as Winter ever got during the contentious public hearing. A few whites at Moorhead expressed support for a new flag, in the interest of "fairness" and "inclusion." A couple of black speakers also spoke out against the existing flag, including state senator David Jordan, who told the largely white audience they did not "have a right to decide everything. I'm for redesigning it because it's the right thing to do." Most of those who spoke at the three-hour session, however, remained adamant that the current flag should remain and that the people of Mississippi should have the right to express their preferences on this topic in a public referendum.[26]

The following week at Gulfport, for the first time in the series of forums, opponents of the existing state flag outnumbered supporters. In a crowd two-thirds black, a black woman who was one of the school integration pioneers on the Gulf Coast, spoke first. Her claim that the flag represented a reminder that "we are not wanted" elicited a chorus of boos from the whites in attendance. A black man said he thought the flag should not contain a symbol offensive to so many people and asked "the good white people" why they continued to support such an icon. A man dressed in black and waving a Confederate battle flag provided a blunt reply. He "ripped" the microphone from the speaker's stand and declared: "This flag is just like my wife. You mess with my wife and you're gonna get your ass kicked." Another white speaker claimed that slavery had benefitted blacks, which elicited angry shouts from the blacks in the audience. At one point, a black man taking his turn at the microphone asked for a standing vote on whether or not to keep the existing flag. Those opposed rose, largely the black majority present. The whites who remained seated began to boo those standing. The last forum was held in Jackson on the campus of Millsaps College. While a number of black Mississippians attended the meeting and voiced their preference for a new state flag, competing white voices dominated the Jackson discussion. A number of whites who spoke favored scrapping the current flag for a new symbol. One white man holding the Mississippi flag told the audience that the symbol he held was "a slap in the face of black Mississippians" and noted that "friendship" and "simple courtesy" were more important values than a strip of cloth. On the other hand, a young white woman, who identified herself as a grocery store worker, with "several black friends," began by asking, "Where would blacks be without slavery?" When she answered her own question—"Africa"—boos rang out. She then made an appeal that seemed to exclude her black acquaintances: "It is time we all stand together once more and defend the heritage and honor we have left."[27]

Even during his service on Clinton's race board, Winter had not seen "dialogues" on race as intense as those at the flag forums. Following the Morehead meeting, an editorial in the *Memphis Commercial Appeal* urged a halt to further hearings, "before someone gets hurt." Security had been in place since the first meeting in Tupelo, but after the often intemperate remarks directed at the former governor and other commission members, law enforcement stepped up their presence to protect the flag panel from any potential violent attacks. Winter himself seemed largely unruffled by the volleys of verbal assaults launched at him and the other commission members during the public forums. The *Biloxi Sun Herald* thought, "Winter has stood his ground at the eye of this emotional hurricane— seemingly undaunted by bigotry and certainly determined to complete his gubernatorial assignment." Winter disagreed with suggestions that the flag hearings had only driven a bigger wedge between the races. He called the forums "messy but necessary," adding that "it has been necessary to give people a forum in which they could really vent their strong feelings." Winter had no problem with the many white speakers who expressed their honest and obvious discomfort with altering the state flag. As he had throughout his public career, Winter hoped, however, that whites would see the value in advancing the cause of racial harmony, which in this instance, meant adopting a new state symbol. At the same time, Winter believed that the small group of vocal opponents to changing the flag, who trailed the forum tour—led by Jim Giles—and made confrontational remarks at every stop, would in the end create a backlash among the "moderate, reasonable people of the state" and lead them to compromise on the flag issue.[28]

From the beginning of its deliberations, the flag commission had decided to come up with a new design to supplant the existing Mississippi flag, and the design adopted by the flag commission had the look of a symbol shaped by a committee. Instead of the Confederate battle flag in the canton, the new banner featured twenty stars: an outer ring of thirteen stars symbolizing the thirteen colonies (though Mississippi was not among them); an inner ring of six stars standing for the "nations or republics that have claimed dominion over Mississippi" (Indian tribes, France, Great Britain, Spain, the United States, and the southern Confederacy); and a slightly bigger star in the middle of these two circles, representing Mississippi itself. After the hearings and further deliberations, the flag commission recommended that the state hold a public referendum after the 2001 legislative session. Voters could chose between the existing flag or the new design created by the commission, with the understanding that the 1894 flag would continue as an "official historic flag to be honored,

protected and flown wherever historic flags are flown." Winter had originally opposed a referendum, but he now realized that most white legislators, given the impassioned opposition on display in the public forums,
would never vote to adopt the new design. After the contentious hearings,
Winter also understood that the new banner could only gain acceptance
if the people voted for it. The legislature, unwilling to touch the controversial issue, eagerly accepted the commission's recommendations and set
a date for a referendum.[29]

A vigorous campaign by both supporters and opponents of the new
design preceded the April 2001 vote, and Winter spoke for the new banner. He told voters, "A vote for the new flag would separate us from the
stereotype that has come about as a result of the old flag being hijacked by
hate groups. When that flag appears as representing Mississippi, it really
does hurt this state." Prominent organizations and individuals endorsing the commission's new flag included not only the state NAACP but
also the Mississippi Bankers Association, the Mississippi Manufacturers
Association, and the Board of Trustees of the State Institutions of Higher
Learning. Coaches at the University of Mississippi (where spectators
waved the Confederate flag at school functions) also favored the new flag
and reminded the state's football-loving citizens that removing the Confederate symbol from the state banner would help Ole Miss recruiting
efforts. Even Donald Wildmon, the head of the conservative Christian
group, the American Family Association, based in Tupelo, endorsed the
new flag. Wildmon claimed that his support for a new flag would "show
to our black brothers that race doesn't make any difference to us. It is the
right practical thing to do. Heritage is not a piece of cloth."[30]

On election day, 65 percent of voters chose to keep the existing flag
with its Confederate symbol. The turnout was relatively light but split
along racial lines, with approximately 85 percent of whites favoring the
existing flag and 90 percent of blacks choosing the new design. Most of
the white support for a new flag came from the Jackson metro area and
in university towns. Returns also showed that a sizeable group of black
Mississippians had sat out the election. A number of black citizens had
told Winter during the public deliberations such things as, "We got a
lot more problems than what the flag looks like. Changing the flag isn't
going to put any more groceries on my dining room table." In the end,

the flag vote was mostly a debate among whites about whether eliminating a symbol offensive to blacks was a worthy action to take. For the vast majority of white Mississippians, the answer to that question was a resounding "No." David Bowen, a former Democratic congressman from Mississippi, had argued before the election that asking whites to make a compromise "to give up a flag they love" was a one-sided affair. To balance the scales, Bowen suggested that black leaders should also volunteer to sacrifice something that contributed to racial discord. His suggested item for elimination: "the morally and constitutionally bankrupt system of racial preferences euphemistically known as affirmative action."[31] Such a tit-for-tat, however, missed the point of the gesture that Winter and a minority of the state's white citizens sought to make in the interest of racial harmony.

Winter's service on Clinton's race board and as chair of the Mississippi flag commission made clear that no magic bullet existed for achieving racial peace in Mississippi and around the country. When Winter spoke in 2004 at the events commemorating the fortieth anniversary of the murders of James Chaney, Andrew Goodman, and Michael Schwerner in Neshoba County, the former governor told the audience that the "most important activity" for all Americans was "the unending work of racial reconciliation." While recognizing how far Mississippi had come since the Ku Klux Klan killed the three civil rights activists forty years earlier, Winter also urged the crowd of fifteen hundred "to recognize how far we still have to go to create a truly united country. There is still too much distrust and misunderstanding among the races; there are still too many situations where we are judged by what we look like rather than who we are; there is still too much stereotyping; there are still too many of us who are indifferent to the importance of the little gestures of kindness and courtesy and civility in our dealings with each other and especially across racial lines." Even the memorial service at which Winter spoke had sparked racial controversy. Ben Chaney, the brother of one of the victims, claimed that the Philadelphia Coalition (composed of blacks, Choctaw Indians, and whites) that had organized the event had not included some local black leaders in the planning and only acted to improve the town's battered image. That same coalition, however, later in the year played a key role in convincing Mississippi Attorney General Jim Hood to reopen the state case against those responsible for the 1964 Neshoba County murders. A year after the memorial service where Winter spoke, a Neshoba County jury convicted Edgar Ray Killen of manslaughter in the 1964 slayings, the first state conviction in the long-ago crime.[32]

For Winter, racial reconciliation became the central yet difficult requirement for further progress in Mississippi and the South. As he told southern legislators in Chapel Hill, North Carolina, in November 2004, "The problem of race, despite all the progress that we have made, is still the thorniest, trickiest, and [most] difficult barrier that we confront to achieve a truly successful and united region . . . . There is still too much misunderstanding between the races, too much white flight, too little trust, too many subtle nuances that signal the continuing gap." Although Winter acknowledged that continued racial conflict was not solely a southern problem, he told the legislators, "I would like to believe that we who live in the South have a special insight into how" racial reconciliation might be achieved, because the region's "history has been most shaped by the factors of race over three centuries." Winter suggested, "The challenge now is for southerners of both races to work to come together with the same commitment and intensity with which a generation ago so many white southerners sought to maintain segregation and so many black southerners sought to end it. The new realities require us to understand our mutual interdependence." David Broder, the *Washington Post* columnist, was present for the talk, and he found it so inspirational that he organized his own speech commemorating Martin Luther King Jr.'s birthday in 2005 around Winter's Chapel Hill remarks.[33]

In the decades after his political career ended, Winter worked tirelessly as a private citizen to promote the causes he thought important: educational improvement and economic change for Mississippi and the South; a strong, biracial Democratic Party; and racial reconciliation. Jesse White, who worked with Winter for much of his political career, told him in 1999 that "if Jimmy Carter is an exemplary former President, you are *the* exemplary former Governor." The comparison was an apt one. Like Carter, Winter stayed actively engaged in the public arena, though he no longer had the trappings of political power.[34]

EPILOGUE

In May 2009, Winter spoke at the fiftieth anniversary celebration of Mississippi's first civil rights protest, the wade-in on the segregated beaches of the Gulf Coast, which was led by Dr. Gilbert Mason, head of the Biloxi chapter of the National Association for the Advancement of Colored People. In Winter's address, he praised Mason and his fellow protestors as heroes, courageous Mississippians who freed the entire state from a system whose values ran contrary to the ideals of the United States. Winter also noted that not many whites joined the Coast civil rights pioneers during their march into the Gulf of Mexico: "You didn't see this white face on the beach with Mason because white people, like me and many others, were intimidated by the massive forces of racial segregation. I have to admit I could not stand up to the pressure for being in public life in Mississippi and come out four-square for the elimination of segregation and for that I apologize today." The predominantly black crowd appreciated Winter's honesty and his heart-felt emotion, but as speaker after speaker who followed Winter revealed, black Mississippians thought the former governor had little for which he needed to apologize. They understood that he had done what he had to in order to remain politically viable, a strategy that allowed him to retain enough power to fight successfully for educational improvement and racial healing in the years ahead. Although not on the front lines of the movement, he also did little to assist the forces of massive resistance to civil rights. In a state consumed by hatred for more than a decade after the *Brown* decision, William Winter had been a voice of reason and cooperation, as he tried to move whites away from massive resistance toward compromise and acceptance.[1]

Winter played a crucial role in the creation of a new Mississippi during the years of civil rights struggle and beyond. Throughout a public career that spanned more than sixty years—the last twenty-five as a private citizen—Winter worked for solutions not only to the racial issues that divided the state's citizens but also to other problems that prevented

Mississippians from realizing their full potential, such as a lack of adequate education. At the 2003 dedication ceremony for the state archives building in Mississippi named for Winter, the journalist and historian David Halberstam told the former governor, "You're my favorite politician, my personal hero. I believed for a long time that America would not be whole until Mississippi became part of it, and you more than any other politician are the architect of the new Mississippi and the new America."[2] Although Winter's ideals for a New Mississippi have not been completely realized, his goals remain worthy objectives.

Winter's long and successful career deservedly led to many awards and accolades. Among the many organizations to recognize Winter's achievements were the National Education Association, which presented Winter with the Martin Luther King Jr. Memorial Award in 2001, and the John F. Kennedy Presidential Library and Museum, which in 2008 honored Winter with its Profile in Courage Award for his work on behalf of promoting improved education and racial understanding. Noted political consultant Peter Hart, a veteran of numerous of political campaigns, including several of William Winter's races, judged that the Mississippi leader "knew what was important and never shrank from doing the important things. And never had the small view and always had the large view of the state. And [he] played to people's better angels, and how much more can you ask of a public servant than that?" Longtime Mississippi journalist Bill Minor summed up the judgment of many observers when he noted in 2004 that Winter "brought a nobility to the calling of politics far in excess of what it deserves."[3]

As these honors and assessments attest, Winter's public career exemplified the kind of political leader that any true democracy needs, one devoted to public service not in the interest of personal aggrandizement or the advancement of narrow special interest but in the belief that government should work to improve the lives of all its citizens. To be sure, Winter, like any political aspirant, had ambitions. He made mistakes. He sometimes took actions that were politically expedient or adopted stands he thought necessary to protect a future political career. Yet William Winter steadfastly used his political offices to further the public interest, and his work in the public arena in the more than twenty-five years after he left politics continued that same objective. Our democracy could benefit from more leaders who emulate the career of William F. Winter.

ACKNOWLEDGMENTS

William F. Winter provided crucial help in the creation of this book. For one thing, he has preserved an extraordinary documentary record of his life and career, a fact perhaps attributable to his training as a historian and his well-deserved reputation as a man of honesty and integrity. When I began this project, many of his papers had already been sent to the Mississippi Department of Archives and History (MDAH), although a good part of the collection remained unprocessed when I examined the materials. Winter had even more treasures in his office and home, and he allowed me to look through all these items, even turning me loose in his office for some unsupervised plunder of his filing cabinets. Among the most notable items I discovered in Winter's possession were several drafts of an unpublished memoir and an extensive correspondence between Winter and his parents during the 1940s and early 1950s.[1]

In addition to the mass of public and private documents concerning Winter's life and career, his own memories, preserved in numerous oral history interviews dating back to the 1970s, have played a major role in constructing this narrative. The interviews are particularly forthcoming for a political figure, no doubt attributable to fact that Winter is at heart a thoughtful intellectual, reflective about Mississippi's past and his role in that history. A particularly useful interview for my purposes was the lengthy and detailed series of discussions Winter recorded with Jack Bass in 1992.[2] Winter also sat for sixteen separate interviews with me between 2001 and 2009, most of them lasting two hours or more. In many cases, I used these conversations to question Winter about the written and oral sources I was examining. For a man with such a substantial oral history record, his memories have remained remarkably consistent over the years, although some discrepancies in his stories do exist. In those cases, I tried to resolve the contradictions by relying on other evidence whenever possible.

In addition to the assistance Winter provided, I could not have completed this project without help from many others. A number of people provided crucial information in interviews with me over the years: Bryan Baker, Fred Banks, William Joel Blass, Senator Thad Cochran, John Corlew, David Crews, Brad Dye, Wilson Golden, Peter Hart, Martin Hegwood, John Henegan, Elbert Hilliard, Charles C. Jacobs Jr., Guy Land, Ray Mabus, Bill Minor, Dick Molpus, Andy Mullins, James A. Peden Jr., H. M. Ray, George Rogers, Jim Simpson, Eleanor Winter, Elise Winter, and Jesse White. I would particularly like to thank Wilson Golden, who not only gave a wonderful interview but also allowed me to conduct research in his unprocessed collection of papers at the MDAH, and Jesse White, who let me examine a detailed scrapbook he compiled of the 1979 gubernatorial campaign.

Like any historian, I am grateful to the dedicated archivists who make historical research possible, including those at Duke University; the Legislative Reference Bureau at the Mississippi Capitol; the University of Southern Mississippi; the National Archives in Washington, D.C. and at College Park, Maryland; the University of North Carolina at Chapel Hill; Mississippi State University; and the University of Mississippi. I spent many weeks conducting research at the MDAH, and every member of the wonderful staff there, from Hank Holmes and Julia Marks Young on down, could not have been more patient, helpful, and knowledgeable in providing assistance—even if they sometimes silently dreaded my periodic arrivals for all the extra work it entailed. I would like to offer special thanks to a few of those many excellent staff members: Anne Webster, for seemingly knowing where everything at the MDAH is located; Elaine Owens, for providing timely help in finding photographs after the Winter collection was reorganized following my initial research in the papers; and Clarence Hunter, for directing me to important documents in Tougaloo College's Aaron Henry Papers that he was processing.

I began work on this project less than a year after I moved from Mississippi to North Carolina. As I returned to Mississippi periodically to work in archives and conduct oral histories, I was fortunate to have the opportunity to stay with family and friends, including my brother, Chip Bolton, and his wife, Jennifer; Kevin Farrell; and Sean and Mary Beth Farrell. I am also indebted to Eleanor Winter for providing me with housing during one of my research trips to Washington, D.C.

A number of individuals read various versions or parts of this work: the three readers from the University Press of Mississippi—an anonymous reader, Joseph Crespino, and Charles Eagles—Curtis Austin, Jim Bissett, Brian Daugherity, Sean Farrell, Jim Hollandsworth, Watson Jennison, Joseph Moore, Jere Nash, and Fred Smith. JoAnne Prichard Morris also offered extensive editorial suggestions about my manuscript. While all these readers gave me invaluable advice, I remain solely responsible for all the outstanding imperfections of this work.

I would also like to thank the University of North Carolina at Greensboro (UNCG) for providing me with a semester-long research assignment, which allowed me to complete an initial draft of this manuscript. In addition, I received important help from two graduate research assistants at UNCG, Jacqueline Spruill and Kim Proctor, who both helped me research microfilm editions of the local Grenada, Mississippi, newspapers. I would also like to acknowledge the assistance of Leila Salisbury, director of the University Press of Mississippi, who has been extremely helpful and supportive throughout the long process of bringing this project to publication, and Anne Stascavage, managing editor at the press, who ably copyedited the manuscript.

Finally, I want to thank my wife Leslie for all her support and encouragement throughout my work on this project. She has read numerous drafts of this book. She also created rough transcripts of all the interviews I conducted, which made finding information on the interview tapes significantly easier. As a result, she is probably as familiar with the stories of William Winter's life and political career as I am. For all these reasons and many more, I dedicate this book to her and to our children, Laura and Ben.

NOTES

DUKE — Rare Book, Manuscripts, and Special Collections Library, Duke University, Durham, North Carolina

LRB — Legislative Reference Bureau, Mississippi State Capitol, Jackson

MDAH — Mississippi Department of Archives and History, Jackson

MOHP — Mississippi Oral History Program, University of Southern Mississippi, Hattiesburg

NA — National Archives and Records Administration, Washington, D.C.

NA-CP — National Archives at College Park, College Park, Maryland

RG — Record Group

SHC — Southern Historical Collection, University of North Carolina Libraries, Chapel Hill

MSU — John C. Stennis Collection, Congressional and Political Research Center, Mississippi State University, Starkville

UM — Department of Archives and Special Collections, University of Mississippi, Oxford

USM — McCain Library and Archives, University of Southern Mississippi, Hattiesburg

WWPC — William Winter personal collection

Introduction

1. Charles C. Bolton, *The Hardest Deal of All: The Battle over School Integration in Mississippi, 1870–1980* (Jackson: University Press of Mississippi, 2005), introduction.

2. William Winter memoir, WWPC; William Winter, Bolton interview, May 18, 2006; William Winter, Bass interview.

3. Bolton, *The Hardest Deal of All*, introduction; William Winter memoir; William Winter, Bolton interview, May 18, 2006; William Winter, Bass interview; Joseph Crespino, *In Search of Another Country: Mississippi and the Conservative Counterrevolution* (Princeton: Princeton University Press, 2007), 119–31; Homer Bigart, "13 Whites Seized in Grenada Strife," *New York Times*, September 18, 1966.

4. Jason Sokol, *There Goes My Everything: White Southerners in the Age of Civil Rights, 1945–1975* (New York: Alfred A Knopf, 2006), 4.

5. Although white Southerners often labeled those whites who offered any criticism of existing social arrangements as "liberals," I have used the term "moderate" to describe William Winter. While some of his political positions could certainly qualify as "liberal," Winter typically thought of himself as a moderate, as someone who sought compromise and consensus. In 1969, he told the *Mississippi Freelance*, a small progressive publication, "I do try to take a reasonable, rational, common-sense approach, steering between the shoals. History shows that our government has always operated best on that basis. . . . When moderation was forsaken, the result was the Civil War." See "Winter," *Mississippi Freelance*, October 1969.

6. Morton Sosna, *In Search of the Silent South: Southern Liberals and the Race Issue* (New York: Columbia University Press, 1977); Charles W. Eagles, *Jonathan Daniels and Race Relations* (Knoxville: University of Tennessee Press, 1982); John T. Kneebone, *Southern Liberal Journalists and the Issue of Race, 1920–1944* (Chapel Hill: University of North Carolina Press, 1985); S. Jonathan Bass, *Blessed Are the Peacemakers: Martin Luther King Jr., Eight White Religious Leaders, and the "Letters From Birmingham Jail"* (Baton Rouge: Louisiana State University Press, 2002). Some white Southerners, including many involved in the labor movement, were even more actively involved in efforts to transform southern race relations and southern power in the decades before the *Brown* decision, though few white politicians could be counted among this group. See Patricia Sullivan, *Days of Hope: Race and Democracy in the New Deal Era* (Chapel Hill: University of North Carolina Press, 1996).

7. Tony Badger, "'Closet Moderates': Why White Liberals Failed, 1940–1970," in *The Role of Ideas in the Civil Rights South*, ed. by Ted Ownby (Jackson: University Press of Mississippi, 2002), 105; Anders Walker, *The Ghost of Jim Crow: How Southern Moderates Used* Brown v. Board of Education *to Stall Civil Rights* (New York: Oxford University Press, 2009); Crespino, *In Search of Another Country*, esp. ch. 1; Jason Morgan Ward, *Defending White Democracy: The Making of a Segregationist Movement and the Remaking of Racial Politics, 1936–1965* (Chapel Hill: University of North Carolina Press, 2011).

8. Matthew D. Lassiter, *The Silent Majority: Suburban Politics in the Sunbelt South* (Princeton: Princeton University Press, 2006), 266–75; Crespino, *In Search of Another Country*, 206–12.

Chapter 1

1. William Winter memoir, WWPC; William Winter, Crews interview; William Winter, Bass interview; "Eyes on Mississippi," *Time* 42 (August 16, 1943): 19–20. Winter's account of the 1932 battle to enact the Mississippi sales tax can be found in William Winter, "Governor Mike Conner and the Sales Tax, 1932," in Dean Faulkner Wells and Hunter Cole, eds., *Mississippi Heroes* (Jackson: University Press of Mississippi, 1980), 159–76.

2. William Winter memoir; William H. Winter to his mother, September 8, 1816, and January 26, 1819, both in WWPC; Malcolm J. Rohrbough, *The Land Office Business: The*

Settlement and Administration of American Public Lands, 1789–1837 (New York: Oxford University Press, 1968), ch. 6; Mary Wallace Kirk, *Locust Hill* (University: University of Alabama Press, 1975), 5.

3. Aunt Blanche to William Winter, n.d., WWPC; William H. Winter, Tax Roll, 1839, Hinds County, MDAH; William Winter, Bass interview; WPA History for Grenada County, MDAH; 1850 and 1860 Federal Censuses for Yalobusha County, Population, Slave, and Agricultural Schedules; Confederate Tax Bill, March 25, 1862, Box 142, William F. Winter and Family Papers, MDAH.

4. William Winter memoir; Melody Rubalcaba, "Mississippi's Ephriam Stone Fisher: Supreme Court Judge," *Yalobusha Pioneer* 8 (Summer 1984): 43–44; 1860 Federal Census for Yalobusha and Tallahatchie Counties, Slave Schedules; John Ray Skates, Jr., *A History of the Mississippi Supreme Court, 1817–1948* (Jackson: Mississippi Bar Foundation, 1973), 75; "Ephraim S. Fisher," Subject File: Ephraim S. Fisher, MDAH.

5. William Winter memoir; William A. Winter to William F. Winter, September 14, 1944, WWPC; receipt for slave labor, February 9, 1864, and Ephraim S. Fisher to General John S. Pemberton, December 5, 1862, copies of both documents in WWPC.

6. William Winter memoir; Aunt Blanche to William Winter, n.d., WWPC; service record for A. S. Fisher and service record for W. Winters, Compiled Service Records of Confederate Soldiers Who Served in Organizations from the State of Mississippi, RG 109, NA, reels 13 and 45 (microfilm); Dunbar Rowland, *Military History of Mississippi, 1803–1898* (Madison, Miss.: Chickasaw Bayou Press, reprint, 2003), 433–34, 437–39; Jack Hurst, *Nathan Bedford Forrest: A Biography* (New York: Alfred A. Knopf, 1993), 196–99, 212–15; John Allen Wyeth, *Life of Lieutenant Nathan Bedford Forrest* (New York: Harper and Brothers, 1909), 470–76. The Civil War service record for W. Winters seems clearly to be that of William B. Winter, despite the misspelled name and the fact that the record lists the hometown of Winters as DeSoto County, Mississippi, which may have instead been where William B. Winter enlisted. Other evidence, including William B. Winter's tombstone in the Odd Fellows cemetery in Grenada, confirms that he served in Company C of the Eighteenth Mississippi Calvary.

7. Eric Foner, *Reconstruction: America's Unfinished Revolution, 1863–1877* (New York: Harper and Row, 1988), ch. 3–4, 9; William C. Harris, *The Day of the Carpetbagger: Republican Reconstruction in Mississippi* (Baton Rouge: Louisiana State University Press, 1979), ch. 3; William A. Winter to William F. Winter, April 3, 1945, WWPC; Julia C. Brown, "Reconstruction in Yalobusha and Grenada Counties," *Publications of the Mississippi Historical Society* 12 (1912): 218–19, 232–37, 241, 255. In this latter source, the author identifies W. H. Winter as one of her informants and as the head of the Pea Ridge Klan in Yalobusha County. Since William H. Winter died in the 1880s, and since Governor William F. Winter independently identified his grandfather, William B. Winter, as the head of the Pea Ridge Klan during Reconstruction, it seems likely that Brown misidentified her informant in her essay. See William Winter, Bolton interview, July 22, 2008.

8. William Winter, Bolton interview, July 22, 2008; William C. Harris, *Presidential Reconstruction in Mississippi* (Baton Rouge: Louisiana State University Press, 1967),

ch. 6; Harris, *The Day of the Carpetbagger*, ch. 9, 380; Brown, "Reconstruction in Yalobusha and Grenada Counties," 237; Allen W. Trelease, *White Terror: The Ku Klux Klan Conspiracy and Southern Reconstruction* (Baton Rouge: Louisiana State University Press, 1971), ch. 24–25.

9. William Winter memoir; deeds from Ephraim S. Fisher to William B. Winter and Amelia P. Winter, February 3, 1870, and February 27, 1873, both in WWPC; William Winter, Bass interview; 1880 Federal Census for Grenada County, Mississippi, Population Schedule; William Winter, Bolton interview, December 5, 2008.

10. William Winter memoir; H. A. Dean, *Ninth Annual Catalog of Iuka Normal Institute, 1890–1891*, DUKE.

11. William Winter memoir; 1900 and 1910 Federal Censuses for Grenada County, Mississippi, Population Schedule; WPA History for Grenada County, MDAH; James C. Cobb, *The Most Southern Place on Earth: The Mississippi Delta and the Roots of Regional Identity* (New York: Oxford University Press, 1992), ch. 4–5; William A. Winter to William F. Winter, September 29, 1945, WWPC; William Winter, Bolton interview, May 18, 2006.

12. William Winter memoir; Mississippi Auditor of Public Accounts, *Expenses and Appropriations of the Mississippi Legislature* (Jackson: Auditor of Public Accounts, 1912).

13. William Winter memoir; William A. Winter to William F. Winter, February 11, 1946, WWPC; Mississippi Legislature, *Journal of the House of Representatives of the State of Mississippi, 1916* (Jackson: The House, 1916), 1825–1827, 1830–1831, 2158.

14. William Winter memoir; biographical memoranda, William Aylmer Winter, Subject File: William A. Winter, MDAH; William Winter, Bolton interview, July 12, 2006; William Winter, Bass interview.

15. Mississippi Legislature, *Journal of the Senate of the State of Mississippi, 1926* (Jackson: The Senate, 1926), 435, 634, 646, 768, 813, 920–21; William Winter memoir, WWPC; Nollie Hickman, *Mississippi Harvest: Lumbering in the Longleaf Pine Belt* (University: The University of Mississippi Press, 1962), 265; Dorothy Nelkin, *The Creation Controversy: Science or Scripture in the Schools* (New York: W. W. Norton, 1982), 30–34.

16. Mark L. Woods to J. P. Coleman, March 3, 1956, Box 38, J. P. Coleman Papers, MDAH.

17. William Winter, Bass interview; William Winter memoir; Aylmer Winter 1941 tax return, WWPC.

18. William Winter, Bolton interviews, July 14, 2006, March 9, 2007, and July 3, 2007; 1920 and 1930 Federal Censuses for Grenada County, Population Schedules; William Winter memoir; tenant account book of William A. Winter, Box 143, William F. Winter and Family Papers; Inez Winter to William F. Winter, 1944, WWPC.

19. Melissa Walker, *Southern Farmers and Their Stories: Memory and Meaning in Oral History* (Lexington: University Press of Kentucky, 2006), introduction; Edward L. Ayers, *The Promise of the New South: Life after Reconstruction* (New York: Oxford University Press, 1992), ch. 8; John Shearer, "Links Go Far Back for 2 at Meeting," *Chattanooga News Free Press*, March 18, 1986; distribution of parity payment, 1935, tenant account book of

William A. Winter, Box 143, William F. Winter and Family Papers; "Grenada County Negro Addresses Letter to Brethren," *Grenada Sentinel*, October 19, 1923; James N. Gregory, *The Southern Diaspora: How the Great Migrations of Black and White Southerners Transformed America* (Chapel Hill: University of North Carolina Press, 2007).

20. William Winter memoir; William Winter, Bolton interview, May 18, 2006; Bryan Baker, Bolton interview. For information on the rural system of segregation, see Mark Schultz, *The Rural Face of White Supremacy: Beyond Jim Crow* (Champaign: University of Illinois Press, 2005). Also see Jennifer Ritterhouse, *Growing Up Jim Crow: The Racial Socialization of Black and White Southern Children, 1890–1940* (Chapel Hill: University of North Carolina Press, 2006), esp. ch. 4.

21. "Presbyterian Church Organized in 1837," *Grenada Sentinel*, May 24, 1929; William Winter, Bolton interviews, July 12, 2006, and December 5, 2008; William Winter, Bass interview.

22. William Winter memoir; William Winter, Bass interview; William Winter, "My Autobiography," 1936, WWPC; William Winter, "The Essays of Ralph Waldo Emerson," in Michael J. Collins and Francis J. Ambrosio, eds., *Text and Teaching: The Search for Human Excellence* (Washington, D.C.: Georgetown University Press, 1991), 101.

23. William Winter, Bass interview; William Winter memoir; William Winter report card, 1929–1930, WWPC; William Winter, Bolton interview, December 19, 2007.

24. William Winter, Bass interview; William Winter memoir; "City's School System Great Asset to Town," *Grenada Sentinel*, May 24, 1929.

25. William Winter memoir; William Winter, Bass interview.

26. William Winter report cards, WWPC; William Winter, Bolton interview, July 3, 2007; "Class History," *Grenada County Weekly*, February 11, 1940; Winter, "My Autobiography"; J. B. Perry Jr. to William Winter, January 16, 1940, WWPC.

27. William Winter, Bass interview; Ralph Waldo Emerson, *Self-Reliance and Other Essays* (Mineola, N.Y.: Dover Publications, 1993), 19–38; Winter, "The Essays of Ralph Waldo Emerson," 101–2.

28. William Winter, Crews interview; William Winter, Bass interview; William Winter memoir; Winter, "My Autobiography"; William Winter, Caudill interview; William Winter, Bolton interview, February 26, 2009; item about Carolyn Whitaker and William Winter, *Grenada County Weekly*, April 4, 1940.

29. William Winter, Bolton interview, December 19, 2007; William Winter memoir.

30. Winter, "My Autobiography"; William Winter, Crews interview; William Winter, Bass interview; William Winter memoir.

31. Winter, "My Autobiography."

32. William Winter memoir; William Winter, Bass interview; William A. Winter to William F. Winter, December 8, 1945, WWPC.

33. Winter, "My Autobiography"; William Winter to Willie Morris, April 29, 1993, Box 40, Willie Morris Collection, UM; William Winter, Bolton interview, May 18, 2006; John Thorn and Pete Palmer, eds., *Total Baseball* (New York: Warner Books, 1989), 144.

34. William Winter memoir; William A. Winter to William F. Winter, November 25, 1945, WWPC; William Winter, Crews interview; transcript of Eudora Welty/William

Winter class at Millsaps College, April 5, 1989, WWPC; Randal L. Hall, *Lum and Abner: Rural America and the Golden Age of Radio* (Lexington: University Press of Kentucky, 2007); Lewis A. Erenberg, *The Greatest Fight of Our Generation: Louis vs. Schmeling* (New York: Oxford University Press, 2006).

35. William Winter, Bass interview; William Winter, Caudill interview; Winter, "My Autobiography"; William A. Winter to William F. Winter, January 25, 1944, WWPC.

36. William Winter, Crews interview; William Winter, Bass interview; William Winter memoir.

37. William Winter, Bass interview; William Winter memoir; James Donald Holley, "The New Deal and Farm Tenancy: Rural Resettlement in Arkansas, Louisiana, and Mississippi" (Ph.D. diss., Louisiana State University, 1969).

38. William Winter memoir; William Winter, Crews interview; Paul M. Gaston, *The New South Creed* (New York: Knopf, 1970).

39. "Eyes on Mississippi," 19–20; Winter, "The Essays of Ralph Waldo Emerson," 102; William Winter, Bolton interview, May 18, 2006; William Winter, Bass interview; Bill Minor, "Winter's Love Affair with Politics Brought 'Nobility' to the Calling," April 11, 2004, WWPC. For an overview of the impact of the New Deal on the South, see Roger Biles, *The South and the New Deal* (Lexington: University Press of Kentucky, 1994).

Chapter 2

1. William Winter, Greenville speech, September 1940, WWPC; "William Winter Addresses Greenville Legion Post," *Grenada County Weekly*, September 12, 1940; William Winter memoir.

2. William Winter, Bass interview; William Winter, Bolton interviews, December 8, 2006, and December 5, 2008; "Committee Chooses Winter, Granberry Outstanding Frosh," *The Mississippian*, April 4, 1941; "William Winter—A Leader as an Ole Miss Student," *The Mississippian*, April 23, 1964.

3. William Winter, Bass interview; William Winter, Bolton interview, December 8, 2006; "Clubs to Discuss Two Party System," and "Freshman 'Y' Cabinet Makes Clothing Drive," both in *The Mississippian*, December 6, 1940; "Committee Chooses Winter, Granberry Outstanding Frosh," and "Freshman Orators Compete Tuesday," both in *The Mississippian*, April 4, 1941.

4. "Winter Is Elected New Hermaean Head," *The Mississippian*, April 17, 1942; "These Men Selected for ODK Recently," *The Mississippian*, November 13, 1942; "Winter Is Named IRC President; Discussion Held," *The Mississippian*, November 15, 1943; William Winter to his father, n.d., April 1943?, WWPC; Charles W. Eagles, *The Price of Defiance: James Meredith and the Integration of Ole Miss* (Chapel Hill: University of North Carolina Press, 2009), 140; William Winter, Bolton interview, December 8, 2006.

5. William Winter, Bass interview; William Winter, Bolton interview, December 8, 2006; William Winter to Inez Winter, November 6, 1940, WWPC; Louis Silver, "Winter Most Valuable on Newspaper Staff," *The Mississippian*, May 9, 1941; William Winter,

"George, Henry Add Lustre to Great Family Tradition," *The Mississippian*, November 29, 1940; "Haile in the Winter," *The Mississippian*, December 13, 1940; William Winter, "A Rebel Writes," *The Mississippian*, Fall 1941; "Wilson, Granberry, Winter Elected to Head Paper," *The Mississippian*, February 13, 1942; "Winter, McCarty, Furr Named Paper Heads as Annual Elects," *The Mississippian*, February 12, 1943.

6. William Winter, Bass interview; "106 Students Make Honor Roll List," *The Mississippian*, February 28, 1941; William Winter to Aylmer Winter, September 9, 1943, and William Winter's graded papers from Ole Miss, both in WWPC.

7. William Winter, Bass interview; William Winter, Crews interview; "Dr. Howerton Praises Winter," *The Mississippian*, April 23, 1964.

8. William Winter, Bass interview; William Winter, Bolton interview, May 17, 2006; James W. Silver, *Running Scared: Silver in Mississippi* (Jackson: University Press of Mississippi, 1984), ch. 2. For an insightful history of Ole Miss during these years, see Eagles, *The Price of Defiance*.

9. "Freshmen Orientation Finished; 1941 Enrollment Shows Decrease," *The Mississippian*, September 19, 1941; "New Courses Aid Future Soldiers Now at Ole Miss," *The Mississippian*, January 16, 1942; David Bunch, "Blasts of Steam Whistle Signal Beginning of Campus Blackout Tuesday Night, 8:30–9:00," *The Mississippian*, February 13, 1942; Frazier Furr, "All Ole Miss Students Asked to Register for Sugar Ration Books," *The Mississippian*, May 1, 1942; "'Meatless Days' Prove Fruitful," *The Mississippian*, November 6, 1942; David G. Sansing, *The University of Mississippi: A Sesquicentennial History* (Jackson: University Press of Mississippi, 1999), 256–57; "Army Enlisted Men Move on Campus Today to Attend the Administration School Here," and "Official Notice to University Students," both in *The Mississippian*, September 25, 1942.

10. William Winter memoir; "ROTC Members Receive Orders," *The Mississippian*, January 8, 1943; William Winter to his parents, March 1943, WWPC.

11. "Depression Is Here," *The Mississippian*, November 6, 1942; William Winter to his father, n.d., May 1943? and April 28, 1944, both in WWPC; "New Student Rulers," *The Mississippian*, April 9, 1943.

12. Joseph E. Lowndes, *From the New Deal to the New Right: Race and the Southern Origins of Modern Conservatism* (New Haven: Yale University Press, 2008), ch. 2; "Rumblings in the South," *The Mississippian*, April 9, 1943.

13. United Sons of the South, "The Southern Negro—How Will This War Affect His Future Status?" *The Mississippian*, April 10, 1942; William Winter to James O. Eastland, April 30, 1942, File Series 1, Subseries 19, Box 3, James O. Eastland Collection, UM. Winter also participated in a forum sponsored by the International Relations Club on the "Negro and Alien in America at War," during October 1942. See "IRC to Hold Forum on Negro and Alien in First of Series," *The Mississippian*, October 30, 1942.

14. "Mississippi," *Time* 42 (April 12, 1943): 25; "Time Strikes Again," *The Mississippian* editorial, April 1943; William Winter to Time, Inc., April 14, 1943, and Ned Lee letter to the editor, *The Mississippian*, April 1943, both in WWPC; William Winter, Bolton interview, December 8, 2006; "This Country Club," *The Mississippian*, April 23, 1943.

15. William Winter memoir; William A. Winter to William F. Winter, April 22, 1944, WWPC; Elbert Hilliard, Bolton interview; William Winter, Bolton interview, July 3, 2007.

16. William Winter, Bass interview; W. A. Winter to John Lee Gainey, May 14, 1942, and W. A. Winter to Joe Brown, June 9, 1942, both in Series File 1, Subseries 19, Box 2, James O. Eastland Collection; Dan W. Smith Jr., "James O. Eastland: Early Life and Career, 1904–1942," (MA thesis, Mississippi College, 1978), ch. 5; William Winter, Bolton interview, May 18, 2006.

17. William Winter to Aylmer Winter, June 8, 1942, WWPC; William Winter, Bolton interviews, December 8, 2006, and December 19, 2007; Eastland schedules, Series File 1, Subseries 19, Box 9, James O. Eastland Collection; William Winter memoir; "Dedication of Eastland Portrait," William Winter speech, August 17, 1992, WWPC.

18. William Winter, Bolton interview, December 19, 2007.

19. Smith, "James O. Eastland," ch. 5; Jesse Lamar White Jr., "Mississippi Electoral Politics, 1903–1976: The Emerging Modernization Consensus," (Ph.D. diss., Massachusetts Institute of Technology, 1979), 285; "Mississippi Elects J. O. Eastland as Junior Senator," *Winona Times*, September 18, 1942; William Winter, untitled essay, 1943, WWPC; Robert L. Fleegler, "Theodore G. Bilbo and the Decline of Public Racism, 1938–1947," *Journal of Mississippi History* 68 (Spring 2006): 1–27.

20. "Mississippi Plans a Run-off," *New York Times*, August 27, 1942; "Results Senatorial Race," *Jackson Clarion-Ledger*, August 28, 1942; "Mississippi Elects J. O. Eastland as Junior Senator," *Winona Times*, September 18, 1942; White, "Mississippi Electoral Politics," 289–92.

21. William Winter, Bolton interviews, May 18, 2006, and December 8, 2006; James O. Eastland to W. A. Winter, November 4, 1942, and Inez Winter to Senator and Mrs. Eastland, September 21, 1942, both in File Series 1, Subseries 19, Box 2, James O. Eastland Collection; William Winter memoir.

22. Special Orders No. 129, May 31, 1943, Military Service Record for William Winter, WWPC; William Winter, Bass interview; William Winter to his parents, July 20, 1943, and November 20, 1946, William Winter to Aylmer Winter, August 5, 1943, September 9, 1943, and April 28, 1944, and W. Alton Bryant to Members of the Graduating Class, September 16, 1943, all in WWPC. Winter's ASTP physical training instructor was Edward Khayat, a former high school coach from Moss Point, who was the father of Robert Khayat, later to become an Ole Miss and National Football League star player and Chancellor of Ole Miss.

In July 1943, after a white woman in the town of Duck Hill accused a black soldier from Camp McCain of raping her, thirteen black soldiers from the camp armed themselves and headed for the nearby town, where they took up positions on the Illinois Central train tracks about three hundred yards from downtown and began shooting, damaging some buildings but injuring no one in a ten-minute assault. The army eventually court-martialed six of the soldiers and sentenced them to hard labor at Fort Leavenworth. See "The Attack on Duck Hill," *Time* 42 (September 13, 1943): 67; and

James Albert Burran, III, "Racial Violence in the South During World War II," (Ph.D. diss., University of Tennessee, 1977), ch. 5.

Chapter 3

1. Neil R. McMillen, ed., *Remaking Dixie: The Impact of World War II on the American South* (Jackson: University Press of Mississippi, 1997).

2. William Winter memoir; William Winter to his parents, September 30, 1943, and December 1, 1943, William F. Winter to William A. Winter, January 23, 1944, and Solly to William Winter, April 15, 1944, all in WWPC.

3. William Winter memoir; William Winter, Bolton interview, December 8, 2006; William F. Winter to William A. Winter, September 24, 1943, and October 4, 1943, both in WWPC.

4. W. Stanford Smith, *Camp Blanding: Florida Star in Peace and War* (Fuquay Varina, N.C.: Research Triangle Publishing, 1998), 118; William F. Winter to William A. Winter, September 24, 1943, and William Winter to his parents, September 30, 1943, October 24, 1943, and November 15, 1943, all in WWPC.

5. William F. Winter to William A. Winter, October 4, 1943, and February 9, 1944, and William Winter to his parents, October 10 and 31, 1943, and November 30, 1943, all in WWPC.

6. William Winter to his parents, October 31, 1943, November 7, 22, and 30, 1943, and December 5, 1943, all in WWPC.

7. William F. Winter to William A. Winter, January 23, 1944, WWPC; William Winter, Bass interview; William Winter, Bolton interview, December 8, 2006.

8. William Winter to his parents, June 19 and 25, 1944, July 25, 1944, and August 13, 1944, all in WWPC; William Winter, Bolton interviews, July 3, 2007, and December 5, 2008; Cpl. Lewis O. Swingler, "News of Mighty Fort Benning," *Atlanta Daily World*, June 14, 1944; "77 Paratroopers Take First Leap at Fort Benning," *Atlanta Daily World*, May 27, 1944; Christopher Moore, *Fighting for America: Black Soldiers—The Unsung Heroes of World War II* (New York: Presido Press, 2005), 208–9; Record, May 13, 1944, RG 407, Box 4413, NA-CP.

9. David M. Kennedy, *Freedom from Fear: The American People in Depression and War, 1929–1945* (New York: Oxford University Press, 2001), 767–69; Neil A. Wynn, *The African American Experience during World War II* (Lanham: Rowman & Littlefield Publishers, 2010).

10. Charles L. Zelden, *The Battle for the Black Ballot: Smith v. Allwright and the Defeat of the Texas All-White Primary* (Lawrence: University Press of Kansas, 2004); William A. Winter to William F. Winter, April 17, 1944, and May 10, 1944, and William Winter to his parents, April 23, 1944, all in WWPC.

11. Burran, "Racial Violence in the South During World War II," ch. 5; "F.D.R., Stimson, Asked to Probe Soldier Lynching," press release, April 18, 1941, Papers of the

NAACP, Part 9, Series B, (microfilm), reel 14; Margaret E. Wagner, et al., *The Library of Congress World War II Companion* (New York: Simon & Schuster, 2007), 295; "Army to South: 'End Jim Crow,'" *Chicago Defender*, June 3, 1944; Bell I. Wiley, *The Training of Negro Troops* (Washington, D.C.: Historical Section, Army Ground Forces, 1946), 52, 78; Robert H. Dunlop to Truman K. Gipson Jr. (Civilian Aide to the Secretary of War), April 1, 1944, RG 107, Box 205, NA-CP.

12. Burran, "Racial Violence in the South During World War II," 157; Wiley, *The Training of Negro Troops*, 53; Morris J. MacGregor, *Integration of the Armed Forces, 1940–1965* (Washington, D.C.: Government Printing Office, 1989), ch. 2; William Winter, Bolton interview, December 5, 2008; Robert L. Shives to Walter White, June 17, 1944, Papers of the NAACP, Part 9, Series B (microfilm), reel 13; Ruth Danenhower Wilson, *Jim Crow Joins Up: A Study of Negroes in the Armed Forces of the United States*, rev. ed. (New York: Press of William J. Clark, 1944), 26–31; Jean Byers, *A Study of the Negro in Military Service* (Washington, D.C.: U.S. Dept. of Defense, 1950), 84.

13. William Winter, Bolton interview, December 5, 2008. This incident was apparently not an isolated one. In October 1944, about the time Winter finished OCS, another graduating class had arranged a party at a nightclub in Columbus. That group also had two black members, and the nightclub's white manager turned them away from the affair. The black graduates left without incident, but two white members of the class challenged the white manager and his wife by telling the woman "that the Negroes were as good as she was." The white officers eventually retreated and further trouble was averted. See Weekly Intelligence Report, 21 October 21 through October 28, 1944, RG 197, Box 262, NA-CP.

14. William Winter, Bass interview; William Winter to his parents, n.d., late June 1944, June 25, 1944, July 2, 9, and 29, 1944, and August 20, 1944, and William Winter to his mother, June 27, 1944, all in WWPC.

15. William Winter memoir; Frank J. Price, *Troy H. Middleton: A Biography* (Baton Rouge: Louisiana State University Press, 1974); William Winter, Bolton interview, July 3, 2007; William Winter to his parents, June 25, 1944, July 25, 1944, and August 13, 1944, all in WWPC.

16. William F. Winter to William A. Winter, September 20, 1944, and William A. Winter to William F. Winter, September 21, 1944, both in WWPC.

17. William A. Winter to William F. Winter, August 11, 1944, September 6 and 14, 1944, November 6 and 13, 1944, and December 20, 1944, all in WWPC.

18. William Winter to his parents, October 29, 1944, WWPC; William Winter, Bolton interview, July 3, 2007; William Winter memoir; Byers, *A Study of the Negro in Military Service*, 44–52.

19. Byers, *A Study of the Negro in Military Service*, 44–52; William Winter, Bolton interview, July 3, 2007.

20. William Winter to his parents, December 17, 1944, January 29, 1945, and December 29, 1945, all in WWPC; William Winter memoir; MacGregor, *Integration of the Armed Forces, 1940–1965*, ch. 2.

21. William Winter, Bolton interview, July 3, 2007; William Winter to his parents, November 19, 1944, December 17, 1944, and February 9 and 18, 1945, and William A. Winter to William F. Winter, November 13, 1944, all in WWPC; William Winter memoir.

22. William Winter to his parents, February 18, 1945, March 12, 1945, April 5, 1945, and n.d., April 1945, all in WWPC; Robert F. Jefferson, *Fighting for Hope: African American Troops of the 93rd Infantry Division in World War II and Postwar America* (Baltimore: The Johns Hopkins Press, 2008), ch. 6 and 7.

23. William F. Winter to William A. Winter, January 29, 1945, and February 9 and 18, 1945, and William Winter to his parents, August 18, 1945, all in WWPC; William Winter memoir. For American attitudes concerning the Japanese during World War II, see John Dower, *War without Mercy: Race and Power in the Pacific War* (New York: Pantheon Books, 1986), part II.

24. William Winter memoir; Wiley, *The Training of Negro Troops*, ch. 4; William R. Boes Jr., interview by Kurt Piehler and James Dunne, October 16, 1995, transcript, Rutgers Oral History Archives of World War II, http://oralhistory.rutgers.edu/Interviews/boes_william.html (Accessed on June 8, 2009).

25. Intelligence Report from Major Daniel Sullivan, December 7, 1944, and Technical Intelligence Report, May 28, 1945, both in RG 107, Box 265, NA-CP; Ulysses Lee, *United States Army in World War II: Special Studies, The Employment of Negro Troops* (Washington, D.C.: Office of the Chief of Military History, 1966), 220–25; William Winter memoir; Wiley, *The Training of Negro Troops*, ch. 4.

26. William Winter, Bolton interview, December 5, 2008; Wiley, *The Training of Negro Troops*, 76–78; James Truehart to Whom It May Concern, June 8, 1944, Papers of the NAACP, Part 9, Series B (microfilm), reel 13; Weekly Intelligence Summary, January 13 to January 20, 1945, RG 197, Box 262, NA-CP; Will Weathers and others to Walter White, April 18, 1945, Papers of the NAACP, Part 9, Series B (microfilm), reel 14.

27. William F. Winter to William A. Winter, June 5, 1945, WWPC; William Winter memoir.

28. William Winter memoir; William Winter, Caudill interview; Fleegler, "Theodore G. Bilbo and the Decline of Public Racism, 1938–1947," 1–27; Harry S. McAlpin, "Congress FEPC Opponents Hasten Its Death," *Atlanta Daily World*, June 29, 1945; "Ironical Contrasts," *Washington Post*, July 3, 1945.

29. William Winter, Bass interview; Weekly Intelligence Summary, August 11 to August 18, 1945, RG 107, Box 263, NA-CP; William Winter, Bolton interview, August 29, 2001.

30. William Winter to his parents, July 31, 1945, August 10 and 18, 1945, and September 25, 1945, William A. Winter to William F. Winter, August 22, 1945, and September 18, 1945, and William F. Winter to William A. Winter, February 21, 1946, all in WWPC; Edward J. Drea, "Intelligence Forecasting for the Invasion of Japan: Previews of Hell," in Robert James Maddox, ed., *Hiroshima in History: The Myths of Revisionism* (Columbia: University of Missouri Press, 2007), 59–75.

31. William Winter to his parents, August 31, 1945, September 3 and 30, 1945, and October 6 and 15, 1945, all in WWPC; William F. Winter, "A Veteran's View of the End of World War II," *Journal of Mississippi History* 57 (Winter 1995): 306; William Winter memoir.

32. Winter, "A Veteran's View of the End of World War II," 307; William Winter memoir; William Winter to his parents, October 30, 1945, and November 1, 1945, both in WWPC; Stanley Karnow, *In Our Image: America's Empire in the Philippines* (New York: Random House, 1989), ch. 11.

33. William Winter to his parents, October 30, 1945, and November 1 and 6, 1945, William F. Winter to William A. Winter, November 8, 1945, and Request for Reassignment, November 3, 1945, William Winter Military Service Record, all in WWPC.

34. William F. Winter to William A. Winter, November 8, 1945, and William Winter to his parents, November 14, 21, and 25, 1945, all in WWPC; William Winter memoir.

35. William F. Winter to William A. Winter, January 23, 1946, and William A. Winter to William F. Winter, June 25, 1946, both in WWPC; Robert W. Rydell, *All the World's a Fair: Visions of Empire at American International Expositions, 1876–1916* (Chicago: University of Chicago Press, 1984), ch. 6.

36. William F. Winter to William A. Winter, January 6 and 23, 1946, both in WWPC; Robert Trumbull, "GI Protests Win Pledge of Return," *New York Times*, January 7, 1946; Robert Trumbull, "20,000 Manila GI's Boo General; Urge Congress to Speed Sailings," *New York Times*, January 8, 1946; Robert Trumbull, "Manila GI's Draft Protest to Army," *New York Times*, January 11, 1946; Sidney Shalett, "Army Seeks a Way Out of Its Morale Crisis," *New York Times*, January 13, 1946; Paul Siegel, "The Greatest Generation? Reflections of a World War II Veteran," *Socialist Action*, July 2001, http://www.socialistaction.org/news/200107/wwii.html (Accessed on June 22, 2009); William F. Winter to William A. Winter, January 13, 1946, and William Winter to Inez Winter, January 17, 1946, both in WWPC.

37. William Winter memoir; Michael Norman and Elizabeth M. Norman, *Tears in the Darkness: The Story of the Bataan Death March and Its Aftermath* (New York: Farrar, Straus, and Giroux, 2009); William Winter to his parents, February 18 and 25, 1946, April 1 and 28, 1946, and July 8, 1946, all in WWPC; Karnow, *In Our Image*, ch. 11.

38. William Winter memoir; James Grant Crawford, "Aguinaldo, Emilio," in John Whiteclay Chambers II, ed., *The Oxford Companion to American Military History* (New York: Oxford University Press, 2000), 12; William Winter, Bass interview; David Haward Bain to Governor Winter, February 6, 1985, WWPC.

39. "Independence for Philippines Hailed Amid Cheers, Gaiety," *Atlanta Daily World*, July 5, 1946; William Winter to his parents, July 8, 1946, WWPC; William Winter memoir; David Haward Bain, *Sitting in Darkness: Americans in the Philippines* (Boston: Houghton Mifflin Company, 1984), 389–90; William F. Winter to Charles C. Bolton, June 1, 2009 (email), in author's possession. The Filipino government later moved the official Independence Day for the nation to June 12, the date Aguinaldo had originally proclaimed independence in 1898.

40. William A. Winter to William F. Winter, May 5, 1946, William Winter to his parents, February 6, 1946, and July 8, 1946, all in WWPC.

Chapter 4

1. *Mississippi Blue Book, 1945–1949* (Jackson: Secretary of State, 1949), 51–63; Kari Frederickson, *The Dixiecrat Revolt and the End of the Solid South, 1932–1968* (Chapel Hill: University of North Carolina Press, 2001), 70–76.

2. Sansing, *The University of Mississippi*, 263; Michael De L. Landon, *The University of Mississippi School of Law: A Sesquicentennial History* (Jackson: University Press of Mississippi, 2006), 82–83; William Winter, Bass interview; W. C. Trotter to W. A. Winter, May 15, 1946, Box 141, William F. Winter and Family Papers, MDAH; William Winter to his parents, April 1, 1946, November 20, 1946, and February 13, 1947, and William A. Winter to William F. Winter, May 5 and 24, 1946, all in WWPC.

3. William Winter to his parents, December 5, 1946, WWPC; William Winter, Bass interview.

4. Ann Waldron, *Hodding Carter: The Reconstruction of a Racist* (Chapel Hill: Algonquin Books, 1993), ch. 9; David Brinkley, *Brinkley's Beat: People, Places, and Events That Shaped My Time* (New York: Knopf, 2003), 18; William Winter, Bolton interview, May 18, 2006.

5. William Winter, Bolton interview, May 18, 2006; ODK flyer, Hodding Carter speech, December 12, 1946, WWPC; "Economic Advancement within Pattern of Segregation Advocated in Speech by Carter," *Delta Democrat-Times*, December 13, 1946; "Hodding Carter Speaks Here Despite Protest; Promotes Awakening of South to Dangers," *The Mississippian*, December 13, 1946.

6. Nellie N. Sommerville to William Winter, December 27, 1946, and Winter's reply to Sommerville, undated, both in Box 141, William F. Winter and Family Papers; Eagles, *The Price of Defiance*, 31–32.

7. "History Group Forms Society," *The Mississippian*, May 9, 1947; "Lawyers Elect Class Officers," *The Mississippian*, October 18, 1946; William Winter, Bolton interview, December 8, 2006; William A. Winter to William F. Winter, September 15, 1946, and January 25, 1947, both in WWPC; "Barnett, Winter Go into Second Primary Tuesday; Taylor Chosen A.S.B. Vice-President Yesterday," *The Mississippian*, January 17, 1947.

8. William Winter, Bass interview; William Winter, Bolton interview, July 3, 2007; "Former First Lady Elise Winter," *Jackson Christian Family*, May 2004, copy in WWPC; Anita Lee, "Democratic Candidate's Wife Takes the Campaign Trail in Stride," *Jackson Daily News*, September 10, 1979; "Celebrate Fiftieth Wedding," article from the *Memphis Commercial Appeal*, 1921, in Subject File: Mrs. Elise F. Winter, MDAH; Elise Winter, Bolton interview; Elise Winter, Meincke interview.

9. William Winter memoir; William Winter, Bass interview; William A. Winter to William F. Winter, January 18, 1946, April 9, 1946, and November 26, 1946, all in WWPC.

10. William Winter memoir; William Winter, Bass interview; *Journal of the House of Representatives of the State of Mississippi, 1940* (Jackson: The House, 1940), 1042–43; William A. Winter to William F. Winter, January 18, 1946, March 6, 11, and 24, 1947, April 9, 1946, November 26, 1946, and January 10, 1947, and William Winter class at Millsaps College, March 1, 1989, transcript, all in WWPC.

11. William A. Winter to William F. Winter, April 28, 1947, WWPC; William Winter, Bass interview.

12. William Winter, "Remembering the Judges," May 4, 2000, speech, and William Winter class at Millsaps College, March 1, 1989, transcript, both in WWPC.

13. William Winter class at Millsaps College, March 1, 1989, transcript, WWPC; election returns, *Grenada County Weekly*, August 28, 1947.

14. William Winter, Bass interview; William Winter to his parents, September 28, 1947, William A. Winter to William F. Winter, October 1, 1947, and John C. Stennis to William Winter, November 22, 1947, all in WWPC; Frank E. Smith, *Congressman from Mississippi* (New York: Pantheon Books, 1964), 70–71; Kenneth Toler, "Stennis Is New Senator; Promises He Will Serve 'Plain People' of State," *Memphis Commercial Appeal*, November 6, 1947; Luke Fowler and Jeffrey Markham, "John C. Stennis and the 1947 Senate Campaign," http://www.msgovt.org/files/200_1236_01_CPB_Stennis_1947Election2.18-1.pdf (accessed on December 30, 2008).

15. *Mississippi Blue Book, 1945–1949*, 51–63; Mary Evelyn Blagg, *The Legislative Process: A Handbook for Mississippi Legislators* (University, Miss.: Bureau of Public Administration, 1947); Boyce Holleman, Caudill interview; William Winter memoir; William Winter, Bass interview; William A. Winter to William F. Winter, January 6, 1948, and Edwards Hotel postcard from William F. Winter to William A. Winter, January 1948, both in WWPC; *Grenada County Weekly*, January–April 1948.

16. William A. Winter to William F. Winter, November 8, 1947, December 11, 1947, and January 6, 1947, all in WWPC.

17. William Winter, Bass and DeVries interview; Wiesenberg quoted in Adam Nossiter, *Of Long Memory: Mississippi and the Murder of Medgar Evers* (Boston: Addison-Wesley, 1994), 166; Charles C. Jacobs, Jr., Bolton interview; *Mississippi Blue Book, 1945–1949* (Jackson: Secretary of State, 1949).

18. William Winter memoir; William Winter, Bass interview; Ward, *Defending White Democracy*, 56–62; John Dittmer, *Local People: The Struggle for Civil Rights in Mississippi* (Urbana: University of Illinois Press, 1994), 6–7.

19. William Winter class at Millsaps College, March 1, 1989, transcript, WWPC; "Miss. Legislators Back Gov. Threat Against Party," *Atlanta Daily World*, January 27, 1948; Mississippi Legislature, *Journal of the House of Representatives of the State of Mississippi, 1948* (Jackson: The House, 1948), 48, 90–91; *Mississippi Blue Book, 1945–1949*, 61; William Winter, Crews interview; Frederickson, *The Dixiecrat Revolt and the End of the Solid South, 1932–1968*, ch. 3.

20. William A. Winter to William F. Winter, January 28, 1948, WWPC; Mississippi Legislature, *Journal of the House, 1948*, 168–78; William Winter, conversation with

author, August 28, 2009; House Concurrent Resolution 22, 1948, LRB; William Winter, "Legislative Notes," *Grenada County Weekly*, February 5, 1948.

21. C. P. Trussell, "Vote on ERP, Taxes by April 1, GOP Aim," *New York Times*, February 7, 1948; "Mississippi Democracy Carries On" (editorial), *Jackson Daily News*, February 13, 1948; William Winter, "Legislative Notes," *Grenada County Weekly*, February 26, 1948.

22. "Judge Says State Must Answer Suit of Fired Instructor," *Pittsburgh Courier*, January 1, 1949; "Anti-Negro Vote Amendment Fails in Legislature," *Jackson Daily News*, March 26, 1948; *Journal of the House, 1948*, 48, 666–67, 740–41, 746, 981–82; Boyce Holleman, Caudill interview.

23. William Winter to his parents, May 2, 1948, WWPC; William Winter, Bailey interview; William Winter, Bolton interview, May 18, 2006; William Winter memoir; Frederickson, *The Dixicrat Revolt*, 104–8.

24. William Winter to his parents, January 26, 1948, WWPC; William Winter, conversation with author, December 2006; "Notes and Announcements," *The Journal of Negro History* 67 (Spring 1982): 84.

25. William Winter, conversation with author, August 28, 2009; *Journal of the House, 1948*, 400–401.

26. William Winter, "Constitutional Law—Fourteenth and Fifteenth Amendments—State Action Where Party Kept Negro from Voting in South Carolina White Primary," *Mississippi Law Journal* 19 (1948): 244–46.

27. William Winter, Bolton interview, July 22, 2008.

28. Mississippi Legislature, *Journal of the Senate of the State of Mississippi, 1940* (Jackson: The Senate), 319, 442; House Bill 351, 1948, LRB; William Winter memoir; Bill Minor, *Eyes on Mississippi: A Fifty-Year Chronicle of Change* (Jackson: J. Prichard Morris Books, 2001), 151; Mississippi Legislature, *Journal of the House, 1948*, 213, 447, 489, 499–500, 714–16, 898–99, 1092–93; *Journal of the Senate of the State of Mississippi, 1948* (Jackson: The Senate, 1948), 607, 669, 673–77; Kenneth Toler, "Mississippi Session 'Spent' $120,000,000," *Memphis Commercial Appeal*, April 11, 1948.

29. William Winter memoir; "House Will Get Bill for Sunday Movies," *Jackson Clairon-Ledger*, n.d., 1948; "Faith and Politics," undated speech, "Kill That Bill (editorial), *Mississippi Methodist Advocate*, February 25, 1948, and telegram from Andrew F. Gallman, pastor Broad Street Methodist Church, Hattiesburg, February 5, 1948, all in WWPC; William Winter, Bolton interview, May 18, 2006; Moon Mullen, "Personally About the Legislature," February 12, 1948, Subject File: Phillip Mullen, MDAH; *Journal of the House, 1948*, 210.

30. William Winter, "Legislative Notes," *Grenada County Weekly*, February 26 and March 4, 1948; William Winter to his parents, February 18, 1948, WWPC; William Winter memoir.

31. J. K. Morrison to W. A. Winter, April 2, 1948, WWPC.

32. William to his parents, December 1, 1948, and William F. Winter to William A. Winter, December 5, 1948, both in WWPC; William Winter to Charles Bolton,

March 4, 2009 (email), copy in author's possession; Walter R. Ruch, "Breakdown Seen in Federal System," *New York Times*, December 5, 1948; "Representative William F. Winter Reports on Legislative Meeting," *Grenada County Weekly*, December 9, 1948.

33. William Winter to his parents, February 18 and 22, 1949, and William A. Winter to William F. Winter, February 24, 1949, all in WWPC; Kathryn S. Olmsted, *Red Spy Queen: A Biography of Elizabeth Bentley* (Chapel Hill: University of North Carolina Press, 2002).

34. William Winter to his parents, October 12 and 24, 1948, and February 18, 1949, William F. Winter to William A. Winter, March 21, 1949, and May 26, 1949, all in WWPC; *Mississippi Law Journal*, Volume 20, 1948–1949.

35. William F. Winter to William A. Winter, April 19, 1949, William A. Winter to William F. Winter, April 21 and 27, 1949, all in WWPC; William Winter, Bolton interview, July 3, 2007; William Winter, Bass interview; William Winter memoir; Smith, *Congressman from Mississippi*, 78.

36. William F. Winter, "The Work of the 1950 Session of the Mississippi Legislature," *Mississippi Law Journal* 22 (December 1950): 1–2; Janis Quinn, *Promises Kept: The University of Mississippi Medical Center* (Jackson: University Press of Mississippi, 2005), 26; House Bill 290, 1950, LRB; William F. Winter, "New Directions in Politics 1948–1956," in *A History of Mississippi*, Richard Aubrey McLemore, ed. (Hattiesburg, Miss.: University and College Press of Mississippi, 1973), 2: 145; William Winter, "Legislative Notes," *Grenada County Weekly*, January 12, 1950.

37. *Journal of the House of the State of Mississippi, 1950* (Jackson: The House, 1950), 266, 487, 1061–62; William Winter, Bass interview; Winter, "The Work of the 1950 Session of the Mississippi Legislature," 16–17.

38. "Solons in Secret Session Here to Hear 'Red' Names," *Jackson Daily News* (early edition), February 2, 1950, and William A. Winter to William F. Winter, November 29, 1946, both in WWPC; "Red Scare Stirs Mississippi Legislature; Student Member Sees Schools 'Infested,'" *New York Times*, February 5, 1950; Eagles, *Price of Defiance*, 148; "26-Year-Old Legislator Starts Furor With Bill Proposing Sweeping Investigations of Colleges," *Delta Democrat-Times*, February 5, 1950; Winter, "The Work of the 1950 Session of the Mississippi Legislature," 16–17; Richard M. Fried, *Nightmare in Red: The McCarthy Era in Perspective* (New York: Oxford University Press, 1990), 109; William Winter, "Legislative Notes," *Grenada County Weekly*, February 16, 1950.

Chapter 5

1. William Winter, Bolton interview, July 14, 2006; "Negro C. of C. to Give Away TV Set Dec. 18," *Grenada County Weekly*, October 16, 1953; "Thousands Expected for Harvest Festival: Both White and Colored Invited," *Grenada County Weekly*, November 19, 1953; "$1900 in Prizes Awarded at Harvest Festival," *Grenada County Weekly*, November 26, 1953.

2. John Stennis to William Winter, January 4, 1950, Series 50, Box 8; "1950 Tour for Stennis," Series 46, Box 94; undated memorandum to William Winter, and John Stennis to William Winter, March 22, 1950, both in Series 46, Box 1, all in MSU.

3. William Winter to his parents, July 25, 1950, n.d., early September 1950, and September 13, 1950, all in WWPC; John D. Morris, "Congress Planning to Quit on Sept. 16 If Agreed on Taxes," *New York Times*, September 3, 1950; William S. White, "Congress Recess Till Late Fall Set As Leaders Refuse Adjournment," *New York Times*, September 21, 1950.

4. Wedding invitation of Elise Varner and William Winter; Aylmer Winter to Inez Winter, October 4, 1950; John Stennis to William Winter, November 20, 1948, all in WWPC; William Winter, Bolton interview, July 22, 2008; William Winter memoir.

5. William Winter to his parents, n.d., November 1950, and December 1, 1950, and William Winter to Aylmer Winter, November 29, 1950, all in WWPC; C. P. Trussell, "Alaska Statehood Blocked in Senate," *New York Times*, November 29, 1950. Also see Ann K. Ziker, "Segregationists Confront American Empire: The Conservative White South and the Question of Hawaiian Statehood, 1947–1959," *Pacific Historical Review* 76 (August 2007): 439–66.

6. William Winter to his parents, April 28, 1951, May 21, 1951, and June 12, 1951, all in WWPC.

7. William Winter to his parents, August 27, 1951, September 16, 1951, and September 28, 1951, all in WWPC; William Winter to John Stennis, September 3, 1951, Series 50, Box 8, MSU; William Winter memoir.

8. William Winter memoir; Andrew H. Myers, *Black, White, and Olive Drab: Racial Integration at Fort Jackson, South Carolina, and the Civil Rights Movement* (Charlottesville: University of Virginia Press, 2006), 81–85.

9. William Winter to John Stennis, February 15, 1952, Series 50, Box 8, MSU; William Winter, Bolton interviews, July 12, 2006, and July 22, 2008.

10. "'States Rights' Defended," *New York Times*, January 10, 1952; Winter, "New Directions in Politics 1948–1956," 148; "Third-Party Bolt Mississippi Threat," *New York Times*, June 27, 1952; William Winter to John Stennis, May 27, 1952, Series 50, Box 8, MSU; William Winter memoir; John N. Popham, "Mississippi Bloc Backs Eisenhower," *New York Times*, August 30, 1952; Frederickson, *The Dixiecrat Revolt*, 226–27; William Winter, Bass and DeVries interview.

11. William Winter memoir; Mississippi Legislature, *Journal of the House of Representatives of the State of Mississippi, 1952* (Jackson: The House, 1952), 50, 119, 133–34, 266, 338, 377.

12. William Winter, Bolton interviews, July 12, 2006, July 3, 2007, and December 19, 2007; "W. F. Winter Named Manager of C. of C.," *Grenada County Weekly*, January 15, 1953; "Winter Resigns as C. of C. Manager," *Grenada County Weekly*, October 7, 1954; "Welcome to Grenada—McQuay, Inc.—Formal Dedication Is Monday Oct. 3," *Grenada County Weekly*, November 29, 1955; James C. Cobb, *Selling of the South: The Southern Crusade for Industrial Development, 1936–1980* (Baton Rouge: Louisiana State University Press, 1982), ch. 1.

13. William F. Winter, "Mississippi's Legislative Approach to the School Segregation Problem," *Mississippi Law Journal* 26 (1954–1955): 172; "Mississippi's $100 Million," *Pittsburgh Courier*, November 14, 1953; Bolton, *The Hardest Deal of All*, 53–54; Winter, "New Directions in Politics 1948–1956," 150.

14. Winter, "Mississippi's Legislative Approach to the School Segregation Problem," 172; Mississippi Legislature, *Journal of the House of Representatives of the State of Mississippi, 1954 and 1953 Special Session* (Jackson: The House, 1954), 1391, 1408, 1504; John Stennis to William Winter, December 8, 1953, and William Winter to John Stennis, December 22, 1953, both in Series 50, Box 8, MSU.

15. William Winter, Bolton interviews, July 12, 2006, and July 3, 2007; *Journal of the House of Representatives of the State of Mississippi, 1954* (Jackson: The House, 1954), 33, 737; "Gates Officially Close at Grenada Dam Wednesday," *Grenada County Weekly*, January 21, 1954; "New Facilities Are Planned for Popular Grenada Lake," *Grenada County Weekly*, September 1, 1955.

16. Numan V. Bartley, *The Rise of Massive Resistance: Race and Politics in the South During the 1950s* (Baton Rouge: Louisiana State University Press, 1969), 55–56; "More Than 100 Bills Introduced, Only One Signed," *Jackson Daily News*, January 20, 1954; "Miss. Votes to Revise Schools on Trial Basis," *Chicago Defender*, May 15, 1954; Bill Middlebrooks, "Solons Ready to Go Home; Start Spending Money; Even Consider the Schools," *Jackson Daily News*, March 26, 1954; Mississippi Legislature, *Journal of the House, 1954*, 44, 47, 77, 650, 1396–97, 1406–8; Winter, "Mississippi's Legislative Approach to the School Segregation Problem," 168.

17. Todd Moye, *Let the People Decide: Black Freedom and White Resistance Movements in Sunflower County, Mississippi, 1945–1986* (Chapel Hill: University of North Carolina Press), 58; William Winter, Bolton interview, March 12, 2008; William Winter to Senator Stennis, July 10, 1954, Series 50, Box 8, MSU; William Winter memoir. Mississippi's massive resistance campaign is detailed in Yasuhiro Katagiri, *The Mississippi State Sovereignty Commission: Civil Rights and States' Rights* (Jackson: University Press of Mississippi, 2001); and Neil R. McMillen's *The Citizens' Council: Organized Resistance to the Second Reconstruction, 1954–64* (Urbana: University of Illinois Press, 1972).

18. William Winter, Bolton interview, May 18, 2006; William Winter to Stanley L. Richards, April 27, 1956, WWPC.

19. William Winter, Bolton interview, August 29, 2001; Winter, "Mississippi's Legislative Approach to the School Segregation Problem," 165–72.

20. William F. Winter, "Development of Educational Policy in Mississippi," *Mississippi Law Journal* 58 (1988): 230; Report of LEAC Subcommittee on Planning, October 12, 1954, Box 7, George Washington Owens Papers, MDAH; William Winter, Nash interview; "Legislature Meets on Miss. School Plans," *Atlanta Daily World*, September 8, 1954; Mississippi Legislature, *Journal of the House of Representatives of the State of Mississippi, 1954 Extra Session and 1955 Extra Session* (Jackson: The House, 1955), 21–23, 32–33, 40, 68–71, 1391–92; Winter, "Mississippi's Legislative Approach to the School Segregation Problem," 169; William Winter, Bolton interview, August 29, 2001. Legislators had to vote on proposed constitutional amendments three separate times, on three separate days. Winter voted for the amendment in the fall of 1954 on the first and second votes, but he was absent on the third vote.

21. *Journal of the House, 1954 Extra Session and 1955 Extra Session*, 482; Mississippi Secretary of State, *Mississippi Official and Statistical Register* (Jackson: Secretary of State,

1956), 428; "Editor Condemned in Mississippi House," *New York Times*, April 2, 1955; William Winter memoir.

22. William Winter memoir; William Winter, Bolton interview, July 3, 2007; McMillen, *The Citizens' Council*, ch. 2. Dave Womack produced a list for Walter Sillers listing Citizens' Council members from the House of Representatives, and William Winter's name is on the list, but no other evidence backs up this claim. It is possible that Womack, from Humphreys County, attended the Greenwood meeting, where he compiled this list. See Dave Womack, "Members of the Citizens Councils in the House," n.d., Box 112, Walter Sillers Papers, Delta State University, Cleveland, Mississippi.

23. "Semmes and Winter Office Started Monday," *Grenada County Weekly*, April 1, 1954; ad announcing opening of Winter/Semmes Law Offices, *Grenada County Weekly*, July 1, 1954; William Winter, Bolton interview, July 22, 2008; William Winter to Senator Stennis, September 8, 1954, Series 50, Box 8, MSU; William Winter, Bass interview.

24. William Winter, Bailey interview; William Winter, Bolton interview, March 12, 2008; William Winter, Bass interview.

25. William Winter, Bass interview; William Winter, Bolton interviews, May 18, 2006, and March 12, 2008; William Joel Blass, Bolton interview.

26. William Winter to Senator Stennis, May 6, 1955, Series 50, Box 8, MSU; William Winter, Nash interview; William Winter, Bolton interview, May 18, 2006; William Winter to Stanley L. Richards, April 27, 1956, WWPC.

27. Stephen J. Whitfield, *A Death in the Delta: The Story of Emmett Till* (New York: Free Press, 1988); William Winter, Bolton interview, December 8, 2006; William Winter to Norrell H. Noble, April 20, 1956, Box 40, William F. Winter and Family Papers, MDAH.

28. Jere Nash and Andy Taggart, *Mississippi Politics: The Struggle for Power, 1976–2006* (Jackson: University Press of Mississippi, 2006), 86–87; William Winter, Bailey interview; William Winter, Bass interview; William Winter, Bolton interviews, August 29, 2001, and May 18, 2006; George Rogers, Caudill interview.

29. Nash and Taggart, *Mississippi Politics*, 86–87; William Winter, Bass interview; William G. Burgin Jr. to Erle Johnston, July 27, 1992, Box 9, Erle Johnston Papers, USM; J. P. Coleman, Caudill interview.

30. William Winter, Bass interview; George Rogers, Caudill interview; William Winter, Caudill interview; letters from various House members to Walter Sillers, November and December 1955, and Sillers statement to Kenneth Toler, December 24, 1955, all in Box 22, Sillers Papers; Walter Sillers to C. B. Newman, September 15 and November 28, 1955, and "Here's What One Editor Hears about the Speaker's Race," n.d., November 1955, all in Box 1, C. B. "Buddie" Newman Papers, MDAH; "New Charges of 'Pressures' Made Against Sillers," *Greenville Delta Democrat-Times*, December 14, 1955.

31. William Winter, Bass interview; *Journal of the House of Representatives of the State of Mississippi, 1956* (Jackson: The House, 1956), 7–10, 1083–1101; William Winter, Bailey interview.

32. Katagiri, *The Mississippi State Sovereignty Commission*, xxxiv, 5–8; *Journal of the House, 1956*, 104–5, 114, 122–23, 137–39; Anders Walker, "Legislating Virtue: How Segregationists Disguised Racial Discrimination as Moral Reform Following *Brown v.*

Board of Education," *Duke Law Journal* 47 (1997–1998): 399–424; House Bills 21, 26, and 33, 1956, LRB.

33. Mississippi Legislature, *Journal of the House, 1956,* 263, 357–58, 572, 659, 688, 726, 787–88, 908; Joe Wroten, Katagiri interview; William Winter, Bolton interview, July 22, 2008; House Bill 880, 1956, LRB; Erle Johnston, *Mississippi's Defiant Years: 1953–1973, An Interpretative Documentary with Personal Experiences* (Forest, Miss.: Lake Harbor Publishers, 1990), 49; William F. Winter to Erle Johnston, October 27, 1987, Box 9, Erle Johnston Papers.

34. William F. Winter, "Recent Legislation in Mississippi on the School Segregation Problem," *Mississippi Law Journal* 28 (1956–1957): 155; William Winter, Bolton interview, May 18, 2006.

Chapter 6

1. William Winter memoir; David G. Sansing, "Thomas Lowry Bailey: Forty-Eighth Governor of Mississippi, 1944–1946," *Mississippi History Now,* http://mshistory.k12. ms.us/articles/265/index.php?s=extra&id=147 (Accessed June 25, 2009); William Winter, Bass interview; Phil Stroupe, "Coleman Appoints Winter to Tax Job," *Jackson Daily News,* April 3, 1956.

2. William Winter, Bass interview; Stroupe, "Coleman Appoints Winter to Tax Job"; William Winter memoir; Norman Ritter, "A Tax on Lawbreakers Only," *Life* 52 (May 11, 1962): 11; William Winter class at Millsaps College, March 1, 1989, transcript, William A. Winter to William F. Winter, January 3, 1946, and December 11, 1946, and William F. Winter to William A. Winter, January 23, 1946, all in WWPC.

3. Phil Stroupe, "Tee-Totaler Winters Will Spend Years Collecting Taxes from Non Tee-Totalers," undated newspaper article, and "Licenses," February 8, 1957, both in Box 6797, Mississippi State Tax Commission Records, MDAH; Ritter, "A Tax on Lawbreakers Only"; Jack Sunn, "Black Market Tax," *Jackson Daily News,* August 27, 1984; William Winter memoir. Statutory local option was the method the state would finally adopt in 1966, which brought an end to prohibition in the state.

4. Ed Cony, "Mississippi Mores: How Busy Mr. Winter Pulls Taxes from Loan Sharks and Bootleggers," *Wall Street Journal,* December 26, 1957; William Winter memoir; Ritter, "A Tax on Lawbreakers Only."

5. William Winter memoir; Ritter, "A Tax on Lawbreakers Only"; "Raids Have Forced Liquor Prices Up," *Greenwood Commonwealth,* May 18, 1956; "Tax Collector Refuses Bootlegger Refund Bid," *Washington Post and Times Herald,* March 10, 1959.

6. "Record Bootleg Liquor Tax," *New York Times,* January 1, 1959; William Winter, Caudill interview; "Winter Aims at Capping Public Career as Governor," undated newspaper clipping, Box 19774, William J. Cole Office Files, MDAH; Summary of Collection and Disbursements, Office of State Tax Collector, 1959 Through 1961, *Journal of the House of the State of Mississippi, 1962 and 1961 Special Session* (Jackson: The House, 1962), 699; Ritter, "A Tax on Lawbreakers Only," 11.

7. William Winter to Charles Bolton, July 1, 2009 (email), copy in author's possession; William Winter, Bolton interview, May 18, 2006; William Winter memoir; "Winter Reveals His Financial Status," undated newspaper clipping, 1975, WWPC.

8. William Winter memoir; *Journal of the House of the State of Mississippi, 1958 and 1957 Special Session* (Jackson: The House, 1958); William Winter, Bass interview; Resolution of the North Mississippi Conference of the Methodist Church, June 5, 1957, and Resolution of the Executive Committee of the Mississippi Baptist Association, Wilkinson and Amite Counties, August 26, 1957, both in Mississippi Prohibition, 1950s, Small Manuscripts, UM; George Rogers, Bolton interview.

9. William Winter memoir; "Judge Charges Winter Violating Whiskey Law," *Jackson Clarion-Ledger*, January 31, 1959; Mississippi Secretary of State, *Mississippi Official and Statistical Register* (Jackson: Secretary of State, 1956), 268.

10. William Winter, Bass interview; George Rogers, Bolton interview; William Winter, White interview; William Winter, Crews interview; William Winter, Bolton interview, July 22, 2008; William Winter, conversation with author, December 14, 2007; Elise Winter, Bolton interview.

11. William Winter, Bass interview; William Winter, White interview; William Winter, Bolton interview, July 22, 2008; F. Glenn Abney, *Mississippi Election Statistics, 1900–1967* (University, Miss.: Bureau of Governmental Research, 1968), 361–63.

12. William Winter, Caudill interview; William Winter, Bolton interviews, May 22, 2006, July 12, 2006, and December 8, 2006; "Wm. Winter Is Mental Health Chief," *Jackson Clarion-Ledger*, April 30, 1969.

13. Bob Spiro to William Winter, October 10, 1957, Box 6797, Mississippi State Tax Commission Records, MDAH; William Winter to Lawrence E. Noble Jr., February 6, 1957, Box 19, William F. Winter and Family Papers, MDAH.

14. Charles Deaton to William Winter, June 22, 1957, and Paul Pittman to William Winter, June 30, 1957, both in Box 6797, Mississippi State Tax Commission Records; Statement of Principles for the Organizing of the Young Democrats of Mississippi, n.d., 1957?, Box 23, J. P. Coleman Papers, MDAH; Paul Pittman, interview by Gordon G. Henderson, July 30, 1965, transcript, Box 1, Paul Howard Pittman Papers, MDAH; Dennis Mitchell, *Mississippi Liberal: A Biography of Frank Smith* (Jackson: University Press of Mississippi, 2001), 138–40; William Winter to Lawrence E. Noble Jr., August 21, 1956, Box 1, William F. Winter and Family Papers, MDAH; Smith, *Congressman from Mississippi*, 214–15; Mark Stern, *Calculating Visions: Kennedy, Johnson, and Civil Rights* (New Brunswick, N.J.: Rutgers University Press, 1992), ch. 1.

15. William Winter, Nash interview; Jesse White, Bolton interview, September 27, 2007; Nash and Taggart, *Mississippi Politics*, 74–79, 201–3; William Winter to James O. Eastland, May 19, 1960, Box 19, William F. Winter and Family Papers, MDAH; John Stennis to William Winter, July 16, 1957, William F. Winter to John Stennis, July 24, 1957, and John Stennis to William Winter, January 25, 1960, all in Box 6797, Mississippi State Tax Commission Records.

16. Gilbert Mason and James Patterson Smith, *Beaches, Blood, and Ballots: A Black Doctor's Civil Rights Struggle* (Jackson: University Press of Mississippi, 2000); Dittmer,

Local People, ch. 4. See also J. Michael Butler, "The Mississippi State Sovereignty Commission and Beach Integration, 1959–1963: A Cotton-Patch Gestapo?" *Journal of Southern History* 68 (February 2002): 107–48.

17. White, "Mississippi Electoral Politics, 1903–1976," 415–16; Smith, *Congressman from Mississippi*, 216; John Stennis to William Winter, January 25, 1960, William Winter to John Stennis, February 9, 1960, and William Winter to John Stennis, August 19, 1960, all in Box 6797, Mississippi State Tax Commission Records; Jeremy D. Mayer, *Running on Race: Racial Politics in Presidential Campaigns, 1960–2000* (New York: Random House, 2002), ch. 2; Bill Minor, Bolton interview.

18. William Winter to Lawrence E. Noble, September 29, 1960, Box 6796, Mississippi State Tax Commission Records; "Hear the Great Debate," flyer, n.d., 1960, WWPC; William Winter, Nash interview; William Winter, Bass interview; Bill Minor, Bolton interview; White, "Mississippi Electoral Politics, 1903–1976," 417; William Winter to John Stennis, August 19, 1960, Box 6797, Mississippi State Tax Commission Records.

19. Gregory Crofton, "Sovereignty Files Reveal Persecution of Former DM Staffer," *Daily Mississippian*, April 21, 1998; William J. Simmons to Albert Jones, August 17, 1960, Sovereignty Commission Files, 7-0-2-86-1-1-1, MDAH.

20. Jim Silver to William Winter, January 17, 1961, and January 28, 1961, both in Box 20, William F. Winter and Family Papers; Malcolm Dale to Ross Barnett, December 6, 1960, Sovereignty Commission Files, 7-0-2-22-1-1-1; "Barnett Denies Barton Smear," *Memphis Commercial Appeal*, March 16, 1961; Hazel Brannon Smith, "State Sovereignty Commission Should Be Abolished," *Northside Reporter*, March 16, 1961; Crespino, *In Search of Another Country*, 38–41; "Three Students Back Billy Barton," *Memphis Commercial Appeal*, March 16, 1961; "Mississippi: Thought Control," *Time*, April 28, 1961.

21. Memorandum, March 6, 1961, March 13, 1961, and October 14, 1961, all in Benjamin Muse Papers, DUKE; Matthew D. Lassiter and Andrew B. Lewis, eds., *The Moderates' Dilemma: Massive Resistance to School Desegregation in Virginia* (Charlottesville: University Press of Virginia, 1998), 196.

22. Erle Johnston, "The Practical Way to Maintain a Separate School System in Mississippi," 1962, Box 58, Paul B. Johnson Jr. Papers, USM; Erle Johnston, *The Defiant Years, 1959–1973: An Interpretive Documentary with Personal Experiences* (Forest, Miss.: Lake Harbor Publishers, 1990), 137–40; Katagiri, *The Mississippi State Sovereignty Commission*, 98–100; Lewis Lord, "Sovereignty Unit PR Chief Praised for Slapping Extremists," *Greenville Delta Democrat-Times*, June 1, 1962.

23. Eagles, *The Price of Defiance*.

24. William Winter to Jimmy Hall, October 8, 1962, Box 19, William F. Winter and Family Papers; William Winter to Wade P. Huie Jr., October 8, 1962, Box 6797, Mississippi State Tax Commission Records.

25. William Winter, "A Time For Responsibility," speech to the Mississippi Library Association, October 27, 1962, and William Winter, "The Problems of Southern Politics," speech at All Saints' Junior College, March 27, 1963, both in WWPC; James W. Silver, *Mississippi: The Closed Society* (New York: Harcourt Brace, 1964), 208; William

and Elise Winter, Edmonds interview; William Winter, Bolton interview, May 18, 2006; memorandum, January 1964, Benjamin Muse Papers; Bolton, *The Hardest Deal of All*, 113–15.

26. William Winter memoir; *Journal of the House of the State of Mississippi, 1962 and 1961 Special Session* (Jackson: The House, 1962), 698, 700; *Journal of the Senate of the State of Mississippi, 1962 and 1961 Special Session* (Jackson: The Senate, 1962), 783; "House Approves Bill Allowing Women Jurors," *Greenville Delta Democrat-Times*, April 25, 1962; "The Periscope," *Newsweek* 67 (June 4, 1962): 15.

27. William Winter, White interview; James A. Peden Jr., Bolton interview; William Winter, conversation with author, December 14, 2007; William Winter, Bolton interview, May 18, 2006.

28. Bethany Lamar Baskin, "The Rise of William Forrest Winter," (MA thesis, Mississippi State University, 1992), 18; James A. Peden Jr., Bolton interview; William Winter, White interview; "William F. Winter for State Treasurer" ad, *Greenville Delta Democrat-Times*, August 4, 1963; "William Winter: Man of Unusual Ability" (editorial), *McComb Enterprise-Journal*, August 2, 1963; William and Elise Winter, Edmonds interview; Glenn Abney, *Mississippi Election Statistics, 1900–1967* (University, Miss.: Bureau of Governmental Research, 1968), 323–24, 361.

29. William Winter, Caudill interview; William Winter, Bolton interview, December 8, 2006; Douglas A. Blackmon, "Silent Partner: How the South's Fight to Uphold Segregation Was Funded Up North," *Wall Street Journal*, June 11, 1999; "Mississippi Returns to Long-Term Market with $10,450,000 Bonds," *Wall Street Journal*, August 17, 1966.

30. Reid Stoner Derr, "The Triumph of Progressivism: Governor Paul B. Johnson Jr. and Mississippi in the 1960s," (Ph.D. diss., University of Southern Mississippi, 1994), 197–231; McMillen, *The Citizens' Council*, 348–49.

31. William Winter, interview by Charles Bolton, July 12, 2006; Shannon Dortch, "William Winter Stays in Touch with Faith and Values," n.d., Subject File: William F. Winter, 1985–1986, MDAH.

32. Martin Luther King Jr. et al., *A Knock at Midnight: Inspiration from the Great Sermons of Reverend Martin Luther King Jr.* (New York: Warner Books, 2000), 21–31; Charles Marsh, *God's Long Summer: Stories of Faith and Civil Rights* (Princeton: Princeton University Press, 1997), 131–41; Clarice T. Campbell, *Civil Rights Chronicle: Letters from the South* (Jackson: University Press of Mississippi, 1997), 186; William Winter, "The Elder as Leader," speech, August 31, 2007, WWPC.

33. William Winter, Bass interview; Randy Sparks, *Religion in Mississippi* (Jackson: University Press of Mississippi, 2001), ch. 10.

34. William Winter, Bass interview; William Winter, Bolton interview, May 18, 2006; Smith, *Congressman from Mississippi*, 315; William Winter to Frank E. Smith, December 10, 1963, Box 27B, William Winter unprocessed collection, MDAH.

35. Dittmer, *Local People*; Smith, *Congressman from Mississippi*, vii–viii, 330–32; Mitchell, *Mississippi Liberal*, 183.

36. Silver, *Mississippi: The Closed Society*, 208; William Winter, Bolton interview, May 18, 2006.

37. Crespino, *In Search of Another Country*, 110–11; Silver, *Mississippi*, 208; William Winter, Bolton interview, May 18, 2006; memorandum, July 11, 1964, Benjamin Muse Papers; Mitchell, *Mississippi Liberal*, 174; William Winter speech to Hinds County Democratic Convention, June 23, 1964, Box 10, William Winter unprocessed collection.

38. Memorandum, January 1964, Benjamin Muse Papers.

39. William Winter memoir; William Winter, Edmonds interview; William Winter, Bolton interview, July 22, 2008; Ed McCusker, "Lay Aside Past, Speaker Urges," *Jackson Daily News*, January 24, 1965; "Winter Cites Defiance's Price," *Greenville Delta Democrat-Times*, February 25, 1965.

40. William Winter memoir; Newsfilm, D33, MDAH; Dick Molpus, Bolton interview.

41. Bernice Saeger to William Winter, March 10, 1965, WWPC. Jules Loh's story appeared in a number of papers around the country in April 1965. For examples, see the following: "New Image: 'The Dead Hand of the Past' Slowly Fading in Mississippi, *Charleston (W.Va.) Gazette-Mail*, April 4, 1965; "'New Mississippi' Emerges from Behind Bombast and Smoke of Burning Churches," *Huron (S.D.) Daily Plainsman*, April 5, 1965; and "Winds of Change Sweep across Stronghold of Segregation," *The Ada (Okla.) Evening News*, April 8, 1965.

42. William Winter, Bass interview; Mitchell, *Mississippi Liberal*, 187–88; Gibson B. Witherspoon (American Bar Association) to William Winter, March 2, 1965, Box 19, William F. Winter and Family Papers.

Chapter 7

1. Larry Noble to William and Elise Winter, September 26, 1966, Box 20, William F. Winter and Family Papers, MDAH; Larry Noble to William Winter, February 4, 1966, and Kenneth Toler, newspaper clipping, *Memphis Commercial Appeal*, July 3, 1966, both in WWPC; William Winter to Jim Silver, April 11, 1966, Box 10, James W. Silver Collection, UM.

2. Bill Waller, *Straight Ahead: The Memoirs of a Mississippi Governor* (Brandon, Miss.: Quail Ridge Press, 2007), 85–86; "Jimmy Swan for Governor: Stand Up for Mississippi," n.d., 1966?, Mississippiana Collection, USM; William Winter, Bass interview; William Winter memoir.

3. William Winter, Bolton interviews, May 18, 2006, and March 12, 2008; Hodding Carter, Bass interview; William Winter, Bass interview; William Winter memoir; William Winter, Caudill interview; White, "Mississippi Electoral Politics, 1903–1976," 467.

4. William Winter, announcement for governor, January 11, 1967, Box 1, William F. Winter and Family Papers, MDAH; William Winter memoir; "Triggs to Manage Winter's Campaign," *Jackson Times*, March 17, 1967; Paul Pittman, "Anything But Dull," *Greenville Delta Democrat-Times*, November 7, 1974; William Winter, conversation with author, December 14, 2007; William Winter, Bailey interview; White, "Mississippi Electoral

Politics, 1903–1976," 478; William G. Riley and John D. McEachin to Thomas F. Puckett, May 15, 1967, Box 3, Series 1, Subseries 20, James O. Eastland Collection, UM; William and Elise Winter, Edmonds interview; Rowland Evans and Robert Novak, "Inside Report: After Mississippi's Johnson," *Washington Post*, April 12, 1967; James Silver to Leslie W. Dunbar, May 9, 1967, WWPC; Wilson Golden to William Winter, February 3, 1967, Box 13, Wilson Golden unprocessed collection, MDAH; "Radio Poll Shows Winter Is Choice," *Jackson Clarion-Ledger*, April 23, 1967.

5. William Winter memoir; William Winter press release, April 25, 1967, Box 10, William Winter unprocessed collection, MDAH; "A New Note or Two," *Time*, August 4, 1967, http://www.time.com/time/magazine/article/0,9171,837157,00.html (Accessed on July 19, 2009); White, "Mississippi Electoral Politics, 1903–1976," ch. 14.

6. Katagiri, *The Mississippi State Sovereignty Commission*, 203; James Dickerson, *Dixie's Dirty Secret: The True Story of How the Government, the Media, and the Mob Conspired to Combat Integration and the Vietnam Antiwar Movement* (Armonk, N.Y.: M. E. Sharpe, 1998), 142; "William Winter Promises to Fight-To-Win for Mississippi," Subject File: William Winter, 1967, MDAH; "Barnett Slips Sizzling Retort into Hot Debate," *Memphis Commercial Appeal*, May 16, 1967.

7. Katagiri, *The Mississippi State Sovereignty Commission*, 203; "William Winter Promises to Fight-To-Win for Mississippi," Subject File: William Winter, 1967; Winter ads, *Greenville Delta Democrat-Times*, June 16, 1967, and August 7, 1967.

8. "The Winter Plan for Better Schools," May 22, 1967, Box 1, William F. Winter and Family Papers.

9. "The Winter Plan for Better Paying Jobs," n.d., late May or early June 1967, Box 1, William F. Winter and Family Papers.

10. "Barnett Says Foe Has Kennedy's Aid," *New York Times*, June 11, 1967; Ross Barnett political ad, *Greenville Delta Democrat-Times*, July 27, 1967; White, "Mississippi Electoral Politics, 1903–1976," 469; Bill Minor, "Here-e-e's William," *Jackson Capital Reporter*, August 30, 1979; David Webb, "Rally Attracts Politicos," *Franklin (Meadville, Miss.) Advocate*, July 13, 1967.

11. "State Politics Turn Bitter on the Stump," *Greenville Delta Democrat-Times*, July 19, 1967; "Progress Stands Up for Winter Candidacy," *Greenville Delta Democrat-Times*, June 22, 1967; Waller, *Straight Ahead*, 98–99; "Williams Rips Two Opponents," *New Orleans Times Picayune*, August 4, 1967; Curtis Wilkie, *Dixie: A Personal Odyssey through Events That Shaped the Modern South* (New York: Touchstone, 2001), 260–61; "Mississippi Will Stage 3-Way Governorship Primary Tuesday," *New York Times*, August 6, 1967.

12. James A. Peden Jr., Bolton interview; Elise Winter, Bolton interview; Anita Lee, "Democratic Candidate's Wife Takes the Campaign Trail in Stride," *Jackson Daily News*, September 10, 1979; William Winter ad, *Greenville Delta Democrat-Times*, June 16, 1967; William Winter memoir; "Win with Winter" sheet music, Box 1, William F. Winter and Family Papers; *You'll Be the Winner When You Vote for William Winter* (comic book), UM.

13. James A. Peden Jr., Bolton interview; Jesse L. White, Holmes interview; White, "Mississippi Electoral Politics, 1903–1976," 476; "The Winter Plan for Waterway and

Natural Resources Development," Box 13, Wilson Golden unprocessed collection; "Winter Plan for Home Rule and States' Rights," June 20, 1967, Box 1, William Winter and Family Papers.

14. Ad by Washington County Young Supporters for William Winter, *Greenville Delta Democrat-Times*, July 28, 1967; Jesse L. White, Bolton interview, August 30, 2007; James Everett to William Winter, January 16, 1968, Box 20, William F. Winter and Family Papers; Dick Molpus, Bolton interview; Ray Mabus, Bolton interview; Thad Cochran, Bolton interview. Also see Wilson Golden, Bolton interview; Guy Land, Bolton interview; John Corlew, Bolton interview; Andy Mullins, Bolton interview.

15. Evans and Novak, "Inside Report."

16. Report, April 25, 1967, Sovereignty Commission Files, 9-31-6-79-1-1-1, MDAH; Report, June 19, 1967, Sovereignty Commission Files, 1-108-0-6-1-1-1; Dickerson, *Dixie's Dirty Secret*, 141; Waller, *Straight Ahead*, 97; Mertis Rubin, "All Negro Candidates Lose; Miss. Voters Pick Williams," *Southern Courier*, September 2–3, 1967; White, "Mississippi Electoral Politics, 1903–1976," 490; "Williams and Winter Lead Governor's Race as Barnett Backing Fades," *Greenville Delta Democrat-Times*, July 17, 1967.

17. Crespino, *In Search of Another Country*, 153–67, 206–12; Bill Rose, "Winter Steals Show at Cleveland Rally," *Greenville Delta Democrat-Times*, July 10, 1967.

18. "Candidates Talk Law Enforcement," *Greenville Delta Democrat-Times*, July 13, 1967; "Critic Winter Draws Fire from Rivals," *Greenville Delta Democrat-Times*, July 27, 1967; "Winter Calls for Law and Order; Hits Williams and Barnett," *Franklin Advocate*, August 3, 1967; "Curbing the Delta Ministry," *Time*, June 10, 1966, http://www.time.com/time/magazine/article/0,9171,942038,00.html (Accessed July 23, 2009); "Presbyterian Action Rapped by Wm. Winter," *Jackson Clarion-Ledger*, June 14, 1967; Mark F. Newman, *Divine Agitators: The Delta Ministry and Civil Rights in Mississippi* (Athens: University of Georgia Press, 2004), 28, 154–55.

19. *Southern Review*, July 15, 1967, Box 14, Wilson Golden unprocessed collection; William Winter, Bolton interview, December 19, 2007; James W. Cook, *The Arts of Deception: Playing with Fraud in the Age of Barnum* (Cambridge, Mass.: Harvard University Press, 2001), ch. 2.

20. William Winter political ads, *Greenville Delta Democrat-Times*, July 21, 1967, and August 5 and 7, 1967; "Barnett Turns Weatherman, Says Winter Won't Be There When Summer Is Departed," *Greenwood Commonwealth*, August 3, 1967.

21. Jere Nash and Andy Taggart, "William Winter and His Campaigns for Governor: 1967, 1975, and 1979," *Journal of Mississippi History* 70 (Winter 2008): 390–91; Waller, *Straight Ahead*, 100; Abney, *Mississippi Election Statistics 1900–1967*, 160–61.

22. Nash and Taggart, "William Winter and His Campaigns for Governor," 390–91; Abney, *Mississippi Election Statistics 1900–1967*, 160–61; Rowland Evans and Robert Novak, "Leaders' Failure to Deliver Negro Vote Led to Williams' Easy Miss. Victory," *Washington Post*, September 1, 1967; Frank R. Parker, *Black Votes Count: Political Empowerment in Mississippi after 1965* (Chapel Hill: University of North Carolina Press, 1990), 31; "Mississippi: They Voted," *Time*, August 18, 1967, http://www.time.com/time/magazine/article/0,9171,840957,00.html (Accessed July 24, 2009).

23. William Winter, Bass interview.

24. Jerry DeLaughter, "Johnson Faces Upset Threat As Black Forges into Lead for Runoff against Sullivan," *Memphis Commercial Appeal*, August 10, 1967; "Most Conservative Appears Likely Governor Runoff Winner," *Tupelo Daily Journal*, August 11, 1967; White, "Mississippi Electoral Politics, 1903–1976," 481; William Winter, Bass interview; "Winter," *Mississippi Freelance*, October 1969; Nathan Levy, Jr. to William Winter, January 15, 1994, WWPC.

25. William Winter memoir; "Winter Stumps through North," *Memphis Commercial Appeal*, August 13, 1967; White, "Mississippi Electoral Politics, 1903–1976," 481; Rowland Evans and Robert Novak, "William Winter's Mississippi Drive Hints an Upset in Tuesday's Runoff," *Washington Post*, August 25, 1967.

26. "Williams Rips Winter's Record," *Greenville Delta Democrat-Times*, August 18, 1967; *Meridian Star* editorial, August 13, 1967, and "Leopard Tries to Change Spots" (political cartoon), both in Box 1, William Winter Campaign Collection, MDAH; "A New Image" (political cartoon), August 15, 1967, Box 39C, William Winter unprocessed collection; Leopard Changing His Spots ad, *Biloxi Daily Herald*, August 23, 1967.

27. William Winter memoir; William Winter, Bass interview; William Winter ad, *Greenville Delta Democrat-Times*, August 25, 1967; Bill Minor, "Winter's Wet Whistle," *Jackson Capital Reporter*, November 27, 1980; "No Whiskey Drinking, No Vote?" (editorial), *Greenville Delta Democrat-Times*, August 27, 1967.

28. Evans and Novak, "Leaders' Failure to Deliver Negro Vote Led to Williams' Easy Miss. Victory"; "Maybe We'll Learn," *Los Angeles Sentinel*, September 21, 1967; Rubin, "All Negro Candidates Lose."

29. "Miss. Governor Race Drawing a Heavy Vote," *Washington Post*, August 30, 1967; account of John Bell Williams rally in the second primary, 1967, Box 13, Wilson Golden unprocessed collection.

30. William Winter memoir; "Awake White Mississippi," n.d., August 1967, Box 24D, William Winter unprocessed collection.

31. William Winter memoir; "How the Black Bloc Voted for Governor," n.d., August 1967, Subject File: William Winter, 1967.

32. Evans and Novak, "William Winter's Mississippi Drive Hints an Upset in Tuesday's Runoff"; William Winter campaign schedule, August 18, 1967, Box 13, Wilson Golden unprocessed collection; John Bell Williams ad, *Greenville Delta Democrat-Times*, August 27, 1967.

33. William Winter, Bass interview; transcript of death threat telephone call to Winter headquarters, August 1967, WWPC.

34. William Winter, White interview; William Winter, Bass interview; James A. Peden Jr., Bolton interview; Elise Winter, Bolton interview.

35. James A. Peden Jr., Bolton interview; reflections of Lele Winter Gillespie, 2005, WWPC; William Winter memoir; Dittmer, *Local People*, 417; William Winter, Bass interview.

36. Abney, *Mississippi Election Statistics 1900–1967*, 162–63; White, "Mississippi Electoral Politics, 1903–1976," 490; Parker, *Black Votes Count*, 31–32, 72; Rubin, "All

Negro Candidates Lose"; "Mississippi Negroes Surprised, Let Down by Complete Defeat in Democratic Runoff," *Wall Street Journal*, August 31, 1967; Richard D. Chesteen to William Winter, October 9, 1967, Box 10, William Winter unprocessed collection.

37. Larry Noble to William and Elise Winter, August 30, 1967, Box 40, Madge O. Stubblefield to Elise Winter, August 29, 1967, Box 101, James R. Howell to William Winter, August 30, 1967, Box 1, and Richard D. Chesteen to William Winter, October 9, 1947, Box 1, all in William F. Winter and Family Papers; Evelyn and Jim Tigrett to William and Elise Winter, November 10, 1967, Box 10, William Winter unprocessed collection.

Chapter 8

1. Marx to John Stennis, November 9, 1967, Series 50, Box 8, MSU; William Winter memoir; Winter's 1968 New Year's Day card, Subject File: William F. Winter, 1968, MDAH.

2. William B. Street, "Winter Bypasses Judgeship Chance to Remain in Political Field," *Memphis Commercial Appeal*, March 5, 1968; William Winter, Bass interview; "Mississippi Plans General Obligation Bonds in Part to Help Litton's Shipbuilding Unit," *Wall Street Journal*, October 27, 1967; William Winter, Bolton interview, May 22, 2006.

3. William Winter, Bolton interview, May 22, 2006; William Winter to R. B. Lampton, April 26, 1968, Box 20, and folder on Partner's Retreat, November 13 and 14, 1987, Box 90, both in William F. Winter and Family Papers, MDAH; William Winter, Bass interview; William Winter memoir; William Winter to Jim Silver, August 4, 1968, WWPC.

4. Crespino, *In Search of Another Country*, 211–12; William Winter, Bass interview; Nash and Taggart, *Mississippi Politics*, 29–30; Paul Pittman, "GOP Looking for Defectors," *Greenville Delta Democrat-Times*, November 20, 1969.

5. Bolton, *The Hardest Deal of All*, ch. 7; Crespino, *In Search of Another Country*, ch. 6; Bruce Galphin, "Mississippi Waiting Out School Storm," *Washington Post*, January 17, 1970.

6. William Winter to John Stennis, January 16, 1970, Box 41, William F. Winter and Family Papers, MDAH.

7. William Winter, Bolton interview, May 22, 2006; reflections of Lele Winter Gillespie, 2005, WWPC; Eleanor Winter, Bolton interview; William Winter, conversation with author, August 28, 2009; William and Elise Winter, Edmonds interview; William Winter, "Before and After *Brown* in Mississippi," (speech), July 1, 2004, WWPC.

8. "Lt. Gov. Winter Has Praise for Public Schools," *Jackson Clarion-Ledger*, February 1, 1973; Bolton, *The Hardest Deal of All*, 221; Fred Banks, Bolton interview.

9. Wilson Golden, Bolton interview; William Winter memoir; William Winter, Bailey interview; William and Elise Winter, Edmonds interview; William Winter, Bolton interview, May 22, 2006; William Winter to H. B. Howerton, December 3, 1971, WWPC; Paul Pittman, "'Wintertime' Has Arrived," *Greenville Delta Democrat-Times*, May 17, 1974.

10. William Winter memoir; Bill Waller, *Straight Ahead*, 105.

11. Parker, *Black Votes Count*, 200; William Winter memoir; Paul Delaney, "Blacks to Decide Mississippi Race," *New York Times*, August 22, 1971; Waller, *Straight Ahead*, ch. 10; "Election Day Beatings," *Kudzu*, January 1, 1972; David Doggett, "Election '71: An Analysis," *Kudzu*, February 29, 1972; Frank L. Stanley, "It's Really a New Day in 'Ole' Mississippi," *Chicago Defender*, September 11, 1971. On the general transformation of southern politics by the 1970 elections, see Numan V. Bartley, *The New South 1945–1980: A History of the South* (Baton Rouge: Louisiana State University Press, 1995), 398–99; and Lassiter, *The Silent Majority*, 266–75.

12. Baskin, "The Rise of William Forrest Winter," 38–41; William Winter political ad, *Greenville Delta Democrat-Times*, August 2, 1971; William Winter press release, June 21, 1971, William Winter press release, n.d., 1971, and County Youth Chairman Campaign Manual, 1971, all in Subject File: Elections 1971 Gubernatorial William Winter, MDAH; William Winter, Bailey interview.

13. William Winter, Bolton interview, May 22, 2006; Baskin, "The Rise of William Forrest Winter," 38; William Winter memoir; *Mississippi Election Statistics 1971–1979* (University, Miss.: Bureau of Governmental Research, 1982), 24–25; William Winter press release, July 1, 1971, Subject File: Elections 1971 Gubernatorial William Winter; William Winter postcard sent to young voters, n.d., July 1971, Subject File: William F. Winter, 1969–1971, MDAH.

14. Roy Reed, "Mississippi Rebuffs Anti-Negro Politics," *New York Times*, August 5, 1971; Jesse L. White, Bolton interview, August 30, 2007; William Winter, Bailey interview; H. B. Howerton to William Winter, November 28, 1971, and William Winter to H. B. Howerton, December 3, 1971, both in WWPC.

15. William Winter memoir; William Winter, Caudill interview.

16. William Winter memoir; William Winter, Bolton interviews, July 12, 2006, March 9, 2007, and December 12, 2007; William Winter, Caudill interview; James A. Peden Jr., Bolton interview; John Corlew, Pyle interview; Herman B. DeCell, interview by Orley Caudill, June 9, 1977, Vol. 207, MOHP.

17. William Winter, Caudill interview; Jesse L. White, Bolton interview, August 30, 2007.

18. Jesse L. White, Bolton interview, August 30, 2007; W. F. Minor, "Winter's Moves Seen Paying Off," *New Orleans Times-Picayune*, March 10, 1974; George Rogers, Caudill interview; William Winter, Bolton interview, December 19, 2007; *Journal of the Senate of the State of Mississippi, 1974 Session* (Jackson: The Senate, 1974), 591–92; Jack Elliott, "Senate OK's Lease Guard," *Jackson Clarion-Ledger*, March 5, 1974.

19. James Saggus, "Stennis Asks Interest Rates Be Graduated," *Jackson Clarion-Ledger*, January 12, 1974; James Saggus, "Interest Rate Move Praised," *Jackson Clarion-Ledger*, February 9, 1974; Charles B. Gordon, "Senate Debates Interest Bill," *Jackson Daily News*, March 13, 1974; John Corlew, Bolton interview; William Winter, conversation with author, August 28, 2009; *Journal of the Senate, 1974 Session*, 754–63, 962, 1360–69; James Saggus, "OK Small Loan Bill," *Jackson Clarion-Ledger*, March 31, 1974.

20. William Winter, Bass interview; William Winter, Caudill interview; Waller, *Straight Ahead*, 129; Jesse L. White, interview by Orley Caudill, October 9, 1974,

transcript, Vol. 65, MOHP; W. F. Minor, "Officials Share 'Non-Relationship,'" *New Orleans Times-Picayune*, October 7, 1973.

21. Paul Pittman, "Winter to End Waller Ties?" *Greenville Delta Democrat-Times*, August 3, 1972; Tom Bourdeaux to William Winter, September 8, 1973, Box 6B, William Winter unprocessed collection, MDAH; Jesse White to William Winter, April 16, 1973, Box 12, Wilson Golden unprocessed collection, MDAH.

22. "Plenty of Issues," *Greenville Delta Democrat-Times*, March 5, 1973; William Winter, "1974 Legislative Report," Box 9111, Lieutenant Governor Office Files, 1972–1976, MDAH; David G. Schueler, *Preserving the Pascagoula* (Jackson: University Press of Mississippi, 1980), ch. 9; "Proposal Backed," *Greenville Delta Democratic-Times*, January 11, 1973; Charles M. Hills, "Governor's Programs Hit Snags, Dispute Road Fund," *Jackson Clarion-Ledger*, April 16, 1972; W. F. Minor, "Miss. to Begin 90-Day Session," *New Orleans Times-Picayune*, January 2, 1973; *Journal of the Senate of the State of Mississippi, 1972 Session* (Jackson: The Senate, 1972), 83; *Journal of the Senate of the State of Mississippi, 1973 Session* (Jackson: The Senate, 1973), 18, 41, 43; *Journal of the Senate, 1974 Session*, 28; *Journal of the Senate of the State of Mississippi, 1975 Session* (Jackson: The Senate, 1975), 6, 8, 14, 17–18, 34, 211; Bolton, *The Hardest Deal of All*, 167–68.

23. George H. Rainwater to William Winter, April 29, 1974, William Winter to Vivian R. McGaugh, June 4, 1974, and William Winter to Powell Roberts, April 19, 1974, all in Box 9110, Lieutenant Governor Office Files, 1972–1976; "Plenty of Issues," *Greenville Delta Democrat-Times*, March 5, 1973; *Journal of the Senate, 1973 Session*, 562–80; James Saggus, "State School Teachers Get Large Pay Raise," *Jackson Clarion-Ledger*, March 23, 1973; Ronni Patriquin, "Deadline Ax Kills School Proposals: No Teacher Hike," *Jackson Clarion-Ledger*, March 6, 1974; Ronni Patriquin, "School Measures Snagged by House-Senate Conflict," *Jackson Clarion-Ledger*, March 5, 1974; Political Survey, 1974, Box 9116, Lieutenant Governor Office Files, 1972–1976.

24. Nash and Taggart, *Mississippi Politics*, 32; Waller, *Straight Ahead*, 128–29; William Winter, Bass interview; "Winter for Nixon," undated UPI newspaper clipping, 1972, Box 13, Wilson Golden unprocessed collection; "Where Is William Winter?" (editorial), *Greenville Delta Democrat-Times*, April 1, 1973.

25. William Winter, Bolton interview, March 12, 2008; Aaron E. Henry to William Winter, August 1, 1973, Box 9105, Lieutenant Governor Office Files, 1972–1976; Patricia M. Derian to Charles B. Gordon, April 29, 1973, Box 7, Aaron Henry Papers, Tougaloo College Archives, Tougaloo, Mississippi.

26. Parker, *Black Votes Count*, 63–66, 102–24; "Evers Ordered Evicted from Senate Chamber," *New York Times*, March 7, 1975; Ronni Patriquin, "After Conflict, Evers Invited to Hearings," *Jackson Clarion-Ledger*, March 7, 1975; Ronni Patriquin, "Solons Hear Evers," *Jackson Clarion-Ledger*, March 8, 1975; "Senate Rejects Reapportionment," *Jackson Daily News*, March 28, 1975; *Journal of the Senate, 1975 Session*, 1238–42.

27. Crespino, *In Search of Another Country*, 171–72; R. Milton Winter, "Division & Reunion in the Presbyterian Church, U.S.: A Mississippi Retrospective," *Journal of Presbyterian History* 78 (Spring 2000): 67–86; William Winter, Bolton interview, July 12,

2006; Joel L. Alvis Jr., *Religion and Race: Southern Presbyterians, 1946–1983* (Tuscaloosa: University of Alabama Press, 1994). Winter's home church in Grenada, First Presbyterian Church of Grenada, initially remained united in its affiliation with the PCUS, but in the early 1980s, part of the congregation left to form a new Presbyterian church associated with the PCA. See M. Thomas Norwood Jr. to William Winter, June 1, 1982, Box 2171, Mississippi Governor, Subject Correspondence, 1979–1983, MDAH.

28. Bolton, *The Hardest Deal of All*, 202–3; Katagiri, *The Mississippi State Sovereignty Commission*, 193–95, 220–26; *Journal of the Senate, 1972 Session*, 267; *Journal of the Senate, 1973 Session*, 948; William Winter, Bolton interview, July 14, 2006; Mississippi State Sovereignty Commission Minutes, June 7, 1973, Sovereignty Commission Files, 99-216-0-5-1-1-1, MDAH.

29. UPI news clipping, August 30, 1974, Box 9112, Lieutenant Governor Office Files, 1972–1976.

30. Eagles, *The Price of Defiance*, 148, 428; Katagiri, *The Mississippi State Sovereignty Commission*, 120; "Lt. Governor Winter Displays Courage" (editorial), *Biloxi Daily Herald*, July 4, 1972.

31. Wallace Dabbs, "Senate OK's Probe Panel," *Jackson Clarion-Ledger*, February 14, 1973; Edward M. Wheat, "The Bureaucracy: Mississippi's Fourth Branch," in *Politics in Mississippi*, edited by Joseph B. Parker (Salem, Wis.: Sheffield Publishing Co., 1993), 88; William Winter, Bolton interview, December 8, 2006; Theodore Smith to William Winter, March 27, 1973, and William Winter to Theodore Smith, March 28, 1973, both in Box 9108, Lieutenant Governor Office Files, 1972–1976; Wayne Weidie "Where Is William Winter?" (editorial), *Greenville Delta Democrat-Times*, April 16, 1973.

32. Bill Winter [no relation to William F. Winter], "Passage of Ethics Bill Is Favored by Winter," *New Orleans Times-Picayune*, June 28, 1973; "County Reform at Last?" (editorial), *Greenville Delta Democrat-Times*, July 11, 1973; Weidie, "Where Is William Winter?"; Dewey E. McKee to William Winter, June 22, 1973, Box 9108, Lieutenant Governor Office Files, 1972–1976.

33. William Winter press release, August 8, 1973, Box 9107, Lieutenant Governor Office Files, 1972–1976; *Journal of the Senate, 1972 Session*, 170; Bill Pardue, "Winter Backs Open Records Legislation," *Jackson Daily News*, January 30, 1974; William Winter, Caudill interview; *Journal of the Senate, 1975 Session*, 94–95.

34. Andrew Reese Jr., "Hearings Begin on Ethics," *Greenville Delta Democrat-Times*, November 1, 1974; Ronni Patriquin, "Winter Says Smith's Charges Inaccurate," *Jackson Clarion-Ledger*, November 2, 1974; "Winter's Plane Trips Criticized," *Greenville Delta Democrat-Times*, November 17, 1974; map detailing William Winter's state appearances, January 1973 thru April 1974, Box 12, Wilson Golden unprocessed collection; William Winter, Caudill interview.

35. William Winter to Larry Noble, December 28, 1972, Box 6A, William Winter unprocessed collection; undated memo, 1973, Box 13, Wilson Golden unprocessed collection.

Chapter 9

1. Minutes, Strategy Session, September 11, 1972, Wilson Golden to William Winter, n.d., 1973?, Wilson Golden to William Winter, March 26, 1973, and Wilson Golden to Peter Hart, November 26, 1973, all in Box 12, Wilson Golden unprocessed collection, MDAH; Wilson Golden, Bolton interview; Jesse L. White, Bolton interview, August 30, 2007; Roy Pfautch to William Winter, January 23, 1973, and Tom Bourdeaux to William Winter, September 8, 1973, both in Box 41, William F. Winter and Family Papers, MDAH.

2. William Winter, Bass interview; Paul Pittman, "Anything But Dull," *Greenville Delta Democrat-Times*, November 7, 1974; Wilson Golden to William Winter, May 27, 1974, Box 12, Wilson Golden unprocessed collection.

3. Hart Research Associates, Inc., analysis of Winter polling data, 1975, Box 7, William F. Winter and Family Papers; notes on William Winter's strengths and weaknesses, n.d., 1974 or 1975, Box 13, Wilson Golden unprocessed collection; Bob Riser to William Winter, February 18, 1975, WWPC.

4. Remarks of William Winter, Campaign Kick-off Rally, June 16, 1975, Box 11, Wilson Golden unprocessed collection; White, "Mississippi Electoral Politics, 1903–1976," 539; William Winter ads, *Greenville Delta Democrat-Times*, July 21, 1975, and August 4, 1975; Wilson Golden, Bolton interview; William Winter, Caudill interview; John Dittmer to Jim Silver, May 17, 1975, Box 11, James W. Silver Collection, UM.

5. "Winter Opposes Limits," *Greenville Delta Democrat-Times*, November 29, 1974; Pittman, "Anything But Dull"; Common Cause of Mississippi, "1975 Election Questionnaire," Box 9116, Lieutenant Governor Office Files, 1972–1976, MDAH; "No Spending Limit?" (editorial), *Greenville Delta Democrat-Times*, December 1, 1974; "Winter Reveals His Financial Status," undated newspaper clipping, 1975, WWPC.

6. "Race Not Issue in Election," *Chicago Defender*, August 6, 1975; "Wintertime May Come in August," *Greenville Delta Democrat-Times*, July 29, 1975; Gene Triggs, Caudill interview; William Winter, Bass interview.

7. William Winter, Bass interview; Wilson Golden to William Winter, May 27, 1974, Box 12, and Wilson Golden to William Winter, January 2, 1975, Box 11, both in Wilson Golden unprocessed collection.

8. William Winter, Bass interview; William Winter campaign budget, and information on campaign documentary, Box 11, Wilson Golden unprocessed collection; Winter political ad announcing fifteen-minute TV special, *Greenville Delta Democrat-Times*, August 4, 1975; White, "Mississippi Electoral Politics, 1903–1976," 548; photo of Winter billboard, 1975, Box 50, William Winter unprocessed collection, MDAH; "Winter Endorsed," *Greenville Delta Democrat-Times*, July 18, 1975; "Winter For Governor" (editorial), *Greenville Delta Democrat-Times*, July 27, 1975.

9. Jesse White to Lucian W. Pye, November 12, 1975, Box 19, William F. Winter and Family Papers; William Winter, Bolton interview, May 22, 2006; White, "Mississippi Electoral Politics, 1903–1976," 543–544; William Winter, Bass interview; Chris Danielson, *After Freedom Summer: How Race Realigned Mississippi Politics, 1965–1986* (Gainesville:

University Press of Florida, 2011), 89; remarks of William Winter, Campaign Kick-off Rally, June 16, 1975, Box 11, Wilson Golden unprocessed collection.

10. Jesse White to William Winter, July 7, 1975, Box 11, Wilson Golden unprocessed collection; White, "Mississippi Electoral Politics, 1903–1976," 540–41; William Winter, Caudill interview; William Winter memoir; Waller, *Straight Ahead*, 116–122; Janet Braswell, "Dantin Takes Vigorous Poke at Winter Here," *Hattiesburg American*, July 24, 1975; Tom Eppes, "Dantin Eyes Winter's Law Firm Fees," *Jackson Daily News*, July 27, 1975; Roy Reed, "Arkansas Giant Killer: Dale Leon Bumpers," *New York Times*, May 30, 1974.

11. "HERE ARE THE FACTS!" n.d., 1975, Box 11, Wilson Golden unprocessed collection; White, "Mississippi Electoral Politics, 1903–1976," 540–41; William Winter, Caudill interview; William Winter memoir; Nancy Y. Stevens, "Political Rivalry Heating Up," *Greenville Delta Democrat-Times*, July 25, 1975; Bill Rose, "Winter Intensifies Campaign," *Greenville Delta Democrat-Times*, July 31, 1975.

12. *Mississippi Election Statistics: State Offices, 1971–1979*, 9–10; White, "Mississippi Electoral Politics, 1903–1976," 548; "General suggestions—now through run-off," n.d., August 1975, Box 11, Wilson Golden unprocessed collection.

13. Philip D. Hearn, "Finch Refuses Winter Debate Offer," *Greenville Delta Democrat-Times*, August 8, 1975; "Bad Inning for the Public" (editorial), *Greenville Delta Democrat-Times*, August 10, 1975; White, "Mississippi Electoral Politics, 1903–1976," 548–49.

14. Philip D. Hearn, "Winter Probes Finch Contributions," *Greenville Delta Democrat-Times*, August 15, 1975; White, "Mississippi Electoral Politics, 1903–1976," 548–49.

15. White, "Mississippi Electoral Politics, 1903–1976," 549; William Winter ad copy, August 7, 1975, Box 11, Wilson Golden unprocessed collection; William Winter, Bass interview; William Winter, Bolton interview, May 22, 2006; Elise Winter, Bolton interview.

16. Glenn Stephens, "Winter: History Won't Repeat Itself," *Greenville Delta Democrat-Times*, August 25, 1975; Ed Issa, "Winter Talks to Workers," *Greenville Delta Democrat-Times*, August 24, 1975.

17. Mike Sturdivant, interview by Orley Caudill, November 23, 1976, transcript, Vol. 109, MOHP; William Winter to Wade P. Huie, Jr., August 29, 1975, Box 19, William F. Winter and Family Papers.

18. John Dittmer to Jim Silver, November 9, 1975, Box 11, James W. Silver Collection; John G. Corlew, Pyle interview.

19. "Black Loyalist Leader Endorses Winter," *Memphis Commercial Appeal*, August 13, 1975; "Finch Gets Evers' Support in Runoff," *Memphis Commercial Appeal*, August 12, 1975; William Winter, Bass interview; William Winter, Bailey interview; William Winter, Bolton interview, July 3, 2007.

20. *Mississippi Election Statistics: State Offices, 1971–1979*, 11–12; William Winter, Bailey interview.

21. William Winter memoir; James Saggus, "Winter Leaving Political Scene; Has No Regrets," *Jackson Clarion-Ledger*, January 11, 1976; "Winter Bows Out" (editorial), *Greenville Delta Democrat-Times*, January 15, 1976.

22. William Winter memoir; Nash and Taggart, *Mississippi Politics*, ch. 3; William Winter to Jim Silver, January 23, 1977, Box 11, James W. Silver Collection.

23. William Winter to John C. Stennis, June 9, 1977, Series 50, Box 8, MSU; William Winter, Bass interview; Warren Weaver Jr., "Side Issues Delay Bill to Create New U.S. Judgeships," *New York Times*, March 19, 1978; "Dividing Up Justice" (editorial), *New York Times*, March 27, 1978; Warren Weaver Jr., "Disagreement Delaying Division of Federal Judgeships for South," *New York Times*, June 19, 1978; William Winter to James Eastland, March 3, 1978, and James Eastland to William Winter, April 22, 1978, both in Series 1, Subseries 22, Box 29, James O. Eastland Collection, UM.

24. Nash and Taggart, *Mississippi Politics*, ch. 4; William Winter, Bass interview; William Winter, Caudill interview; Jere Nash and Andy Taggart, "William Winter and His Campaigns for Governor: 1967, 1975, and 1979," *Journal of Mississippi History* 70 (Winter 2008): 396–97; William Winter, Bolton interview, May 22, 2006.

25. William Winter memoir; William Winter, Bass interview; Nash and Taggart, *Mississippi Politics*, 89–90; Bill Minor, "Winter Comeback: Dramatic Political Story," *Capital Reporter*, August 23, 1979.

26. William Winter, Bass interview; William Winter memoir; Peter Hart, Bolton interview.

27. Jesse L. White, Bolton interview, September 27, 2007; William Winter, Bass interview.

28. William Winter memoir; William Winter, Bass interview.

29. William Winter memoir; William Winter, Bolton interview, May 22, 2006; David Crews, Bolton interview; "Winter Outlines Plan to Move State Ahead," *Memphis Commercial Appeal*, July 18, 1979; "Voters Must Study Economic Plans" (editorial), *Jackson Clarion-Ledger*, July 26, 1979; David W. Kubissa, "Winter: Giving It One More Try," *Jackson Clarion-Ledger*, July 12, 1979; "Winter Unveils Program to 'Uplift' Education," newspaper clipping, July 1979, Jesse White scrapbook, Jesse White Personal Collection.

30. Jo Ann Klein and David W. Kubissa, "Gandy, Winter Take Different Route to the Runoff," Jesse White scrapbook; Wayne King, "Mississippi Public Apathetic Despite Novel Primary Race," *New York Times*, August 3, 1979; "Phone Calls to Be Made by WFW," July 23, 1979, Box 19774, William J. Cole III, Office Files, MDAH; *Mississippi Election Statistics: State Offices, 1971–1979*, 17–18.

31. William Winter memoir; Peter D. Hart Research Associates, Inc., Analysis of Poll Conducted between June 18 and June 22, 1979, Box 19774, William J. Cole III, Office Files; William Winter, Bass interview.

32. David Crews, Bolton interview; William Winter, Bass interview; Kathleen Hall Jamieson, *Eloquence in an Electronic Age: The Transformation of Political Speechmaking* (New York: Oxford University Press, 1988), 85; Lois Romano, "Robert Squier's Literary Campaign," *Washington Post*, May 15, 1985; Nash and Taggart, "William Winter and His Campaigns for Governor," 397–98; William Winter, Crews interview; "Winter Quote Clarified," newspaper clipping, August 1979, Jesse White scrapbook; Steve Sanders, "Past Administrations Defended by Winter," *Jackson Daily News*, August 14, 1979; Lloyd Gray,

"It'll Be an Intriguing Two Weeks," *Biloxi Sun-Herald*, August 12, 1979; Lisa Belkin, "In Politics, Women Run By a Different Set of Rules," *New York Times*, September 9, 1984; David W. Kubissa, "Winter Fortifies the Delta Troops," *Jackson Clarion-Ledger*, August 18, 1979.

33. "Winter Promises to Restore Order to State Government," newspaper clipping, August 14, 1979, and Keith Harstein, "Voters Show Apathy, Pessimism, Cynism," newspaper clipping, 1979, both in Jesse White scrapbook; Bill Minor, "Finch Turns Loose Forces for Gandy," *Jackson Capital Reporter*, August 12, 1979; "Past Administrations Defended by Winter"; "Campaign Notes," *Jackson Clarion-Ledger*, August 11, 1979; Klein and Kubissa, "Gandy, Winter Take Different Route to the Runoff"; William Winter, Bolton interview, July 12, 2006.

34. Klein and Kubissa, "Gandy, Winter Take Different Route to the Runoff"; William Winter, Bolton interview, May 22, 2006; Dick Molpus, Bolton interview; Baskin, "The Rise of William Forrest Winter," 66–67; Jesse L. White, Bolton interview, September 27, 2007; Peter Hart, Bolton interview.

35. *Mississippi Election Statistics: State Offices, 1971–1979*, 19–20; Baskin, "The Rise of William Forrest Winter," 67; Michael Flagg, "3rd Time's the Key," newspaper clipping, August 1979, Jesse White scrapbook.

36. Chris Danielson, "'Lily White and Hard Right': The Mississippi Republican Party and Black Voting, 1965–1980," *Journal of Southern History* 75 (February 2009): 95; Nash and Taggart, *Mississippi Politics*, 88–89; King, "Mississippi Public Apathetic Despite Novel Primary Race"; Bill Peterson, "Miss. Election Turning into Case of GOP Southern Discomfort," *Washington Post*, November 2, 1979.

37. David W. Kubissa, "Winter Getting Campaign Rolling Again," *Jackson Clarion-Ledger*, September 12, 1979; William Winter, Bass interview; Jo Ann Klein, "Mansion's Price: $870,000—Winter," *Jackson Clarion-Ledger*, January 5, 1980; William Winter memoir.

38. David W. Kubissa, "Carmichael Scolds Winter on Bond Profits," newspaper clipping, October 1979, Jesse White scrapbook; M. J. Daltel to William Winter, October 19, 1979, Box 1B, William Winter unprocessed collection; David Hampton, "Winter Claims Carmichael Using Desperation Politics," *Jackson Daily News*, October 18, 1979; William Winter memoir; William Winter, Bass interview.

39. Danielson, "'Lily White and Hard Right,'" 95–112; Peterson, "Miss. Election Turning into Case of GOP Southern Discomfort."

40. *Mississippi Election Statistics: State Offices, 1971–1979*, 21–22; Wendell Rawls Jr., "Winter Wins Mississippi Governor Race," *New York Times*, November 7, 1979; Wendell Rawls Jr., "Mississippi Governor-Elect Plans to Guide State to Turning Point," *New York Times*, November 8, 1979.

41. Parker, *Black Votes Counts*, ch. 4; Rawls, "Winter Wins Mississippi Governor Race"; "The Voters Speak, Gently" (editorial), *New York Times*, November 8, 1979.

42. George M. Street to William Winter, November 7, 1979, Box 7, George Street Collection, UM; Rhea Grimsley Johnson, "Winter in Mississippi," *Atlanta Journal*, April 1, 2001; William Winter, Bolton interviews, May 22, 2006, and July 3, 2007.

Chapter 10

1. David W. Kubissa, "Winter Starts Plans for Next Four Years," *Jackson Daily News*, November 8, 1979; William Winter memoir; Michael Flagg, "Winter and Friends Await the Big Day," *Jackson Clarion-Ledger* news clipping, January 1980, Jesse White scrapbook; Eudora Welty, "Mississippi Has Joined the World," *Jackson Capital Reporter*, January 24, 1980.

2. William Winter memoir; David Bates, "Soggy Inauguration Didn't Seem to Dampen Spirit of Winter's Day," *Jackson Clarion-Ledger*, January 23, 1980; William Winter, Bass interview; William Winter, Bolton interview, August 29, 2001; William Winter, Crews interview.

3. William F. Winter inaugural address, 1980, Series 67, Box 2143, MDAH; David W. Kubissa, "Winter Sworn in as 58th Governor," *Jackson Clarion-Ledger*, January 23, 1980.

4. William F. Winter inaugural address; William Winter memoir.

5. Bill Minor, "Governor Winter's Intellectualism Capturing Mississippi's Affection," *Natchez Democrat*, April 2, 1980; Governor's Office Staff, July 1, 1980, Box 13001, Mississippi Treasury Department, Office Files—Executive Assistant/Chief of Staff to the Governor, 1980–1981, MDAH; Lloyd Gray, "Winter Emphasizes Confidence in Staff," *Jackson Daily News*, July 30, 1980; William Winter, Bass interview; David Crews, Bolton interview; Dick Molpus, Bolton interview; Ray Mabus, Bolton interview; William Winter memoir; Andy Mullins, Bolton interview; William Winter, Bolton interviews, May 22, 2006, and March 9, 2007; Andy Kanengiser, "Architects of Education Reform," *Jackson Clarion-Ledger*, December 15, 2002.

6. Governor's Office Staff, July 1, 1980, Box 13001, Mississippi Treasury Department, Office Files—Executive Assistant/Chief of Staff to the Governor, 1980–1981, MDAH; Lloyd Gray, "Winter Emphasizes Confidence in Staff," *Jackson Daily News*, July 30, 1980; William Winter, Bass interview; William Winter memoir; William Winter, Bolton interviews, May 22, 2006, and March 9, 2007; Bill Minor, "Winter's Honeymoon Fading," *Jackson Capital Reporter*, July 17, 1980.

7. "Winter Emphasizes Confidence in Staff"; Andy Mullins, Bolton interview; Dick Molpus, Bolton interview; William Winter, Bolton interviews, May 22, 2006, and March 9, 2007; John Henegan, introduction of William Winter at the Mississippi Press Association Convention, June 21, 2002, John Henegan Personal Collection; David Crews, Bolton interview; John Henegan, Bolton interview.

8. William Winter, Sansing interview; C. Thompson Wacaster to William Winter, March 10, 1980, and April 18, 1980, both in Box 2323, Mississippi Governor, Subject Correspondence, 1979–1983, MDAH.

9. William Winter, Bass interview; W. L. Jones to William Winter, June 20, 1980, and William Winter to W. L. Jones, August 20, 1980, both in Box 2181, Mississippi Governor, General Correspondence, 1980, MDAH; William Winter, Bolton interview, August 29, 2001.

10. William Winter, Bolton interview, December 8, 2006; William Winter, Sansing interview.

11. "Winter Signs Bill," *Memphis Commercial Appeal*, February 9, 1980; William Winter, Bass interview; William Winter, Bolton interview, July 12, 2006; Mitchell, *Mississippi Liberal*, 242.

12. Baskin, "The Rise of William Forrest Winter," 79–82; William Winter, Bass interview; David W. Kubissa and Don Hoffman, "State Tax Commission to Assume MVC's Duties," *Jackson Clarion-Ledger*, May 6, 1980; William Winter, Nash interview; Don Hoffman, "House Passes Bill to Scrap Bank Comptroller's Office," *Jackson Clarion-Ledger*, February 8, 1980; Office of the Governor, *Highlights of the 1980 Mississippi Legislative Session*, 10–12; Lloyd Gray, "Governor's Office Will Be 'Reorganized,' Winter Says," newspaper clipping, November 17, 1979, Jesse White scrapbook; "Winter Outlines Reorganization," *Memphis Commercial Appeal*, December 22, 1979; Dale Krane and Stephen D. Shaffer, *Mississippi Government and Politics: Modernizers Versus Traditionalists* (Lincoln: University of Nebraska Press, 1992), 260–61; Dick Molpus, Bolton interview.

13. "Major Economic Development Programs during Winter Administration," n.d., Box 9A, William Winter unprocessed collection, MDAH; William Winter, Bolton interviews, August 29, 2001, and July 12, 2006.

14. William Winter, Bass interview; Ada Reid to William Winter, February 11, 1980, Matthew J. Page to William Winter, February 7, 1980, Fred L. Banks Jr. to William Winter, February 7, 1980, Walter E. Gardner to William Winter, April 4, 1980, and Minutes, Governor's Minority Economic Development Task Force, April 18, 1980, all in Box 2156, Mississippi Governor, Subject Correspondence, 1979–1983; David Bates and Don Hoffman, "Second Black Group Raps Makeup of Economic Board," *Jackson Clarion-Ledger*, February 8, 1980.

15. "Winter Begins to Outline Programs," *Vicksburg Evening Post*, November 17, 1979, Jesse White scrapbook; "Black Leaders Think Winter Will Grant Minorities a Say," *Jackson Clarion-Ledger*, December 2, 1979; "Winter's Record" (editorial), *Jackson Daily News*, June 30, 1980; "Extremely Pleased/Winter Reflects," *Jackson Clarion-Ledger*, May 19, 1980; Minor, "Winter's Honeymoon Fading." The approximate number of female appointees was calculated from the information on the membership of state boards and commissions contained in *Mississippi Official and Statistical Register, 1980–1984* (Jackson: Mississippi Secretary of State, 1981).

16. William Winter, Bass interview; William Winter to Alfred G. Nicols Jr., August 28, 1980, Box 2181, Mississippi Governor, General Correspondence, 1980; Jo Ann Klein, "Winter Names Black Attorney to Commission," *Jackson Clarion-Ledger*, February 13, 1980; "Winter Names Woman to Head Agency," *Jackson Clarion-Ledger*, February 13, 1980; "Trailblazers of the Mississippi Legal Frontier: Reuben V. Anderson," *The Mississippi Lawyer* 9 (February 2003): 16.

17. Bill Minor, "Beginning of a Mississippi Camelot?" newspaper clipping, WWPC; "Running Around with Winter Part of the Job," *Jackson Clarion-Ledger*, November 24, 1980; Ronnie Miller, Governor's Council on Physical Fitness and Sports, flyer, n.d., Subject File: Governor's Council on Physical Fitness, MDAH; David Crews, Bolton interview; Andy Mullins to Governor Winter, June 5, 1981, Box 2221, Mississippi Governor, Staff Memoranda, 1980–1983, MDAH.

18. Andy Mullins, Bolton interview; Reuben V. Anderson, "Governor William Winter," *Journal of Mississippi History* 70 (Winter 2008): 404.

19. Elise Winter, *Dinner at the Mansion* (Oxford, Miss.: Yoknapatawpha Press, 1982), 7–9; William Winter, Bass interview; Mitchell, *Mississippi Liberal*, 243–44; Raad Cawthon, "Elise Winter's Style, Grace Seen in 'Dinner at Mansion,'" *Jackson Clarion-Ledger*, October 10, 1982.

20. Paul Pittman, "The 'Real Mississippi' Has New Image," *Oxford Eagle*, November 5, 1980; Bill Minor, "Governor Winter's Intellectualism Capturing Mississippi's Affection"; Winter, *Dinner at the Mansion*; John Emmerich, "Winter Shows Style in Governor's Mansion, *McComb Enterprise-Journal*, August 19, 1981; Raad Cawthon, "I Wish Everyone Could See the True Mississippi I Have Seen," *Jackson Clarion-Ledger*, May 2, 1983; William F. Winter, "Not Forgotten: Reimagining the South," *Southern Cultures* 11 (Fall 2005): 88–100.

21. Minor, "Governor Winter's Intellectualism Capturing Mississippi's Affection"; Bill Ferris, Leontyne Price, Eudora Welty, Willie Morris, Dinner at the Mansion, April 1, 1981, and Muddy Waters reception, September 18, 1981, both in Box 2196, Mississippi Governor, Speeches—Cassette Tapes and Transcriptions, 1980–1983, MDAH.

22. William Winter, Bolton interview, August 29, 2001; William Winter memoir; Elise Winter, Bolton interview; Raad Cawthon, "I'm Proud to Be Winter's Running Mate in Governor's Cup," *Jackson Clarion-Ledger*, August 29, 1983; Philip Shenon, "For Homesick Mississippians, A Day Full of Grits and Grins," *New York Times*, June 19, 1983.

23. Howard Scarborough to William Winter, July 8, 1980, Box 2181, Mississippi Governor, General Correspondence, 1980; Mrs. James R. (Esther) Baugh to William Winter, November 10, 1983, Box 2171, Mississippi Governor, Subject Correspondence, 1979–1983; Cawthon, "I'm Proud to Be Winter's Running Mate in Governor's Cup."

24. Lou Young to William Winter, March 25, 1980, Box 2167, Mississippi Governor, Subject Correspondence, 1979–1983.

25. Press release from Grenada NAACP, May 11, 1981, Box 2221, Mississippi Governor, Staff Memoranda, 1980–1983.

26. Nash and Taggart, *Mississippi Politics*, 116; William Winter, Bolton interviews, August 29, 2001, December 8, 2006, and July 3, 2007; Parker, *Black Votes Count*, 147–50.

27. Nash and Taggart, *Mississippi Politics*, 116–17; Aaron Henry to Robert Strauss, May 14, 1980, Box 7, Aaron Henry Papers, Tougaloo College Archives, Tougaloo, Mississippi; Bill Minor, "Democrats in Mississippi Feud Over New Chairman," *Washington Post*, May 11, 1980; William Winter, Bolton interview, December 8, 2006.

28. Aaron Henry to William Winter, May 16, 1980, Box 7, Aaron Henry Papers; Resolution, Hinds County Democratic Executive Committee, May 16, 1980, WWPC; Jo Ann Klein, "Apologize, Hinds Dems Tell Winter," *Jackson Clarion-Ledger*, May 20, 1980; William Winter to Robert C. Wilkerson III, May 19, 1980, Box 2199, Mississippi Governor, Daily Schedules and Message Sheets, 1980–1983, MDAH; "Resolution Condemns Governor Winter's Actions in Dem. Party," *Jackson Advocate*, June 26–July 2, 1980.

29. Nash and Taggart, *Mississippi Politics*, 116–17; Aaron E. Henry and other Democrats to Judicial Council, Democratic National Committee, n.d., 1980, WWPC;

Danny E. Cupit to David Bowen, June 27, 1980, David R. Bowen Collection, Congressional and Political Research Center, Mississippi State University, Starkville; Aaron Henry to Jack Harper, June 25, 1980, Box 7, Aaron Henry Papers.

30. Howell Raines, "Among Southern Delegates, Enthusiasm Is Hard to Find," *New York Times*, August 14, 1980; Wilson F. Minor, "Winter Takes Key Role in National Party Politics," *Jackson Capital Reporter*, August 21, 1980; William Winter, Bolton interviews, May 22, 2006, and December 8, 2006; Baskin, "The Rise of William Forrest Winter," 83–84; David Hampton, "Winter Wants State in Mainstream," *Jackson Daily News*, September 1, 1980; Aaron Henry to fellow participants in the 1980 Democratic National Convention, September 15, 1980, Box 7, Aaron Henry Papers; Mrs. Ollye B. Shirley to President Jimmy Carter, September 17, 1980, Box 2152, Mississippi Governor, Subject Correspondence, 1979–1983, MDAH.

31. Minor, "Winter Takes Key Role in National Party Politics"; Baskin, "The Rise of William Forrest Winter," 83–84; Edward Walsh, "Carter: Appealing to the South to Support One of Its Own," *Washington Post*, September 2, 1980; "Reagan Jabs Carter on Choice of Area with Klan Strength," *Washington Post*, September 2, 1980; Martin Schram, "Reagan Beats a Retreat on Klan Remark," *Washington Post*, September 3, 1980; Democratic Victory Rallies, October 1980, Box 13001, Mississippi Treasury Department, Office Files—Executive Assistant/Chief of Staff to the Governor, 1980–1981, MDAH; Gov. Winter's Carter tour, Oct. 24–25, and Governor Winter's schedule, week of Oct. 27–Nov. 2, both in Box 2199, Mississippi Governor, Daily Schedules and Message Sheets, 1980–1983, MDAH.

32. A Winter Supporter in Many Elections to William Winter, August 15, 1980, Box 2152, Mississippi Governor, Subject Correspondence, 1979–1983, MDAH; James Moye, interview by Orley Caudill, April 2, 1981, transcript, Vol. 216, MOHP; William H. Morris Jr. to William Winter, August 25, 1980, Box 2181, Mississippi Governor, General Correspondence, 1980, MDAH.

33. William Winter to Charles Evers, August 9, 1982, WWPC; E. C. Foster, "A Time of Challenge: Afro-Mississippi Political Developments since 1965," *Journal of Negro History* 68 (Spring 1983): 195.

34. Foster, "A Time of Challenge," 195; "Mississippi Nominee Poses Test for Black-White Ties," *New York Times*, August 19, 1982; Johanna Neuman, "Demo Leaders Gather in D.C. for Clark Rally," *Jackson Daily News*, September 29, 1982; Karen Hinton, "Democrats Crossing Over, Says Republican Franklin," *Jackson Daily News*, September 29, 1982; Adam Clymer, "Race Raised as an Issue in Mississippi House Contest," *New York Times*, October 14, 1982; Curtis Wilkie, "Change Comes to Mississippi, But Race Remains Key Issue," *Boston Globe*, October 24, 1982; James H. Cleaver, "Blacks Seek Offices in Bay Area, Deep South," *Los Angeles Sentinel*, October 28, 1982; Mary and John Dye to William Winter, November 6, 1982, WWPC.

35. Cleaver, "Blacks Seek Offices in Bay Area, Deep South"; Sam J. Foose Jr. to William Winter, August 31, 1982, Box 2153, Mississippi Governor, Subject Correspondence, 1979–1983; Willie and Cornelia Dillard to William Winter, December 29, 1982, RG 27, Vol. 1255, MDAH.

36. William Winter memoir; C. B. Newman, Bolton interview; Brad Dye, Bolton interview; William Winter, Bass interview; David Crews, Bolton interview; Bill Minor, "Winter's Wet Whistle."

37. Office of the Governor, *Highlights of the 1980 Mississippi Legislative Session*, 12–14; David Hampton, "Legislature Still in No Mood for Winter," *Jackson Daily News*, January 19, 1981; Don Hoffman, "Open Records Wars Saga: Try, Try Again," *Jackson Clarion-Ledger*, December 27, 1981; Don Hoffman, "Mississippi Government May Be Dull, But . . .," *Jackson Clarion-Ledger*, January 25, 1981; Bill Minor, "Nice Guy Winter Is Accomplishing Little," *McComb Enterprise-Journal*, May 4, 1982; Wayne W. Weidie, "Winter Described as 'Caretaker' Governor," *Scott County Times*, May 19, 1982; James Dickerson, "Will Gov. Winter Change His Tactics?" *Jackson Daily News*, April 14, 1981.

38. Office of the Governor, *Highlights of the 1980 Mississippi Legislative Session*, 8; Bill Minor, "Winter May Find Tax Increase Unavoidable," *Jackson Capital Reporter*, December 11, 1980; John Herbers, "Mississippi Fears U.S. Cuts Imperil Its Fiscal and Racial Gains," *New York Times*, April 14, 1982; William Winter, Bass interview.

39. Lloyd Gray, "Pay Attention, Washington, to Mississippi's Tax-Cut Woes," *Biloxi Sun-Herald*, July 5, 1981; William Winter, Bass interview; William Winter, Shaw interview.

40. Cobb, *The Selling of the South*; Sayuri Guthrie-Shimizu, "From Southeast Asia to the American Southeast," in *Globalization and the American South*, ed. by James C. Cobb and William Stueck (Athens: University of Georgia Press, 2005), 144–47; William Winter, Bolton interviews, July 12, 2006, and December 8, 2006; Anthony Ramirez, "Mississippi Pushes for Growth, But Can't Lose 'Poorest' Label," *Wall Street Journal*, June 16, 1981; "Winter: Worst Is Behind, Economic Future Looks Rosy," *Jackson Clarion-Ledger*, September 24, 1980.

41. Cobb, *The Selling of the South*; Herbers, "Mississippi Fears U.S. Cuts Imperil Its Fiscal and Racial Gains"; William Winter, Bass interview; Brian Williams, "Winter: We've Been 50th Long Enough," *Jackson Clarion-Ledger*, January 6, 1982.

42. Orley Hood, "Governor Winter's Legacy Is the Best and the Brightest," *Jackson Daily News*, January 6, 1984.

Chapter 11

1. Nash and Taggart, *Mississippi Politics*, 133; Bolton, *The Hardest Deal of All*, 217; William F. Winter, "Development of Educational Policy in Mississippi," *Mississippi Law Journal* 58 (1988): 234; *Journal of the House of the State of Mississippi, 1982 Session* (Jackson: The House, 1982), 59–63.

2. William Winter, Bolton interview, August 29, 2001; Danny McKenzie, *A Time to Speak: Speeches by Jack Reed* (Jackson: University Press of Mississippi, 2009), 57–64; Andrew P. Mullins Jr., *Building Consensus: A History of the Passage of the Mississippi Education Reform Act of 1982* (Mississippi: A. P. Mullins, 1992), 9; Office of the Governor, *Highlights of the 1980 Mississippi Legislative Session*, 17.

3. *Report of Special Committee on Public School Finance and Administration* (Jackson: The Committee, 1980); Wilson Minor, "Mississippi: Activist Governor," *New York Times*, November 13, 1983.

4. William Winter, Bolton interview, August 29, 2001; McKenzie, *A Time to Speak*, 57–64; Winter, "Development of Educational Policy in Mississippi," 232; William Winter, Bass interview.

5. Andy Mullins, Bolton interview; John Henegan to Governor Winter, December 6, 1981, Box 2201, Mississippi Governor, Education Reform Act Files, 1979–1982; Judy Putnam, "Elise Winter—First Lady, First Lobbyist," *Jackson Clarion-Ledger*, February 1, 1982; Mullins, *Building Consensus*, 30–31.

6. William Winter, Nash interview; William Winter, Bass interview; William Winter, Shaw interview; Gray, "Pay Attention, Washington, to Mississippi's Tax-Cut Woes"; Brian Williams, "Winter Considers Gas Severance Tax before Legislature," *Jackson Clarion-Ledger*, September 19, 1981; William Winter, Bolton interview, July 12, 2006; Bill Minor, Bolton interview; Mullins, *Building Consensus*, 42; letter to the editor from Guy McLendon, *Jackson Clarion-Ledger*, January 8, 1981.

7. Endorsement Group Efforts, 1981, Box 2230, Mississippi Governor, First Lady's Subject Files, 1979–1983, MDAH; "Resolute Reach for Bootstraps" (editorial), *Jackson Clarion-Ledger*, November 12, 1981; Mullins, *Building Consensus*, 48–51; David Crews to William Winter, December 9, 1981, Box 2221, Mississippi Governor, Staff Memoranda, 1980–1983, MDAH; Tom Dulin to William Winter, September 9, 1982, Box 2158, Mississippi Governor, Subject Correspondence, 1979–1983, MDAH.

8. Fred Anklam Jr., "Mississippi Senate Passes Creationism Bill," *Jackson Clarion-Ledger*, January 6, 1982; William Winter, Bolton interview, July 12, 2006.

9. Mullins, *Building Consensus*, 74–78; Jim Simpson, Bolton interview.

10. William Winter, Bolton interview, July 12, 2006; William Winter, Bass interview; Bill Minor, Bolton interview; Williams, "Winter: We've Been 50th Long Enough"; Letter from Charles H. Williams, Jr., to members of the Mid-Continent Oil & Gas Association, December 28, 1981, and Jerome C. Hafter to John Henegan, January 11, 1982, both in Box 2201, Mississippi Governor, Education Reform Act Files, 1979–1982; Mullins, *Building Consensus*, 72–73.

11. Mullins, *Building Consensus*, 81–82; Winter, "Development of Educational Policy in Mississippi," 233.

12. William Winter, Bolton interview, August 29, 2001; Norma Fields, "Winter's Non-Stands Puzzle Admirers," *Northeast Mississippi (Tupelo) Daily Journal*, June 15, 1982; John Henegan, introduction of William Winter at the Mississippi Press Association Convention, June 21, 2002, transcript, John Henegan personal collection.

13. Fields, "Winter's Non-Stands Puzzle Admirers"; Judy Wall, "Mississippi House Dominated by Power Clique Rotarians Told," *Amory Advertiser*, July 19, 1982, Subject File: William F. Winter—1982 (May–August), MDAH; Jere Nash and Andy Taggart, "Education Transforms the Mississippi Legislature," *Journal of Mississippi History* 68 (Fall 2006): 180; William Winter, Bass interview; Mullins, *Building Consensus*, 97–101; Paul

Pittman, "Gov. Winter's Education Crusade Belies Low-Profile Image," *Jackson Clarion-Ledger*, October 10, 1982.

14. Dick Molpus, Bolton interview; Herman Glazier to Governor Winter, June 11, 1982, and Kelley Walton to the PACK Bureau, June 11, 1981, both in Box 2221, Mississippi Governor, Staff Memoranda, 1980–1983; John Henegan, Bolton interview; Mullins, *Building Consensus*, 48, 94; speaking commitments, June–October 1982, Box 2158, Mississippi Governor, Subject Correspondence, 1979–1983; Ray Mabus, Bolton interview; David Crews, Bolton interview; William Winter, Bass interview.

15. Herman Glazier to Governor Winter, June 11, 1982, Box 2221, Mississippi Governor, Staff Memoranda, 1980–1983; Mullins, *Building Consensus*, 109–11; William Winter, Bass interview; William Winter to Mrs. R. Glenn Miller, December 28, 1992, Box 41, William Winter unprocessed collection, MDAH.

16. William Winter, Bass interview; Mullins, *Building Consensus*, 115–18; William Winter, Nash interview.

17. McKenzie, *A Time to Speak*, 63; William Winter, Bolton interviews, March 9, 2007, and March 12, 2008; Mullins, *Building Consensus*, 125; John Henegan, Bolton interview; William Winter, Bass interview.

18. Cliff Treyens and Fred Anklam Jr., "Special Session's Outcome Tied to Key Players," *Jackson Clarion-Ledger*, December 6, 1982; William Winter, Bass interview; Mullins, *Building Consensus*, 141–44; Jack Elliott, "Key Legislator Opposes Tax, Could Scuttle Winter's Plan," *Jackson Daily News*, December 3, 1982.

19. Mullins, *Building Consensus*, 144–48; "New South at the *Clarion-Ledger*," *Time* 121 (May 2, 1983): 78; Nancy Weaver and Fred Anklam Jr., "Mississippi Schools: Hard Lessons," *Jackson Clarion-Ledger*, November 28, 1982. The *Jackson Clarion-Ledger* won a Pulitzer Prize in 1983 for its eight-part story on Mississippi education.

20. William Winter, Bass interview.

21. Winter, "Development of Educational Policy in Mississippi," 235–36; Mullins, *Building Consensus*, 154.

22. Lucy Hovious and Jack Elliott, "Amid 'Good Signs,' Pressure on State Senate Increasing," *Jackson Daily News*, December 14, 1982; Mullins, *Building Consensus*, 161–66; William Winter, Bass interview; William Winter, Bolton interview, August 29, 2001.

23. William Winter, Bass interview; Ray Mabus, Bolton interview; William Winter, Bolton interview, August 29, 2001; Willie and Cornelia Dillard to William Winter, December 29, 1982, RG 27, Vol. 1255, MDAH.

24. Mullins, *Building Consensus*, 163–64; William Winter, Bass interview; William Winter, Bolton interview, July 12, 2006.

25. Mullins, *Building Consensus*, 167–70; William Winter, Bass interview.

26. William Winter, Bass interview; Lucy Hovious, "Education Package Stripped of Kindergartens before Senate," *Jackson Daily News*, December 16, 1982; Mullins, *Building Consensus*, 171–75.

27. Mullins, *Building Consensus*, 175–76; Dick Molpus, Bolton interview.

28. William Winter, Bass interview; Robert Clark, Tanzman interview; Mullins, *Building Consensus*, 176–81; Bolton, *The Hardest Deal of All*, 218.

29. Mullins, *Building Consensus*, 180–84; Minor, *Eyes on Mississippi*, 174; Jack Elliott, "Winter Waiting Anxiously to Sign Education-Tax Bill," *Jackson Daily News*, December 21, 1982.

30. Elliott, "Winter Waiting Anxiously to Sign Education-Tax Bill"; Mitchell, *Mississippi Liberal*, 245; Mullins, *Building Consensus*, 185–86; Wendell Rawls Jr., "Mississippi Governor Is Big Winner on Education," *New York Times*, December 27, 1982; Hamilton Jordan, "To: Democratic Presidential Candidates," *Washington Post*, February 10, 1983.

31. Bolton, *The Hardest Deal of All*, epilogue; "Winter's Legacy," *Memphis Commercial Appeal*, December 24, 1982; Larry Noble to William Winter, December 29, 1982, Box 2171, Mississippi Governor, Subject Correspondence, 1979–1983, MDAH; Dick Molpus, Bolton interview.

Chapter 12

1. Bill Minor, "New Winter-Allain Alliance Could Spell Trouble for Cochran in '84," *Jackson Clarion-Ledger*, November 1983, Subject File: William F. Winter, 1983 September–December, MDAH.

2. *Journal of the House of the State of Mississippi, 1983 Session* (Jackson: The House, 1983), 951; Fred Anklam Jr., "Winter Signs into Law '83 Utility Reform Act," *Jackson Clarion-Ledger*, April 7, 1983; "Public Records Bill Goes to Winter," *Jackson Clarion-Ledger*, March 12, 1983; Cliff Treyens, "Budget Saga Ends; Prison Bill Passes," *Jackson Clarion-Ledger*, April 16, 1983.

3. Proceedings of the dedication ceremonies, Mississippi State Capitol restoration and renovation, 1980–1983, June 3, 1983, MDAH; Norma Fields, "Winter Addresses Crowd of 2,000 at New Capitol Dedication," *Northeast Mississippi (Tupelo) Daily Journal*, June 4–5, 1983.

4. James S. Granelli, "Justice Delayed," *ABA Journal* 70 (1984): 51–55; Ben Owen to William Winter, May 9, 1983, Box 2171, Mississippi Governor, Subject Correspondence, 1979–1983, MDAH; William Winter, Bolton interview, December 8, 2006; William Winter to Larry Noble, February 14, 1983, Box 2171, Mississippi Governor, Subject Correspondence, 1979–1983, MDAH; John Henegan, Bolton interview; Tom Oppel, "Winter Standing Firm on Clemency Denial," *Jackson Clarion-Ledger*, July 1, 1983.

5. John Henegan, Bolton interview; Brad Dye, Bolton interview; "Mississippi Executes Child Slayer Gray," *Atlanta Daily World*, September 4, 1983; Donald A. Cabana, "The History of Capital Punishment in Mississippi: An Overview," *Mississippi History Now*, http://mshistory.k12.ms.us/articles/84/history-of-capital-punishment-in -mississippi-an-overview (Accessed September 14, 2009); E. R. Shipp, "Killer of 3-Year-Old Mississippi Girl Executed after Justices Reject Pleas," *New York Times*, September 2, 1983.

6. Tom Oppel, "Winter Warns of Need for Tax Increase," *Jackson Clarion-Ledger*, October 6, 1983; Susan Tifft, "Restoring a Delicate Balance," *Time* 122 (November 28,

1983): 27; Tom Oppel, "Winter Vows to Tackle Budget Woes," *Jackson Clarion-Ledger*, October 19, 1983.

7. Jack Elliott, "Sales Tax Hike Gains Support," *Jackson Daily News*, November 16, 1983; "Text of Gov. Winter's Address before Joint Assembly," *Jackson Clarion-Ledger*, November 17, 1983; *Greenwood Commonwealth* editorial reprinted in "Winter, Legislature Acted Decisively When Necessary," *Jackson Clarion-Ledger*, November 26, 1983.

8. William Winter, Bass interview; Nash and Taggart, *Mississippi Politics*, 224–25; James R. Crockett, *Operation Pretense: The FBI's Sting on County Corruption in Mississippi* (Jackson: University Press of Mississippi, 2003); Ray Mabus, Bolton interview; John P. Judis, "Campaign '88: White and Wrong," *New Republic* 199 (October 24, 1988): 16–18.

9. Nash and Taggart, *Mississippi Politics*, 161, 251–55; Stephen D. Shaffer et al., "Mississippi: From Pariah to Pacesetter?" in *Southern Politics in the 1990s*, edited by Alexander P. Lamis (Baton Rouge: Louisiana State University Press, 1999), ch. 9; William Winter, Shaw interview; Douglas Demmons, "Winter's Proteges Ring Up Victories," *Jackson Clarion-Ledger*, August 25, 1983; "Rosenblatt Seeking Senate Seat," *Jackson Northside Sun*, April 7, 1983, Subject File: Cy Rosenblatt, MDAH; Curtis Wilkie, *The Fall of the House of Zeus: The Rise and Ruin of America's Most Powerful Trial Lawyer* (New York: Random House, 2010).

10. Nash and Taggart, *Mississippi Politics*, 161, 193–95; Luix Overbea, "Education Reform Tops List of Progress for Mississippi Governor," *Christian Science Monitor*, October 3, 1983; William Winter, Bass interview.

11. William Winter, Bass interview; Nash and Taggart, *Mississippi Politics*, ch. 9; E. R. Shipp, "Mississippi Attorney General Claims Nomination," *New York Times*, August 24, 1983; "Mississippi Officials in Gubernatorial Runoff," *New York Times*, August 3, 1983; William Winter, Bolton interview, July 3, 2007.

12. Nash and Taggart, *Mississippi Politics*, ch. 9; William Winter, Bolton interview, July 3, 2007; Ray Mabus, Bolton interview; Minor, "New Winter-Allain Alliance Could Spell Trouble for Cochran in '84"; John Howard, *Men Like That: A Southern Queer History* (Chicago: University of Chicago Press, 1999), 280–96. Billy Mounger maintains the truth of the allegations against Allain and claims that his revelations about the gubernatorial candidate were not politically motivated. See William D. Mounger with Joe Maxwell, *Amidst the Fray: My Life in Politics, Culture, and Mississippi* (Brandon, Miss.: Quail Ridge Press, 2006), ch. 24.

13. Wendell Rawls Jr., "Mississippi Governor Is Big Winner on Education," *New York Times*, December 27, 1982; Danny Cupit to William Winter, February 9, 1983, WWPC; William Winter, Bolton interview, July 14 2006; William Winter to Edward H. Hobbs, June 7, 1983, Box 2171, Mississippi Governor, Subject Correspondence, 1979–1983, MDAH.

14. Sansing, *The University of Mississippi*, 330; William Winter, Bolton interviews, August 29, 2001, and May 22, 2006; Frank Smith to Governor Winter, September 19, 1983, Box 2221, Mississippi Governor, Staff Memoranda, 1980–1983, MDAH; Andy Kanengiser, "Winter Asked for Ole Miss Job in Letter, Source Says," *Jackson Daily News*, November 14, 1983; William Winter, Bass interview.

15. William Winter, Bolton interview, August 29, 2001; William Winter, Shaw interview; "In Bilbo's Path?" (editorial), *Memphis Commercial Appeal*, November 30, 1983; Tom Oppel and Coleman Warner, "Board, Winter Still Undecided on Ole Miss Post," *Jackson Clarion-Ledger*, December 6, 1983.

16. William Winter, Bolton interview, August 29, 2001; William Winter, Shaw interview; "In Bilbo's Path?"; Oppel and Warner, "Board, Winter Still Undecided on Ole Miss Post"; Coleman Warner, "Winter Wavers after Accepting Chancellorship," *Jackson Clarion-Ledger*, December 15, 1983; Andy Kanenigiser, "Winter Officially Accepts UM Job," *Jackson Daily News*, December 15, 1983.

17. William Winter, Bass interview; William Winter, Bolton interview, August 29, 2001; Jack Elliott, "Winter Lacked Enthusiasm for UM Post," *Jackson Daily News*, December 20, 1983; Andy Mullins, Bolton interview; George M. Street to Norman E. Shaw, January 10, 1984, Box 9, George Street Collection, UM; Tom Oppel, "Winter Move Revives Dems' Senate Hopes," *Jackson Clarion-Ledger*, December 20, 1983; David Crews, Bolton interview; Dick Molpus, Bolton interview.

18. Tom Oppel, "Party Urges Winter to Run for U.S. Senate," *Jackson Clarion-Ledger*, December 8, 1983; Ron Suskind, "The Power of Political Consultants," *New York Times*, August 12, 1984.

19. Cliff Trevens, "Dem Leaders Meet with Winter about Senate Candidacy in '84," *Jackson Clarion-Ledger*, June 16, 1983; Curtis Wilkie, "Democrats Urge 3 Governors to Oppose GOP Senators," *Boston Globe*, June 23, 1983; Andy Mullins, Bolton interview; William Winter, Bolton interview, August 29, 2001; "Reagan Pollster Says He'd Beat Mondale or Glenn," *Washington Post*, December 8, 1983; Bill Minor, "Winter Has Two Tempting Plums, and Now He Must Chose," *Jackson Clarion-Ledger*, December 4, 1983; Suskind, "The Power of Political Consultants."

20. Oppel, "Party Urges Winter to Run for U.S. Senate"; William Winter, Bass interview; William Winter, Bolton interview, August 29, 2001; David Crews, Bolton interview; Andy Mullins, Bolton interview.

21. Thad Cochran, Bolton interview; John H. Chafee, "New Cast of G.O.P. Leaders in Senate," *New York Times*, November 29, 1984.

22. William Winter, Bass interview; Bill Minor, "Old Governor: What Ever Happened to Our Cochran Challenger?" *Jackson Clarion-Ledger*, March 25, 1984; Randy Patterson to Governor Winter, January 4, 1984, Box 9A, William Winter unprocessed collection, MDAH; Bill Minor, "Decisions, Decisions: They Nag Winter Even Out of Office," *Jackson Clarion-Ledger*, January 15, 1984.

23. William Winter, Bass interview; Andy Mullins, Bolton interview; Thad Cochran, Bolton interview; Tom Oppel, "Winter Says He's in Race for Senate," *Jackson Clarion-Ledger*, February 7, 1984.

24. Minor, "Old Governor"; Thad Cochran, Bolton interview; Guy Land, Bolton interview; Guy Land to Governor Winter, April 22, 1984, Box 5A, William Winter unprocessed collection, MDAH; Democratic Senate Campaign Committee, "Mississippi Opposition Research Project: The Views and Record of Senator Thad Cochran, A Briefing Prepared for Governor William Winter," 1984, Box 30, William Winter

unprocessed collection; Tom Oppel, "Cochran's Expenses 5 Times Those of Winter," *Jackson Clarion-Ledger*, October 18, 1984; Michael Barone and Grant Ujifusa, *The Almanac of American Politics, 1986* (Washington, D.C.: National Journal, 1985), 738; Suskind, "The Power of Political Consultants"; Wallace Dabbs, "Winter: No Political Plans in the Forseeable Future," *Jackson Daily News*, November 7, 1984.

25. Guy Land to Governor Winter, April 22, 1984, Box 5A, William Winter unprocessed collection, MDAH; Democratic Senate Campaign Committee, "Mississippi Opposition Research Project"; Winter Campaign Newsletter, July 1984, Subject File: William F. Winter, 1984, MDAH; Martin Tolchin, "Who Has Done More for a State That Has Little?" *New York Times*, April 29, 1984.

26. William Winter, Bolton interview, August 29, 2001; Andy Mullins, Bolton interview; William Winter, Bass interview; Guy Land, Bolton interview; "Ex-Governors," Script for Winter TV spot on WJTV, 1985, and William Winter to Hodding Carter III, December 3, 1984, both in WWPC; Peter D. Hart Research Associates, Inc., analysis of May 1984 poll, Box 30, William Winter unprocessed collection.

27. William Winter, Bolton interview, August 29, 2001; Paul Taylor, "Mississippi Tests Its 'Long-Term' Tradition," *Washington Post*, June 16, 1984; Jack Elliott, "Winter's Age Is First Target for Cochran," *Jackson Daily News*, June 17, 1984; Sid Salter, "Winter Gives 'Em That Old 'High Popalorum and Low Popahirum,'" *Jackson Clarion-Ledger*, June 24, 1984.

28. Helen Dewar, "In Mississippi Contest, a Touch of Class," *Washington Post*, October 25, 1984; Thad Cochran, Bolton interview; Ronald Smothers, "The 1984 Elections: Reagan's Coattails Put to the Test; Republican Mississippi Senator Holds Off Ex-Governor's Challenge," *New York Times*, November 7, 1984; Tom Wicker, "In the Nation: Fighting White Drift," *New York Times*, October 26, 1984.

29. Nash and Taggart, *Mississippi Politics*, 170–71; Ronald Smothers, "Jackson Joins Carolina Leaders in a Call for Unity," *New York Times*, September 8, 1984.

30. James R. Dickenson, "Mondale Appeals for South," *Washington Post*, August 6, 1984; William Winter, Bolton interview, August 29, 2001; Guy Land, Bolton interview; Peter D. Hart Research Associates, Inc. to The Winter for Senate Campaign, October 4, 1984, Box 30, William Winter unprocessed collection.

31. Peter D. Hart Research Associates, Inc. to The Winter for Senate Campaign, October 4, 1984, Box 30, William Winter unprocessed collection.

32. Nash and Taggart, *Mississippi Politics*, 171; "The Senate: Riding High with Reagan," *Time* 124 (October 29, 1984): 34; William Winter to Tom Wicker, November 29, 1984, WWPC.

33. William Winter, Bass interview; William Winter, Bolton interview, August 29, 2001; Erle Johnston to William Winter, November 9, 1984, WWPC.

34. Rabb, "Winter"; David Crews, Bolton interview.

Chapter 13

1. William Winter, Bass interview; syllabus for "The South and the Nation," Harvard Institute of Politics, Spring 1985, and William Winter to Jonathan Moore and Theresa Donovan, July 10, 1985, WWPC; Tom Oppel, "Harvard Assignment Gives Winter Chance to Appreciate Spring," *Jackson Clarion-Ledger*, April 29, 1985.

2. Jeff Edwards and Joe Atkins, "WJTV Hires William Winter as Editorial Commentator," *Jackson Daily News*, January 3, 1985; William Winter, Bolton interview, July 14, 2006; Scripts for Winter TV spots on WJTV, 1985, WWPC.

3. William Winter, Bolton interview, July 14, 2006; Robert R. Korstad and James L. Leloudis, *To Right These Wrongs: The North Carolina Fund and the Battle to End Poverty and Inequality in 1960s America* (Chapel Hill: University of North Carolina Press, 2010), 354; William A. Link, *William Friday: Power, Purpose, and American Higher Education* (Chapel Hill: University of North Carolina Press, 1995), 378; MDC Panel on Rural Economic Development, *Shadows in the Sunbelt: Developing the Rural South in an Era of Economic Change* (Chapel Hill: MDC, Inc., 1986); "Roads, Roots Cited as Key to New South," *Jackson Daily News*, May 15, 1986.

4. "Panel Studies South's Economic Potential," *Jackson Clarion-Ledger*, December 4, 1985; William Winter, Bolton interview, September 13, 2001; Jesse White, Bolton interview, September 27, 2007; Doris Betts, *Halfway Home and a Long Way to Go: The Report of the 1986 Commission on the Future of the South* (Research Triangle Park, N.C.: Southern Growth Policies Board, 1986); William Winter class at Millsaps College, April 26, 1989, transcript, WWPC; William Winter, Bass interview.

5. William Winter, Bass interview; William Winter and Jesse White addressing Joint Session of Mississippi Legislature, January 11, 1989 (videotape), Box 133, Southern Growth Policies Board Records, SHC; William Winter, Bolton interview, September 13, 2001; Joe Atkins, "Winter Uses 'Old South' in Warnings of Troubled Future in South," *Jackson Clarion-Ledger*, March 8, 1987; Ferrel Guillory, "William F. Winter: Mississippi's Elder Statesman Preaches the Gospel of Economic Reform," *Governing* 1 (February 1988): 36–40; "The South: Another Exodus," *The Economist* 303 (May 16, 1987): 47; William F. Winter, "Closing the South's Economic Gap," *Southern Business and Economic Journal* 11 (January 1988): 34–40.

6. William Winter to H. Brandt Ayers, February 21, 1986, WWPC.

7. David T. Gordon, ed., *A Nation Reformed: American Education 20 Years after a Nation at Risk* (Cambridge, Mass.: Harvard Educational Publishing Group, 2003); *Implementation* (SGPB newsletter) 1 (November 1987): 1–28; William Winter, Bolton interview, July 14, 2006; William Winter, Southern Growth Policies Board speech, December 10, 1992, WWPC; Ferrel Guillory, "Panel Thinks South Should Aim High," undated newspaper clipping, December 1992?, Box 7, William Winter unprocessed collection, MDAH.

8. William Winter, Bass interview; Foundation for the MidSouth, summary of accomplishments, 1990–1998, Box 2, William Winter unprocessed collection; William Winter, Bolton interview, July 14, 2006.

9. Nancy Cotten Hirst, "Foundation for the Mid South: Helping Build Infrastructure for Personal and Economic Growth," *Delta Business Journal*, 1 (June 1998): 1, 24; press release on the creation of the Foundation for the MidSouth, n.d., late 1980s, Box 44, William Winter unprocessed collection; Jack Bass, "To Regenerate a Region," *Foundation News* 34 (March/April 1993): 17–19; William Winter, "Foundation for the Mid South Raises Hope," *Delta Business Journal* 3 (May 2000): 10; William Winter, Bolton interview, July 14, 2006.

10. William F. Winter, "Delta: A Reservoir of Great Potential," *Delta Business Journal* 2 (August 1999): 9; Bill Minor, "Winter's at It Again in Boosting Funding for Adequate Education," *Jackson Clarion-Ledger*, September 19, 2004; McKenzie, *A Time to Speak*, 71–75.

11. William Winter, Bolton interviews, May 22, 2006, and July 3, 2007; Theodore Smith to William Winter, June 12, 1990, WWPC.

12. Theodore Smith to William Winter, June 12, 1990, DEC to William Winter, Wilson Golden, Leslie King, and Bobby Moak, November 11, 1991, Frank A. Riley to William Winter, December 11, 1991, and Lisa Walker to William Winter, February 27, 1992, all in WWPC; Nash and Taggart, *Mississippi Politics*, ch. 15 and 16.

13. David S. Broder, "Moderate Democrats Trying to Grow Grass Roots," *Washington Post*, December 12, 1990; file on Democratic Leadership Council, Box 26, Wilson Golden unprocessed collection, MDAH.

14. William Winter, Bass interview; William Winter memoir; William Winter class at Millsaps College, March 15, 1989, transcript, WWPC; Shearer, "Links Go Far Back for 2 at Meeting."

15. William Winter memoir; "Mississippi Ex-Governor Brings Tenacity to Race Panel," *Atlanta Constitution*, August 24, 1997.

16. John Hope Franklin, *Mirror to America: The Autobiography of John Hope Franklin* (New York: Farrar, Straus, & Giroux, 2006), ch. 28; Steven A. Holmes, "Clinton Panel on Race Urges Variety of Modest Measures," *New York Times*, September 18, 1998; William Winter, Bolton interview, September 13, 2001.

17. William Winter, Bolton interview, September 13, 2001; Franklin, *Mirror to America*, ch. 28.

18. William Winter to Bill Clinton, November 26, 1997, Box 9, William Winter unprocessed collection; Gregory Freeman, "Member of Race Panel Hopes to Start Movement," *St. Louis Post-Dispatch*, January 8, 1998; Franklin, *Mirror to America*, ch. 28; Louis Freedberg, "Race Panel Gets an Earful in San Jose," *San Francisco Chronicle*, February 11, 1998. For a sampling of the negative press coverage, see Jodi Enda, "Race Initiative Slow to Hit Stride," *Charlotte Observer*, November 30, 1997; Susan Kauffman, "Historian Gets Flak for Piloting of Race Panel," *Raleigh News and Observer*, December 27, 1997; and Ellen Warren, "Race Panel's Report Thick but Lightweight: Nothing Startling Emerges from 15 Months of Work by a Presidential Advisory Group," *Chicago Tribune*, September 18, 1998.

19. Franklin, *Mirror to America*, ch. 29; Gail Russell Chaddock, "Will 'Year of Dialogue' Matter? Race in America," *Christian Science Monitor*, June 12, 1998; Advisory

Board to President's Initiative on Race, *One America in the 21st Century: Forging a New Future* (Washington, D.C.: The Initiative, 1998); William Winter and Michael Wenger, "Healing Racial Rifts: What Unifies Us?" *Christian Science Monitor*, March 25, 1999; John M. Broder and Don Van Natta Jr., "Clinton Staff Derides 'Lurid' Account of Lewinsky Case," *New York Times*, September 12, 1998; William Winter, Bolton interview, September 13, 2001; Bill Clinton, *My Life* (New York: Alfred A. Knopf, 2004), 948; William Winter speech to Memphis Rotary Club, September 2007, WWPC.

20. William Winter speech to Memphis Rotary Club, September 2007, and William Winter, "Reflections at the End of the Century" (speech), December 16, 1999, both in WWPC; David DuBuisson, "Despite Shortcomings, Clinton Commission on Race Made Real Progress: 'One-America' Found Scores of Things That Work," *Greensboro News and Record*, November 1, 1998; William Winter, Bolton interview, July 14, 2006.

21. William Winter speech to Memphis Rotary Club, September 2007, WWPC; William Winter, Bolton interview, July 14, 2006; The Birmingham Pledge, http://www. birminghampledge.org/ (Accessed on October 21, 2009).

22. Eagles, *The Price of Defiance*, 437; Winter and Wenger, "Healing Racial Rifts"; Chaddock, "Will 'Year of Dialogue' Matter? Race in America"; William Winter, "Cultural Change, Community Building and Civic Responsibility" (speech), n.d., 2005?, "Institute for Racial Reconciliation Named for Former Gov. William Winter," magazine clipping, Summer 2003, and William Winter speech, February 20, 2003, all in WWPC.

23. Sansing, *The University of Mississippi*, 326–27; "Mississippi's State Flag and Coat of Arms: History of the Advisory Commission on the Mississippi State Flag and the Coat of Arms," n.d., Box 25885, Mississippi Governor, Advisory Commission on the Mississippi State Flag and the Mississippi Coat of Arms Files, 2000–2001, MDAH; David Firestone, "Debating Flag, Mississippi Finds It Doesn't Have One," *New York Times*, May 5, 2000.

24. William Winter, Bolton interview, September 13, 2001; Jack Elliott Jr., "Winter's Roots Run Deep into Mississippi History," *Biloxi Sun Herald*, September 26, 2000.

25. Mississippi Educational Television, "Flag Flap" (videorecording), 2000; McKenzie, *A Time to Speak*, 132–33; "Civility and Fairness Are Woefully Missing from Fiery Debate over State Flag" (editorial), *Biloxi Sun Herald*, October 22, 2000.

26. Mississippi Educational Television, "Flag Flap"; "Flag Panel Hit by Another Round of Insults," *Biloxi Sun Herald*, November 4, 2000.

27. Mississippi Educational Television, "Flag Flap"; Esther Campi, "Winter Calls Flag Hearings 'Messy But Necessary,'" *Biloxi Sun Herald*, November 11, 2000.

28. Rheta Grimsley Johnson, "Surely the State Flag Isn't Enough to Stir Mississippians to the Brawling Point," *Atlanta Journal Constitution*, November 19, 2000; "Mississippi Flag Conflict," *Pittsburgh Courier*, December 30, 2000; "Whatever He Recommends, Winter's to Be Commended" (editorial), *Biloxi Sun Herald*, November 19, 2000; Campi, "Winter Calls Flag Hearings 'Messy But Necessary.'"

29. William Winter, Bolton interview, September 13, 2001; "Mississippi's State Flag and Coat of Arms: History of the Advisory Commission on the Mississippi State Flag and the Coat of Arms," n.d., Box 25885, Mississippi Governor, Advisory Commission on the Mississippi State Flag and the Mississippi Coat of Arms Files, 2000–2001; Esther

Campi, "Mississippi Lawmakers Bow to Public Preference on Flag," *Biloxi Sun Herald*, December 12, 2000; Melissa M. Scallan, "Winter: New Flag Will Boost State," *Biloxi Sun Herald*, February 7, 2001.

30. Scallan, "Winter: New Flag Will Boost State"; Rheta Grimsley Johnson, "Winter in Mississippi," *Atlanta Journal*, April 1, 2001; Steve Miller, "The Rebel Symbol Gains in Mississippi Favor," *Washington Times*, April 14, 2001.

31. Douglas G. Feig, "Race, 'the New South,' and the Mississippi Flag Vote," *Politics & Policy* 32 (December 2004): 671; Miller, "The Rebel Symbol Gains in Mississippi Favor"; Esther Campi, "Flag of Choice—65 Percent Vote to Keep Old Banner," *Biloxi Sun Herald*, April 18, 2001; Nash and Taggart, *Mississippi Politics*, 282–83; William Winter, Bolton interview, September 13, 2001; Bradley G. Bond, ed., *Mississippi: A Documentary History* (Jackson: University Press of Mississippi, 2003), 303–4.

32. William Winter speech at Chaney, Goodman, Schwerner Memorial, June 20, 2004, WWPC; Richard Cotton, "Miss. Memorial Turns Divisive," *Atlanta Journal-Constitution*, June 21, 2004; "Mississippi Community Commemorates 40th Anniversary of Civil Rights Murders," *Los Angeles Sentinel*, June 24, 2004; Shaila Dewan, "Ex-Klansman Guilty of Manslaughter in 1964 Deaths," *New York Times*, June 22, 2005. Also see Howard Ball, *Justice in Mississippi: The Murder Trial of Edgar Ray Killen* (Lawrence: University Press of Kansas, 2006).

33. William F. Winter, "Not Forgotten: Reimagining the South," *Southern Cultures* 11 (Fall 2005): 88–100; David Broder, "William Winter: An Inspiration for Us All," *Washington Post*, January 16, 2005.

34. Jesse L. White Jr. to William Winter, April 1, 1999, WWPC.

Epilogue

1. Michael Newsom, "Marker Honors Struggle of Many," *Biloxi Sun Herald*, May 18, 2009; author's observations of Wade-In Commemoration Event, May 2009.

2. "Address by David Halberstam," November 7, 2003, WWPC.

3. Peter Hart, Bolton interview; Bill Minor, "Winter Helped 'Shake Loose the Old Chains,'" *Biloxi Sun Herald*, April 8, 2004.

Acknowledgments

1. Most of the material that had been in William Winter's possession has since been transferred to the MDAH.

2. I utilized a rough transcript of this interview prepared by Winter that he had in his personal possession, although the MDAH is currently preparing a transcript that will be publically available.

LIST OF ORAL HISTORY INTERVIEWS

Bryan Baker, interview by Charles Bolton, December 5, 2008, tape, in author's possession.

Fred Banks, interview by Charles Bolton, March 5, 1998, transcript, Vol. 706, MOHP.

William Joel Blass, interview by Charles Bolton, March 14, 2008, tape, MOHP.

Hodding Carter, interview by Jack Bass, April 1, 1974, transcript, SHC.

Robert Clark, interview by Harriet Tanzman, February 11, 2000, transcript, Civil Rights Documentation Project, Tougaloo College Archives, Tougaloo, Mississippi.

Thad Cochran, interview by Charles Bolton, October 16, 2007, tape, in author's possession.

J. P. Coleman, interview by Orley Caudill, November 12, 1981, transcript, Vol. 203, MOHP.

John Corlew, interview by Charles Bolton, December 15, 2007, tape, in author's possession.

John Corlew, interview by R. Wayne Pyle, October 10, 1979, transcript, Vol. 221, MOHP.

David Crews, interview by Charles Bolton, March 9, 2008, tape, in author's possession.

Brad Dye, interview by Charles Bolton, July 24, 2008, tape, in author's possession.

Wilson Golden, interview by Charles Bolton, October 15, 2007, tape, in author's possession.

Peter Hart, interview by Charles Bolton, October 15, 2007, tape, in author's possession.

John Henegan, interview by Charles Bolton, December 17, 2007, tape, in author's possession.

Elbert Hilliard, interview by Charles Bolton, March 13, 2008, tape, in author's possession.

Boyce Holleman, interview by Orley Caudill, August 9, 1976, transcript, Vol. 484, MOHP.

Charles C. Jacobs Jr., interview by Charles Bolton, September 23, 1999, transcript, Vol. 748, pt. 2, MOHP.

Guy Land, interview by Charles Bolton, October 15, 2007, tape, in author's possession.

Ray Mabus, interview by Charles Bolton, July 23, 2008, tape, in author's possession.

Bill Minor, interview by Charles Bolton, March 2 and April 13, 2000, transcript, Patchwork Oral History Project, Delta State University, Cleveland, Mississippi.

Dick Molpus, interview by Charles Bolton, July 21, 2008, tape, in author's possession.

Andy Mullins, interview by Charles Bolton, March 10, 2008, tape, in author's possession.

C. B. Newman, interview by Charles Bolton, June 18, 1992, transcript, Vol. 447, MOHP.

James A. Peden Jr., interview by Charles Bolton, December 17, 2007, tape, in author's possession.

George Rogers, interview by Charles Bolton, October 14, 2007, tape, in author's possession.

George Rogers, interview by Orley Caudill, November 16, 1977, transcript, Vol. 652, MOHP.

Jim Simpson, interview by Charles Bolton, May 11, 1992, transcript, Vol. 497, MOHP.

Gene Triggs, interview by Orley Caudill, October 16, 1975, transcript, Vol. 385, MOHP.

Eleanor Winter, interview by Charles Bolton, October 14, 2007, tape, in author's possession.

Elise Winter, interview by Charles Bolton, March 10, 2007, tape, MOHP.

Elise Winter, interview by Stephanie Meincke, May 3, 2007, transcript, MOHP.

William Winter, interview by Robert J. Bailey, November 1, 1977, tape, MDAH.

William Winter, interview by Jack Bass and Walter DeVries, March 27, 1974, tape, SHC.

William Winter, interview by Jack Bass, early 1992, transcript, WWPC.

William Winter, interview by Charles Bolton, August 29, 2001, transcript, MOHP.

William Winter, interview by Charles Bolton, September 13, 2001, transcript, MOHP.

William Winter, interview by Charles Bolton, May 17, 2006, tape, MOHP.

William Winter, interview by Charles Bolton, May 18, 2006, tape, MOHP.

William Winter, interview by Charles Bolton, May 22, 2006, tape, MOHP.

William Winter, interview by Charles Bolton, July 12, 2006, tape, MOHP.

William Winter, interview by Charles Bolton, July 14, 2006, tape, MOHP.

William Winter, interview by Charles Bolton, December 8, 2006, tape, MOHP.

William Winter, interview by Charles Bolton, March 9, 2007, tape, MOHP.

William Winter, interview by Charles Bolton, July 3, 2007, tape, MOHP.

William Winter, interview by Charles Bolton, December 12, 2007, tape, MOHP.

William Winter, interview by Charles Bolton, December 19, 2007, tape, MOHP.

William Winter, interview by Charles Bolton, March 12, 2008, tape, MOHP.

William Winter, interview by Charles Bolton, July 22, 2008, tape, MOHP.

William Winter, interview by Charles Bolton, December 5, 2008, tape, MOHP.

William Winter, interview by Charles Bolton, February 26, 2009, tape, copy in author's possession.

William Winter, interview by Orley Caudill, August 9 and 16, 1978, transcript, Vol. 417, MOHP.

William Winter, interview by David Crews, November 21, 2006, transcript, copy in author's possession.

William Winter, interview by Jere Nash, April 14, 2004, tape, copy in author's possession.

William Winter, interview by David Sansing, September 26, 1980, transcript, Box 5, Verner S. Holmes Collection, UM.

William Winter, interview by Robert Shaw, December 9, 1981, transcript, Box 2222, Mississippi Governor, Press Secretary's Subject Files, 1979–1983, MDAH.

William Winter, interview by Jesse White, n.d., transcript, WWPC.

William and Elise Winter, interview by Bill Edmonds, April 17, 1999, transcript, WWPC.

Jesse White, interview by Charles Bolton, August 30, 2007, tape, in author's possession.

Jesse White, interview by Charles Bolton, September 27, 2007, tape, in author's possession.

Jesse L. White, interview by H. T. Holmes, August 7, 1973, transcript, OH 74-06, MDAH.

Joe Wroten, interview by Yahuhiro Katagiri, November 4, 1993, transcript, Vol. 476, MOHP.

INDEX